Bringing the Body to the Stage and Screen

Expressive Movement for Performers

Annette Lust

With Movement Consultant Jo Tomalin
Illustrations by C. Yeaton

The Scarecrow Press, Inc.
Lanham • Toronto • Plymouth, UK
2012

Published by Scarecrow Press, Inc.
A wholly owned subsidiary of The Rowman & Littlefield Publishing Group, Inc.
4501 Forbes Boulevard, Suite 200, Lanham, Maryland 20706
http://www.scarecrowpress.com

Estover Road, Plymouth PL6 7PY, United Kingdom

British Library Cataloguing in Publication Information Available

Library of Congress Cataloging-in-Publication Data

Lust, Annette.
  Bringing the body to the stage and screen : expressive movement for performers / Annette Lust.
      p. cm.
  Includes bibliographical references and index.
  ISBN 978-0-8108-8124-2 (cloth : alk. paper) — ISBN 978-0-8108-8212-6 (pbk. : alk. paper) — ISBN 978-0-8108-8125-9 (ebook)
  1. Movement (Acting) 2. Mime. 3. Movement, Aesthetics of. I. Title.
  PN2071.M6L87 2011
  792.02'8—dc23
                                                                          2011019898

Printed in the United States of America.

For Jean and my loving family

To know the parts of the body for dramatic expression is to throw the spectator into magic trances.

—*Antonin Artaud*

Contents

Foreword

Thank you and congratulations, Annette Lust, for providing another extraordinary guide to further develop and refine our perception of movement and its great and multiple expressive potential. It is a great honor to introduce to a vast readership the fascinating aspects of human behavior that Lust has studied through her in-depth research and eloquently documented in her workbook on expressiveness derived by means that the human body explores.

We comedians, actors, mimes, singers, dancers, clowns, and whoever else is acting on a stage of any kind always must bring our body in front of an audience. Apart from the voice, it is the most elaborate and sophisticated tool of immediate natural expression we have. It is therefore absolutely imperative to learn to use it consciously and as much in depth as possible; we need to discover the many more muscles we are able to singularly command and conduct, from complete relaxation almost up to contraction and back again, respecting a scale of seven holds, as in music. Playing the body like an instrument and with the language of exuberance, we will automatically enhance the expressiveness and beauty of whatever the nature or kind of performance we create.

The show must go on, and get better and better each time it is performed.

Bernie Schürch, Mummenschanz

Preface

God bless the roots! Body and soul are one.

—Theodore Roethke

Among the ancients, mime and expressive movement were never separated from dance, song, dialogue, acrobatics, and animal disguises. Midst the Greeks and Romans, mime and expressive movement infused life into tragedy, comedy, and dance as well as existed in the form of mime sketches and pantomimes. As the Greek theatre continued to harmonize expressive movement with rhythmic dance and scanned verse, it became the pillar for Occidental theatre.

The word *theatre* stems from the Latin *theatrum* and the Greek *theatron*, derived from the Greek verb *theasthai*, signifying "to behold or see." At its origin, the theatre was a synthesis of visual and auditory elements (poetry, dance, and music) rather than an auditory art with a visual component. The spoken word was born from movement rather than the contrary. From the ancient ceremonies emerged the actor who was also a dancer, singer, and mime. With the addition of a text and of protagonists and stage sets, miming and dance still remained intrinsic to tragedy and comedy. In the Greek theatre, movement was thus basic to the actor's art. And just as the Greek theatre harmonized movement with the text, so Shakespeare and Molière in their works integrated the physical with verbal expression.

More evidence that movement is essential in the actor's art may be found in the derivation of the word *actor* from the Latin *agere*, signifying "to do" or "a doer" and implying someone who acts or performs. The original meaning of the word *actor* thus alludes to someone involved in action. One of the synonyms for *act* is *movement*. According to the initial signification and primary function, an actor is a stage artist who moves.

The twentieth-century French actor, poet, and drama theoretician Antonin Artaud criticized Occidental theatre for being a branch of literature engaged primarily in performing plays with emphasis placed on the playwright's text. During the second half of the twentieth century, literature no longer had as important a place in speaking theatre as in the preceding century. A number of twentieth-century avant-garde theatre companies such as Grotowski's Polish Laboratory Theater, the Living Theater, and the Open Theater, rather than rely on the playwright's text, experimented with content improvised by actors and directors, utilized gestures and sounds rather than words alone, developed the playing space in relation to the audience, and revived theatre as ritual. All this was done to unite the body with the voice and render theatre an experience that stimulates feeling and the senses. Through the influence of animators and companies such as Jerzy Grotowski, Eugenio Barba and the Odin Theatre, the Living Theatre, Etienne Decroux, and Jean-Louis Barrault, actors made use of the body to the fullest, and they integrated movements with voice. Stage directors and companies such as Robert Wilson, Tadeusz Kantor, and the Canadian Theatre Beyond Words combined movement and silence with a spoken text utilized minimally.

In the mid-1940s, inspired by the teachings of Jacques Copeau, Etienne De-croux, mime master of Marcel Marceau, had created a mime grammar that obliged mime-actors to develop body expression in order to make their art worthy of being called an art. Decroux believed that if the actor abandoned the text and other so-called alien stage arts to concentrate on physical expressivity exclusively for a period of thirty years, his or her art could be as self-sufficient and as creative as music, painting, or sculpture. Until actors possessed their own technique and the freedom to create through the body, they would remain suppressed by sets, costumes, texts, lighting, and other stage elements. Decroux's teachings, parallel to those of Grotowski on the importance of the actor's body and physical training to access emotional expression and incite creativity, influenced twentieth-century theatre. Theatre animators, performers, writers, and teachers such as Anne Dennis, former director of the London Rose Bruford College of Speech and Drama and author of *The Articulate Body*, considered Decroux mime technique as valid for "speaking actors as it is for mime actors" (Anne Dennis 1995, 96).

Trained in mime by Decroux, Jean-Louis Barrault is one of the best examples of a stage and screen actor and stage director who enriched his roles and verbal productions by allying gestures to words. Barrault's corporeal mime training, rather than deform the actor and director's art, rendered it one of the most vital forms of twentieth-century theatre in Europe.

Differing from Decroux's codified teaching method, but sharing a common aim to revitalize theatre through movement, Jacques Lecoq taught mime as a research tool to further dramatic creativity as well as combine it with other arts. He trained international mimes, clowns, actors, dancers, and people of diverse professions in a pedagogical method he devised that established movement as the root of silent, spoken, written, and plastic expression. Text, decor, costumes, and other elements could be added to movement only after the body's creative potential had been reestablished. His training program included acrobatics, stage combat, juggling, mask work, character creation, pantomime blanche, *commedia*, antique and modern chorus, clown and buffoon work, mime and music, mime and text, classic and modern text, and writing for the stage. His global method united the body's expression with theatre, music, plastic arts, poetry, and all of life. In his revival of total theatre, Lecoq played an important role in the synthesis of mime with other theatre and art forms.

These theatre aimators have made us aware that in speaking theatre (with the exception of such forms as radio theatre, dramatized literature, and philosophical and literary theatre in which the text is primordial), whenever physical expression is subordinated to the text and to words, the staged piece risks the loss of dramatic power and vitality. Placing emphasis on a text can also limit the role of creative movement that stirs the imagination. The theatre that has flourished over the centuries harmonized the physical with the verbal, as in the ancient Greek theatre, the commedia dell'arte, and the classical masterpieces of Shakespeare and Molière, in which the word matches the physical action.

The basic premise of this book, which could be subtitled "From Mime, Pantomime, and Physical Performance to Acting, Speaking, Total Theatre, and Beyond," is that movement is fundamental to the life of all theatre, whether it is movement theatre or theatre movement. While the movement theatre artist and the pantomimist are mainly concerned with the use of movement, the stage and screens actor's craft comprises voice (a portion of the body) and gesture, that of the dancer of dance and expressive movement, that of the clown of clowning combined with movement and miming skills, and the art of the puppeteer and other stage and screen artists may be enlivened by physical expression. Through this book's program of exercises as well as essays and interviews with movement experts and artists, I hope to convey the importance of physical expression to breathe life into their various arts and render them whole. Yet the object of this program is not to encourage an exclusive or exaggerated use of physicality that could counteract other movement choices or needs. Nor is it intended to impose a restrictive training method on participants but rather to help each discover and enrich his or her talent and ability through an expanded physical training program that offers a number of approaches and a broad choice of exercises. Devised to serve as a guide for anyone utilizing movement to train or perform, some of these exercises may also serve as a supplement to an existing program practiced by the participant.

Designed to help explore means to express freely and fully with one's body in acting, mime, dance, clowning, and all of the stage and screen arts, at the same time, through the opportunity they offer to invent movement and gestures, these exercises release and activate the participant's creative potential. Besides exercises enabling stage and screen actors, dancers, clowns, singers, and performers to incorporate expressive movement into their particular art forms, there are exercises that may aid mimes and pantomimists in perfecting their nonverbal art and technique.

This program may also offer personal as well as professional benefits beyond artistic needs or enrichment. It can help participants acquire a fuller and more integrated physical, mental, and emotional lifestyle. They can strengthen and render expressive the individual parts of the body and help reeducate, liberate, and bring spontaneity to bodies curbed or limited by habitual and conventional movement. As they integrate the physical and expressive corporal elements, they may stimulate physical and mental activity as well as promote the unity of body and mind.

Physical expression has become all the more important since the advent of twentieth-century postmodernism, which refuses limitations and frontiers among art forms. It encourages the combining of varied styles and expressions and expects stage and screen performers to be multitalented and trained in more than one stage art. Also, with the crossing over of barriers and intermixing of theatre arts, mimes and dancers began to speak, actors and singers mimed, and performing artists and clowns engaged in several art forms, including mime. Since art forms have blended, interacted, sometimes even clashed, and may no longer be separated from one another, we have found it difficult to identify them as one art or another.

Performers need physical expression to complete their art, integrating body with mind. The essential importance of movement expression in combined stage forms, as well as in all the theatre and film arts, is a primary reason for bringing the body to stage and screen. My hope is that this program will provide a keener awareness of physical expression to aid future stage and film artists revitalize their art by restoring the body to its proper place on stage and screen.

Acknowledgments

I am profoundly grateful to all those who have offered their support and contributions in the preparation of my book, *Bringing the Body to the Stage and Screen*. Among these are colleagues, friends, artists, teachers, and scholars who have shared their knowledge on the role of movement in the theatre and on screen. These colleagues, friends, artists, teachers, and scholars have enriched my creation and contributed to the compilation and editing of what first began as a secondary dissertation to accompany my primary doctoral dissertation, *The Art of Mime*, presented at the Sorbonne University for my Doctorat de l'Université and first published in 2000 under the title *From the Greek Mimes to Marcel Marceau and Beyond*.

I wish first of all to thank Robert Fleshman, professor emeritus of the Drama Department at Loyola University in New Orleans, for his continued guidance as consulting editor and for his essay "Etienne Decroux and the Contemporary Theatre" written for this book. I would also like to express my indebtedness to Jo Tomalin, professor of theatre arts performance at San Francisco State University, who trained at the Ecole Internationale de Théâtre Jacques Lecoq in Paris and at the Laban Centre at Goldsmith's College, University of London. Dr. Tomalin provided invaluable suggestions in examining the exercises, editing my book, and producing the website media along with the help of C. Yeaton, her San Francisco State University MFA student in theatre, who created the exercise illustrations. I, likewise, deeply appreciate the continual guidance of Stephen Ryan, Andrew Yoder, and Christen Karniski at Scarecrow Press in the preparation of my manuscript. Thanks are also due to film/stage director and executive producer Linda A. Vito for looking over the technical and expressive exercises.

I am grateful to Bernie Schürch and Floriana Frasseto of Mummenschanz for the insightful foreword and interview, and I am equally grateful to Bill Irwin, Geoff Hoyle, Joanna Sherman and Michael McGuigan of the Bond St. Theatre, Joan Shirle of the Dell'Arte International School of Physical Theatre and Company in Blue Lake, Liebe Wetzel who founded the Lunatique Fantastique puppeteers, mime-puppeteer-dancer Ilka Schönbein, filmmaker Karina Epperlein, dance choreographer Joe Goode, Jeff Raz of the Clown Conservatory, Theatre Critic Ken Bullock, movement specialists Dan Kamin, Mark Jackson, and Jo Tomalin, JoAnne Winter who co-founded Word for Word Company, and author Barry Gurdin for their enlightening contributions on the role of movement in theatre, cinema, dance, puppetry, and clowning.

Thanks are also due to Peter Bu and Etienne Bonduelle, the artistic directors of the Périgueux Mimos Festival, who invited me to write about the artists in their annual international mime festival and provided photos of their festival artists. I am grateful as well to the Association of Movement Theatre Educators and to Jean Wolski of *Atme News*; to Kim Corsaro, Albert Goodwyn, and Tom W. Kelly of the San Francisco *Bay Times*; to Phyllis Sherman and Mitch Bull of the *Westside Observer*; to Doreen and Al Burgin of the *Commuter Times* and to Sheryl Case of *Women's Voices*, who published my theatre reviews; and to Joseph Cillo and Mary Buttaro, who created a theatre critics column for me on *For All Events.com* and *the Fringe of Marin* and *Annette Lust* websites for my *Fringe of Marin Festivals* and my publications on theatre.

Dominican University of California and Sister Aaron Winkelman, chair of the English Department, were highly supportive of my research and publication on movement theatre. At the request of Dean Katherine Henderson at Dominican University, I began a theatre production course in 1990 that provided me with the opportunity to teach mime and include mime in our university and community Fringe Festivals. In this respect, I would like to thank stage directors Greg Angeo and Sasha Litovchenko, who, in their direction of my *Pantry Tale* plays and other productions, helped student and community actors understand the importance of movement in their work. In turn, these students and actors aided me in concretizing my movement exercises and theories.

I also thank my daughter, pianist and musical director Evelyne Luest, for her fine compilation of musical pieces to accompany the exercises and mime pieces. I shall be forever grateful to my late husband, Jean, for his devoted encouragement during the many hours I spent preparing the pages of my book. I am as well grateful to my son, Jean Claude, and daughters Eliane and Evelyne for their care and understanding when I was buried in my papers.

Finally, I am indebted to the photographers, artists, authors, teachers, and mime and movement enthusiasts, living and dead, without whose work this book would not exist. And I am thankful to those I may have neglected to mention but whose contributions to my work do not go unappreciated.

Introduction: Goals and Objectives for Learning to Move Expressively

Learning to move expressively in some respects entails the same basic approach for future artists engaged in physical theatre, improvisation, miming or moving with or without a text, or pantomime, and for the training of the mime, stage and screen actor, clown, dancer, singer, or performance artist, as well as for those engaged in this study for educational, nonprofessional, or recreational aims. For those pursuing any of these aims, this basic approach provides the teacher, students in a class, or those working independently with a practical program of exercises to develop a relaxed, flexible, and responsive body before beginning any movement expression. It is also helpful for the teacher, as well as for individuals working on their own, to have some training in dance, yoga, or gymnastics along with an understanding of the body's function and of acting, miming, and movement techniques.

Learning to move expressively, akin to dance or circus arts programs, consists first in developing and training the different parts of the body. Secondly, it requires communicating ideas and emotions through the body and face as in miming. However, in the exercises in this book, the word *miming*, when utilized in a broader sense, does not refer solely to moving or acting without words. It may also include movement and gestures utilized in acting and improvisational exercises that may or may not be combined with words. This differs from pantomimic movement that is stylized, performed without words, and is a means as well as an end in itself.

My approach to physical training in this program, conceived for beginning and intermediate students and beyond, encompasses experimentation with a variety of movement forms. It also aims to develop physical technique and expressivity to empower the stage and screen performer's art. Beyond this, it is hoped that experimentation with a number of movement forms will help the student and future performer to better understand and direct his or her own talent and discover what best suits his or her artistic needs and capacities that may be further developed with specialists of these movement styles. The exercises are devised to assist the student to become familiar with movement and acting styles from realistic to stylized, from pantomime and nonverbal to verbal theatre, from conventionally styled period plays to popular farce and physical improvisation, and to move with ease from naturalistic, realistic, expressionistic, farcical, theatrical, romantic, and period theatre forms to physical theatre, mime, pantomime, clowning, and dance-theatre.

However, although future stage and screen artists can enrich their art by training in stylized or more formal mime, depending on the kind of theatre or film work they intend to pursue, they may wish to concentrate on less stylized movement exercises. Contrarily, pantomime artists, clowns, and dancers of formal style ballet may choose to work in pantomime. I have included both nonstylized physical exercises and texts as well as stylized pantomime exercises and original pantomimes that may be selected and utilized to suit the needs of assorted stage and film performers.

Movement training is essential not exclusively for mimes and clowns working in stylized mime and pantomime. In its broader sense and with some adjustments, movement training is also beneficial for stage and screen actors whose performances contain a physical component. In accordance with the more obvious differences between acting on stage and screen, such as the need to minimalize the actor's movements and gestures in films and magnify them in stage plays, one of the main differences between the two arts is that of degree concerning the movement used in an acting style. Michael Chekhov in *On the Technique of Acting* suggests that although the stage actor in front of a camera should be extremely economical in use of gestures and facial expression, the emotional content of the role should never be lessened or killed (Chekhov 1991, 165).

Acting styles vary on the screen, where the film actor, like the stage actor, performs in movement forms from Greek, medieval, romantic, realistic, or naturalistic to all types of comedy. James Naremore in *Acting in the Cinema* describes James Stewart as an expert pantomimist in *Vertigo* (1958), Gary Grant as a modern practitioner of the Delsarte technique in *North by Northwest* (1958), Marlene Dietrich as using theatricality in *Morocco* (1930), and James Cagney as one of Hollywood's most mannered actors. Marlon Brando is characterized as a Method actor in *On the Waterfront* (1954), while Lillian Gish in *True Heart Susie* (1919) employs both pantomime and a natural acting style.

Many of our finest screen actors learned their art on the stage and relied on their stage training when performing on the screen. French mime/actor Jean-Louis Barrault, who began studying and performing mime with Etienne Decroux in the 1930s and gradually moved into speaking theatre, utilized his mime training in his total theatre productions of, for example, Racine's *Phèdre*, and in his roles in such films as *Les Enfants du Paradis*. Charles Chaplin, who began in English Music Hall pantomime, later had speaking roles in movies, and Jacques Tati, who at first mimed in the Music Hall, brought their talents as pantomimists into their films. Clown-mime Bill Irwin enhanced Beckett's *Texts for Nothing* and Molière's *Scapin* through his clown-mime movement skills. Geoff Hoyle utilized his circus clowning and pantomime to enrich his speaking theatre roles. A number of mimes who began with the Decroux and Marceau styles gradually added dialogue and acting techniques to their work. Among these are Kari Margolis and Tony Brown of the Margolis Brown Co., Leonard Pitt, Tony Montanaro, and Alvin Epstein, the first

American Decroux student who utilized his unique physical expression to create Beckett and other speaking theatre roles.

Dancers from Martha Graham to Alwin Nikolais incorporated dramatic movement in their dance-dramas. Graham created a moving interpretation of Aphrodite in *Ardent Song* and Nikolais provided stirring dance-theatre in *Galaxy* and in *Sanctum*. In the nineteenth century, ballerinas Carlotta Grisi and Fanny Elssler were known for their talent as pantomimists. Martha Graham, the "Goddess of Gestures," expressed the soul's emotions in her dance-dramas and Mary Wigman encouraged dramatic expressivity in her dance students and in the dancers she inspired, such as Hanya Holm, Lotte Goslar, Harald Kreutzberg, and Kurt Joos, who founded the modern dance-drama. Doris Humphrey utilized pantomime in her choreographies and Trudi Schoop was called the female Charlie Chaplin.

Toward the end of the twentieth century, Steve Krieckhaus, Helmut Gottschild, and Terry Beck, a former student of the Mary Wigman technique, mimed as well as danced in their creations. Pina Bausch's "tanztheater" combined theatre and dance in her *Bluebeard* piece, which violently depicts the physical and emotional abuse in the female and male relationship. Wendy Houstoun's 1997 social commentary trilogy *Haunted, Daunted, and Flaunted* combined dance, acting, and a text. Peter Martins in his 2007 New York City Ballet choreography of *Romeo and Juliet* with a Prokofiev score included scenes entirely acted out with expressive movement, such as the scene in which Juliet takes a sleeping potion and Romeo, believing she is dead, kills himself. Choreographer Joe Goode integrated movement with speaking theatre and puppetry in his 2008 *Wonder Boy*.

Examples of opera successfully combined with mime clowning include the character Pagliacci and numerous characters in operas such as Rossini's *Barber of Seville* and Mozart's *Marriage of Figaro* among other comical opera buffa. A more resent example is that of Philip Glass's chamber opera *Orphée*, presented by Ensemble Parallele in February 2011, in which the menacing underworld, imaginatively performed by cirque artists of the San Francisco Circus Center, greatly enlivened the production.

Miming has always been a part of puppetry and traditional Punch and Judy shows in which humpback, hook-nosed Punch fights with his wife Judy. The Bread and Puppet Theatre utilized pantomime to animate giant puppets along with live actors, storytelling, dance, painting, and sculpture to voice political issues. Liebe Wetzel and her Lunatique Fantastique puppeteers took movement in puppetry a step further by transforming everyday objects such as toilet paper rolls, kitchen articles, hardware, newspapers, and clothing into characters that move and interact in silence to depict current issues in a world of fantasy. Inversely, actors and mimes may make use of dance, clown, and other stage arts to enrich their own art as long as these skills are at the service of acting and miming and utilized according to the nature and needs of a particular stage or film work.

Although anyone may benefit from this program of exercises, learning to mime or engage in physical theatre for educational or personal purposes differs from miming for professional purposes. While the student in mime or physical theatre may learn the fundamentals of movement expression as well as derive educational and personal benefits from these exercises, to develop a professional career he or she will need to pursue it in programs that offer more advanced training.

Nonetheless, for the student of acting, mime, dance, clowning, singing, storytelling, and other stage and screen arts, such a program is beneficial because of the increasing popularity of multimedia performances that combine theatre or film with other arts and the need for movement skills in a number of image and visually oriented theatre and film productions.

Moreover, this program will help develop characterization and the physical aspect of role interpretation, and will help improve style, concentration, coordination and control, body alignment and centering, body strength and muscle tone, flexibility, confidence, ease. It will also help establish physical discipline and increase range and freedom of movement. The program will help channel the mental, emotional, and imaginative forces toward creative expressivity, develop an ability to communicate silently, render movement meaningful, increase physical sensitivity and responsiveness, and relate movement to words in speaking theatre and film.

Beyond this, the personal and educational gains in learning to move expressively are manifold. This learning process will develop in students a keener sense of perception, observation, physical interrelationship and reaction, use of imagery, a more energized and vibrant physical presence. It will reduce stress and foster a better balance between physical movement, thought, emotions, and verbal expression. Practicing the expressive exercises, improvisations, and pantomimes in groups will also teach the student to collaborate with others and to seek partners to participate in creating projects and a peer audience to offer constructive criticism. One of the greatest satisfactions that I have experienced as a mime teacher, besides observing students discover dramatic and meaningful movement and develop creative ways of utilizing their bodies, is to watch them grow and enrich their physical expression and works while developing the above-mentioned qualities.

Learning to mime and work with movement likewise may provide a deeper comprehension of art, music, dance, history, and literature. Concentrated attention focused on the creation of a visual image will help the student acquire a better notion of line and form. Moving to music will sharpen one's sense of rhythm and timing, developing qualities also provided by the study of dance. History, mythology, geography, and religious studies may also be taught and learned more vividly through mimed tableaux of famous events, places, and characters. Mime may be used to accompany and illustrate a literary text. For example, the members of the National Theatre of the Deaf in West Hartford, Connecticut, staged programs in which the performers mimed to narrations of works by Ogden Nash, Dylan Thomas, E. E. Cummings, and other poets and authors. Word for Word Company in San Francisco, as well as other American companies, stage productions in which they dramatize stories and novels through physical movement and narration. I have utilized mime to accompany the recitation of La Fontaine's fables as well as employed movement to animate literary works such as Saint Exupéry's *The Little Prince* for schools as well as public programs.

The exercises in this program do not require preliminary training or specialized skills. If a teacher or coach is not available, students may practice them on their own. They are not based on any particular physical theatre method or school of mime but are exercises that I devised and compiled influenced by diverse methods in which I trained, observed, or researched. Among these are the French schools of mime of Georges Wague, Etienne Decroux, Jean-Louis Barrault, Marcel Marceau, and Jacques Lecoq as well as modern dance, yoga, and the movement training classes of Mamako and Leonard Pitt. Inspired by their methods, I then adapted and created exercises in a program that would be flexible enough to serve aspiring stage and screen performers as well as other participants. It was out of my introductory mime and improvisation classes and play rehearsals and performance warm-ups that my exercises evolved along with the addition of original pantomimes and selections of plays, poetry, and prose texts for miming. They are presented in an order similar to the one I used along with supplementary exercises I created to offer a broader selection for the particular movement orientation of teachers and students.

In these physical and expressive exercises for each part of the body, the expressive exercises introduce feelings and emotions related to the basic physical exercises that remain the springboard for expressive movement. Both the physical and expressive aspects of movement are also included in the pantomimes, improvisations, and texts suggested for physical interpretation. However, rather than rely solely on the expressive exercises, scenes for miming, improvisations, and pantomimes in this program, or resort to imitating teachers demonstrating them, the object is for participants to create their own expressive exercises, mimed scenes, improvisations, and pantomimes and to develop a personal expression and style.

THE GOALS AND OBJECTIVES OF PART I

Part I of this book focuses on stage and screen movement, mime, pantomime, corporeal mime, improvisation, basic physical and expressive exercises, and utilizing movement to create a visual image.

1. To develop a strong, coordinated, controlled, supple, animated, and responsive body and technical skills by exercising the individual parts of the body.
2. To access emotional reactions through physical and muscular work.
3. To develop a totality or wholeness of expression by relating the physical development of the individual parts of the body to the performer's expressive movement skills through the use of interdependent physical and expressive exercises.
4. To become familiar with the different kinds of movement on stage and screen in mime, pantomime, physical theatre, and improvisation, and to choose a movement style and practice these forms in a class or on one's own.

The third goal also incites the student to develop his or her creative talent through the invention of expressive exercises and the utilization of improvisational skills in order to achieve a natural and spontaneous acting style. Jacques Copeau believed that it is through the use of gesture that the actor could best be a creator. As Michael Chekhov states in his book *Etre Acteur*, dramatic art is no more than permanent improvisation, and the actor should not be deprived of the right to invent (Chekhov 1980, 66).

In part I, the exercises begin with relaxation, warming up, body alignment, breathing, and body centering exercises. They are then divided into:

1. Exercises focusing on the use and training of the individual parts of the body along with related movements.
2. Expressive exercises pertaining to these individual parts of the body to be further developed and created by the student.
3. Exercises in creating a visual image that develop the expressive nature of movement further and in regards to sense perception, physical sensation, weight, volume, space, and time, sound, descriptive and occupational subjects, objects and colors, slow and rapid rhythm, the creation of characters, types, and animals, costumes and styles, and finding the basic psychological gesture and movement.

Part I includes a large number of basic fundamental introductory exercises to provide a broad choice for beginners and more advanced participants desirous of reworking and reviewing them. They proceed from elementary to more advanced exercises and may be utilized progressively or selected according to need, time allotment, and how rapidly they can be mastered. The expressive exercises of the individual parts of the body as well as the visual image exercises in part I may also be selected as needed and could serve to develop physical improvisations or pantomimes in part II.

THE GOALS AND OBJECTIVES OF PART II

Part II focuses on improvisation, pantomime, movement for acting, and mime and text.

1. To develop the student's confidence and ease and enlarge expressive skills and movement vocabulary through improvisations, the performing of pantomimes, and the "physicalizing" of scenes for stage and screen acting.
2. To familiarize the student with the incorporation of movement into text and how the use of movement can render a text meaningful and alive. Just as in music the silence between the notes empowers the notes, so the silence between words filled with expressive movement gives the words their dramatic power.

Part II includes themes for solo and group improvisations, original solo and group pantomimes, classical and modern scenes combining mime and text, and miming to poetry and prose texts. Improvisation and acting have been introduced here not only to aid the actor to develop movement skills and physical expressivity but as a means to release the subtextual impulses that bring out the meaning of a text. In the section on miming with a text, the choice of using mime or movement for acting will depend on the text, the teacher, and student options. The exercises involving pantomime will require more stylized movement and the development of a pantomime technique. Again, all of the exercises in this section should be selected according to the aims and needs of those utilizing the program for class or individual work or for school or public performances. (For permission to stage the author's original pantomimes for public performances, please contact the author by e-mail at jeanlust@aol.com.)

GOALS AND OBJECTIVES OF PART III

Part III demonstrates the major role of movement in a number of artistic areas through essays and interviews by renowned actors, mimes, clowns, dancers, theatre critics, movement teachers, puppeteers, and filmmakers who present their beliefs on the importance of expressive movement in their particular art forms.

AIMS OF THE BOOK

The overall aim of *Bringing the Body to Stage and Screen* is not to impose a training method or a "How to Become a Mime or Movement Theatre Artist" recipe. Rather it is to offer a varied and wide choice of exercises and training methods to help participants, future actors, mimes, and stage and film performers become more physically adept, expressive, and complete in their artistic performance. The exercises are thus arranged so as to interrelate the preparatory physical exercises of the various parts of the body to creative and expressive movement.

A second aim is to aid the student in becoming aware of and eliminating physical obstacles in order to freely develop his or her own creativity and expand characterization and other stage and film talents through the channel of expressive movement.

A third aim is to ease the barriers that separate the stage and film arts through the use of movement, which by the same token enriches each of these arts.

A fourth aim is to offer a training program flexible enough to benefit not only students interested in mime and acting but also those involved in other kinds of stage performance, public speaking, and professional and educational activities. It may also enliven the teaching of academic and other subjects, or simply offer a personal artistic or physical benefit.

Part I

PHYSICAL AND EXPRESSIVE EXERCISES

Chapter 1

Definitions of Stage and Screen Movement, Mime, Pantomime, Corporeal Mime, Stage Combat, Physical Theatre, and Physical Improvisation

The word *mime* may at times be utilized broadly, even throughout this book, to refer generally to both stylized and less stylized body and facial movements. Yet, to distinguish between the two forms, stylized movement conforms to a distinctive style or mode and is more elaborate and formal while nonstylized movement is not as crafted and appears to be more natural. For example, an actor's realistic movement on stage or screen, whether or not it accompanies spoken words, is nonstylized, but the mime artist communicates in stylized or more elaborate movement not dependent on spoken language. And in pantomime, the pantomimist utilizes still more structured conventional, physical, and gestural signs to create in silence the illusion of objects or persons not present. The mime artist and pantomimist also differ from the stage and screen actor in that the actor's nonstylized, less crafted movement or action may accompany spoken words or may be used in the silences before, between, or after the actor's or other actors' words.

Some of the mime exercises in this program involve the use of stylized or conventional pantomime (especially in the illusion pantomime sections in parts I and II). If at times the terms *mime* and *pantomime* seem to be used interchangeably, their meanings and differences need to be clarified. Distinctions between mime that is stylized and nonstylized movement on stage and screen, pantomime, and the more abstract and corporeal forms of mime follow.

STAGE AND SCREEN NONSTYLIZED MOVEMENT

Although modern mime is perceived as a more specialized or ornate form of silent movement, in its broader, historical meaning and use, it is not limited, except perhaps in period plays and films, to silent performance and to a stylized formal expression without the use of props. Nonstylized movement in stage and film acting and business may also be seen as a form of miming that may or may not directly accompany a spoken text and can be performed with or without the use of real props.

There are nonetheless inherent differences in the use of mime or physical movement on screen and on stage. Film acting can be as theatrical as stage acting, but acting on screen ordinarily appears more natural and intimate than stage acting. This is due to the use of confined space with actors in close proximity projecting their detailed movements to a camera rather than to an audience. And while on stage the dialogue may play an important role in developing and projecting dramatic action and characters, on screen these elements are visually developed and projected with less theatrical and more lifelike physical movement. According to Linda A. Vito, assistant artistic director of the Fringe of Marin Play Festival and executive producer of *On the Starting Line Movie*, "on stage the actor needs to dramatize and magnify gestures and movements to project immediately to a live audience whereas in film the camera dramatizes and projects the actor's more subtle gestures and movements to a future film audience."

STAGE AND SCREEN STYLIZED MIME

Mime, as a more specialized form of movement that depends less on a text or words to communicate an action, is more stylized or theatrical than the movement ordinarily used in stage or screen acting but less stylized than that found in pantomime. This use of more or less stylized movement that differs from that used in stage and screen acting and in pantomime is exemplified in Chaplin's later films such as *City Lights* (1931) and *Modern Times* (1936). In *City Lights*, in addition to his comical theatrical movements, Chaplin delivers a speech full of unintelligible words to mock spoken language, and in *Modern Times* his movements, along with the creation of an imaginary language, satirize the machine age. Although in these scenes Chaplin's movements are less stylized or exaggerated than in his early films and he incorporates words to heighten his satire, his miming and movements differ here in their degree of stylization from the more theatrical pantomimic style of his early short films influenced by the English Music Hall slapstick style, such as *Kid's Auto Race* (1914), *The Pawnshop* (1916), *The Immigrant* (1917), and *The Cure* (1917). Again, although some of Chaplin's abrupt, jerky pantomimic movements and the extravagant dance mime of these earlier films reappear in *The Great Dictator* (1940) and *Monsieur Verdoux* (1947), in these films his miming, combined with spoken dialogue, is no longer a highly stylized, independent movement art form. (See Dan Kamin's essay "How Charlie Chaplin Spun Stagecraft into Cinematic Gold" in part II.)

Another example of stylized mime in the cinema is D. W. Griffith's silent film *True Heart Susie* (1919). In certain scenes, Lillian Gish uses theatrical mime with her hands and face to portray a country girl's desperation over losing her boyfriend. Film actors Katharine Hepburn and James Stewart are likewise remembered for their highly theatrical physical styles in many screen performances.

Among the stage companies utilizing stylized mime, Canstage from Canada toured internationally in 2004–2005 with an adaptation of Gogol's *The Overcoat* that deployed expressionistic mime and dance with no text. The San Francisco Mime Troupe that performs in parks began in 1959 as a silent mime troupe based on commedia dell'arte physical and vocal characterizations, but it now adds text and political issues to their retention of broad, exaggerated movement and gestures that reinforce the farce element of their work. The Dell'Arte Players in Blue Lake, California, at first staged traditional *commedia* plays and then moved to combining verbal and movement theatre in modern and classical plays grounded in stylized *commedia* technique, as in their 2006 staging of Molière's *Tartuffe*.

PANTOMIME

Pantomime communicates an action mainly through bodily movement and gestures and by creating the illusion of real objects and characters to portray ideas or emotions in a literal and anecdotal manner. It also deals with selected conventional and occupational movements performed in a more formal physical manner. An example in the cinema is Jean-Louis Barrault's nineteenth-century Pierrot pantomimes in Marcel Carné's *Children of Paradise* (1945). On stage, illusion pantomime is often performed in whiteface (whitening the face with makeup), as seen in Marcel Marceau's Bip pantomimes and in street and stage artist Robert Shields' sketches. In stage mime/actor Geoff Hoyle's solo sketch *Two Waiters*, Hoyle creates the illusion of two waiters who appear and disappear behind a screen as they pursue one another.

CORPOREAL MIME

Twentieth-century Decroux school corporeal mime—also called pure mime because it strives for a purity of form and conveys ideas and emotions principally through a grammar of body movements without music, words, or other means—represents a more abstract form of silent expression. The performer of corporeal mime challenges the spectator's imagination by creating universal emotions or ideas presented in a nonliteral and nonanecdotal manner with unconventional movements of the entire body rather than with familiar and tangible movements of the hands, face, or other more communicative parts of the body. For example, in Marceau's *The Hands*, sometimes referred to as *The Hands of Good and Evil*, the mime evokes through original hand gestures that are not concretely interpreted (as in his Style and Bip pantomimes) intangible and poetic images. In Decroux-trained Daniel Stein's *Timepiece*, the mime moves from one sculptural attitude to another, animating like a puppeteer chairs, ropes, discs, and a swinging plumb line (in an exceptional nonrealistic use of props) to present an abstruse interpretation of the passing of time in a man's life. (See "Etienne Decroux, Father of Corporeal Mime" in Annette Lust's *From the Greek Mimes to Marcel Marceau and Beyond*, Lanham, Md.: Scarecrow 2003; and Thomas Leabhart's *Etienne Decroux*, New York: Routledge Performance Practitioners, 2007.)

DIFFERENCES BETWEEN NONSTYLIZED MOVEMENT AND STYLIZED MIME, PANTOMIME, AND CORPOREAL MIME

The nonstylized movement in stage and screen acting and the more stylized mime differ depending on whether the movement is natural and tangible and includes props and words, or more artful and performed in silence without props. The actor's nonstylized movement and the mime's stylized mime are likewise distinct from the pantomime style of, for example, Marcel Marceau and the silent film work of Chaplin, Buster Keaton, and Jacques Tati, or the corporeal abstract mime of Decroux-trained mimes.

The differences between nonstylized movement (referring here to acting in a broad general sense), stylized mime, pantomime, and abstract and corporeal mime are illustrated in the following examples of a scene in which the protagonist plucks the petals of a flower to determine if his girlfriend loves him.

- An actor using movement in a broad sense would pluck the petals of a real flower with natural stage movement while saying "She loves me; she loves me not" with a facial expression of worried inquiry.
- The mime would enact the same scene with more artful movement and most likely without the use of his voice or a real flower.
- The pantomimist would create the illusion of plucking the petals from an imaginary flower with no words and with conventional and elaborate hand movements and a facial expression of anxiety.
- The abstract or corporeal mime performer would convey this action without words or props and with nonliteral movements that express inner and more general or universal feelings and thoughts about the uncertainty of being loved.

The following are examples in nonstylized movement and stylized mime, pantomime, and corporeal mime of a character opening a package to pull out a ticking ball.

- The stage or screen actor utilizing concrete stage and screen movement (more enlarged for the stage actor and less expanded and more intimate for the screen actor) would play the character opening a real package, pulling out the ticking ball, and quickly throwing it far away with uncrafted and concrete movements of the arms, hands, body, and facial expression. He or she would communicate this action with, before, or after the lines of a text and with props such as a package and ball.
- The mime would mime the character opening the package and quickly throwing it far away for fear it is a bomb by utilizing more crafted theatrical movements of the arms, hands, body, and facial expression. He or she would communicate this action without or depending less on words, and most likely without real props.
- The pantomimist would perform this scene without words or props, creating through conventional and exaggerated pantomimic movements of arms, hands, body, and facial expression, often in whiteface, the detailed illusion of the character unwrapping a package, pulling out a ticking ball, and fearfully hurling it away.
- The performer of corporeal and abstract mime would not anecdotally depict the specific dramatic action of a person unwrapping the package and fearfully hurling the ticking ball away. Extending this theme, he or she would

express, for example, the inner emotions of astonishment and fear underlying the creation of a universal image of terror. In a silent interpretation (performed most often without props unless they are utilized abstractly), the performer would employ the unconventional movements of the entire body and a neutral facial expression characteristic of a highly stylized corporeal mime style that, along with its abstract content, has been likened to modern dance.

Although it will depend on the teacher's, actor's, and students' choices, in the beginning stages, it is recommended that one practice the exercises in nonstylized movement and stylized mime and pantomime that can be more readily mastered and more useful before moving into abstract and corporeal mime exercises.

STAGE COMBAT

As in pantomime and stylized mime, stage combat utilizes codified movement techniques that create the illusion of fighting, often violently, on stage or screen. Codified movements help the performer choreograph and incorporate fighting into a dramatic action. Stage combat is utilized in period as well as modern plays and films in which actors perform moves involving combat styles, armed or unarmed, that are safe, theatrical, and believable regarding the dramatic action.

The Society of American Fight Directors (SAFD), founded by David Boushey and others just over thirty years ago, provides safety, historical accuracy, and period movement as well as training workshops and standardized Skills Proficiency Testing for certification of actor-combatants, teachers, and fight directors. The SAFD is recognized the world over and has counterparts in almost every country where professional Western theatre is regularly performed.

PHYSICAL THEATRE

Physical theatre, like all forms of mime as well as pantomime, is a visual form that expresses emotions, ideas, and character mainly through body movement. It may include dance, mask, music, text, clowning, *commedia*, multimedia, costumes, and scenery. Performers train in diverse movement styles and techniques such as Decroux corporeal mime, Marceau mime and pantomime, Lecoq mime and clowning, *commedia*, Laban, Feldenkrais, Suzuki, Tai Chi, and various dance styles and forms of Eastern theatre that develop flexibility, physical coordination, and control, and that provide tools for self-expression and creativity.

The term *physical theatre* has become more predominant for those who have felt the limitations of such forms as twentieth-century Decroux corporeal mime and the whiteface pantomime of Marceau. Rather than remaining a specialized or limited movement expression, it may be seen as an extension of mime that seeks a broader, freer vision by embracing other movement theatre genres. Physical theatre and mime styles also often overlap in the work of some twenty-first-century movement theatre performers.

While physical theatre appears to be a broader form of movement theatre than mime, we should recall that mime among the Greeks also included the use of a text, dance, buffoonery, and other elements. Among the Greeks and Romans, mime was a short comedy written in prose or verse that portrayed life and consisted, especially among the Romans, of expressive gestures and dance that were more prevalent than the spoken text. The Greek author Lucian describes the *pantomimus* as a dancer who is, above all, an actor.

Thus, if as well as speaking, singing, dancing, or performing acrobatics, their gestures and movements play a role in their art, these artists may be said to engage in the art of mime. Yet *physical theatre* is a more modern term used to describe movement theatre that embraces other arts to become a broader stage form. Contrary to physical theatre, twentieth-century Decroux corporeal mime, the Deburau classical nineteenth-century and the twentieth-century pantomime, although their mime styles differed, were restricted to silent movement and a structured mime form.

And just as the twentieth and twenty-first centuries have given rise to numerous mime styles that are broader than the twentieth-century corporeal mime style, the combinations of movement forms in physical theatre are varied and limitless. Among the many companies that engage in image-based theatre that includes mime, dance, circus arts, and storytelling is the Bond Street Theatre, which incorporates styles and traditions of other countries. And the Dell' Arte Players have expanded its *commedia* and mask work to include other kinds of physical theatre. (See Franc Chamberlain's essay on "Gesturing towards Post-Physical Performance," in *Physical Theatres: A Critical Reader*, edited by John Keefe and Simon Murray, New York: Routledge, 2007.)

PHYSICAL IMPROVISATION

In physical improvisation, the improviser or player creates movement spontaneously and without any previous preparation nor preconceived scenario or action. It consists of inventing on the spur of the moment movement and content that are not based on a given plot or story line but are derived from extemporaneous physical action discovered through immediate and intuitive means.

The purpose of physical improvisation, utilized for example in improvisational games, is to free the improviser from mechanical performance and achieve a natural and spontaneous style. It renders the improviser physically responsive and alert, vitalizes his or her work, releases creativity, and teaches him or her to adjust to the needs of the moment while performing. It also helps the player gain confidence, learn to utilize space, and interact with other players.

The commedia dell'arte with masked characters is one of the best examples of the use of physical improvisation that in more traditional forms employs more structured movement. (For information on commedia dell'arte resources and actor training with masks, see www.theater-masks.com/about_commedia_dell_arte.)

The expressive exercise sections in this program may also serve as departure points for creating short or longer improvised movement. They may be used freely and followed through with the actors' or students' own findings or utilized as subjects to create improvisations. In improvisational work, the use of a mask also helps to free the expression of the entire body. (See part II for more exercises and information on improvisation.)

For video clips on YouTube of some of the movement forms above, see appendix A, lesson 1, exercise 3, Discussion.

For the history and definitions of mime and pantomime, see in the bibliography works by Margarete Bieber, Walter Parker Bowman and Robert Hamilton Ball, Pierre-Louis Duchartre, Douglas Hunt and Kari Hunt, Joan Lawson, Annette Lust, Irene Mawer, Allardyce Nicoll, Katherine Sorley Walker, and Albert E. Wilson.

Chapter 2

Conducting a Class and Practicing on One's Own

Individuals interested in developing the physical and expressive aspects of movement without joining a class or working with a teacher or coach may profit from these exercises by practicing them on their own (preferably with a group and a group leader). Whether in a class or working on one's own, the physical and expressive exercises should be selected, adapted, and practiced according to the needs and the particular stage or screen art and movement expression the participant, teacher, and students are pursuing.

The selection of exercises for those working on their own or for a class program should be based on the age, training background, and needs of the participants. Dance and physical education students, for example, may require less basic physical training than actors. The training of adults also differs from that of children, who may not be able to endure as strenuous or as long periods of physical exercises. Since most young people have a vivid imagination and express freely, their interest is readily captured and stimulated by imaginative exercises with a game-like approach.

The exercises should be practiced in a well-lit and ventilated room with enough space to practice and perform safely as well as comfortably. An uncarpeted, unpolished wood or linoleum floor is preferable, with a mat for exercises that may include falls, acrobatics, or gymnastics. One end of the room may be used for performing or demonstrating student work. Although the program of exercises may be conducted without a large mirror, video recorder, tapes, and chairs or benches, the latter are useful.

For guidance in setting up a program, a lesson plan with sample introductory exercises is provided in appendix A. Also see the website www.AnnetteLust.com. The lessons consist of a minimum of four-hour periods of exercises practiced once a week (with breaks) or broken down to two hours twice a week, with shorter periods for children. The number of exercises to be completed in each lesson is not as essential as working on them technically and creatively. Although the choice of exercises and time allotment for them will vary, this sample lesson plan offers guidance in setting up a program to initiate participants into movement expression.

If a mime, physical theatre, improvisation, or movement course cannot be of-fered at a school, selected exercises may be incorporated into theatre games or added as warm-ups and physical expression sections in beginning, intermediate, and advanced acting, dance, clown, or other stage and screen classes. These exer-cises may also be adapted to dance, clown, and other stage and screen workshops.

ATTIRE, PROPS, SETS, MASKS, MAKEUP, AND MUSIC

Tights or leotards, T-shirts, sweatpants or shorts, or other loose clothing permit-ting flexibility of movement are recommended, as are soft-soled shoes or bare feet. For performances, costume items that allow the body to move freely may be worn to indicate a character or period.

Movements may be practiced at first with real props or objects, but in mime the latter should not be utilized once the movements are created. Exercises should also be practiced on a bare or almost bare floor or performing area.

Wearing a mask or demi-mask when preparing the expressive movement exer-cises (except for those requiring facial expressions) in acting, mime, pantomime, physical theatre, and improvisation as well as in dance, clowning, and other stage and screen arts can be helpful. It is an actor's training technique developed by Jacques Copeau at the Vieux Colombier to aid his actors to become more fully en-gaged in their roles and to train them to make better use of the entire body. French mime masters Etienne Decroux and Jacques Lecoq later utilized masks in their training programs. Use of masks also relieves tension and self-consciousness, develops concentration, helps build characterization and communication of inner motives, increases physical dramatic expression, and helps release one's creative impulses and expand one's personal acting and performance style. (See appendix C for suggestions on making masks and applying whiteface makeup.)

Although music is not necessary to accompany warm-ups and basic technical and expressive exercises in class, it may have a relaxing effect on students work-ing out. For the creation of mime, pantomime, or improvisations, music, from jazz to rock to classical works, may serve to inspire the discovery of expressive movement and make the movement more rhythmic. Such instruments as drums, percussion, cymbals, piano, tambourines, and flutes may serve as rhythmic ac-companiment but should be adapted to the movement and gestures rather than the contrary to create a mood or atmosphere, underscore a dramatic action, and heighten the dramatization of a movement piece or a play. (See appendix C, les-son 4, Use of Music, for suggestions of musical selections.)

ORGANIZATION, PRACTICE, AND PURPOSE OF EXERCISES

If students in a mime and physical improvisation class can train for only a mini-mum of two hours per week, rather than four or more, to fully benefit from such a program it is suggested that they practice selected physical and expressive exer-cises on their own as well as create their own related exercises. Creating expres-sive exercises may begin by deriving them from everyday movement. The use of a mask for the creation of expressive movement exercises and in acting, mime, pantomime, physical theatre, and improvisational work can help discover and enrich physical expression.

If participants have had little or no preparatory physical training, a good portion of the first meetings should be devoted to practicing a selection of introductory physical exercises of, for example, shoulder, back, trunk, and arm movements combined with related expressive exercises. (See the sample lessons in appendix A.) The physical and expressive exercises will also be more beneficial if participants begin working on them directly rather than discussing at length how to proceed or what kind of movement to utilize.

Beginners may practice the physical and expressive exercises, sense perception, physical sensation, and other exercises in part I individually or in small groups (which helps develop confidence and a sense of working together) before attempting to create more advanced improvisational mime or pantomime, stage and screen acting, and mime and text exercises in part II.

If participants have sufficient weekly training in dance, gymnastics, or a physical education program, the preparatory physical exercises may be practiced for a shorter period of time. To improve their movement work in class, students may work on selected physical and expressive exercises that may be given as homework assignments. Participants may create their own mime exercises, scenes, improvisations, and pantomimes by adapting plays, children's stories, poems, and historical or other material into mime and movement forms.

The study of all movement forms comprises first of all the development of the body as an instrument. Only after one has acquired flexibility and muscle control of each part of the body through physical exercise is one prepared to move and express well. However, if the following program of physical exercises is too extensive or if some exercises are not useful for the teacher or students' purposes, the exercises may be selected according to need and utilized for classroom, individual training, or as a basis to create material for school performance. If the student requires improvement in specific areas of physical training such as flexibility, relaxation, balance, or muscle control, the exercises addressing these needs may be selected with the help of a teacher or coach and, in addition to class work, can be practiced on one's own. Besides utilizing this program to develop flexibility, muscle control, balance, and other physical elements, participants will also find benefit in the movement practices of yoga, Tai Chi, martial arts, and movement techniques such as Laban, the Alexander Technique, and Feldenkrais, as well as physical activities such as swimming, ice skating, skiing, tennis, fencing, gymnastics, tumbling, and dance (ballet, jazz, folk, or period).

When practicing these exercises, the student should allow physical movement to discover feeling and thought rather than the contrary. Students should also maintain a sound balance between physical and imaginative work, the one never being sacrificed to the other. Precision, clarity, and vitality of expression are all essential, movement being related to feeling and thought rather than created solely for physical effect. Physical and expressive movement should not be conventional, generalized, exaggerated, or disrupted (except for comic or special effects) but rather be particularized, continuous, and creative.

CHOOSING A MOVEMENT STYLE: WHEN TO USE STAGE AND SCREEN MOVEMENT, MIME, PANTOMIME, CORPOREAL MIME, PHYSICAL THEATRE, AND IMPROVISATION

Choosing a movement style depends on the training and movement skills the teacher and participants wish to develop and improve upon for educational or artistic purposes. The choices as to which kind of movement to select for the gestures and movements in the expressive exercises in this program are multiple. For example, to interpret the expressive hand movements of washing one's hands, turning the pages of a book, or picking up a telephone receiver while also portraying character and emotions, consider the following choices for gestures and movement:

- The stage and screen actor's concrete, nonstylized ones utilized with real props, sets, and a text.
- The mime's stylized movement that interprets the action more emphatically and formally through movement and gestures without props or words.
- The pantomimist's autonomous and conventional pantomimic ones that create the illusion of the existence of props, sets, and other characters to depict the action and that may be performed with whiteface.
- The corporeal mime's unconventional, more universal corporeal movement that expresses inner emotions.
- The physical theatre performer's physical theatre style that combines mime, dance, clowning, or other stage forms.
- The improviser's spontaneous physical improvisation (see chapter 1).

The expressive occupational gestures and movements of, for example, sawing a log or carrying a ladder, utilizing trunk, shoulders, and arms, could be illustrated by the stage actor's larger movements to project to an audience and the screen actor's diminished and less expansive gestures. And their words and use of props would equally portray in a realistic manner the character, for instance, of a person frantically trying to finish sawing a large real log before nightfall or a person hurriedly carrying a real ladder and climbing it to save a child in a burning house.

When chopping a log or carrying a ladder are interpreted without (or with lesser) props and words, the mime performer's mime style would require more emphasis on the use of movement that is enlarged and more crafted. And when the pantomime performer, usually wearing whiteface makeup on an empty stage, creates the detailed illusion of the presence of a log and a saw that he or she uses, and of a ladder that is carried and climbed, he or she would recur to more exaggerated conventional pantomimic movements of sawing and climbing. The abstract and corporeal mime would also interpret these actions without props and words. But rather than doing so concretely through occupational movement, the latter would construe them more abstrusely to depict inner feelings such as the fear and anxiety of facing death under the pressure of time. The spectator may interpret these nuances of the universal feelings of death and anxiety according to his or her imagination.

Thus, contrary to acting accompanied by spoken dialogue and the use of props, or dance combined with mime, or storytelling, or clowning that includes juggling and other circus antics, in stylized mime in which the performer does not utilize props and words, he or she must rely on crafted movement and gestures as the main means of communication. In pantomime, where words are also not employed and the pantomime artist is creating the illusion of props as well as characters that are present, the movement and gestures need to be clear, precise, and well defined. For example, in acting, either verbal or silent, real steps are provided when climbing a staircase. In stylized mime, and even more explicitly in pantomime, the illusionary effect of the steps one climbs as well as the climbing of the steps needs to be established (as indicated in the pantomime exercise on climbing steps in part I).

Again, while a mime would interpret, for example, a painful toothache by holding his or her jaw in agony with larger, crafted movement, and a pantomimist would employ conventional illusion type gestures, the speaking or silent actor, working with props and words, would not need to employ enlarged or conventional and pantomimic gestures but rather more natural and realistic movement to communicate suffering. When creating pantomime, one should also choose a subject that is familiar and may be clearly communicated along with the development of characterization and the introduction of a dramatic conflict. For example, a dental patient entering the dentist's office holding his or her jaw in pain may be depicted by an actor as a fearful person struggling to face the dentist. This pantomimic action could still contain the same basic emotions as those expressed by the actor, with the difference that the actor would employ nonstylized, more natural, and less exaggerated movement along with the use of words or exclamations and props such as an ice pack or scarf held on the patient's jaw.

When interpreting this same scene in abstract mime, to depict physical pain the mime would not convey the details of a patient's visit to a dental office with the precise movements and gestures of having a toothache but rather create a less explicit and more imaginative rendition of suffering. Differing from the actor's realistic, occupational movements of holding the jaw and using props and words to express pain would be the stylized mime's interpretation without props and words, and the pantomimist's conventional, illusionary pantomimic movements to create the illusion of a dental patient suffering from a toothache. The abstract mime would express anguish through unconventional movements and gestures that depict universal physical and emotional suffering, leaving much of the interpretation up to the spectator. The abstract mime performer could, for example, enter crouching with an immobile masklike expression and periodically raise his or her torso and rock from side to side. Spectators' interpretations of this action could include, for example, imagining they are viewing a scene of physical suffering, or one of lamenting or mourning for the loss of a mate or child, or some other kind of sorrow.

In physical theatre, which may comprise movement derived from physical improvisation or spontaneous physical action, the performer could include text, dance, buffoonery, and other movement forms and stage arts to communicate a dental patient's painful toothache in a more concrete manner than in corporeal or abstract mime.

Chapter 3

Basic Physical
and Expressive Exercises

This program provides choices in a large selection of basic physical exercises interspersed with related expressive exercises intended for all kinds of movement students and artists. It will be beneficial even if only a limited number of physical and related expressive exercises, along with the visual image exercises, are selected and practiced during each session. The basic physical and expressive exercises should be repeated several times at first and if needed more often later. (See the sample lessons in appendix A, also available at www.AnnetteLust.com with several exercise illustrations.)

The concentrated practice of physical exercises not only improves one's technique but also helps release emotions and free the imagination. The coordination of the physical with emotional expressivity is also essential to the organic wholeness of the stage and screen performer's art. Because it is important to link physical and expressive exercises as well as connect body training with other aspects of the performer's training in voice, acting, clowning, dance, and other stage arts, the corresponding expressive exercises should be practiced along with the physical exercises. To integrate body work with emotional expression, it is important to intersperse the technical exercises with related expressive and eventually with visual image exercises (see appendix A, lessons 3 through 10).

The suggestions for expressive exercises are offered here as a starting point to be further developed by students. The sooner students can devise their own expressive exercises connected with the physical exercises involving the particular parts of the body, the faster they will begin to develop their own creativity. And to acquire a sense of collaboration, whenever possible and with the exception of solo pieces, two or more students should perform the expressive exercises.

The expressive exercises that accompany the physical exercises and the visual image exercises created by the participants may be enacted in nonstylized, informal acting for those interested in stage as well as screen movement. Students who reap the benefits of learning to work for both stage and screen will develop a better sense of their bodies and of movement that enables them to react naturally and be spontaneous and resourceful. It will also help them take direction from directors needing different types of movement. Working with a screen director will likewise develop an awareness of how to create and repeat body or head movement for multiple screen acting takes. When utilizing screen acting, the students should imagine they are projecting to a camera rather than to an audience and utilize reduced movement when performing in close proximity to one another.

These expressive and visual image exercises may be adapted to stylized or more formal mime and to pantomime for those who wish to specialize in mime, clowning, or ballet pantomime. Suggestions for the use of pantomime or more stylized mime are included in the following exercises for individual parts of the body.

The expressive and visual image exercises in chapters 3 and 4 may also serve as subjects to further develop into short scenes or to use as a basis to create spontaneous physical improvisations. Subjects for solo and group improvisations may likewise be found in part II.

ESTABLISHING AN AIM

Before beginning this program of exercises, the teacher and students need to establish what they wish to accomplish, how they will realize that aim, and the results they hope to obtain.

If participants wish to learn multiple movement styles, from movement for stage and screen to corporeal mime, to prepare their bodies for all kinds of movement genres, they may utilize all of the exercises included in parts I and II and suggested in appendix A. This will provide them with a well-rounded physical training background that allows their bodies to adapt to varied physical expression genres and diverse movement styles. This exploration of multiple movement forms will also help students better understand themselves and their talents to make future choices as stage and screen performers.

If participants aim to ameliorate their movement expression to act on stage and screen, they may engage in all of the basic physical exercises for the different parts of the body in this chapter. They may also work on improvisation, movement for acting, the mime and text exercises, and the selected scenes and prose and poetry sections in part II and in appendix A. As a result, they will be prepared to utilize nonstylized movement combined with spoken words to achieve a total form of stage and screen acting.

Students who wish to engage in practicing and performing pantomime and express ideas and emotions through exaggerated and stylized pantomimic movement and gestures, as in the art of a Chaplin or Marcel Marceau, may concentrate on the pantomime exercises and original pantomimes in parts I and II and suggested in appendix A. If more pantomime exercises are needed, they may select the basic physical and expressive exercises and visual image exercises in part I and adapt them to pantomime. As a result, the students will be able to create movement of the whole body solely by means of a stylized and silent physical means of expression. The appendix lesson plan and the videography and bibliography also offer suggestions to view videos and books with illustrations of pantomime.

To develop their improvisational skills, students may practice the improvisational exercises and utilize improvisation to expand on the expressive exercise themes in this chapter for individual parts of the body, work on the improvisational exercises and develop the scenes for improvisation in chapter 5, as well as the *commedia* scenarios in the "Working with a Mask" section of this chapter, and the themes for improvisation in appendix B. All of these exercises will free the students' physical expressivity and develop their physical spontaneity and creativity.

For those interested in corporeal mime, the corporeal mime section in this chapter is only an introduction to this form of mime that requires more advanced training. Suggestions for other books, videos, and DVDs to consult are provided in appendix A, appendix F, the bibliography, and in the list of schools and training centers. Corporeal mime will render students' physical expression articulate and serve as excellent training for other forms of mime and stage and screen acting.

All the exercises in this program may be helpful for students who wish to engage in physical theatre that could contain mime, dance, mask, music, text, clowning, *commedia*, and multimedia. Physical theatre may also include movement styles that range from Decroux corporeal mime, Marceau pantomime, Lecoq mime and clowning, *commedia*, and Laban, Feldenkrais, Suzuki, and Tai Chi. Physical theatre does not exclude various dance styles and forms of Eastern theatre, some of which are mentioned in the videography in this program.

All of the basic physical and expressive exercises for the individual parts of the body are useful for students interested in learning stage combat. Suggestions are offered in the list of training centers for those who wish to pursue the study of stage combat.

The exercises in "Body Relaxation and Warm-ups," "Aligning the Body," "Breathing," and "Working with the Body Center" that precede the physical and expressive exercises for individual parts of the body should not be practiced as a habitual routine but with fresh vitality. They may also serve as an introduction to the exercises in each section.

BODY RELAXATION AND WARM-UPS

Body relaxation exercises, intended to relieve body tension and help the performer function well physically, mentally, and emotionally, should be practiced in an unstrained manner. A relaxed body may be maintained during all the exercises by beginning with several exercises intended to relieve tension and that render the body unconstrained but not limp. The following physical exercises should begin with deep and slow inhaling and exhaling in order to warm up muscles and relax joints. If desired, several breathing exercises may be added before beginning relaxation exercises (see "Breathing").

After working on the relaxation exercises, one way to verify whether muscles and limbs are no longer tense is to have students lie down and one of the participants or the teacher gently lift each student's hand, arm, or foot a few inches to check if these parts of the body fall back loosely to the floor. To prevent or relieve muscle tension that may develop after practicing certain exercises, gently shake the involved body muscles and relax the entire body after each lesson.

It is important to visualize each exercise in the program before beginning.

Basic Relaxation Exercises

Exercise #1

Lying

(See Figure 1. Illustrated Exercise #1)

1. Lying with your upper and lower back touching the floor, extend legs straight ahead and turn them outward. Place arms at sides, drop chin, slowly inhale and exhale as you relax your entire body and feel it sink into the floor.
2. Lying with your arms extended above head, gently stretch out legs; point right and left toes forward and draw them back. Repeat and relax.
3. Lying, with your arms dropped at sides, close eyes and inhale slowly from the diaphragm. Exhale mental, emotional, and physical impurities as you relax first your toes, and move up body to relax feet, legs, thighs, buttocks, stomach, chest, arms, shoulders, neck, face, and head. Hold entire body in relaxed state for 15 to 30 seconds.
4. Tense, hold five seconds and relax left toes; repeat with left foot, next left leg from the knee down, and thigh. Repeat on right side.
5. Lift left leg slightly and drop back limply to the floor. Repeat with right leg.
6. Tense, hold five seconds and relax separately buttocks, stomach area, chest muscles, fingers, hands, forearms, upper arms, shoulders, neck, head, open mouth and tense lips, close eyes, move eyebrows and forehead up and down. Tense the entire body; hold five seconds, and relax.
7. Lying, inhale a deep breath and slowly bring arms up overhead to touch hands; exhale and drop arms to sides. Inhale and slowly raise right leg; exhale and drop leg to the floor; repeat with left leg, repeat with both legs.

Standing

8. Legs comfortably apart, inhale, rise on toes, and stretch arms upward as far as possible, tensing all upper body and arm muscles; alternate reaching upward with right and left arms for 30 seconds. Relax, exhale and fall forward from waist down, slowly swinging from side to side like a limp Raggedy Ann doll.
9. Muscles relaxed, inhale and move from waist down in large circles from right to left; exhale and repeat left to right; inhale and make circles from waist up right to left; exhale and repeat left to right.
10. Make large circles with each shoulder separately, first backward and then forward, arms hanging limply at the sides. Repeat with both shoulders simultaneously.

Figure 1. ILLUSTRATED EXERCISE #1

1   Lying with your upper and lower back touching the floor, extend legs straight ahead and turn them outward.

Place arms at sides, drop chin, slowly inhale and exhale as you relax your whole body and feel it sink into the floor.

2   Lying with your arms extended above head, gently stretch out legs; point right and left toes forward and draw them back. Repeat and relax.

3   Lying, with your arms dropped at sides, close eyes and inhale slowly from the diaphragm. Exhale mental, emotional, and physical impurities as you relax your toes, feet, legs, thighs, buttocks, stomach, chest, arms, shoulders, neck, face, and head...

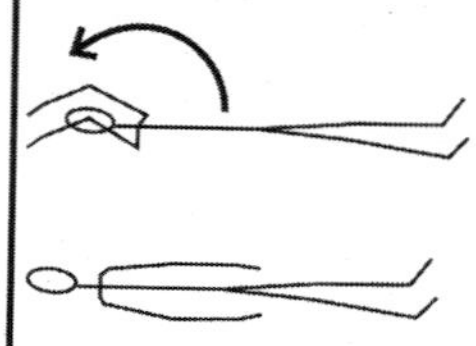

4   ...Tense, hold five seconds and relax left toes; repeat with left foot, next left leg from the knee down, and thigh. Repeat on right side.

5   Lift left leg slightly and drop back limply to the floor. Repeat with right leg.

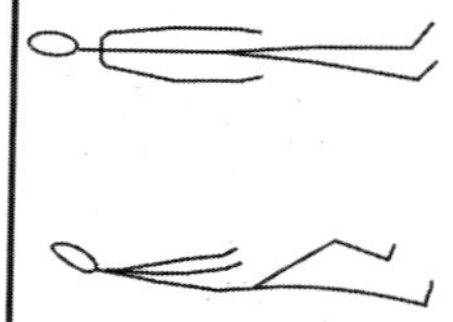

6   Tense, hold five seconds and relax separately buttocks, stomach area, chest muscles, fingers, hands, forearms, upper arms, shoulders, neck, head, open mouth and tense lips, close eyes, move eyebrows and forehead up and down.

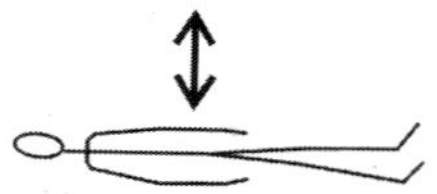

Tense the entire body; hold five seconds, and relax.

7 Lying, inhale a deep breath and slowly bring arms up overhead to touch hands;	
exhale and drop arms to sides.	
Repeat.	
Inhale and slowly raise right leg; exhale and drop leg to the floor; repeat with left leg, with both legs.	

8   Legs comfortably apart, inhale, rise on toes, and stretch arms upward as far as possible, tensing all upper body and arm muscles;

alternate reaching upward with right and left arms for 30 seconds.

Relax, exhale and fall forward from waist down, slowly swinging from side to side like a limp Raggedy Ann doll.

9   Muscles relaxed, inhale and move from waist down in large circles from right to left;

exhale and repeat left to right;

inhale and make circles from waist up right to left;

exhale and repeat left to right.

10   Make large circles with each shoulder separately, first backward ...

...and then forward, arms hanging limply at the sides.

Repeat with both shoulders simultaneously...

Repeat with both shoulders simultaneously...backward

...and forward

11   Make circles gently from neck up, right to left and left to right...

...dropping head limply forward...

...and backward.

12 Stretch arms out to the sides, drop forearms limply from elbows down,

...and bring back up and circulate arms outward and inward;

in same position move wrists up and...

down and...

...circulate outward and inward.

13 Legs comfortably apart, inhale, raise arms, and clasp hands tightly over head, tightening all muscles and hold for thirty seconds;

relax muscles, bend knees,

and exhale as you swing arms down between legs.

Hands clasped above right shoulder, swing down...	
...as in chopping wood;	
alternate with hands clasped above left shoulder.	
Repeat swinging arms higher from upper left to upper right side of body twisting trunk from left to right and...	
...from upper right to left side of body twisting trunk from right to left.	

14 Inhale and gently undulate all of body by pushing thighs forward...	
...followed by chest and shoulders pushing backward,	
and exhale as chest and shoulders move forward...	
followed by thighs moving backward.	
Repeat several times.	

15 Sitting on floor, legs extended and wide apart (bend knees if legs cannot be fully extended), grasp ankles, bend forward from hips and gently bounce;

sit up...

...and repeat toward right leg...

(sit up)

and left legs.

Relax.

16 On knees, place your hands on floor in front of you and lower head;

inhale moving head up and stomach and chest outward;

exhale and contract chest by rounding back and pull in stomach.

Return back to flat position.

Repeat sequence several times.

END OF EXERCISE #1

11. Make circles gently from neck up, right to left and left to right, dropping head limply forward and backward.
12. Stretch arms out to the sides, drop forearms limply from elbows down, and bring back up and circulate arms outward and inward; in same position move wrists up and down and circulate outward and inward.
13. Legs comfortably apart, inhale, raise arms, and clasp hands tightly over head, tightening all muscles and hold for thirty seconds; relax muscles, bend knees, and exhale as you swing arms down between legs.

    Hands clasped above right shoulder, swing down as in chopping wood; alternate with hands clasped above left shoulder. Repeat swinging arms higher from upper left to upper right side of body twisting trunk from left to right and from upper right to left side of body twisting trunk from right to left.
14. Inhale and gently undulate all of body by pushing thighs forward followed by chest and shoulders pushing backward, and exhale as chest and shoulders move forward followed by thighs moving backward. Repeat several times.

Sitting:

15. Sitting on floor, legs extended and wide apart (bend knees if legs cannot be fully extended), grasp ankles, bend forward from hips and gently bounce; sit up and repeat toward right and left legs. Relax

On Knees:

16. On knees, place your hands on floor in front of you and lower head; inhale moving head up and stomach and chest outward; exhale and contract chest by rounding back and pull in stomach. Repeat several times.

Expressive Relaxation Exercises

Develop the action in the following expressive exercises.

1. Walk very slowly as the sun beats down on you and you feel as if you are melting; breathless, drag your feet after jogging halfway up a hill.
2. Roll limply around on the green grass, enjoying its cool softness.
3. Fall onto a couch or floor, exhausted after working out.
4. Sitting in an automobile that just passed a red light and missed hitting a car crossing before you, take a big breath, exhale, and drop head and body forward, relieved.
5. Float on a lake, all muscles relaxed, feeling the soft waves ripple against your body, soothing you as the warm sunlight streams down.
6. Slowly doze off as you watch a boring movie, all muscles relaxed and your head drooping to one side.

7. Tense your whole body as you feel a large branch brush hard against your back. Bend your body forward, relieved after moving away from the branch.
8. Tense arms, shoulders, back, and facial muscles as you reach high up to pick an orange on a tree. Relax body after you pick it.
9. Tense leg and feet muscles as you try to squeeze into tight boots. Relax leg and feet muscles after you succeed.
10. Tense your whole body as you suddenly see a snake move across your path. Relax as it moves away.
11. Tense your arms, trunk, and shoulders as you hear a door slam. Relax when you discover it was only the wind that blew the door shut.
12. Locked out of your house after losing your key, tensely pound on the door with hands and feet frantically trying to be let in. Relax your whole body when someone opens the door.
13. Walk with your body limp after coming out of a steaming hot sauna.
14. Undulate and swing your body to and fro as you dance a hula dance in a relaxed manner.
15. Create other expressive relaxation exercises.

ALIGNING THE BODY

Before beginning exercises of the different parts of the body, the body should be aligned and the posture erect, relaxed, and natural. To align the body, begin in a neutral position by standing erect, motionless, and without any tension, to be ready for action. Stand with your feet six to eight inches apart, knees forward and relaxed (not hyperextended or locked), stomach muscles pulled in toward the spine, and shoulder blades drawn back together. The chest should be raised, the back broadened and lengthened, shoulders and neck relaxed, and the head forward and up.

Another way of aligning the body is to stand for sixty seconds, gently pressing your back and the remainder of the body in a relaxed manner against a wall, and then walk away maintaining the same position.

Observe your front and profile postures in a mirror. Correct (with the help of a teacher or student) back, neck, chest, and knee positions that are not erect, relaxed, and natural. Think positively about your posture and create an image of an aligned body for yourself. To acquire a poised and free body according to the Alexander technique, try Walter Carrington's *Thinking Aloud* (see the bibliography).

The following seven-step exercise may be practiced standing and in its entirety.

Exercise #2

(See Figure 2. Illustrated Exercise #2 for numbers 1–6)
The following 7-step exercise may be practiced standing and in its entirety

1. Standing, feet approximately six inches apart in semi-V position, your body straight and bent slightly forward without arching your back, the body's

weight placed on the center of the feet, inhale. Exhale, relaxing all of body and face, feeling your spine lengthening and your shoulders widening, and continue inhaling and exhaling.

2. Without moving your feet, lean your body backward and forward and from side to side.
3. Inhale, hold and exhale, slowly moving thorax (chest) backward; inhale moving back to center and pushing out chest; exhale and repeat from beginning.
4. Inhale slowly moving head (keeping upright position) from center to right; exhale moving head back to center. Repeat from center to left.
5. Slowly move head (keeping upright position) upward, back to center, downward, and back to center.
6. Slowly drop head to right shoulder and back to center, to left shoulder and back, drop forward to chest and return, backward and return.
7. Return to a neutral relaxed position attempting to center your body as you continue to inhale and exhale while feeling your spine lengthening and your shoulders widening.

Expressive Alignment Exercises

1. Slouch, dropping head and shoulders forward, knees bent, feeling depressed. Straighten up, move head up, widen and lengthen back, straighten knees, feeling cheerful and free.
2. Pull head up and back, and raise shoulders, feeling defensive and ready to strike back at someone for having insulted you. Relax head and shoulders, feeling relieved after the person who insulted you has apologized.
3. Jut upper body, head, and jaw forward as you question someone you think has been extorting money from you. Relaxed, straighten upper body, head, and jaw when you discover the person is innocent.
4. Frown and tilt head and upper body to one side, trying to understand what a wounded person is mumbling to you. Relax forehead and straighten head and upper body as you begin to understand him or her.
5. Shift weight backward, pull shoulders up, draw in pelvis, and lock knees as a bee flies around you. Relax, straighten body, and drop shoulders and release knees as the bee flies away.
6. Draw head and shoulders back; pull in pelvis and lock knees, feeling tense and proud to receive a long-awaited award at an awards ceremony. Center head and shoulders, relax pelvis, and release knees as you leave the awards ceremony stage.
7. Utilize the following scene for posture and alignment changes. In *Tartuffe*, Act IV, scenes 5 and 6, as Tartuffe pursues Elmire to seduce her, he is crouched over, shoulders and head bent, joyfully and tensely wringing his hands as he approaches her. When her husband, Orgon, emerges from under the table, Tartuffe straightens his body, standing upright, seemingly guiltless, relaxed, and in control as he prepares to defend himself.
8. In the above scene, as Elmire, frightened, tries to escape from Tartuffe, she cowers each time he approaches her but stands erect and relaxed when her husband comes out from under the table to protect her.

Figure 2. ILLUSTRATED EXERCISE #2

1   Standing, feet approximately six inches apart in semi V position, your body straight and bent slightly forward without arching your back, the body's weight placed on the center of the feet, inhale.

Exhale, relaxing all of body and face, feeling your spine lengthening and your shoulders widening, and continue inhaling and exhaling.

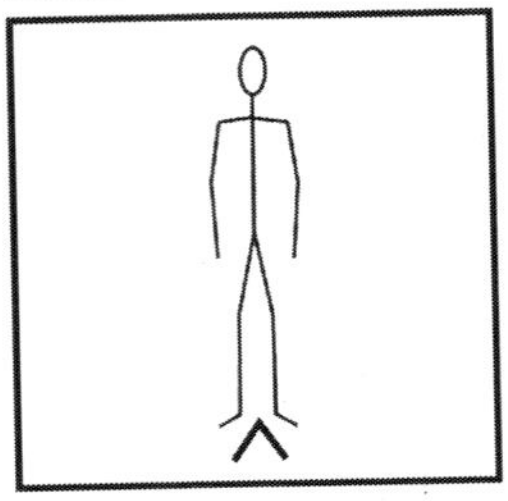

2   Without moving your feet, lean your body backward...

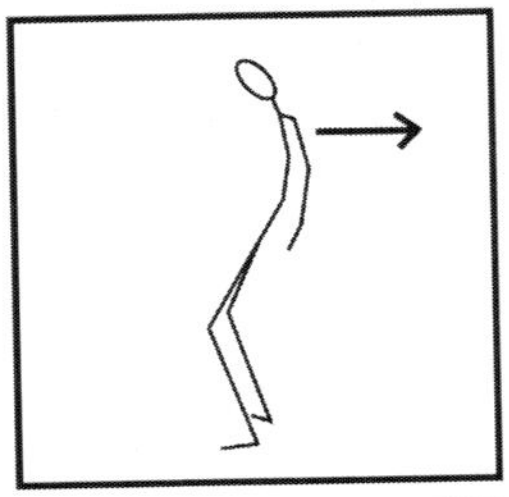

...and forward...

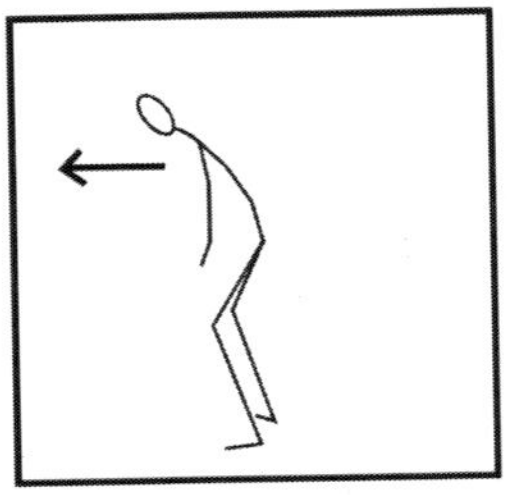

...and from side to side.

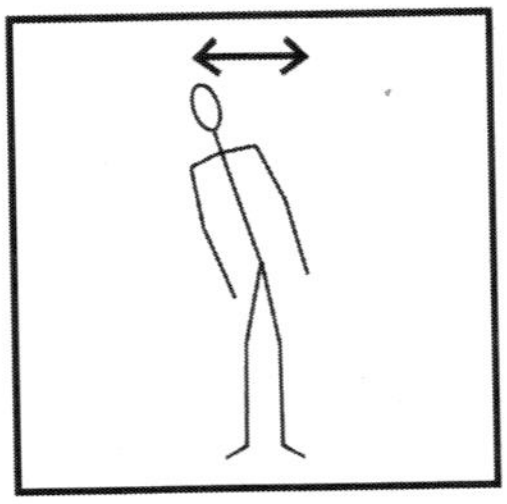

3 Inhale, hold and exhale, slowly moving thorax (chest) backward;	

inhale moving back to center and pushing out chest; exhale and repeat from beginning.	

4 Inhale slowly moving head (keeping upright position) from center to right;	

exhale moving head back to center.	

Repeat from center to left.	

5   Slowly move head (keeping upright position) upward,

back to center,

downward, and back to center.

6   Slowly drop head to right shoulder and back to center, to left shoulder and back, drop forward to chest and return, backward and return.

7   Return to a neutral relaxed position attempting to center your body as you continue to inhale and exhale while feeling your spine lengthening and your shoulders widening.

END OF EXERCISE #2

9. In Chekhov's one-act play *The Proposal*, Natalya stiffens, pulling back her head, shoulders, and upper body and locking her knees when her neighbor Ivan claims the land between them is his and she angrily replies that it belongs to her. After Ivan leaves and her father reveals that Ivan came to propose marriage to her, she relaxes, centering her head, shoulders, and upper body and releasing her knees as she now calmly asks her father to bring him back.

10. Find or create other scenes in which the actor or actors transform the alignment of their bodies.

BREATHING

Breathing influences movement and the vitality of the whole body that depends on the respiratory mechanism. In order to perform with our entire being, we need to develop our breathing to its full capacity. To relax, cleanse the mind and body, and help direct body movements, begin a class or a rehearsal or performance with several of the following exercises based on the practice of yoga. As mentioned earlier, physical and expressive exercises benefit when preceded by a few moments of deep and slow inhaling and exhaling. Throughout all the exercises in the program, remember to inhale when engaged in dynamic movement and to exhale on relaxed movement. It is also important to be aware of the rhythm and breathing needed for the physical, expressive, and visual image exercises in chapters 3 and 4 as well as in working with improvisation, pantomime, and physicalizing the spoken word in chapters 5 through 7.

Repeat the following exercises several times or more.

Exercise #3

Repeat the following exercises several times or more.

Standing:

(See Figure 3. Illustrated Exercise #3a for numbers 1–6)

1. Legs slightly apart, muscles relaxed, arms at sides, breathe deeply from the diaphragm, slowly inhaling through the nose to the count of four, retaining breath for four to six counts or as long as it is comfortable; slowly exhale through the mouth to the count of four. As you inhale, keep chest and shoulders motionless, expanding the ribs sideways. With practice, double the length of inhaling, retaining, and exhaling.

2. Inhale and rise up on tips of toes, holding breath for four to six counts or as long as it is comfortable. Exhale and return to standing position.

3. Inhale and raise both arms above head, placing one palm against the other, holding breath from four to six counts or as long as it is comfortable. Exhale and drop arms.

Figure 3. ILLUSTRATED EXERCISE #3A + #3B

ILLUSTRATED EXERCISE #3A

1   Legs slightly apart, muscles relaxed, arms at sides, breathe
deeply from the diaphragm, slowly inhaling through the nose to
the count of four, retaining breath for four to six counts or as long
as it is comfortable;

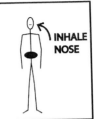

INHALE
NOSE

slowly exhale through the mouth to the count of four.
As you inhale, keep chest and shoulders motionless, expanding
the ribs sideways. With practice double the length of inhaling,
retaining, and exhaling.

EXHALE
MOUTH

2   Inhale and rise up on tips of toes, holding breath for four to six
counts or as long as it is comfortable.

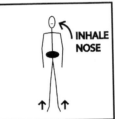

INHALE
NOSE

Exhale and return to standing position.

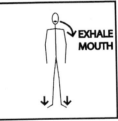

EXHALE
MOUTH

3   Inhale and raise both arms above head, placing one palm against the other, holding breath from four to six counts or as long as it is comfortable.

Exhale and drop arms.

4   Cleansing and revitalizing breath. Stand, legs apart, and inhale, stretching arms above the head.

Dropping arms, bend forward from the waist and expel breath rapidly repeating the sound of HA. Hang from the waist and swing arms loosely repeating HA several times.
Rise and repeat.

Hang from the waist and swing arms loosely repeating HA several times. Rise and repeat.

5 With your right hand thumb close right nostril and inhale slowly through left nostril, holding breath from 4 to 6 counts,	INHALE
and then slowly exhale through right nostril as you close left nostril with the little finger of the right hand.	EXHALE
Repeat closing left nostril and inhaling through right nostril. (holding breath from 4 to 6 counts)	INHALE
(and then slowly exhale through left nostril as you close right nostril with the little finger of the right hand.)	EXHALE

6   Inhale from diaphragm to the count of five...

**INHALE
TO 5**

...and exhale (to the count of ten) through the mouth a little breath on each of the ten counts and the remainder on the last count.

END OF EXERCISE #3A

**EXHALE
TO 10**

ILLUSTRATED EXERCISE #3B

1   Lying on back, legs extended and slightly apart, arms at sides, begin inhaling from the diaphragm continuing the intake from the lower chest, and then from the upper chest.

Hold and exhale some air from the upper chest, continuing to exhale air from the lower chest, and then exhale the remainder of your breath from the diaphragm.

**INHALE
NOSE**

2   Repeat the exercise inhaling to the count of 4 (increasing to 6 counts or more with practice), holding it to the count of 4 (increasing with practice to 6 counts or more), and slowly exhaling to the count of 6 (increasing with practice to 8 counts or more).

**EXHALE
MOUTH**

3	Lying on back, knees bent, feet flat, arms extending at shoulder height, inhale and to the count of four to six, raise hips...	
	...and slowly draw circles with hips from right to left;	
	exhale and return to original position. Repeat drawing circles from left to right.	
4	Lying on stomach, arms stretched out to sides, inhale lifting chest and right leg; hold 3 to 5 counts...	
	...and exhale as you return to original position. Repeat with left leg.	

5   The Cobra. Lie down on the abdomen, chin touching the floor, arms bent with elbows raised + palms on the floor at either side of your chest, legs straight + together + toes pointed. Inhale + to the count of five slowly lift upper body, leaning on your hands + arching your back, the lower part of the body from the navel down touching floor, head up with eyes looking upward;

Inhale and to the count of five slowly lift upper body, leaning on your hands and arching your back, the lower part of the body from the navel down touching the floor, head up with eyes looking upward; hold five counts;

exhale and slowly descend to the count of five. Repeat.

6   The Cat.
On knees and all fours, back flat, hands flat on the floor, arms straight, head centered...

...inhale counting to six as you slowly lower head and curve the spine up to a hump; hold six counts...

...exhale as you slowly move the spine back down to flat position to the count of six, keeping the rest of the body still. Repeat several times.

END OF EXERCISE #3B

4. Cleansing and revitalizing breath. Stand, legs apart, and inhale, stretching arms above the head. Dropping arms, bend forward from the waist and expel breath rapidly repeating the sound of HA. Hang from the waist and swing arms loosely repeating HA several times. Rise and repeat.
5. With your right hand thumb close right nostril and inhale slowly through left nostril holding breath from 4 to 6 counts, and then slowly exhale through right nostril as you close left nostril with the little finger of the right hand. Repeat closing left nostril and inhaling through right nostril.
6. Inhale from diaphragm to the count of five and exhale through the mouth a little breath on each of the five counts and the remainder on the last count.

Lying:

(See Figure 3. Illustrated Exercise #3b for numbers 1–6)

1. Lying on back, legs extended and slightly apart, arms at sides, begin inhaling from the diaphragm continuing the breath intake from the lower chest, and then from the upper chest. Hold and exhale some air from the upper chest, continuing to exhale more air from the lower chest, and then exhale the remainder of your breath from the diaphragm.
2. Repeat the exercise inhaling to the count of 4 (increasing to 6 counts or more with practice), holding it to the count of 4 (increasing with practice to 6 counts or more), and slowly exhaling to the count of 6 (increasing with practice to 8 counts or more).
3. Lying on back, knees bent, feet flat, arms extending at shoulder height, inhale and to the count of four to six, raise hips and slowly draw circles with hips from right to left; exhale and return to original position on the count of four to six. Repeat drawing circles from left to right.
4. Lying on stomach, arms stretched out to sides, inhale lifting chest and right leg; hold 3 to 5 counts and exhale as you return to original position. Repeat with left leg.
5. The Cobra. Lie down on the abdomen, chin touching the floor, arms bent with elbows raised and palms on the floor at either side of your chest, legs straight and together and toes pointed. Inhale and to the count of five slowly lift upper body, leaning on your hands and arching your back, the lower part of the body from the navel down touching the floor, head up with eyes looking upward; hold five counts; exhale and slowly descend to the count of five. Repeat.

Kneeling:

6. The Cat. On knees and all fours, back flat, hands flat on the floor, arms straight, head centered, inhale counting to six as you slowly lower head and curve the spine up to a hump; hold six counts; exhale as you slowly move the spine back down to flat position to the count of six, keeping the rest of the body still. Repeat several times.

Sitting:

Sitting on the floor with feet comfortably apart and arms relaxed at sides, inhale slowly to the count of 4; exhale to the count of 8, dropping head forward until it is between the knees. Inhale slowly to the count of 4 as you raise your head. Exhale rapidly after you sit up.

The following exercise will gradually augment your breathing capacity.

7. Exhale, relax, take a breath and pronounce with precise diction a line from your favorite play or poem once. Exhale and take a deeper breath and repeat the line twice. Remain relaxed as you continue taking a breath, keeping shoulders down and augmenting the number of times you repeat the line as you hold your breath.

Expressive Breathing Exercises

1. Take a deep breath to summon up courage to dive into the ocean from a pier.
2. Breathe short and irregularly, as you grow more and more frightened by a mysterious tapping noise against the wall.
3. Exhale a deep sigh of exasperation as you hear a complaint from your neighbor about your barking dog. Quicken your breath as you forcefully defend your dog.
4. Pant as if out of breath from running to catch a bus you are about to miss. Gradually slow down panting as you reach the bus.
5. Breathe as if breathing is painful because of a sore throat. Breathe more easily after you swallow medicine.
6. Gasp several times, happy over hearing that your lost dog has been found.
7. Inhale a deep breath of relief as you finish writing a long paper.
8. Breathe tensely, your breath becoming shorter as you jump into a cold shower.
9. Breathe slowly and heavily, feeling giddy from sitting in the hot sun.
10. Breathe and hold your breath after opening a bottle of vinegar. Close the bottle and breathe a sigh of relief.
11. Inhale a deep breath as you push open a heavy wooden gate to rescue a cat behind it. Exhale as you pick up the cat and go out and close the gate.
12. As you bend down into a pool to find a ring you just dropped, inhale before you place your head in the water; exhale as you raise your head out of the water.
13. Read aloud passages of poetry, prose, or plays, inhaling before and exhaling after each line or short passage.
14. Create other expressive breathing exercises.

WORKING WITH THE BODY CENTER

In order to strengthen, stabilize, and harmonize the body and physical movements, the actor, mime, and performer should work from the body center from which certain movements and gestures are initiated. You may begin by locating the body center (or centers) that is the source of movement and energy in your own body. This source may be, for example, the head, chest, heart, abdomen, or another area. After discovering your own body center (or centers) and source of energy, you may experiment with imagining different body centers to create various characters and their emotional reactions. These centers that command movements should be integrated into the movements of each character and remain basic to emotional reactions.

The next set of exercises describes generalized feelings identified with certain body centers and, depending on the character and the circumstances, may likewise relate to other body centers. For example, intense emotional feelings may originate from the chest as well as from the heart, while strength and authority may originate from the loins as well as from the chest or head. The use of a mask in these exercises helps to clarify and fortify the physical reactions related to the body centers. (See chapter 2 and appendix C for information on creating and using masks.)

1. To find your own body center, as you rise from a sitting position, attempt to discover where the movement originated (chest, abdomen, legs, etc.). Do the same when you sit down, walk, or lie down.
2. Stretched out on your back, slowly inhaling and exhaling, direct your attention to the centers of your body from which certain movements originate, such as raising arms from the chest, arching your body upward from the abdomen, pressing the head down from the neck, and other movements.
3. Feel qualities corresponding to each center: for example, strength coming from the loins; intense emotions from the stomach, the center of visceral feelings; empathy from the heart; calm determination from the head; confidence from the chest; sensuality from the genitals, and so on. Add arm, hand, leg, feet, and other body movements to accompany the feelings originating from each of these centers.
4. Feel fear originating from the stomach, and with the chest, stand up to face someone attempting to attack you.
5. Standing upright, smile and begin to move your trunk forward to shake the hand of a new acquaintance. Next frown, pull back your trunk, and withdraw your hand when someone impolitely walks between both of you.
6. Move loins forward as you pull hard on the knob of a door that is stuck. Next draw back loins and almost fall backward as the door suddenly opens.
7. Standing, walking, sitting, and lying, create reactions in accordance with the centers of vitality where the movements originate, showing intention and utilizing movements in a precise situation (for example, fear of a rat under a bed with movements originating in the stomach; admiration for a hero's photo with movements originating in the chest).

Expressive Body Center Exercises

1. Advancing with the stomach, devour slices of chocolate cake from a buffet table. Feel your stomach pull in and stop as you realize that others are watching you stuffing yourself.

2. Feel the body center in your shoulders, shifting shoulders up and down as you nervously try to find an excuse to tell your boss you can't work overtime. Drop shoulders reluctantly when your boss tells you he needs your help.

3. Move with head and mouth leading as you walk toward an ice cream parlor to purchase your favorite ice cream. Drop head and mouth when you find the ice cream parlor closed.

4. Reacting from your heart, sway your upper body from side to side and pace up and down, ready to break down after receiving news of a close friend's car accident.

5. React from your chest, disturbed as you see someone shove a person who falls down in the street.

6. Interpret the following scene and the scenes in items 7 through 11 first without and then, if desired, with words, utilizing various body centers to express the characters and their reactions. In Neil Simon's *The Prisoner of Second Avenue*, Act I, scene 2, Edna has just returned from the supermarket to find her apartment has been ransacked. Her movements originate in her solar plexus or chest as she desperately calls the police and begs for help because her husband is not home yet and she is afraid she will be killed.

7. In the above scene, Mel, who is depressed because he has lost his job and not told Edna that he has been out of work for four days, returns to learn that they have been robbed. His reaction stems from his shoulders and chest, which cave in as he receives this second blow.

8. In Shakespeare's *The Merchant of Venice*, Act IV, in the court scene as Shylock declares he requires a pound of flesh rather than money from Antonio, the controlled and calculated movements of his decision stem from his head.

9. In Bernard Shaw's *Saint Joan*, scene 6, during her inquisition, Joan is accused of heresy but is relentless in her intrepid faith and refuses to deny that she has had visions and revelations from God. She stands staunchly upright, her physical movements originating from her chest, which moves up and forward to show her courage.

10. In Jean Racine's *Phaedra*, Act I, scene 3, Phaedra's physical movements portraying her desperation in confessing her secret love for Hippolytus to her confidant Oenone originate from her throat.

11. In the same scene, as Phaedra's confidant Oenone listens to her confession and pities her, Oenone's physical movements, such as her arms extended to give solace, originate from her heart.

12. Act out other scenes with emotions originating from various body centers.

PHYSICAL AND EXPRESSIVE EXERCISES FOR INDIVIDUAL PARTS OF THE BODY

The physical exercises for individual parts of the body help develop flexibility, an awareness of the different parts of the body, and precision of movement. They also serve for warming up and provide motivation for creating expressive movement. They may be done progressively or selected at the teacher's or participant's discretion, repeated as often as needed, but should always be related to and alternated with the expressive exercises in the lesson or created by participants. For example, legs, feet, and running exercises may be followed by an expressive exercise depicting a person running to catch a dog or a departing train.

Since the movements of each part of the body depend upon the trunk, the following exercises begin with trunk movements, which include arm and shoulder exercises. They are followed by exercises involving the end parts of the body, the arm movements preceding those of the hands and fingers, which are often inseparable from the latter. Leg, foot, head, and neck movements are succeeded by facial expression and imaginary and real mask exercises.

To relieve tension and fatigue, selected relaxation and breathing exercises may be repeated after each session. Whether the expressive exercises are practiced in nonstylized movement or in stylized mime or pantomime, they should be done as much as possible in character and represent a precise situation. If the exercise calls for joy or anger, find a reason or particular circumstance to be joyful or angry to motivate each of your character's movements. Establishing a specific body center from which your character's movements originate will also render the movements more focused and forceful.

To obtain clarity of intention, each movement in the expressive exercises should be envisaged physically and emotionally or preceded by an inner reaction prior to being expressed physically. For example, to mime burning your hand on a hot pot, envisage the physical feeling and emotional reaction of the character touching the imaginary object before interpreting it. Or prior to raising your hand to prevent someone from coming closer, enact the gesture and intention inwardly before exteriorizing it. This gives movement and gestures more depth of meaning and credibility.

To gain in amplitude and dramatic tension, a movement may be made opposite to its intended completion. For instance, when tugging a rope toward you, allow the hands to slide from time to time in the opposite direction to show the difficulty of pulling it to you. Or when climbing stairs, move your body down slightly while raising your foot to show your body's effort to reach up to the next step.

When utilizing stylized mime or pantomime, there should be little or no physical contact with your own body or that of another mime. When striking another mime, for example, execute the movement several inches away.

Whenever movements are repeated (except when needed for comical or other effects), they should be enlarged or underplayed the next time so as not to become repetitive.

To encourage the development of creative movement, real props should not be used in the following exercises requiring interaction with objects. They may be utilized in part II in the sections pertaining to mime and text and in improvisation or exercises that prepare students for stage or film scenes that require the use of props.

These basic physical exercises should be done slowly at first and repeated as much as needed with an aim toward continual improvement. They should never be practiced mechanically but with concentration on how a particular physical exercise is functioning and how it is affecting the other parts of the body. And since corresponding expressive exercises are suggested for the physical exercises that pertain to individual parts of the body, the student can, while practicing the basic exercises, begin to imagine how, for example, lifting an arm upward may unleash a feeling of despair or joy, or how when bending the arm and the torso sideways, the student may express a fear of being attacked. In this way, practicing the purely physical aspects of movement can lead to the body's discovery of a corresponding natural and more spontaneous emotional expression of a particular part of the body.

Again, whenever possible, students should be given the opportunity to improvise their own expressive exercises related to the different parts of the body in class or as a homework assignment. Continual observation of one's own and others' movements will enrich one's inventiveness and physical creativity.

TRUNK, SHOULDERS, AND ARMS

The exercises to develop muscle control and widen and lengthen the back and render the trunk and spine flexible should be practiced slowly at first and repeated as often as needed. The expressive exercises and those invented by the students should be done with only the most essential movements.

Begin this segment and all the physical exercises for the individual parts of the body from the neutral or zero position by remaining still, expressionless, and ready for action. Although the entire body is related to the smallest gesture or movement, while moving a particular part of the body the sections of the body not in use should remain motionless. Inhale and exhale deeply from the diaphragm during each exercise. From time to time, shake and relax the part of the body being utilized. A few selected relaxation and breathing exercises may precede and follow sections of the technical and expressive body exercises here as well as in other exercise sections in parts I and II.

Exercise #4

An illustrated version of this exercise is available at www.AnnetteLust.com.

Standing:

1. Begin by standing with legs slightly apart; inhale and expand chest and shoulders; exhale and draw in chest and shoulders.
2. Arms extended overhead, rise on toes and reach upward as far as possible; alternate reaching upward with right and left arms.
3. Arms clasped overhead, pull body straight upward from waist, upward to right, back to center, and upward to left.
4. Slowly lift right arm to shoulder height at side, slightly tensing muscles; slowly drop arm and relax muscles. Repeat with left arm; repeat with both arms. Repeat slowly lifting arms forward at shoulder height separately and then together.
5. Hands clasped behind head, tense your muscles and slowly bring elbow tips forward until they touch and then back and relax muscles. Repeat still more slowly.

6. Arms placed across chest, fingertips touching, elbows up and out, push fingers of both hands hard against one another; release and extend arms to sides and drop.

7. Arms extended at sides, palms down, pull inward as if tugging heavy ropes toward you. Push arms out as though clearing away heavy brush with shoulders, arms, and hands; drop arms to sides.

8. Stretch arms upward and lean and stretch to the left; drop arms and head to left in a relaxed manner. Repeat to the right, backward, and forward.

9. Place left foot forward; stretch right arm toward the back and move to the front several times. Repeat with right foot forward, stretching and moving left arm.

10. Raise arms forward to shoulder height; drop arms from elbows down and move lower part of arms in circles several times inward and outward.

11. Place left foot forward; swing right arm fully from back to front and front to back. Repeat with right foot forward and left arm swinging from back to front and front to back.

12. Arms down at sides, slowly shrug right shoulder and drop; shrug left shoulder; shrug both shoulders. Repeat several times.

13. Arms down at sides, shrug and slowly draw circles with right shoulder, moving it forward and drop. Repeat with left shoulder; repeat with both shoulders. Repeat moving shoulders backward separately and then together.

14. Arms down at sides, simultaneously bring right shoulder forward and left shoulder back; repeat bringing left shoulder forward and right shoulder back.

15. Extend and swing right arm up, back, and around, drawing circles. Repeat with left arm, both arms. Repeat exercise swinging and circling arms forward.

16. Swing left arm to shoulder level at side and swing inward while turning head to left; swing left arm outward and back while turning head to right. Repeat with right arm.

17. Arms at sides, rising on toes, bring shoulders and arms forward and up and bend head down as though ready to dive; drop arms, lift head, expand chest, and straighten shoulders.

18. Lift arms over your head and move trunk in a relaxed manner to the left, to the back, to the right, and forward. Dropping arms at sides, allow body to drop forward from waist down. Repeat, beginning from the right.

19. Using hands and arms to strengthen, widen, and lengthen back, stand in a doorway, place palms as far down as possible on both sides of the frame, and press against it for thirty seconds. Move up two inches and press again for thirty seconds. Continue moving up and pressing against the sides of the frame as far up as you can reach.

Lying:

20. Lying face down, hands clasped on lower back, contract shoulder blades by drawing elbows together behind you. Hold for ten to twenty seconds and then relax.

21. Lying face down, extend arms forward and raise upper chest, shoulders, arms, legs, and feet one to two inches or more. Hold for ten to thirty seconds and then relax.

22. Lie on a bench or stool face down. Extend arms outstretched at sides up toward the ceiling and down ten to fifteen times. Extend arms forward beyond head and back to sides ten to fifteen times. Swing arms up over head toward ceiling until hands touch and bring back down ten to fifteen times. Stretch right arm forward beyond head and then back alternating with left arm ten to fifteen times.

23. Lie on the floor on your back, legs bent, hands clasping back of neck. Flatten back and then raise head and shoulders from floor, hold for five seconds, and then slowly drop back to floor. Repeat moving to right and left.

Sitting:

24. Sitting on the floor, legs apart, hands behind neck, alternate bending trunk to right and to left leg.

Kneeling:

25. On all fours with back flat, swing right arm up, back, and down, twisting right side of trunk to look at moving arm. Repeat with left arm. Repeat moving trunk from center to extreme right, to center, to extreme left. Repeat moving trunk around in clockwise direction and then counterclockwise.

26. On all fours with your back flat, slowly move your back upward like a cat, then bring your back down and hold. Repeat ten to fifteen times.

Standing:

27. Arms bent in front of chest, place fingers of one hand against the fingers of other hand and with shoulders, arms, and hands, push fingers against one another; hold five seconds and release. Repeat ten to fifteen times. Shake and relax shoulders, arms, and hands.

Expressive Trunk, Shoulders, and Arm Exercises

Covering the face with a mask may be utilized in practicing the following exercises to emphasize the expressivity of the trunk, shoulders, and arms. These exercises may be adapted to pantomime and performed with stylized and exaggerated movement that give the illusion of making the invisible visible while expressing dramatic emotions.

1. Chop a big log with a hatchet, bearing down rapidly in a desperate effort to finish cutting it before dark.

2. Carry and set up a heavy ladder, at times almost falling under it.

3. Pull on the rope of a heavy church bell with trunk, arms, shoulders, hands, and legs to alert the villagers of a fire.
4. Shrug shoulders indifferently, angrily, mockingly, in other ways.
5. Drop shoulders meekly as a timid person. Hold shoulders straight up as a courageous person. Move shoulders, back, and trunk as a calm, aggressive, happy, sad, angry person, and as other character types and emotions.
6. Hold arms outstretched to help a child take his or her first steps; to help an older person crossing over a ditch.
7. Balance yourself with arms as you fearfully cross a river on small stones,; as you walk on narrow boards on a newly painted surface; on a burning hot pavement.
8. Beat angrily on a door, nervously, cautiously, in other ways.
9. Shake a dirty dust rag out of a window, moving your face, trunk, and shoulders to one side not to breathe in dust. Impatiently shake and fold bed sheets with a lazy person.
10. Disgusted, wipe or brush away spiders and cobwebs on the ceiling and walls, using trunk, shoulders, and all of upper body as well as arms.
11. Set a table angrily, throwing down dishes and silverware.
12. Throw various objects into the air (e.g., a pillow, books, dishes, etc.) happily, desperately, in other manners.
13. Pick up a wounded animal and place it on a blanket to care for its wounds.
14. Wave good-bye to a friend sadly, cheerfully, in other manners.
15. Stretch arms and yawn, feeling rejuvenated after a nap.
16. Slap or hit someone on the back in a jovial manner; angrily, to catch his or her attention; in other manners.
17. Place hands on hips indignantly, in surprise, with authority, and in other manners.
18. Raise and lower arms while laughing hilariously, while screaming hysterically.
19. Greet a child with open arms. Push away an intruder.
20. Raise arms and back away as a car swerves in front of you. Raise arms in happy surprise at the sudden arrival of a friend.
21. Shake hands with another person cheerfully, indifferently, timidly, and hypocritically.
22. Swim the crawl in a relaxed manner in a lake; swim the backstroke. Swim the crawl against a strong current in the ocean; swim the backstroke in the ocean.
23. Swing a scarf around to the left and right overhead to signal that you are in distress.
24. Step into a tub of water and splash water and scrub your feet and legs to remove mud. Scrub your perspiring body under a shower.
25. Throw a ball up for a dog (played by another student) to jump up and catch with its mouth. Repeat. Throw the ball across a lawn for the dog to run and bring back. Repeat.

Illusion Pantomime for Trunk, Shoulders, and Arms

Illusion pantomime that may be helpful training for actors and other kinds of performers requires a specific and conventional mime style. It differs from expressive stage movement in that it is played with exaggerated and stylized movements and gestures and sometimes with counterweight to clearly communicate the illusion of making the invisible visible. While expressive movement may accompany a spoken text or other art forms and may be utilized with real props, illusion style pantomime is most often practiced in silence, without props, and as an independent form of communication and art.

When engaging in illusion pantomime, first visualize the movements and the object or objects you will be miming and select only essential and a minimum of gestures and movements to create the action. A gesture or movement in pantomime may be highlighted with a light bounce or click at the beginning and end of the gesture or movement portraying an action. For example, to open a door, reach out, lightly bounce and flex (bend) your wrist as you place your hand around an imaginary doorknob; turn the knob and pull it toward you; stop; release, bounce, and drop your hand from the knob. Apply this technique when applicable to the following illusion style pantomime exercises. (For more information on illusion pantomime, see chapter 6.)

After practicing the following exercises, select several of the following examples to develop with characterization and dramatic content.

Standing:

1. Lift a big log, carry it, drop it on a bench, and saw off a piece.
2. Push a heavy table; draw it back to you; open a drawer in the table; close it. Show weight in shoulders, arms, and all of your body by pushing and then drawing the table to you, opening and closing the drawer with counterweight movements (contrasting movements such as thrusting arms forward to push table while leaning upper body backward to gain strength and moving arms toward you to draw table to you while pushing thighs and lower body forward).
3. Pull toward you an imaginary rope held at the other end by a partner, pulling back with trunk and arms as lower part of body moves forward. In the same manner, pull toward you the string of a balloon blowing in the wind.
4. Play a vigorous tug of war with a partner, pulling, losing rope, gaining rope, falling. Utilizing counterweight, as arms, shoulders, and trunk pull back, the lower part of body moves forward, and as arms, shoulders, and trunk are tugged forward, the lower part of body moves backward.
5. At a party, lean casually on a mantelpiece, raising one elbow to shoulder level behind you, forearm dangling downward. Holding a glass of wine in the other hand, sip the wine and place your glass on the mantelpiece with a slight bounce of the hand. Place the other elbow on the mantelpiece with forearm dangling downward; smiling and relaxed, gaze around the room at people partying.

6. Reach high up to pick pears from a tree; shake branches, gather up pears that fall on the ground, and place them in a bag.
7. Push imaginary heavy objects (piano, cabinet) and push light objects (plastic bags, empty shopping cart), showing weight differences in shoulder, arm, and body movements.
8. With a partner, lift imaginary tables of different sizes and turn them upside down. Put them back on legs. Show differences in table weights in your arms.
9. Play tennis, golf, basketball, and other sports with trunk, shoulder, and arms.
10. Conduct an orchestra, playing classical and other kinds of music.
11. Use arms to simulate a duck spreading its wings to move away from someone.

Sitting:

12. Play a monkey sitting on a branch and removing bugs from a younger monkey.
13. Sitting on a cliff, throw a fishing line into the sea and pull out a big fish.
14. Row a boat, utilizing more and more effort as the sea grows rougher.
15. Play a harp, an accordion, and other instruments with trunk, shoulder, and arms.
16. Sit on a stool or bench with your back to viewers and show tension in your back, shoulders, and arms as you drive through a blinding blizzard.

HANDS, WRISTS, AND FINGERS

Exercise #5

An illustrated version of the exercise is available at www.AnnetteLust.com.

1. Arms stretched forward, palms facing downward, clench fists, open them, and repeat. Repeat with palms facing upward. Repeat with arms stretched upward and to sides.
2. Arms stretched forward, palms facing downward, flex hands from the wrist upward and downward and repeat. Repeat moving hands from the wrist to left and to right. Circle hands to the right; repeat to left.
3. In same position, move fingers of right hand upward and downward; repeat with fingers of left hand; repeat moving fingers of both hands together. Move each finger of right hand separately up and down; repeat with left hand. Circle each finger of right hand to the right and then to the left. Repeat with left hand.
4. Spread fingers of right hand like a fan; close; repeat with left hand; repeat with both hands. Undulate right hand from wrist down in waves; undulate left hand; undulate both hands.

5. Form an "O" by touching first and second fingers of right hand, then first and third fingers, then first and fourth fingers, then first and fifth fingers. Repeat with fingers of left hand; repeat with fingers of both hands.
6. Place one palm of hand against the other at chest level. Push hard, hold, and relax. Repeat holding hands above head; repeat holding hands behind head.
7. Hands crossed at wrists in front of chest, pulse against pulse and held at an angle, vibrate and flutter fingers and move hands around like a bird flying slowly, then faster, and then as a bird wounded in the air that falls.
8. Start to clap hands but do not let the hands actually touch. Stop when the hands are two inches apart, then a foot apart, then several feet apart.
9. Juggle imaginary ice cubes in your hands. Open and close hands as you roll balls on a table; squeeze a sponge.
10. Scratch yourself; massage yourself; tickle someone under the arms; tap fingers on a door to enter; try to warm up by shaking freezing fingers.
11. With your hands and fingers, create a duck's beak; the mouth of a fish opening and closing; other shapes.
12. Create other movement exercises with your hands and fingers.

Expressive Hand, Wrist, and Finger Exercises

Wearing a mask in the following exercises will bring out the expressivity of the hands, wrists, and fingers. Develop characterization and dramatic content in these exercises.

1. Pull on fingers nervously as you wait for a doctor to give you results of your medical exam. Clap hands to kill a moth, joyfully, angrily.
2. Caress a cat, dog, horse, and other pets lovingly; tap on their backs to correct them.
3. Open a letter and read news of a friend's death; show emotion in hands by trembling, dropping the letter, and lowering hands. Sit down at a computer to type out a letter of condolence to your friend's family.
4. Pick up a telephone and try to call someone, impatiently tapping fingers on the phone and moving it from hand to hand as you try to get information from the operator.
5. Steal a purse or briefcase from someone, moving your hands slowly and stealthily. Throw a purse or briefcase angrily at someone.
6. Pick up a dollar bill on the street and, looking around, quickly put it in your pocket. Pick up a dollar bill and run ahead to ask a person if he or she lost it.
7. Burn your finger on a stove; apply ointment to subdue the pain.
8. Sign a contract reluctantly, willingly, fearfully, with enthusiasm.
9. Dig into sand and run it through your fingers until you find a surprise object.
10. Wring your hands in a frenzied manner, impatiently, happily, greedily.
11. Slip, fall, and place hands on forehead in shock, surprise, pain.
12. Frustrated, rub hard to remove stubborn spots on a garment.
13. Beckon for help as you see a person fall in the street. A second pair of hands helps you lift up the person and carry him or her from the street.

14. Roll an imaginary piece of paper into a ball and throw it at someone playfully to get the person's attention, to annoy someone.
15. Pick up and set down various objects such as a book, pen, suitcase, or other object cheerfully, sadly, hesitatingly, disgustedly.
16. Open a door sadly, prudently, suspiciously, happily, with curiosity. Open and push a door outward; open and pull a door toward you; open a sliding door, swinging door, and trap door, each with different feelings.
17. Grow more and more impatient as you attempt to hammer a nail that is bent.
18. Portray sad, hesitating, kind, nervous, frightened, angry, busy, indifferent, and other types of hands as you interact with another person.

Sitting:

19. Sit down and unlace shoelaces in a casual, hurried, preoccupied manner.
20. Work on a crossword puzzle; suddenly hear footsteps and stop to listen with curiosity and fear; show relief after you recognize the footsteps and continue the puzzle.
21. Sew a button showing impatience, nervousness, boredom.
22. Move a pencil pensively, playfully, dreamily, annoyingly.
23. Peel potatoes or another vegetable hurriedly, carefully, awkwardly.
24. Press palms against the window to see the mail carrier bringing a letter you have been awaiting; to see a police officer ringing your bell, an angry neighbor.
25. Create other hand and finger exercises displaying an emotion.

Illusion Pantomime Exercises for Hands, Wrists, and Fingers

Create imaginary objects and situations in the following pantomimes. (For more information on illusion pantomime, see chapter 6.)

1. Create a precise image of the size and texture of a table and feel its flat, hard surface as you move your hands over it. Without overgesticulating, repeatedly flex and open one hand at a time, spreading fingers and extending your hand while keeping it flat as you thrust it on the table with an abrupt and sharp click or bounce and hold at the same level as the other hand. Keep hands still as you touch the table and do not change the level of the table. Place one hand on the table and move around it; kneel and rise with one hand on the table.
2. Holding hands up vertically before you, flex and open one hand at a time with a click or bounce to feel the flat hard surface of a wall as you move upward and rise on toes. Place one hand against the wall and move body to right and left.
3. Locked in a dark closet, feel the walls and ceiling as you try to find a way out.
4. Pick up a pole with one hand; after placing the other hand on it, turn and hold it before you horizontally with both hands about one foot apart, fin-

gers facing the floor and hands remaining at the same level. Roll the pole toward you repeatedly by releasing and grabbing the pole that you turn with one hand at a time. To turn the pole up vertically, remove the right hand from the pole and then grab it again with fingers facing the ceiling to push it up vertically by moving the right hand up over the left hand about one foot apart; hold and move back down to horizontal position and repeat with left hand moving above right hand. To pass the pole from one hand to another, hold the pole up vertically with one hand and open hand as you release and pass it to the other hand that closes with a slight bounce as it grabs it. Throw it in the air with one hand and catch it with a slight bounce; balance it vertically on your open palm as you walk about. In a group, pass the pole from one to another.

5. Pick up and, holding it horizontally with both hands, pull at the ends of a flexible rubber tube that you elongate, slowly closing hands over it to show it is becoming narrower. Move back slowly as you shorten it, gradually opening hands to show it is growing thicker. Transform the tube into an umbrella, magic wand, and other objects.

6. Pick up a ball, throw it from one hand to the other, opening and releasing it with one hand and closing the other hand and bouncing it slightly as you catch it; throw it up, bouncing hand slightly as you catch it. Bounce it on the floor, indicating how high it bounces with your hand, head, and eye movements; balance ball on the end of a stick; continue playing with the ball.

7. Take hold and turn a doorknob with right hand; open the door and pull it to you with shoulders and arms, chest slightly concave or hollowed; release hand from knob, straighten up, and pass through the door, weight on leg shifting and chest concave as you turn and pull the doorknob to close the door. Straighten up as you release hand from knob.

8. Enter and push on a revolving door, hand flat against door and chest slightly concave. Releasing hand, move along with door, exit, and straighten up, moving head in a circle as you look back at door continuing to swing around.

9. In the following immovable point exercise, walk about with a tray or another object (book, plate, etc.) on the palm of one hand held out to the side. At one point, feel the object almost drop and suddenly stop you with a slight back and forth body movement and up and down bounce of your hand, freezing your movements as you try to prevent the object from falling while balancing it in midair. Push a cart; drag a chair; walk with a kite and other imaginary objects during which your movements are suddenly arrested by a stone or other object in your path.

10. Open and close a faucet by placing hand on it, turning to right and left, and releasing hand; wash and dry hands slowly, rapidly, under cold water, hot water.

11. Stir gravy, mashed potatoes, and other ingredients, showing the difference in amount and thickness of liquid or food as you stir.

12. Remove your wristwatch, adjust the time, and put it back on wrist. Remove an antique wall clock, adjust the time, wind it up, and put it back on the wall.

13. Turn the pages of a book slowly, rapidly.
14. Cut, comb, and style hair; braid hair.
15. Cut different shaped figures out of paper. Cut material for a dress or shirt.
16. Make a cake, knead dough, mix it with milk, eggs, and sugar. Make cookies, pie, bread, and other food.
17. Remove objects (statue, dish, candle and holder, a bell, and other objects) from a mantelpiece and dust them with a cloth. Convey the size, shape, and weight of each object with hands and dust cloth.
18. Cover the seat of a chair with material. Turn over the seat and use hammer and nails to attach material.
19. Massage another person's back and neck.
20. Remove a tiny splinter from your finger with a pin.
21. Wrap and unwrap boxes of different sizes.
22. Wash, wring, and hang socks. Iron a shirt and slacks.
23. Thread a needle and mend a hole; thread a sewing machine and then sew something with it.
24. Play a piano or another instrument, varying the tempo. Have others guess what kind of instrument and music you are playing.
25. Sweep and mop a kitchen floor; wipe kitchen surfaces and clean the sink.
26. Knit and fold a sweater, a scarf, or other woolen articles, varying your pace.
27. Write in large letters, small letters, and other kinds of styles; type words on a computer.
28. Cut, clean, file, and paint your nails.
29. String beads.
30. Communicate with someone in a foreign country with your hands. Ask him or her where to find a restaurant or a particular street, or where to find the subway or a bus.
31. Carry on a conversation with a foreign person looking for work and a room to rent. Through gestures, tell the person that he or she may rent a room in your house, earn some money washing windows, cleaning the house, painting, or doing other jobs.
32. Create other illusion pantomime occupational exercises with hands, wrists, and fingers.

Improvisation with Trunk, Shoulders, Arms, Hands, and Fingers

Develop dramatic action and movement in these subjects for improvisations. (For more information on physical improvisation, see chapter 6.)

1. Improvise situations with a partner using an imaginary stick to climb a mountain; use the stick to lift a large rock with the partner to search for a hidden cave. Use the stick for other purposes such as a blind person's cane or to train a dog to do tricks.
2. Garden clippers in hand, step up on an imaginary bench or small ladder to trim imaginary leaves on a bougainvillea vine growing on a wooden lattice. For example, reach up to the top of the vine and stretch to the right and left

to cut protruding leaves. Remove a roll of wire from your pocket, then with your clippers clip off pieces of wire to attach loose stems of the vine to the lattice. As you ward off a mosquito, almost fall off your bench or ladder. Descend and drag a hose to water the vine. Find more gardening activities.

3. In a restaurant kitchen, with two or three other cooks, prepare salads, soup, meat dishes, potatoes, rice, and desserts.
4. With partners, portray hairdressers and manicurists in a beauty salon who wash, cut, blow dry, style hair, and file and paint clients' nails.
5. Push a little child on a swing. As the child suddenly falls off the swing, help her or him to get back on the swing.
6. As a construction worker, working with others, saw and hammer away to build a house.
7. You and others enter a laundromat with your bundles of clothes. You each place your clothes in washers and dryers, remove them, and fold them.
8. Massage a person with severe muscular pain.
9. Create other improvisations with trunk, shoulders, arms, hands, and fingers.

TOES, FEET, LEGS, AND HIPS

Exercise #6

An illustrated version of the exercise is available at www.AnnetteLust.com.

Standing:

1. Buttocks slightly tucked under, legs a bit apart, slowly rise on toes and, bending knees, descend as far as possible and return to standing position. Bending and lifting right foot, rise on left toes and, bending left knee, slowly descend as far as possible and return to standing position; repeat with other leg. (If necessary at first, hold on to wall or chair for support.)
2. Place right foot forward and bend right knee, keeping back straight, and return; repeat with left knee. Legs apart and turned out, slowly move to right while bending right knee; straighten; move to left bending left knee; straighten. Repeat, bending knees a little more each time.
3. Slowly lift right leg, bend the knee, moving knee up as high as possible; extend leg forward and return to beginning position. Repeat with left leg. Repeat gradually bending and straightening supporting leg with arms extended at sides to maintain balance. Repeat rising on toes of supporting leg with arms overhead to balance body.
4. Standing with feet parallel, left side close to wall and left hand placed flat on wall, slowly turn right leg outward while moving right foot up along left leg until it reaches left knee; repeat with other leg; repeat rising on toes of each supporting leg.
5. Holding onto a chair or wall for support, lift and bend right knee to waist; circle right leg from knee down to right and then to left several times. Repeat with left leg. Repeat with each leg stretched out forward.

6. Stand on left foot and reach toward the ceiling with left arm. Bend right leg and place it on right buttock with right hand; hold for fifteen seconds. Repeat with other leg.
7. Hands forming a circle above your head with palms together, lift right leg and wrap right foot around the ankle of left leg; hold ten to twenty seconds. Repeat with right leg.
8. Heels together, hands on hips, slowly rise on toes and descend to sitting position and return.
9. Standing, slowly alternate movement from waist down to left and to right, and right to left, without moving body from waist up. Create figure eights from waist down to left and right.
10. Kneel and move knees together; slowly lower buttocks to heels. Rise to knee position.
11. Standing, inhale and straighten spine, then exhale slowly on five counts, pulling in tummy and belly button toward spine, and hold without moving other parts of body. Repeat ten times.

Sitting:

12. Sit down and curl toes under, hold, release. Try to pick up small objects with toes (eraser, pencil, marble). Move forward and back on outer edges of feet.
13. Lift right foot, point toes, and draw circle in the air; repeat with left foot. Draw numbers and letters with each foot; write your name with each foot.
14. Feet apart, lift heel of right foot and lower; repeat with left heel; repeat with both heels.

Lying:

15. Lie on back, arms stretched parallel above head; bend knees to slowly bring body to sitting position, feet not touching floor and head rising while arms lower to clasp knees as body reaches sitting position. Slowly lower body to floor while extending legs and moving arms overhead, feet not touching floor until body is outstretched.
16. On back, arms stretched above head, slowly raise one leg straight up and lower it; raise the other leg and lower it. Raise one leg and draw a circle in the air; repeat with the other leg.
17. On back with feet flat on floor, knees bent, and arms at sides, inhale and lift buttocks for five seconds and return to floor.
18. On back with knees bent, pull right knee to chest, hold five seconds, and return. Repeat with left knee.
19. On back with knees bent, pull both knees toward chest, hold five seconds, and lower and straighten legs one at a time.
20. On back with knees bent, to the count of five seconds, straighten and lift right leg to height of left knee; slowly lower straightened right leg to floor and slide foot back to buttocks and bend knee. Repeat with left leg.

WALKING, TURNING, RUNNING, CLIMBING, DESCENDING, ROWING, JUMPING, BICYCLING, AND HORSEBACK RIDING

Walking

1. To warm up legs, walk briskly two minutes in place. Stretch right leg to rear and hold fifteen seconds. Repeat with left leg.
2. Chest erect, begin walking from the hips down, slowly moving around the room in a relaxed manner, the body held slightly forward. Repeat using the glide walk and lifting your heel after each step.
3. Walk in a straight line balancing an object (book, dish) on head or on back of hand.
4. Walk over real or imaginary objects of different sizes without breaking the rhythm.

Walking in Place and Other Walking Illusion Pantomime

For information on illusionary walks and other illusion pantomime, see Montanaro YouTube videos.

1. Forward Pressing Down Walk. Facing forward and standing with feet slightly apart and parallel, raise right foot and then press down on toes with heel up. Next press right heel down and straighten knee, keeping left foot parallel to the ground as you slide it back and then move it forward to repeat same movements with left foot. Move slowly and smoothly, right arm swinging forward when pressing down left foot and left arm swinging forward with pressing down right foot. The emphasis and the body's balance are on the stepping foot with the other foot sliding backward, giving the illusion of moving forward.
2. Backward Pressing Down Walk. This walk is the same as the Forward Pressing Down Walk with the emphasis on the foot opposite the stepping foot sliding forward, giving the illusion of moving backward.
3. Front to Back Profile Walk. Standing in profile with feet together and slightly apart, thrust right foot forward and slide it back with heel leading. As right foot slides back, slowly raise left heel. When right foot is back in place, thrust left foot forward and slide it back with heel leading as you continue. Swing left arm forward as right foot moves back and right arm forward as left foot moves back. Continue, moving from hips down, chest erect, head high, eyes focusing on a point ahead and emphasizing moving back by holding foot a second at back. Practice the walk slowly, feeling movements of muscles in legs and feet as you progress, pushing one thigh forward followed by accentuating the other leg sliding back.
4. Back to Front Profile Walk. This walk is the same as the preceding except that the emphasis is on sliding the feet forward. Standing in profile, thrust right foot forward and then slide foot back along floor to starting position while simultaneously pushing forward with left thigh and rising on left toes before

sliding left foot back as right thigh pushes forward and right leg rises on toes. Swing left arm forward as right foot moves forward and right arm forward as left foot moves forward. Progress with one thigh pushing forward followed by accentuating the other leg sliding to the front.

5. Pushing Thighs Walk. With legs a good distance apart, push out thigh and lift heel of right leg without moving feet; bring right heel and thigh back to starting position as left heel and thigh push up and out. Alternate arm movements with leg movements, moving left arm forward when right leg pushes forward and vice versa. Feel as though you are progressing in space by pushing thighs forward and lifting heels with effort while feet and legs remain in place.

6. Walking against the Wind. For Walking in Place against the Wind, lean forward with head down, shoulders drawn in, and fists clenched. Create movements with arms and other parts of the body. For Pushing Thighs Walk against the Wind, push the thighs out forcefully and bend torso backward as though being pressed back by the wind. Push arms and hands out before you to guard against the wind. When the wind becomes too strong, step back two steps with torso concave and repeat pushing forward hard against wind.

7. Utilizing one of the illusion pantomime walks, walk forward on an imaginary tightrope; walk backward. Walk on a tightrope with another person at the other end facing you and walking, each reacting to the other's movements. Walk on a tightrope with someone behind you whose movements cause the rope to quiver as you try to keep your balance.

8. Utilizing the illusion pantomime walks, walk with various parts of the body leading in order to create different types: for example, chin leading for a stubborn person, nose leading for a nosy person, shoulders leading for an athlete, chest leading for a proud person, feet and legs leading with long strides for an ambitious person, bent shoulders leading for a tired older person, hips leading and swinging for a coquette, head leading for a determined person, and so on. Find other types led by various parts of the body.

Turning

1. Walk and turn the head first to the right, the shoulders and chest next, with the rest of the body following as you pivot on the leg bearing weight and the other leg takes the next step. Repeat turning to the left.

2. Walk slowly around room and suddenly pivot on leg bearing weight and walk in opposite direction; walk rapidly and turn.

Turning Illusion Pantomime

Incorporate turning with walking, running, or other illusion pantomime.

Running

1. Begin with body in a slightly oblique or inclined position with weight on the lower back, in the center of the body, and on the back leg. As you run,

the legs should push the body forward and upward. To suddenly stop, bear down on the leg that is supporting the body's weight, bending the knee and centering the body that remains vertical to the ground.

2. Run across the room balancing an object (book or cup) on your head; repeat balancing object on back of your hand.

Running Illusion Pantomime

Run in place using walking in place illusion pantomime and quickening the rhythm, lifting legs higher, and bending slightly forward.

Climbing and Descending Steps

1. Climb and descend steps balancing an object (book or cup) on your head or shoulder.
2. Climb onto and descend smoothly from a riser, footstool, and other objects.

Climbing and Descending Illusion Pantomime

In the following climbing and descending exercises, punctuate foot and hand movements with a click or bounce.

1. To climb stairs, bend body slightly back and, moving in place, lift right foot a few inches, step down on imaginary step on right toes, then on ball of right foot, body rising as right heel touches ground and hand takes hold of railing at chest height and slides back downward to hip height, followed by left foot rising on toes and body moving upward to repeat this action. Head and eyes focused upward, with a continuous rhythm, move one leg and arm downward while the other leg moves upward on toes and the hand takes hold of banister and moves downward before taking the next step.
2. As in Front to Back Profile Walk (item 3 under "Walking in Place and Other Walking Illusion Pantomime," above), descend stairs, falling heavily on each foot after sliding it back and moving arm from hip height upward to chest height as hand takes hold of railing and slides upward with each step moving downward. Head and eyes focused downward, continue with one foot rising on toes and then pressing down while hand moves upward before the next step is taken.
3. Climb a ladder with similar foot and leg movements as climbing stairs. Raising head and looking upward, take hold of imaginary rungs with hands held up firmly above one another on two rungs approximately one foot apart just above your head (or in a second version, with hands held up at the same level above head and moving down together); lift right foot to step on imaginary rung, descending first on right toes and next to ball and heel of right foot, body rising as right heel touches ground and left foot rises on toes, both hands (either one foot apart or in second version held at the same level) sliding down simultaneously and the lower hand moving above the upper hand

to reach the next rung while maintaining the same distance between both hands (or in second version with both hands held at the same level moving down together). Lift left foot to move to next rung as lower hand is placed one foot above upper hand (or with both hands at the same level) sliding down simultaneously as left foot descends from toe to ball and heel of foot. Continue to climb as right foot rises and right hand moves above left hand and slides down with left hand (or both hands move down together) as you climb to the next rung.

4. Descend a ladder (see Back to Front Profile Walk) by holding hands steadily one foot apart on imaginary rungs, sliding hands simultaneously up each time you take a step, and maintaining the same distance between hands (or in second version with both hands moving together) as right foot descends from toes to heel, kicks back, and then moves forward to step down to next rung followed by left foot as you continue down the ladder.

5. Climb a tree with similar foot and hand movements as climbing a ladder, placing hands one foot apart above your head as you take hold of imaginary branches above and place feet on branches below or dig feet into the tree trunk to move upward. Descend as though descending a ladder, holding hands a foot apart on upper branches and placing feet on lower branches or digging feet into the trunk to move downward.

Climbing and Descending a Rope Illusion Pantomime

1. To climb an imaginary rope hanging from a tree, place the rope between your knees and lock them together; look up and stretch hands above head as you grab the rope with one hand and place the other hand a foot below it. As you pull yourself up the rope and slide hands straight down toward chest, open and close legs as you move up on your toes and down. Hands apart as you lower your feet, move legs around the rope again and reach up placing the lower hand on top, keeping the same distance between hands, and sliding both hands downward as you pull yourself up.

2. To descend the rope, grab the rope before you, one hand placed above the other and knees locked together. Slide both hands upward and open and close legs as you move downward on the rope. Repeat placing upper hand below lower hand and sliding both hands upward.

Rowing Illusion Pantomime

Sit on floor with legs apart and knees bent and grab imaginary oars; leaning trunk forward, pull imaginary oars to you, moving trunk and hips back; continue to move forward and back. Row with a partner through stormy weather.

Jumping

1. Jump down from a step, two steps, a chair; jump from imaginary levels.
2. Jump rope in place; jump rope running around the room; jump and try to make a complete turn to return to starting position; jump over different-sized imaginary objects (books, small stool, etc.).

Jumping Rope Illusion Pantomime

Jump rope with one foot at a time (see "Running Illusion Pantomime," above) and add arm movements to turn imaginary rope. Jump rope with both feet.

Bicycling Illusion Pantomime

1. Standing in profile, mount bicycle from left side by placing hands one foot apart on imaginary handlebar, keeping them firmly in this position without moving them; lift left foot to step on pedal, swing right foot over bicycle, and sit down with a slight bounce; slightly raise and descend body as you pedal by circling foot of leg that faces the audience. Move handlebar to right and to left to show change of direction. To go around a corner, extend one foot to side and pivot on other leg. To go up and down hills, slow down or accelerate circling of foot, and lean body forward or backward.
2. Ride in tandem, one bicycle rider behind the other, utilizing the same movements simultaneously.
3. Facing front, place hands steadily one foot apart on imaginary handlebar as you mount bicycle; rising on left toes and bending forward, circle right leg and foot once; rising on right toes and bending forward, circle left leg and foot once. Repeat, keeping hands in same position on handlebar and turning slightly as body shifts from one leg to the other. Feel body rise and descend as you pedal. See previous exercise for going around corners, up and down hills, and accelerating and slowing down.

Horseback Riding Illusion Pantomime

Grab the imaginary saddle on the horse with left hand and place left foot in the stirrup, then swing right leg over the saddle and place right foot in stirrup; bend both knees at the sides of the horse. Lift reins, and kick the horse gently with right foot; walk the horse, slightly moving your body from side to side. Lift the reins, kick the horse gently, and trot with the horse, moving body forward and up and lifting heels up and come back down in the stirrups. Leaning back slightly, lift the reins, kick the horse, and gallop with the horse, rocking your body back and forth. Pull back on reins and stop. To get off the horse, with left foot in stirrup and holding onto the saddle, swing right leg over the saddle, place right foot on the ground, and then remove left foot from stirrup and place it beside right foot. Take hold of the reins and walk the horse to the stable.

SITTING, BOWING, KNEELING, FALLING, SOMERSAULTING, DANCING, AND SKATING

Sitting

1. Standing, hands on hips, heels together, bend legs and descend, attempting to sit on heels and rise slowly. Spread legs apart; bend them to squatting position and rise.

2. Lying with legs bent and feet flat on the floor, rise to sitting position without help of hands.
3. Sit on stools or objects (boxes, pillows) that are progressively lower, balancing a book, cup, or other object on your head.

Sitting Illusion Pantomime

1. Back straight, bend knees just enough to keep your balance and sit down on an imaginary chair, the foot nearest chair maintaining weight, the opposite foot sliding along the floor to other foot, chest and arms relaxed, shoulders erect. To rise, move toward front of chair; the leg on which the weight is placed pushes the body upward as the other leg prepares to receive weight of the body. Use same movements to sit down again on the chair, crossing legs at the ankle or knees or placing one foot on the opposite knee.
2. Inclining forward from the waist up and bending right knee slightly, raise the left knee almost to hip level; lean your left elbow and arm on your left thigh and cross right arm over left arm. To appear as if you are sitting cross-legged, cross left knee over right knee with arms in same position.
3. Sit on imaginary chairs and sofas of different styles, beginning with a straight chair, then an armchair, a rocking chair, a straight-back sofa, a wide and deep-seated sofa, and other kinds of chairs and sofas with corresponding positions.

Bowing

1. Taking a step forward with left foot, bow as you take another step forward with right foot and extend right arm across waist.
2. Stepping back with left foot, and placing weight on right foot, bow as you extend right arm across waist.
3. Without moving, bow as you extend right arm across waist.
4. Curtsy, moving one foot behind the other in fourth ballet position, leaving space between feet and bending legs, with arms at sides, hands turned to front, and head inclined forward.

Kneeling

Exercise #7

An illustrated version of the exercise is available at www.AnnetteLust.com.

1. On all fours, extend right leg back and circle leg clockwise and counterclockwise from hip. Repeat with left leg.
2. On all fours, extend and stretch left leg to rear and return. Repeat with right leg. Repeat, accelerating pace.
3. Kneel with knees apart, trunk erect; lean trunk back as far as possible without bending it. Repeat, attempting to move still closer to floor.

4. Kneel on right leg and rise; kneel on left leg and rise. Kneel and rise holding various objects (book, etc.) on your head.
5. While holding a cup or other object in your open palms, kneel and rise without dropping it. This exercise, which develops balance and control, when mastered may also be done rising from lying on the back and on the stomach.

Falling

Exercise #8

An illustrated version of numbers 1–3 of the exercise is available at www.annette lust.com. All falls should be practiced smoothly and slowly at first and progressively more rapidly and continuously in a space that is clear of furniture or other objects.

1. To fall sideward, take a deep breath and relax all body muscles until they are limp. In a single movement, kneel on right knee, drop head and shoulders toward right, sit on right side, brush floor on right by extending side and arms, drop head onto right arm, and roll onto back. Lying on the floor with body relaxed, exhale. To rise, inhale and in a single movement roll from back to right shoulder, right elbow, and hand, and slowly bring up upper part of the body. Bend legs, placing weight on one leg as the other rises and stands. Exhale. Repeat on left side.
2. To fall backward, take a deep breath, relax, and kneel on right knee, dropping head and shoulders; sit back on kneeling leg and then lie back, right leg folded under left leg, arms brushing the ground on each side until they are over your head (use hands to slide down on floor to protect head). Exhale. Repeat kneeling on left knee.
3. To fall forward, take a deep breath, relax, and kneel on right knee, dropping head and shoulders; move left foot back along floor as body falls forward, head dropping on arms (to protect the head and face) that slide forward along the floor. Exhale.
4. To fall in a faint, utilizing the above falls, relax muscles and total body as if feeling weak and dizzy, dropping head, shoulders, and knees limply to the ground in a heap.
5. Practice above falls inhaling and counting to thirty, completing the fall on the thirtieth count. Exhale and rise on thirty counts.
6. With practice in subsequent lessons, repeat item 5, attempting to fall and rise on fifteen counts, on eight counts, on four counts.

Somersaulting

1. Do a somersault by throwing hands down to the right on a mat, then swing the feet over the head and rise from the mat to land back on feet. Repeat to the left.
2. Weaving an object through your fingers (pencil, paper, etc.), somersault and rise still holding the object.
3. After mastering the side somersault, try to do a somersault forward and backward. To roll forward, take one step forward, bend, place hands on

ILLUSTRATED EXERCISE #8 PAGE 1

1 All falls should be practiced smoothly and slowly at first and progressively more rapidly and continuously in a space that is clear of furniture or objects.
To fall sideward, take a deep breath and relax all body muscles until they are limp.

In a single movement kneel on right knee, drop head and shoulders toward right...

sit on right side, brush floor on right by extending side and arms...

drop head onto right arm...

and roll onto back.

Lying on the floor with body relaxed exhale.

To rise, inhale and in a single movement roll from back to right shoulder, right elbow, and hand...

and slowly bring up upper part of the body.

Bend legs...

placing weight on one leg as the other rises and stands.

Exhale.

Repeat on left side.

continued on next page

2   To fall backward, take a deep breath,

relax and kneel on right knee, dropping head and shoulders;

sit back on kneeling leg and then lie back, right leg folded under left leg,

arms brushing the ground on each side...until they are over your head.

(Use hands to slide down on floor to protect head)

EXERCISE #8 PAGE 4

Exhale.

Repeat kneeling on left knee.

3   To fall forward, take a deep breath, relax and kneel on right knee, dropping head and shoulders;

move left foot back along floor as body falls forward,

head dropping (gently) on arms (to protect the head and face) that slide forward along the floor.

Exhale.

END OF EXERCISE #8

floor before you, roll forward and stand. To roll backward, step back, bend, sit, push back with legs, roll onto shoulders and head, place hands on floor beside head, and then push back and stand.

Dancing

Dance your favorite dance (tango, waltz, or others). If you dance with a partner in illusion style pantomime, keep a few inches distance from him or her to create a mimed version of dancing.

Skating

To ice-skate or roller-skate, bending knees, lean forward and, leading with heels, slide one foot obliquely back and then slide same foot forward and outward to one side while inclining in the direction of the slide; repeat with the other foot; swing both arms up to side of foot sliding forward and back down and to opposite side with the other foot moving forward. Maintain an even rhythm, accelerating to go faster and standing erect and progressing less rapidly to slow down. To indicate you will be ice-skating, when putting on ice skates, lace up shoes. For roller skates, adjust strap across each foot.

EXPRESSIVE TOES, FEET, LEGS, AND HIPS EXERCISES

Expressive exercises follow for walking, turning, running, climbing and descending, rowing, jumping, bicycling, horseback riding, sitting, bowing, kneeling, falling, somersaulting, dancing, skating. Covering the face with a mask will emphasize the expressivity of the legs and feet. These exercises may serve first for expressive, nonstylized leg and feet movement and then repeated for expressive illusion pantomime (see illusion pantomime sections above).

Walking

1. Walk, stop, and shift from one foot to the other as a nervous person, a timid person, a worried person, and other character types.
2. Fearfully approach a mysterious package that may contain a bomb; jump for joy after searching and finding a ring you lost.
3. Shyly walk up steps onto a stage to make a speech; courageously tiptoe toward a bee to swat it before it stings you.
4. Sadly react and back away after hearing about the illness of a friend; back away, feeling relief over narrowly escaping a falling branch.
5. Stamp foot angrily as you walk. Express surprise, delight, impatience, and other feelings as you walk about.
6. Walk slowly as if depressed, body bent forward. Walk happily, body erect, head high. Express other emotions while walking.
7. Walk as if attempting to move your injured leg courageously, fearfully, and in other manners.

8. Walk as in a nightmare, desperately searching for a lost child.
9. Walk in a desert under a hot sun. Walk in pouring rain, through heavy snow.
10. Create walks with certain parts of the body leading or accentuated according to character and emotion: an angry proud person leading with chest, a fearful older person leading with hand and cane, a curious person leading with the nose; an irritated nervous person with head leading and turning rapidly in different directions. Create other character types leading with corresponding parts of the body.
11. Cross a street with walks of different ages: a child, limbs moving freely and arms swinging happily; a carefree, bouncing teenager; a confident twenty-year-old; a mature person moving cautiously, chest slightly concave; a hesitant senior, shoulders drooping, chest concave, knees bent, slow gait; a fearful person of eighty-five progressing very slowly, chest sunken in, upper part of body slouched over, cane used to help balance body with each step, hand and head shaking.
12. Walk as an old man or woman attempting to be younger than your age, holding head upright while the rest of body and legs show older age, pelvis concave, and knees bent.
13. Walk as a little girl or boy trying to look older, chest, shoulders, and head held upright while leg and feet movements are quick and carefree.
14. Move like a cat, lion, rooster, frog, monkey, spider, duck, and other animals, birds, and insects.
15. Move about in a toga (long loose robe) like a Roman citizen hailing the emperor who is passing by in a chariot. Enter, bow, and sit like a person in a seventeenth-century French salon, graciously greeting other guests. Enter and sit down to tea with a family in a nineteenth-century English living room.
16. Walk and move like persons of various historical periods. Consult costume books and images. Movements should be related to attire worn during the period. For example, long skirts require shorter steps; a cape or redingote (eighteenth-century men's double-breasted coat) would require more stylized movement.

Turning

1. Turn and look around as you are blown about by a hurricane and run for shelter.
2. Feeling dizzy, turn and sway as you attempt to regain your equilibrium.
3. Turning to right, hear a sound and freeze; next turn to left to check behind you.

Running

1. Run away from a police officer, a kidnapper, and other pursuers.
2. Run to catch a bus, and jump on it just as it is taking off.
3. Run happily through a meadow, breathlessly up a hill, in other manners.

Climbing and Descending

1. Climb up from branch to branch on a tree as you try to catch a frightened cat and come back down with it.
2. Climb and descend stairs in place, portraying a society lady, a homeless person, a happy teenager, a cranky elderly person using a cane, other characters.
3. Climb and descend a ladder in place on your first job painting or washing windows on a high building. Show fear, exasperation, and fatigue as you work.
4. Climb and descend a wall as a robber running from a house; a child returning late from school.
5. Climb steps; see a ghost on an upstairs landing and freeze; descend steps rapidly.

Rowing

Row on smooth bay water; row against mounting waves in a storm.

Jumping

1. Jump in place as you watch your favorite team win points in a basketball game. Jump to keep warm in freezing temperature.
2. Jump back as a car races close by you.
3. Jump about as someone turns a hose with cold water on you.
4. Angrily jump up and down; happily spring up and down with your dog as you run through grass in a park.

Bicycling

1. Bicycle up a hill with effort and descend fast, almost losing control.
2. Bicycle along and see a friend; turn your head to call to your friend and quickly steer your bicycle away from a tree.
3. Race along with another bicyclist, then stop and jump off your bicycle to avoid crashing into a wall.

Horseback Riding

1. Mount and trot a horse until it sees a snake and gallops so fast you nearly fall off.
2. Mount a horse and begin running in a race with other horses and riders, moving ahead and then falling behind the others, then moving ahead and winning.

Sitting

1. Sit down as a middle-aged person complaining to the store manager about being mistreated by a salesperson. Sit down as a salesperson trying to sell a car to a customer. Sit down as a desperate person reporting to the police that

your car has been stolen; as if about to tell your spouse you want a divorce; as a young person being interviewed for a first job.

2. Sit as a child about to eat a piece of cake, happily kicking legs; a teenager told to sit down and scolded by a parent for missing class; a middle-aged person collapsing into a chair after hearing of the death of his or her spouse; an elderly person relieved that his or her spouse's medical operation has succeeded.

Bowing

1. Bow or curtsy before a king or queen who has granted you an audience.
2. Bow and kiss the statue of a saint.
3. Bow as a waiter or waitress serving dinner to a couple in a fancy French restaurant.
4. Bow or curtsy before your partner at a formal ball.

Kneeling

1. Kneel to help a person who has fainted.
2. Kneel to beg mercy from someone to spare your life.
3. Kneel in a church where you have come to pray for your sick child.
4. Kneel to pick up the pieces of an important document that someone has torn up.

Falling

1. Faint as you are told that someone you know died in an accident; faint from hunger and fatigue; faint from walking in desert heat; faint in other ways.
2. Fall forward after being hit by a car.
3. Fall backward from a punch on the jaw.

Somersaulting

1. Do somersaults, happy over good news.
2. Walk along reading a newspaper and suddenly trip and do a somersault; rise, the paper still in your hand.

Dancing

1. Portray a young person dancing on his or her first date, a young person at a formal ball.
2. Portray a macho tango dancer; a ballerina or ballet dancer on opening night; other dance forms.

Skating

1. Ice-skate for the first time, slipping, falling, and losing balance.
2. Ice-skate like an expert skater.

EXPRESSIVE IMPROVISATIONAL THEMES COMBINING MOVEMENTS OF INDIVIDUAL PARTS OF THE BODY

For more information on physical improvisation, see chapter 5.

Expressive Group Improvisational Themes

1. Workers shovel dirt as they dig into the ground in search of a leak in a pipe and find human bones.
2. Guests move about at a cocktail party, sipping drinks and eating appetizers, when there is a sudden earthquake. As people, furniture, and objects are thrown about, the guests get up and run up or down stairs and out of the house. The earthquake stops and each one attempts to move through the debris.
3. Thieves pursued by the police run along a street, down the steps and corridors of a subway station, hop onto the subway train, and move from one compartment to another. At the next station, they jump out of the train, race up the subway steps, and run down an alley.
4. Demonstrators sit on the sidewalk and walk up and down the street waving signs to protest a political action. A riot breaks out. The police arrive.
5. Spectators at a bullfight push their way through the entrance of the amphitheater and rush to their seats. The bull enters the arena and races toward the bullfighter, who waves a red cloth while spectators stand and cheer.
6. Gunshots have people in the street bumping into one another and running about.
7. Seated at a cafe table in Rome, American tourists utilize their hands and facial expressions to communicate to an Italian waiter.
8. A group of teenagers hold hands and run around in a circle, moving in, out, under, and between each other. As they entangle themselves, they fall all over one another.
9. Musicians play on drums, gongs, cymbals, woodwind, brass, and other instruments to a cheering crowd in an outdoor theatre until a loud marching band passes by.
10. Improvise other group scenes combining individual parts of the body. (See more about improvisation in chapter 5.)

Body Expression through Static Attitude

An immobile body and face may be as expressive as a body that moves. To help create a static or immobile attitude, begin by looking at a fixed point before you and remain immobile in a chosen position; add, for example, an expression of fear, content, disappointment.

1. As a preparatory exercise, walk freely about the room, aware of the space, the distance between the walls, objects, and other students or participants. When the teacher or leader calls out "freeze," freeze your body with muscles relaxed, breathing quietly as you express your inner feelings. Continue mov-

ing throughout the room, working up to a run. Whenever the teacher calls out "freeze," portray a dramatic attitude in the body and face, such as desire, fear, or love of someone or something. Freeze and portray a dramatic action along with another student to two or three other students.

2. Strike a dancer's pose (ballerina, modern dancer, other dancers).
3. Portray your favorite figure in a painting (*Primavera* by Botticelli, *Lady with a Fan* by Velazquez, *The Absinthe Drinker* by Picasso, or figures in other paintings).
4. Create the static attitudes of persons, insects, and animals (a person frozen by the sight of a large falling branch, a fly caught under a flyswatter, a deer poised to listen to approaching footsteps, and other static attitudes).
5. Fixing your eyes on a given point, stand in neutral zero position in a statue-like pose; sit, lie, kneel, and create other attitudes in a statue-like pose. Re-create a famous statue (*Winged Victory of Samothrace, The Thinker* by Rodin, *David* by Michelangelo). Utilize images of statues to re-create other statue-like poses.
6. Portray static attitudes of abstract ideas such as freedom, heroism, slavery, brotherhood, hunger, tyranny, and others.
7. Portray the following emotions through static body attitudes:
   - *Happiness.* The body is relaxed and open, palms and feet loose, head and shoulders erect. Portray related feelings such as optimism, enthusiasm, and satisfaction.
   - *Sadness.* The body is relaxed and turned inward, with palms, head, and shoulders drooping. Portray related feelings such as gloom, depression, and mourning.
   - *Arrogance.* The body is erect, chin high, chest high and forward. Portray related feelings such as vanity and conceit.
   - *False courage.* The upper portion of the body conveys assurance, movement outward; the lower portion conveys fear, movement inward; the face shows mixed feelings of fear and assurance.
   - *False approval.* Smile tensely; the upper part of the body conveys agreement with a person's ideas; the lower part conveys disapproval, limbs tense, hands clenched.
   - *Portray other double feelings* such as false admiration, the upper body expressing hypocrisy with movement outward, the lower body expressing deception by, for example, clasping hands in a devious manner or hiding them. Portray false happiness, false generosity, false surprise, and other false emotions.
8. Portray the following emotions and create your own in relation to a character and situation:
   - *Guilt.* You have just robbed someone's wallet and remain immobile as he or she discovers the robbery.
   - *Fear.* Your body is suddenly paralyzed with fear at the sound of a loud explosion.
   - *Anger.* Angry with someone, you are motionless, with fists and teeth clenched.
   - *Pity.* Stand still as you pity your best friend who has just told you bad news.

- *Exasperation.* After your boss does not believe your explanation that you are late for work because of an accident, you are annoyed, your eyes and fists are closed, your head and shoulders and all of your body turned downward.
- *Stubbornness.* Stand erect with arms folded, lips tight, refusing to budge as someone pleads with you to change your mind about a decision.
- *Shock.* Your body is immobile as you receive news of the divorce of a relative.
- *Surprise.* Freeze, eyes wide open, as you see a tiger.
- *Suffering.* Stand paralyzed from a sudden cramp or sharp pain, body tense and face distorted.

Head, Neck, and Face

Head carriage and facial expression are, along with hand gestures, among the most complex and revealing. Character, social class, occupation, nationality, and other factors influence these as well as other gestures and body carriage.

Standing or sitting:

1. Inhale, and slowly and gently drop head forward, exhaling when chin meets the chest; inhale as head raises; exhale as head drops to right; inhale as head raises; exhale as head drops to left; inhale as head raises; exhale as head gently drops backward, keeping eyes looking forward; inhale as head raises.
2. Inhale and exhale as you slowly and gently move head and neck from left to right and back to center, then from right to left and back to center.
3. In a pecking movement, head upright, push chin and head forward and then pull chin and head in, keeping eyes straight ahead at same level. Repeat pushing chin and head backward. Repeat both exercises, accelerating rhythm.
4. Without bending neck, move head up, down; to left, up, down; to right, up, down. Repeat gently several times.

Lying:

5. Lying on back, knees bent, feet flat on floor, press back of neck to floor, hold; release and exhale. Repeat. Lift head up and down gently. Repeat.
6. Lying on a bed or sofa, slowly drop head backward over edge. Bring head forward. Repeat.

Standing or sitting:

7. Shake head. Nod head. Chew vigorously on chewing gum.
8. Move all muscles and parts of face clockwise; move in opposite direction. Move all facial muscles upward, downward, to left and right.
9. Pucker and relax mouth. Tense all facial muscles; relax. Move face, lips, and all facial muscles forward; move back toward ears.

10. Move each part of face and head up, beginning with eyebrows and fore-head, eyes, ears, nose, cheeks, mouth, chin, and neck; move down in reverse order.
11. Grimace with all of face. Make distorted faces.

Expressive Head, Neck, and Face Exercises

1. Shake head in disagreement with a political speech; nod in enthusiastic agreement.
2. React in depressed, joyous, disappointed, and other ways as you listen to voice mail.
3. Portray someone receiving a boss's orders while feeling underpaid and asked to do too much.
4. Shift telephone to other ear; shake head in exasperation and react in other ways to show your boredom, impatience, enthsiasm, and other feelings
5. Listen to another person's story about almost being run over by a car. React with surprise, shock, and empathy.
6. Move head nervously and fearfully as your boss reprimands you.
7. Desperately bend head down to look for a diamond ring you have lost in the sand; a needle you have lost in a thick rug and fear walking on.
8. Watch a plane take off into the sky with a friend on board. Raise head to indicate the plane is moving up into the sky and disappearing into the distance.
9. Nod as you watch a bee fly around you and you try to avoid it.
10. Create the head carriage and facial expressions of a boxer, a millionaire, a professor, a businessperson, a count or countess, a soprano, and other character types displeased with a waiter in a restaurant.
11. Create the head carriage and facial expressions of famous statues or figures in paintings (*Saint Dominic* by Fra Angelico, front figures in Rembrandt's *Night Watch*, Christ's head in Michelangelo's *Pieta*, Giotto's *Betrayal of Christ*, Géricault's *Madman-Kidnapper*, Rouault's *The Old Clown* or *Weary Bones*, Manet's *M. et Mme Auguste Manet* or *Lola de Valencia*, Paul Gauguin's *Self Portrait* or *Tahitian Women*, the child cult art of Paul Klee, the figures in the works of Salvador Dali and Dubuffet and in those of other artists such as Picasso, Matisse, Renoir, Andy Warhol, John Currin, Marlene Dumas, Dana Schutz, Chuck Close, and Gerhard Richter).

Eye Movements

1. Open and shut eyes rapidly and repeatedly. Shut eyes and open wide slowly and repeatedly.
2. Slowly move eyes up and down, from left to right, from right to left; roll eyes clockwise, counterclockwise.
3. Fix eyes attentively on an imaginary scene or object (water in a shady brook, a silver coin gleaming in the sun, a peaceful landscape); stare at someone; watch cars pass by.
4. Wink at someone with one eye and then with the other; alternate winking each eye rapidly and slowly.

5. Look up at a tall building; look down at an ant.
6. Watch an object (kite, bird) approach and grow bigger, a train arrive and then move into the distance, a bird flying above you and then away.
7. Watch a tennis or ping-pong game, a baseball game, a football or other game, nodding head as the ball moves from one place to another.
8. Nod as you watch a plane dive down and move up; a bouncing ball go up and down.
9. Change eye level and nod and shake head as a butterfly moves from one point to another, closer and farther away.
10. Watch a speeding car move closer from the left, suddenly stop in front of you, and move to the right and then move faster in the distance.

Expressive Eye Movements

1. Narrow eyes as if suspicious of someone; as if seeing with difficulty as you enter a smoke filled room; as if the sun blinds you.
2. Open eyes wide in surprise as you run into a long-lost friend; stare in horror at the sight of a neighbor's burning house.
3. Blink as tears come to your eyes while peeling an onion.
4. Suddenly blinded by an explosion, grope about to find your way.
5. Try to find your lost eyeglasses; read like a near-sighted person, a far-sighted person.
6. Wake up and open your eyes wide on a bright sunny morning.
7. Wake up in the dark in the middle of the night after having a nightmare.
8. Recover from an eye operation and slowly discover each object around you.
9. Try to swat a mosquito as it flies closer and away from you. Repeat the action as an elegant lady, a nervous person, a marching soldier.
10. Express sadness, pity, fear, hurt, jealousy, other emotions with your eyes; express each in a specific situation.
11. Change eye expressions from happiness to sadness, from trust to mistrust, from calmness to anger, from belief to doubt, and create other opposite eye expressions, each in a specific situation.
12. Portray the eye expressions of a tired old person, a proud general, a naive child, a jolly sea captain, a haughty aristocrat, a menacing criminal, and other characters, each in a specific situation.

Mouth, Jaws, Lips, and Tongue

The following exercises help render the mouth, jaws, lips, and tongue more flexible and mobile for facial expression as well as improve vocal articulation.

1. Combine vowel sounds with consonants alphabetically, inserting an L after each consonant and before each vowel. Stressing each consonant, begin with bla, ble, bli, blo, blu; cla, cle, cli, clo clu; dla, dle, dli, dlo, dlu, fla, fle, fli, flo, flu, etc., and proceed through the alphabet.
2. Open mouth wide; close mouth. Repeat.

3. Open mouth, extend corners of mouth, and grit back teeth. Close mouth and relax. Repeat.
4. Pucker lips and relax. Form O's with lips as in making smoke rings.
5. Widen lips as in a grimace and hold; relax. Draw lips in, tightly closing mouth; relax. Repeat.
6. Stick tongue out and in. Push tongue hard against back of front upper teeth; relax; against lower teeth; relax. Try to touch nose with tip of tongue. Repeat.

Expressive Mouth, Jaw, Lip, and Tongue Exercises

1. Open mouth wide in surprise over winning the lottery.
2. Burn your tongue after tasting very hot soup.
3. Stick out your tongue at someone who insults you.
4. Flirt with someone with mouth and lips.
5. Grate your teeth as a passenger on a bus grabs the seat before you.
6. Smile and laugh happily as your friends arrive to give you a surprise birthday party.
7. Bite lips nervously as the plane you are on suddenly dives downward.
8. Pucker lips and pout when refused a second helping of your favorite dessert.
9. Close lips tightly while doing something you do not want to do.
10. Cry over sad news with mouth and lip movements.
11. With trembling lips, show fear of falling through holes in a dilapidated floor.
12. You are a cat eagerly licking milk, your fur, and your owner's hand.
13. Eagerly remove wrapping from a piece of bubblegum and chew hard on the gum. Push your tongue through the gum and blow a bubble, which grows bigger and bigger. Feel the top and side of the bubble to show its size. You jump as the bubble suddenly pops. Laughing, continue chewing gum and blowing bubbles.
14. Show mixed emotions of hesitation and delight before eating a big ice cream cone, fear and courage before jumping into ice cold water, anger and regret over having argued with a friend, and other feelings combining mouth, lips, and tongue movements.

Basic Facial Expressions

To avoid creating a stereotyped expression without motivation, each of the facial expressions indicated should be related to a precise emotion in a specific situation (e.g., sadness over the loss of a pet, fear of heights).

In practicing these expressions, it may help to pick up an imaginary mask with both hands and place hands over face while composing an expression. First move hands downward from forehead to chin to put on mask and reveal expression and next move hands upward to remove mask and return to natural expression (recall Marcel Marceau's use of the imaginary mask in *The Mask Maker*). This may also be practiced as a mask game (see the sections on imaginary masks in "Working with a Mask").

Another procedure is to create a facial expression gradually, beginning by showing expression in forehead, eyebrows, eyelids, eyes, mouth, jaw, and all of face. For example, to express sadness, begin by dropping lines of forehead, eyebrows, and eyelids, then jaw and mouth descending at corners, and then all of face dropping as if on the verge of crying. Joy may be expressed by raising forehead, eyebrows, and eyelids and opening eyes wide, and then by moving mouth, jaw, and all of face upward, with mouth open as though ready to laugh.

For the following exercises, the use of a mirror could be helpful. Begin with a calm restful expression, muscles completely relaxed as though listening to soothing music.

1. *Sadness.* Eyelids are half-closed; mouth and all the lines of the face and head are drooping (news of a friend's sickness, loss of a job).
2. *Fear.* Eyes express fear, eyebrows slightly raised, face muscles tense, forehead wrinkled (seeing a mountain lion, a sudden oncoming car as you cross a street).
3. *Happiness.* Eyes smile, the facial, head movements, and corners of the lips move upward, nostrils open, forehead calm (seeing beautiful scenery, a raise in salary).
4. *Boastfulness.* Head high, eyes express confidence, one or both eyebrows raised, lips smiling (bragging about buying a new car, winning a sports competition).
5. *Hatred.* Eyes fixed intensely on the object of hatred, with head somewhat lowered (a person you suspect of stealing your money, a boss who fires you).
6. *Exaltation.* Eyes and mouth wide open, face muscles tense with delight (winning the sweepstakes, news of being cast in a role).
7. *Sympathy.* Eyes and mouth drop, head bent to one side, as you empathize with a person's loss (loss of a pet, kidnapping of child).
8. *Surprise.* Mouth and eyes wide open, muscles tense, eyebrows raised in an expression of astonishment. The nuance will vary: for example, in angered surprise (finding your wallet is gone) or happy surprise (finding your lost kitten).
9. *Disappointment.* Muscles of the face drop and eyes show chagrin (news that your favorite aunt is unable to visit you, failing an exam).
10. *Envy.* Eyes flash and eyebrows, mouth, and lower part of the face move upward in a sneer and then downward in bitterness (envy over another person's popularity, another person's winning an election over you).
11. *Aggressiveness.* Facial expression is authoritative, resolute, and combative (accusing someone of stealing, accosting someone to sell a product).
12. *Hypocrisy.* Eyes and upper and lower parts of the face show conflicting expressions, the lines of the face crooked and the facial expression false (paying a compliment to someone you don't like, agreeing to do something you hate).
13. *Worry.* Facial muscles dropped, lips down at corners, eyes slightly narrowed, forehead wrinkled (rushing to catch a plane at the airport, fear of failing an exam).

14. *Suspicion.* Lower part of face remains serene. One eyebrow is raised and the eye half-closed (suspecting a person of cheating you, of making fun of you).
15. *Timidity.* Lower part of face is drawn inward, forehead slightly wrinkled, eyes express hesitation (facing an angry neighbor, fear of speaking in public).
16. *Stubbornness.* Face remains set, muscles tense (refusing to admit you were wrong in an argument, refusing to make up with someone).
17. *Love.* Muscles of the face move upward, eyes elated, expression giving and open (returning from a trip to see one's family, thinking of someone you love).
18. *Menacing.* Muscles are tense, expression of the eyes narrowed (threatening to punish someone for disobeying, to report someone for trespassing).
19. *Pride.* Head carried high, facial expression resolute, and facial muscles moving upward with a smile (receiving a degree or a national award).
20. *Shame.* Facial muscles drop, expression is submissive, almost fearful (being reprimanded for being noisy, breaking a glass at a party).
21. *Suffering.* Facial muscles move downward, eyes half-closed, showing pain from moral or physical suffering (loss of a parent, falling off a bicycle).
22. *Accusation.* Facial muscles are tense, eyes glaring and narrowed, and expression aggressive (accusing someone of lying, of talking behind your back).
23. *Curiosity.* Facial muscles, lips, and eyes are alert and poised to discover information (questioning a neighbor about why the police have been summoned).
24. *Effort.* Facial muscles are contracted and rigid (lifting a heavy trunk, solving a difficult problem).
25. *Mockery.* Eyes gleam, eyebrows are raised, lips smile (mocking a self-important politician, mocking an exotic dish everyone praises).
26. *Patience.* Facial muscles are relaxed, expression calm (patience with a person who repeatedly asks questions, patience as you thread a small needle).
27. *Enthusiasm.* As in happiness, the face and head movements are directed upward, eyes smiling, nostrils open. Face is alive, eyes bright and eager (watching your favorite team score a point, preparing for a trip to Paris).
28. *Hilarity.* Laugh hilariously from the stomach, all of body shaking, facial muscles moving up and tensely elated (hearing a funny joke, watching a stand-up comedian).
29. *Grief.* Cry with all of facial muscles dropping (the departure of a friend, the sickness of a child you have been baby-sitting).

Head, Neck, and Face Improvisation

Incorporate the above facial expressions and your own in developing the following suggestions for improvisations. (For more information on physical improvisation, see chapter 5.)

1. Combine shock, pride, and despair as your boyfriend or girlfriend announces that he or she wants to break up.
2. Combine shock and horror upon entering a room to find a stranger lying on the floor.

3. Combine disappointment and anger as you tell one of your friends that he or she insulted you.
4. You are being unjustly tried for a serious crime and are waiting for the jury's verdict. React with head, neck, and facial movements as you watch the jury enter, the judge ask for the verdict, and you hear the verdict.
5. Fearfully and cautiously observe a wild cat moving about in your garden. Pick up a broom and hold it up as you prepare to chase it away.
6. Watch a tennis game in which your brother or sister is playing for the world championship. React when he or she loses or wins points.
7. Horrified, watch members of a gang threaten someone. Cautiously wait for a chance to slip away to call the police.
8. Create other improvisations combining head, neck, and face.

WORKING WITH A MASK

Working with a mask helps performers to be less inhibited and free to concentrate and create as well as master movements and gestures and render them more authentic, purposeful, and exact. Mask work also helps performers economize their movements, play with the entire body, and make better use of space. Employing masks can also be helpful in play rehearsals for developing characterization and a believable interpretation. Masks were used in actor training by Jacques Copeau, Meyerhold, Etienne Decroux, and Jacques Lecoq.

The order of the various sections on mask work may be changed according to participants' needs. It begins with exercises with the neutral, character, and counter masks followed by the creation of imaginary masks that I devised in relation to working with facial expressions but are more exaggerated and require set facial expressions. These are followed by original *commedia* scenarios that have been created to use with half masks. For more advanced or in-depth mask training in commedia dell'arte, it is advisable to attend a mask workshop.

Real or mimed simple props and character clothing items are helpful in improvising with masks. Like masks, props and character clothing items may also help to create characterization. For example, Groucho Marx had large horn-rimmed glasses and a big cigar, Harpo Marx wore a curly blond wig, and Carol Burnett in her Eunice role dressed in a motherly housedress and wig. Performers use these and other items along with characteristic clothing to establish their characters.

Neutral or Universal Masks

The purpose of starting mask work with simple neutral or universal expressionless masks is to separate oneself from one's own personal habits and traits; to diminish an overuse of movements and gestures; to utilize gestures and movements economically; to rely more on body movement and expression; to convey general states, feelings, and objects with simple gestures and movements; and to help clarify one's body movements.

If neutral or expressionless masks are not available, you can create a mask by covering the face with a paper bag or a plain paper plate with eyes cut out, or you can utilize gauze, a veil, a nylon stocking, or a kerchief tied around the head.

Wearing a neutral mask, face spectators and convey what you are experiencing (e.g., a cat crossing your path). Engage spectators into seeing the image you are creating solely through a simple gesture or movement of the body.

Create a single, minimal, concentrated, slow-moving gesture or movement for each of the following:

1. See a beautiful bird high in the sky and follow its flight.
2. Feel the sun warm your body and face.
3. Watch a friend disappear in the distance and sadly wave good-bye to him or her.
4. Hear a familiar step behind you.
5. Feel a cramp in your leg.
6. Create other images with single gestures and movements.

Wearing a neutral mask, create simple slow-moving gestures or movements depicting or relating to the following images and themes. Invent other images and themes.

1. Suffering
2. Defeat
3. Gratitude
4. Disappointment
5. Hesitation
6. A reed bending in the wind
7. Cowardice
8. Day Dreaming
9. Praying
10. Forgiveness
11. A snowstorm
12. A soft breeze

Real Character Masks

With ready-made or homemade masks, begin by allowing the expression of the mask to guide your imagination in creating a character or emotion uniquely through movements and gestures of the body. (For information on how to make simple masks, see appendix C or www.AnnetteLust.com.) If several real masks are used, they should be laid out on a table for actors to choose or change masks.

1. Choose a mask and begin to move according to the character your mask represents.
2. Have the character with the mask you chose in item 1 prepare a meal, eat the meal, clear the table, wash dishes, and perform other activities, such as rising in the morning, dressing and undressing, going to sleep at night.
3. With the same mask as in items 1 and 2, introduce a second character that the mask may represent and, employing different body movements to differentiate between the first character and the second character, improvise a scene in which the two characters interact.

4. Choose a second mask with a different expression and, as in item 1, use accompanying body movements for the character your mask represents.
5. With a partner, each choose a mask and interact with one another spontaneously.
6. Choose a mask to improvise situations around job-related activities such as (a) being told by your boss that you have to meet a deadline faster than expected, (b) arriving late for work and attempting to give an excuse, (c) trying to phone your boyfriend or girlfriend while your boss is in an adjacent room. Interpret other job-related situations.
7. Repeat item 6 utilizing the same mask but with different body movements to depict your response to the boss's request in (a), your reaction to his or her response to your excuse in (b), your reaction to the boss hearing your call to your boyfriend or girlfriend in (c).
8. Choose a mask to portray a character's accidental encounters, such as arriving at a formal party in jeans and T-shirt and apologizing to the host; accidentally stepping on a yapping dog and excusing yourself to the owner; sitting on a hat on a park bench and ignoring the owner who begs you in another language to return the hat. Interpret other embarrassing encounters with masks.
9. Choose masks to create characters in plays or novels, then improvise original scenes. Possible characters are Shylock, Medea, Pozzo in Beckett's *Waiting for Godot*, the Hunchback in *The Hunchback of Notre Dame*, Lady Macbeth, Emma Bovary, Tartuffe, Sherlock Holmes.

Counter Masks

A counter mask is used to interpret opposite or contradictory expressions through body movements. Choose a mask that may represent several characters or interpretations. Or use a two-sided mask or two or three masks, rapidly switching from one to the other. In the following, use one of these counter mask arrangements to create opposite, changing, or conflicting characteristics of a character or several characters through their body movements.

1. A waiter who dislikes and is critical of the boss but smiles and flatters the boss when he or she approaches.
2. A girl or boy who cries over having lost his or her dog and laughs for joy when the dog returns.
3. A young man flirting and putting his arm around a young woman when her father suddenly appears causing the young man to withdraw his arm and change his facial expression.
4. A sales clerk who smiles while a client cannot decide which wristwatch to buy, then brings forth more wristwatches, waits for the decision, and impatiently turns away and taps his or her fingers on the counter.
5. A crook selling a fake diamond necklace in a sincere manner to an unsuspecting customer, completing the deal, and laughing at the duped customer while walking away.

6. The husband of an older couple who politely asks a young passerby for directions and becomes offended when the latter replies that they should buy a map.
7. With one mask representing several characters, or a two-sided mask, or by switching two masks, play both a mother trying to gently persuade her child to eat dinner and the child who screams and pushes the food away.
8. Improvise a scene by switching two masks that interact: for example, an aggressive car salesman and a disinterested client, an argument between an angry husband and a calm wife over who lost the house key or who forgot to close the back door, or another disagreement.
9. With one mask or by switching three masks, play a young woman who bumps into a female friend and talks with her when a homeless person approaches them. They shrug their shoulders and move away. The homeless person follows them, taps them on the shoulder, and asks for money. They ignore him and walk on. The homeless person follows them until they run to hide in a doorway and watch the homeless person go down the street.
10. Improvise counter masks with opposing characters and reactions: for example, two drivers interacting after a car accident; commuters at a bus station reacting differently as they wait for a late-night bus; demonstrators versus police; a student being reprimanded by a teacher.
11. Improvise other characters and situations with counter masks.

Imaginary Character Masks

The use of imaginary masks simplifies the need to change masks in a scene. Once the emotional facial expression is created, it should be held firmly in place as if wearing a mask. As with half masks that allow for the accompaniment of the voice, they may be accompanied by voice sounds and eventually used with words.

Stand with feet parallel and slightly apart, weight of body a bit forward. Pick up an imaginary mask with both hands and hold it a little above your forehead. Pull mask down over your face by moving hands downward from forehead over neutral or expressionless facial expression to create, for example, an expression of surprise with accompanying body movement and gestures. To remove the mask, take hold of the mask, move hands upward, and return to a neutral facial expression. In the following, put on and remove the imaginary masks in the same manner.

1. Create imaginary mask expressions of pain, jealousy, pity, suspicion, misery, admiration, fear, violence, and other emotions. Accompany and develop these mask expressions with matching body movements and gestures.
2. Develop dramatic action or short scenes with the above or other imaginary mask expressions.

Imaginary Type Character Masks

Create and develop dramatic action or short scenes with the following type character masks:

1. A grumpy character making his or her way around at an art exhibit with a cane that he or she thrusts about, moving lips and mumbling when someone is in the way.
2. A happy-go-lucky, confident teenager selling lemonade and motioning to passersby to buy a drink for a fund-raiser.
3. A teacher in class pursued by a buzzing bee, growing more impatient while trying to fight off the bee with a ruler, and regaining students' attention.
4. A swindler smiling and attempting to charm someone to obtain money.

Opposite Mask and Body Expression

With the following masks, create conflicting emotions between the face and the body, such as a person smiling at someone while body movements and gestures express irritation.

1. A courageous mask for entering a room to save a child being held as a hostage by someone armed with a gun. Contrast the courageous mask with fearful body movements and gestures as you open the door and see the scene.
2. A generous mask with greedy movements and gestures.
3. A calm mask with impatient body movements and gestures.
4. A happy mask with discontented movements and gestures.
5. Other contrasting mask and body expressions.

Masks That Change into Opposite Expressions

1. Open and move hand across face over neutral facial expression to create an expression of joy and back across face to create an expression of sadness.
2. Enthusiasm to indifference.
3. Boldness to timidity.
4. Agreement to disagreement.
5. Create and develop other opposite mask expressions.

Group Exercises with Imaginary Masks

The following exercises are done in small groups or with a partner. For items 3 through 6, create short scenes.

1. Standing in a circle, the first student passes an imaginary mask with a fixed expression to the next one, who puts it on attempting to repeat the same expression. The student then passes it to the next one and so on until it returns to the first student. Was the original expression of the imaginary mask retained or transformed after it returned to the first student? Repeat if the original expression was lost.

2. Facing a partner who puts on an imaginary mask, react to the expression of your partner's mask as you put on your own imaginary mask. For example, as your partner puts on a mask of hate, you react by putting on a mask of fear. Continue reacting to one another and to others with different masks.
3. Improvise scenes for a robot with mechanical masks that change when an operator pushes a control button (e.g., to react to a person passing by, a rude person, a baby cat, a giggling child).
4. A client enters a store where a vendor with a welcoming salesperson mask shows the client a suit. The client puts on a mask that reveals his or her approval. The client tries on the suit and now puts on a mask of disapproval, causing the salesperson to react with a mask of disappointment.
5. A couple with happy masks socialize with others at a party. The husband moves away to flirt with another woman, causing both husband and wife to change their masks. The wife joins the husband and indicates she is his wife. The husband puts on a mask expressing an apology, and the other woman reacts with a surprised mask. Follow through with mask changes that reflect other reactions between the three characters.
6. Create other group scenes with imaginary masks that interact.

Half Masks and Commedia dell'Arte Scenarios

Students may construct or procure their own half masks, which have the bottom half cut off above the actor's mouth. Half masks may be worn with any of the above exercises with the advantage that sounds or dialogue may be utilized. Typically worn in commedia dell'arte, half masks may be useful when preparing roles to aid the actor find movement for a character. They may also help develop different vocal dynamics as the actor uses a voice that works with the character and can be louder than the regular speaking voice. The speech pattern, rhythm, and tone may differ from the actor's regular voice.

Sixteenth-century commedia dell'arte was based on character types such as Harlequin, Pantalone, Pulcinella, and Colombine, who improvised both physically and through the use of spontaneous dialogue, depending on the actor or performer's talent for improvisation. Commedia dell'arte is a genre that is an extension of acting, and through its use of improvisation, masks, and acrobatics, it helps a performer develop his or her creativity.

However, the interpretation of *commedia* characters with masks, based on sixteenth-century stock or traditional characters with physical and vocal characteristics, requires special training. The following scenarios with *commedia* characters and masks serve as an introduction to *commedia*. They should be performed with broad and exaggerated physical movements.

If *commedia* masks are not available, handmade masks depicting the characters may be utilized along with characteristic gestures and movements. For information on making masks, see appendix C.

For more information on *commedia* characters, masks, and scenarios, see John Rudlin's detailed *Commedia dell'Arte: An Actor's Handbook* (2000), Barry Grantham's *Playing Commedia* (2001) and *Commedia Plays: Scenarios, Scripts, Lazzi* (2007), and www.AnnetteLust.com. See video clips on YouTube of commedia dell'arte scenes such as *Pulcinella's War* with Antonio Fava and Merve Engin, *Truffaldino U Smeraldina Malta*, *Truffaldino Beaten*, *Pantalone*, and *Arlecchino*. Also see YouTube clips of *Commedia dell'Arte Production Café Floriani*, *The Masks of Arnold Sandhaus*, and Dario Fo's *Mistero Buffo* among others.

The following original *commedia* scenarios by the author may be played with half masks.

Pantalone and Arlecchino

Pantalone is an old, mean, hunchbacked miser wearing a mask with a long nose and beard. Arlecchino is a fun-loving, agile, clown-like character wearing a dark mask with rounded cheeks and face and who likes to play tricks on others.

Arlecchino enters to complain that his miserly master Il Dottore has not paid him for some time. When will he get his money from Il Dottore? When Arlecchino sees Pantalone enter with a cane, he suddenly thinks of a solution. Arlecchino approaches Pantalone to tell him he will introduce him to a beautiful lady. However, he will need money to invite her for tea in an elegant cafe to speak to her about Pantalone. Pantalone agrees to pay him after he sees the lady.

Arlecchino faces the audience. Where to find a lady? He thinks of a solution. He tells Pantalone he will have the lady walk by so Pantalone can see her.

As Pantalone excitedly paces back and forth while waiting for the lady, Arlecchino returns wearing a dress, shawl, and female wig and walks by Pantalone. But when the excited Pantalone approaches to kiss the lady's hand, Arlecchino withdraws his big heavy hand and shyly backs away. Pantalone brushes the lady's hair aside to whisper into her ear, causing Arlecchino's wig to fall off his head. When Pantalone realizes that the lady is Arlecchino in disguise, he screams and chases away Arlecchino, angrily waving his cane.

Colombina and Arlecchino

Colombina is a petite, clever, pretty servant who wears makeup in place of a mask and often flirts with the male characters.

Arlecchino enters to find Colombina trimming Pantalone's front hedge. Colombina is angry with Arlecchino because he has not come by for several days. He apologizes and gives her a big kiss on the cheek. As she throws her arms around him, a pretty female passes by and Arlecchino turns to look at her. Colombina angrily stomps her feet, screams at Arlecchino, and pounds her fists on his chest. She then turns away and refuses to speak to him.

Pantalone and Colombina

Pantalone enters as Colombina is on her knees scrubbing the kitchen floor. He bends over and caresses her arm. Colombina shrugs her shoulders and withdraws her arm. Pantalone continues to follow Colombina around the kitchen floor, trying to caress her. Exasperated, she stands and holds out her hand for money he owes her for her work. Pantalone reluctantly gives her a few coins. She shakes her head and puts out her hand for more coins. Pantalone pulls out his empty pockets. She shakes her head and pushes Pantalone so hard that he almost falls over. Colombina runs off stage with the coins as Pantalone rubs his sore shoulder.

Il Dottore, Brighella, and Pantalone

Il Dottore, a talkative, pompous character, likes to give advice to others. He wears a mask that covers his nose and forehead and has white sideburns. Brighella is crafty, cynical, pedantic, and immoral, likes to eat and drink, and enjoys the company of women.

Pantalone visits Il Dottore to buy a potion for more vigor. Il Dottore will give him a bottle of expensive potion if he pays for it immediately. After Pantalone reluctantly pays for the expensive potion, Il Dottore hands it to him and prescribes one spoonful each day. On the way home, Pantalone drops and breaks the bottle of expensive potion.

As Pantalone laments the broken bottle, he looks around to see if anyone is looking and then bends over and rapidly licks up the entire potion. He rises and jumps up and down, full of vim and vigor, and walks home. As he passes Brighella's house, he catches sight of the back of a figure in a nightgown and nightcap in the doorway. Thinking it is Brighella's female cook, he approaches and begins to pat the figure on the backside. Brighella turns around and slaps him.

Pedrolino and Pantalone

Pedrolino is an honest, poetic, naive character wearing a loose white tunic and pantaloons, a skullcap, and whiteface makeup in place of a mask.

Pedrolino enters and pulls out his empty imaginary pockets. Could his master Pantalone, who hobbles by, help him earn some money? He approaches Pantalone to ask for work. Pantalone asks what Pedrolino can do. He replies he can write poetry for him. Pantalone shakes his head. Pet his dog? Pantalone shakes his head. Pick flowers for him? Pantalone shakes his head. Play his mandolin to serenade and attract young women for Pantalone? Pantalone reflects. Maybe that could help him win young women? Pantalone nods and takes Pedrolino to his front garden.

Pedrolino plays his mandolin and dances about in Pantalone's garden while Pantalone sits nearby. A young woman passing by walks right past Pantalone and approaches Pedrolino, clapping her hands and throwing Pedrolino kisses while Pantalone throws Pedrolino a few coins as he plays. A second woman arrives and walks right past Pantalone to Pedrolino, clapping her hands and throwing him kisses while Pantalone throws Pedrolino a few more coins. After a third woman arrives and does the same, Pedrolino quickly picks up the coins and runs off arm in arm with the women while Pantalone curses and waves his cane at him.

Other Scenarios with *Commedia* Characters

Create other scenarios with *commedia* characters. See the pantomime *Pantaloon's Christmas Dinner* in chapter 6.

CORPOREAL MIME AND
DISASSOCIATION OF MOVEMENT: INCLINATIONS, ROTATIONS, UNDULATIONS, AND SEPARATIONS

Decroux-inspired isolation or disassociation exercises, in which one section of the body moves at a time while the rest of the body is immobile, can help performers better understand the function and relationship of one part of the body to another. Although corporeal mime is considered a more specialized form of mime that requires a teacher trained in the method to initiate a performer into it, the introductory exercises presented here may help familiarize participants wishing to know more about the physical movements utilized in this technique.

For a more thorough understanding of the corporeal mime technique and practical exercises with immediate applications along with descriptions of two mime pieces, see corporeal mime teacher Thomas Leabhart's *Etienne Decroux* (2007). Leabhart believes that it is impossible to learn corporeal mime without years of daily lessons with a qualified teacher. For an insightful description of Decroux corporeal mime, see corporeal mime teacher Robert Fleshman's essay "Etienne Decroux and the Contemporary Theatre: Decroux Corporeal Mime" (included in part III of this book), particularly the section on the scales. To view corporeal mime artists, see video clips on YouTube of Mime Corporel (Hippocampe, Charlotte Irvoas), Corporeal Mime, Cours de Mime Corporel, Etienne Decroux, *Le Combat Antique*, and Moveo Teatro. For the above and other movement artists, also consult the videography and DVDs in appendix F of this book.

Since inclinations, rotations, undulations, and separations (also known as translations or slides) are more difficult to master than the preceding individual parts of the body exercises, it is not advisable to engage in them until students or participants are sufficiently prepared in movement training. They should be done slowly at first and repeated until mastered. *Inclinations* are the directed bending of the body to the front, side, and back. *Rotations* are the directed turning of the body to the right or left. *Undulations* are the flowing, wavelike motions of different parts of the body, principally the pelvis that is thrown forward and the chest backward followed by the pelvis moving backward while the chest moves forward in smooth and connected motion. *Separations* (also called isolations) are the movements that separate selected parts of the body from the rest of the body.

These disassociation of movement exercises, simplified adaptations of Decroux corporeal mime that attempt to clarify the function and relationship of each part of the body to one another, require moving one section of the body at a time while keeping the rest of the body immobile. They isolate in order to gain control of the different parts of the body to develop flexibility, body control, and coordination. Through the practice of these exercises, movement becomes more articulate. Mime artists such as Marcel Marceau, Jean-Louis Barrault, Leonard Pitt, and Daniel Stein, renowned for the precision and aesthetic appeal of their movements, were trained by Decroux in corporeal mime.

Begin the following exercises in a neutral or zero position, keeping the sections of the body not being utilized motionless. To obtain a neutral or zero standing position, relax the whole body, place feet comfortably apart with weight centered and evenly distributed on both feet, knees slightly bent, buttocks and stomach pulled in, chest and shoulders wide, head and chin parallel to the floor, face and eyes expressionless.

Inclinations

1. Forward Inclination. Standing in neutral or zero position, move heels together with feet open in a V position and bend head forward and downward without moving neck; next bend neck forward allowing head to move further toward chest; next bend shoulders and chest and bend head and neck still further toward chest, which sinks inward; bend forward at waist, inclining hips forward. Return to starting position by reversing the order of the exercise.

2. Back Inclination. With left foot twelve inches in front of right foot and weight placed on both feet, slowly drop head back; next bend chest backward, then waist and hips, bending the back knee and keeping the body in a straight line. Return by straightening the back knee, the hips, waist, chest, head, and chin.

3. Side Inclination. Stand facing forward, heels together, with feet open in a V position and hands at sides and bend head to right shoulder; next bend neck, chest, waist, and hips to right, lifting left heel and bending left knee. Return in the opposite order. Repeat inclining to left side.

Rotations

Standing in neutral position, heels together with feet open in a V position, turn head to right with the neck helping the head to move as far as possible to the right. Next move shoulders and chest to far right with head and neck following and with the rest of the body facing forward. Next rotate waist and then hips, lifting left heel and rotating and bending left knee. Return in the opposite order. Repeat reversing the rotation order to left side.

Undulations

Undulations resemble the rising and falling of waves. This wavelike movement moves smoothly from one end of the spine to the other. Undulations may also be done separately with the arms and hands, the hands and fingers, and even with the legs from the hips down.

Exercise #9

An illustrated version of the exercise is available at www.AnnetteLust.com.
   For the following undulations, do items 1–4 on all fours (similar to the cat); do 1–5 lying down and sitting.

1. Total Body Undulation. Standing in neutral position, undulate body by thrusting upper body forward as lower body moves backward; next thrust upper body backward as lower body moves forward. Repeat with each movement smoothly flowing into the next.
2. Upper Body Undulation. Undulate from the pelvis upward by moving the pelvis forward with the neck and head slowly moving backward; move the pelvis back again, the neck and head following forward. Continue moving smoothly only from the pelvis up and then with head and neck.
3. Lower Body Undulation. Undulate from the pelvis downward by moving the pelvis forward and the lower body backward; move the pelvis backward and the lower body forward. Continue moving smoothly only from the pelvis down. Repeat with lower body.
4. Side Undulation. Moving continuously, smoothly, and snake like, move hip out to left while curving shoulders, head, and trunk to right; then slide hip in, pushing out right hip while curving shoulders, head, and trunk to the left. Repeat on other side. Repeat undulations diagonally.
5. Arm, Hand, and Finger Undulations. Undulate arms, hands, and fingers together. Undulate only hands and fingers. Undulate only fingers.
6. Do the above undulation exercises (1–4) on all fours (similar to the Cat), lying down (1–5), and sitting (1–5).

Separations

Separations (also called isolations) are more difficult to master than inclinations, rotations, and undulations and should be practiced after developing enough muscular control through work on inclinations, rotations, and undulations.

The separation exercises of the trunk, extending from the neck to the hip, may be divided into three main sections: the upper trunk or chest, the center torso or abdomen, and the lower torso or hips.

Chest, Abdomen, Shoulder, Arm, Hand, and Fingers Separations

Exercise #10

Standing in neutral or zero position, heels together with feet open in a V position, facing front, make all movements parallel and vertical to the floor. An illustrated version of the exercise is available at www.AnnetteLust.com.

1. Without moving waist or hips, slide chest backward, expanding the chest as you move and breathe in, and contracting it as you return and breathe out.
2. Repeat, moving chest forward.
3. Slide chest and shoulders to left, back to center, to right, and back to center.
4. Move chest and shoulders in circular movement to right, to back, to left, forward, and return to original position. Repeat, moving chest and shoulders to left.
5. Raise one arm above head and hold onto an imaginary rope at a fixed point (hold arm up in place motionless) as you repeat the above chest and shoulder movements. Repeat with the other arm.

6. Move the center torso forward and back, to left and right, and with circular movement in the same manner as the above chest and shoulder movements.
7. Pull the shoulders up and down. Pull the shoulders back and forward.
8. Arms held out at sides, bent at elbows and hanging at sides with elbows pointing up, swing lower arms from elbows down, forward, and back and from side to side.
9. Arms in same position as in item 8, move hands from wrist forward, back, and from side to side. Move fingers forward, back, and from side to side.

Hip, Leg, and Feet Separations

Exercise #11

An illustrated version of the exercise is available at www.AnnetteLust.com.

1. (See figure 3.) Standing in neutral or zero position, heels together with feet open in a V position, move hips back, forward.
2. Swing one leg back and forward. Repeat with other leg.
3. Swing each leg from side to side.
4. Hold onto an imaginary rope as you repeat the above movements.
5. Standing on one leg, lift, bend, and swing other leg from the knee down, back and forward and from side to side. Repeat with the other leg.
6. In same position as in item 4, move foot of one leg from the ankle down, back and forward and from side to side. Repeat with other foot.

Head, Neck, and Face Separations

1. Move head slowly up and down as though nodding; from side to side as though shaking head. Repeat.
2. Drop head to left side and return; to right side and return. Repeat.
3. Move head halfway forward; next slide head and neck totally forward; return in opposite order. Repeat.
4. Move head halfway back; next slide head and neck totally back; return in opposite order. Repeat.
5. Keeping face forward, move head halfway to right side, then head and neck as far as possible to right; return in opposite order. Repeat, moving left.
6. Sink neck down while pulling shoulders up, then elongate neck and move shoulders down. Repeat.
7. Move head forward and in circular movement to right, back, left, forward, and back to original position. Repeat to left.
8. Move facial features first up and down and next from side to side beginning with chin and lips, next nose, eyes, and forehead.
9. Combining head, neck, shoulders, chest, waist, and hip separations, move head slightly forward; next move both head and neck more forward; next add shoulders and chest and move more forward; add waist and tuck in hips to move far forward. Return reversing the order. Repeat, moving backward.
10. Slide head slightly to right; next head and neck; add shoulders and chest, waist and hips. Return reversing the order. Repeat on left side.

Combining Inclinations, Rotations, Undulations, and Separations

Standing in neutral or zero position, move heels together with feet open in a V position.

1. Undulate body forward and back rapidly while inclining head slowly to left, right, forward, and back. Undulate body slowly while inclining head rapidly to left, right, forward, and back.
2. Rotate body from waist down slowly to left while rapidly separating head, neck, and chest to right. Rotate body from waist down rapidly to right while slowly separating head, neck, and chest to left.
3. Progressively slide head, neck, chest, shoulders, waist, and hips forward while rotating hips, legs, and feet to right. Return in reverse order. Repeat, rotating to left. Repeat, moving backward.
4. Progressively incline head, neck, chest, shoulders, waist, and hips forward while rotating hips, legs, and feet to right. Return in reverse order. Repeat, inclining backward and rotating to left.
5. Progressively slide head, neck, chest, shoulders, waist, and hips forward while inclining the same parts forward. Repeat, sliding and inclining backward and to sides.
6. Rotate head, neck, chest, and shoulders to right while waist and hips rotate to left (start by rotating each section separately and slowly). Repeat, rotating upper body to left and waist and hips to right.
7. Pull an imaginary object to you with one hand and push away another object with the other hand (e.g., draw a baby buggy to you with right hand and push away a chair with left hand; catch a ball with right hand while throwing another ball with left hand; pull on a rope with right arm, hand, and leg while pushing on a wall with left arm, hand, and leg).
8. Draw a square with right arm and hand and simultaneously draw a circle with left arm and hand. Reverse arms and hands. Add inclinations, rotations, undulations, and separations to the arm and hand movements.
9. Invent combinations of inclinations, rotations, undulations, and separations.

Expressive Disassociation of Movement: Inclinations, Rotations, Undulations, and Separations

1. Incline to one side several times, each time quickly moving back up so as not to be seen trying to pick up a five-dollar bill someone dropped.
2. Rotate head, neck, chest, and shoulders as you attempt to swat a mosquito. Repeat in reverse order and rotate to other side attempting to swat it.
3. Be assured with upper part of body and fearful with lower part. For example, smile, nod, and extend right hand and upper body in a gesture of willingness to speak on TV while nervously rotating left hand and drawing back lower part of body.
4. Refuse an object with one part of body and desire it with another part. For example, play a cleaning lady or handyman being offered a tip by moving head backward and shaking it while sheepishly opening left hand and moving it and upper body forward.

5. Smile falsely, inclining head to one side while hands, lower body, and feet move backward expressing mistrust of a person.

6. Laugh and cry simultaneously, eyes crying while moving head back and forth, mouth laughing nervously, and body undulating ecstatically over winning first prize in a competition.

7. Portray anger by clenching fists and thrusting arms forward and show hurt by inclining head and chest backward for being accused of doing a bad job.

8. Slide head and neck from side to side enthusiastically while rotating upper body and wringing hands nervously as you watch the ball being hit back and forth in an exciting tennis match.

9. Incline body forward and downward while sliding upper body to the right and left as you anxiously look for your ring, which has fallen into the sand, and move head, then neck, chest, shoulders, waist, and hips upward when you find it.

10. Combine inclinations, rotations, undulations, and separations as you ride on the Big Dipper.

11. Interpret contrasting emotions through the use of separations, inclinations, and rotations: sarcasm followed by pity; enthusiasm and refusal; lightheartedness and moroseness; and other opposing feelings in specific situations.

12. To play a robot or a mechanical figure, utilize separations, inclinations, and rotations with a neutral expression; remain immobile in a statue-like position with eyes fixed on a given point and begin by moving one part of your body at a time. For example, first move up hand, next lower arm, upper arm; rotate head, next neck, next torso, next lower body, and freeze each movement with an abrupt stop. Continue moving other parts of your body one section at a time and freeze each movement, moving each part of the body abruptly and rigidly.

13. To play a marionette, have a real or imaginary person manipulate your strings. Begin by bending forward, swinging hands and arms loosely and bending legs. Feel the strings pull up first left shoulder and arm, hand, fingers; next right shoulder and arm, hand, fingers; straighten left leg, right leg; pull up head and body from waist up. Wave, nod your head, shrug your shoulders, and walk forward and backward. Move all parts of body in a frenetic dance with angular and mechanical movements. Follow each of these movements by completely relaxed ones, ending with all of the body falling limply forward as a marionette no longer being manipulated.

14. Introduce a modified form of inclinations, rotations, undulations, and separations into scenes or monologues.

For information on Decroux corporeal mime exercises, an overview of Decroux's life and work, and an analysis of his book *Words on Mime*, see Thomas Leabhart, *Etienne Decroux* (2007). For key material on Decroux and corporeal mime, see *The Decroux Sourcebook*, edited by Thomas Leabhart and Franc Chamberlain (2008). Also see "Etienne Decroux, Father of Corporeal Mime" in *From the Greek Mimes to Marcel Marceau and Beyond* by Annette Lust (2003).

Chapter 4

Utilizing Movements to Create a Visual Image

This chapter examines body movements that give rise to the creation of visual images. It includes exercises that evoke the illusion of movement and are based on sense perception, physical sensation, weight, volume, space, and time, descriptive and occupational gestures and movements, imaginary objects and colors, movement and sound, slow and rapid rhythm. Exercises also help performers in creating people, animals, insects, and other creatures. The chapter also looks at costume and style, character and type, and finding the basic psychological gestures and movements to create a character.

A visual image of the mobile or even static quality of persons, objects, and activity may be created through body movement or nonmovement. For example, swaying the body upward and downward while riding on an imaginary horse and performing a trotting or galloping movement may create a mobile image of the horse. Climbing imaginary steps may evoke the immobile rungs of a ladder, and raising one arm and standing still may evoke the immobility of a tree.

If some of the following exercises that provide practice in utilizing movement to create visual images resemble those suggested in the expressive exercises for the individual parts of the body, they may be omitted or repeated as needed.

EVOKING THE ILLUSION OF MOVEMENT

1. Ride along with a friend in a fast sports car, eyes narrowed and head braving the wind as the car races along. Brace yourself, and lean to one side, back, and forward as the car moves around a curve and up and down a hill.
2. Watch someone go down a circular staircase. Your hands on an imaginary railing, lean over and nod your head in a circular descending movement as your eyes follow the person downward.

3. Enter an old-style elevator, slide the inner gate closed, and press a button to choose a floor and start the elevator. Move your body up and down with the vibration of the elevator as it mounts; throw your body upward with a short jerk as it stops. Exit by sliding open the inner gate and pushing the heavy door.

4. Sit on a teeter-totter (seesaw) with another person on the other side. Move up and down, at times swiftly, other times slowly, in relation to the person opposite you. You are thrown into the air, fall back down, and slowly rise and continue.

5. To rescue your cat on a tree branch, rapidly climb an imaginary rope (see "Climbing and Descending a Rope Illusion Pantomime" in chapter 3). Bend your knees and open and close them as you wrap legs around the rope and place one hand above the other. Pull hands straight down while rising on toes as though hoisting body upward, alternating placing one hand above the other and sliding both hands downward as you thrust your lower body downward and upward. Repeat the above movements to continue climbing. With your cat inside your jacket, slide back down rope by wiggling body with knees bent and rising on toes, hands placed one above the other and moving upward, alternating placing one hand above the other and sliding both hands upward as you thrust your lower body upward and downward. Repeat these movements as you continue to descend.

6. Walk up and down stairs (see "Climbing and Descending Illusion Pantomime," chapter 3) first as a small child and then as an old man or woman; slide hands from upward downward at a slight angle along an imaginary railing. Move down stairs, sliding hand from downward upward at an angle along an imaginary railing.

7. Look up as you cautiously climb a wiggling ladder (see "Climbing and Descending Illusion Pantomime," chapter 3), nervously wobbling as you step up first on toe and then heel, placing hands on two rungs, approximately one foot apart, and sliding them downward as the body moves up. Look down as you descend ladder by stepping back and down, first on toe and then heel, while placing hands on two rungs and sliding them upward as the body moves down.

8. Jump into the ocean against big waves and a strong current. Feel the water against your legs and all of your body as you swim forward.

9. Ski down a steep hill at full speed, knees bent, head against the wind, turning and leaning to the right, to the left, and coming to a full stop at the bottom.

10. Open an umbrella and hold it over your head. As you turn a corner, the umbrella turns inside out, pulling you along with it. Turn in the opposite direction to blow the umbrella into place. Continue using the umbrella as a shield against the wind and rain.

11. Climb a wooden fence (see "Climbing and Descending Illusion Pantomime," chapter 3), hands grabbing the top of the fence. Lower your hands as you lift one leg to push your foot against the middle board and swing the other leg over the top of the fence. Sit with legs dangling from each side.

Descend, swinging one leg to other side, hands grasping top of the fence and moving upward as you slide downward and jump to the ground.

12. Watch a hummingbird fly up and down by nodding your head to indicate each level it attains as your eyes follow the flight.

13. A ball in each hand, throw each ball up and catch with a bounce. Throw a ball up to right and then to left and catch with opposite hand with a bounce. Throw a ball behind you from left hand upward to right and catch with right hand behind you. Repeat from right hand up to left and catch with left hand behind you. Throw ball in other ways.

14. Hold a dog on a leash and feel it pull you one way and the other; it stops to smell a hedge, then pulls you harder as it runs off to join another dog and sniff passersby.

15. Pull a heavy hose toward you, drawing body forward each time you gain more of it. Move body back and forth as you water trees and flowers.

16. Mount a horse (see "Horseback Riding Illusion Pantomime," chapter 3) by placing left foot in stirrup and left hand on saddle; swing body onto the horse and place right foot in stirrup. As you pick up the reins and trot away, the horse suddenly gallops very fast. Pull hard on the reins to finally stop the horse, then dismount shaken up.

17. In a crowd, feel others push you forward, from side to side, from behind.

18. Throw a kite up into the sky and feel it pull you along faster and faster, almost off the ground. Kneel down on one leg and pull the kite toward you. Fall on back and pull on the kite. Stand and push back with legs and thighs as the kite pulls you here and there.

19. You and other passengers are on a plane in rough weather. Sway as you walk in the aisles; grab seats and do whatever you can to balance yourselves.

20. Several workers ride in the back of a truck, some sitting, others kneeling; bodies are thrown forward as the truck stops and backward as it starts up again; all lean to the left as it turns sharply to the right and lean to the right as it turns to the left. The workers fall against one another as the truck abruptly stops.

SENSE PERCEPTION

Practice the following sense perception (sight, smell, sound, hearing, taste) exercises and build short scenes around them. To achieve more precision depicting imaginary objects, practice them at first with real objects or imagine them as you experienced them. For example, when sawing real wood, the saw should gradually descend as the wood is cut; when heating and stirring a cream sauce, the effort to stir should increase as the sauce thickens.

1. Taste overpeppered spaghetti. Try to get rid of the pepper taste by adding cheese, a bland sauce, wine, and other ingredients.

2. Smell a putrid odor (decaying fruit, rotten eggs, etc.).

3. Put on a wool coat in freezing weather. Run your fingers over the soft wool.
4. Hear a familiar tune; move your head in keeping with the tune as you recall romantic moments with a former girlfriend or boyfriend.
5. Smell a mysterious perfume; try to identify it and trace its whereabouts in a room. Is it coming from a flower, from someone in the room?
6. Hear the sound of a plane approaching the airport to land. Follow its course with head and eye movements. Watch it fly lower as it approaches and lands.
7. Bump into and feel various objects (a chair, table, statue, wall) as you and a couple of friends move about in a dark room.
8. Taste and eat more of your favorite dessert until you are full.
9. Touch ice, sandpaper, moss, thorns, and other items, showing the texture of each. Run your fingers over sand to find a diamond ring; through tall grass to find an earring.
10. With others, watch fireworks in the sky; raise and lower your heads and eyes as the fireworks travel up, light up, and fall downward.
11. Feel hot oil burn your arm; cold metal on your neck; a hand massaging your sore back; a bee stinging your finger.
12. You and others hear a mouse. Quietly move around the room looking for it.
13. Drink a shot of whiskey, cold milk, hot chocolate, root beer, unsweetened lemon juice, spicy soup, distinguishing between the tastes of each.
14. Search for a needle on a thick carpet; suddenly feel it prick your finger. Search through bushes to find a wallet and find a kitten.
15. You and a friend are hungry and smell freshly baked French bread as you pass a bakery. Imagine you are eating it.
16. Cringing, hear two people fighting and screaming at one another nearby.
17. You and a friend taste various kinds of food at a buffet table (pizza, spaghetti with meatballs, stuffed snails, crackers and camembert cheese, and other kinds of food).
18. Taste wine that has turned to vinegar; a mousse au chocolat dessert that melts in your mouth. Find a piece of hair in your salad.
19. Be champagne being poured into a glass. Be steaming hot soup, spicy sauce, tangy lemon juice, iced tea being slowly sipped up, other liquids.
20. Be potatoes being mashed, a hot dog being boiled, spaghetti being tossed about in a dish, an onion being cut up, a banana being peeled, whipped cream being placed on pudding, a doughnut being covered with sugar, other kinds of food.

Combining Sense Perceptions

1. While watching a bird flying in the sky, bump your foot against a curb.
2. While you play on the piano, hear a motorcycle roaring by.
3. While hammering a nail on the garden fence, hear a storm and feel rain fall.
4. While sunbathing on a lawn, jump as someone sprays you with a hose.
5. While watching a romantic scene on TV, hear an automobile collision.
6. While tasting peppery soup, feel your dog licking your foot.

Physical Sensation

Practice the following physical sensation exercises and build short scenes around each one. Create your own physical sensation exercises.

1. As you climb up a steep mountain, feel your legs grow tired and heavy and the perspiration roll down your temples.
2. Plod through deep snow against the wind in a snowstorm. Walk backward against wind and snow. Walk sideways against wind and snow.
3. Drive a car with the top down, your hair blowing in the wind and your body swaying with the fast car movements. Ride a bicycle along a narrow, curvy mountain road.
4. Jump rope as the hot sun beats down on you, forcing you to slow down.
5. After digging ditches to help stop a fire, jump under a cold shower, slapping your arms and legs to warm up.
6. Put on a pair of ice skates. Skate, balancing yourself, almost falling; hold onto a railing; try to skate across the rink; lose your balance, regain it; fall on the ice.
7. Wrestle to free yourself from someone who has grabbed you.
8. Drive a speedboat to right and left to avoid other boats; feel the waves splash against you.
9. Run through woods full of underbrush and tangled branches.
10. Dodge bees flying out of a beehive as you attempt to perform in a play outdoors.
11. Step on a thistle or a prickly plant. Walk barefoot on rocks in a cold brook, on a splintered floor, through soft mud.
12. Make your way through flames to save a child.
13. Hike down a steep, windy hill; try not to slip on small pebbles or leaves.
14. Fall into a big mud puddle; get up and wipe yourself.
15. React to someone pounding on your back; gently caressing your back.
16. Climb a small, wobbly tree that bends to one side as you move up.
17. Ride in a buggy drawn by a horse; on a sled, a ski lift, a tricycle.
18. You are a caveman waking up in your cave; go out and stretch in the sunlight, drink spring water, build a fire, throw in meat, and tear it off the bone as you chew it; continue other activities.

WEIGHT, VOLUME, SPACE, AND TIME

In the next exercises, emphasis should be placed on feeling imaginary weight, volume, and space. Build situations around them and then create your own weight, volume, and space exercises.

Utilizing Weight and Volume

1. Lift a heavy box from the floor and carry it to another spot; lower it to the floor. Pick up, blow, and throw a balloon into the air and catch it.

2. Lift an iron bar over your head, a bamboo stick with one arm, a long heavy metal pipe that you pass to another person. Lift a wooden cane and walk with it.

3. Carry a glass of wine on a tray and serve it; carry full plates of soup on a tray and serve.

4. Lift a heavy person from the floor, a medium-sized person, a baby.

5. Pull on the rope of a heavy church bell. Pull on a small lamp chain.

6. Unwrap a large box. Remove and unwrap smaller and smaller boxes.

7. Push a toy cart, a baby buggy, a wheelbarrow loaded with stones, an upright piano.

8. Throw different-sized plastic balls, heavier rubber balls, metal balls, and objects of various sizes to another person. Show the differences in size and weight.

9. Lift heavy objects (a case of wine, an armchair); light objects (ping-pong ball, a feather duster).

10. Pull a toy train tied to a string; a cart full of heavy wood.

11. Walk balancing a pitcher of water on your head, an encyclopedia, other heavy objects; walk balancing a piece of cardboard, a plastic container, other light objects.

12. A heavy canvas falls on you. Free yourself by pushing out with your arms and legs.

13. Feel the top of a wobbling table and then cautiously lean on it to verify if it will support you (utilizing illusion pantomime if desired). The arm of your hand touching the table remains straight and tense while the remainder of your leaning body relaxes.

14. Feel a wet wall with one hand to verify if there is a leak (utilizing illusion pantomime if desired). Your arm and your hand touching the wall remain straight and tense while the remainder of your leaning body relaxes.

15. Walk through a flood, pushing legs and arms against the force of the water.

16. Open, close, spray, and wipe a small window; a middle-sized and a large one.

17. Feel the edges of a small plastic table to indicate its size and lift it; a wooden table; a large marble slab.

18. Put clothes and toothbrush, toothpaste, comb, alarm clock, and other personal objects of different sizes and weight into a small overnight bag and carry the bag to your car; open your car trunk and place it inside.

19. Walk around a table, a sofa, and other furniture looking for a book; walk about in an empty room.

20. Feel the sides and top of a large trunk or crate in which you are hiding; the walls and ceiling of a dungeon in which you are imprisoned.

21. Run after a piece of paper that suddenly flies out of your hands up into the air in all different directions. Reach for it and almost fall down as you grasp it.

22. Form a circle with players whose backs are turned to the center. Ask one participant to pass an imaginary object (glass of water, book, big ball), without telling what it is, to the person on her or his right. Have observers guess

what the original object was after it returns. Pass around other imaginary objects.

Utilizing Space and Time

To become familiar with the space in which you are working, begin by observing the length and width of the space, the walls, floors, and ceiling. A number of games may be played to familiarize yourself with your space and to relate to others playing with you.

1. Run around the space with other students, attempting not to bump into one another; repeat purposely bumping into one another.
2. Move slowly with others in a large circle, walking, jumping, running, and skipping without bumping into each other. Repeat in smaller circles without bumping into one another. Move from smaller circles back to larger circles. Repeat moving rapidly.
3. Play games such as tag and throwing a ball to others while running around the space.
4. Play tennis, basketball, and other sports that require the use of a large space.
5. Do yoga movements slowly, push-ups, and other exercises rapidly that require a smaller space.
6. Engage in work that requires a large range of space, such as raking or mowing a large lawn; work with a reduced use of space, such as weeding or planting flowers.
7. Imagine you are in an ocean swimming, and the shore is several hours away. Move with long, slow gestures, feeling that the time is interminable.
8. Jump into freezing ocean water and swim back to shore as rapidly as you can.
9. Slowly cross over one stone after another on a long river shore. Quickly jump from one river stone to a second one.
10. Dance with an imaginary or real partner in a small room; in a spacious hall, waltzing slowly and then jitterbugging or dancing other rapid dances.
11. Create situations using different dimensions of space and time.

DESCRIPTIVE AND OCCUPATIONAL EXERCISES

Occupational gestures and movements should be precisely communicated. The use of real props at first can help develop the following exercises. Avoid employing stereotyped gestures and movements. Create other descriptive and occupational exercises.

1. Repair an object (screw on a door hinge, change faucet washer, hammer a board, sand a ceiling, hose down a wall).
2. Remove a light bulb and install a new one in its place on a lamp, on a ceiling fixture, inside a refrigerator.

3. Get up and rapidly wash and dress, showing each piece of clothing you put on as you rush to get to class or work on time.
4. Play a card game or your favorite game with a partner. Combine occupational movements with moments of defeat or victory.
5. Sit down to eat a meal, showing the kind of foods you are eating (soup, salad, meat, vegetables, ice cream) and which you enjoy or like less.
6. Wash your hair; dry it with a towel, a hair dryer; brush, comb, and style it.
7. Give a friend a haircut. Brush, comb, cut, and style the hair.
8. Prepare your favorite dish (boil water for spaghetti, fix a salad and dressing, bake cookies or a cake), showing the ingredients and utensils you use.
9. Decorate a room; add or remove a lamp, cushion, flowers, furniture.
10. Build an object (bookshelf, fence). Use hammer, nails, and other tools.
11. Clean a kitchen (sink, stove and refrigerator inside and outside, floor, shelves, windows, and other parts of the kitchen).
12. Exaggerate gestures to make yourself understood by a hearing impaired neighbor as you ask if you can borrow a pan to fry a big fish and show how you will fry it.
13. As a sidewalk artist, sketch a passerby's face.
14. Create a piece of pottery such as a vase or bowl; sculpt a statue.
15. Baby-sit two-year-old twins. Feed them as they spill food, fight, and cry. Undress and bathe them, help them put on their pajamas, and put them to bed.
16. Carefully dust, polish, and shine antique furniture (piano, buffet, chair).

Descriptive and Occupational Improvisations Performed Blindfolded with Real Props to Improve Perception and Sense of Observation and Memory

After handling and observing the places of the real props in the following scenes, use the props after you are blindfolded or your eyes are closed. Utilize other objects or imaginary ones to represent props not available.

1. Yard Sale. *Props: boxes of clothing, shoes, hats, books, dishes, jewelry, belts, dishes, and other small articles; a computer, microwave, TV, and other large articles.* You and passersby move about at a yard sale, handling articles in each box, trying on clothes and jewelry, and examining other articles.
2. Home Gardening. *Props: gardening gloves, flower seeds, small shovel or spade, hoe, rake, real or imaginary plants in buckets, hose, hedge clippers.* You and another gardener pull up and rake imaginary weeds and leaves on a lawn. Pick up a shovel or spade to dig holes, throw seeds inside, fill the holes with dirt, and smooth them out with a hoe. Dig more holes to plant new plants that you remove from buckets. Pick up the hose and water seeded area and plants. Continue trimming imaginary bushes, cutting tree branches, and mowing the lawn.
3. A Day at the Office. *Props: table, chair, pencils, pens, paper, telephone, real or imaginary computer, printer, and fax machine on table.* Improvise a scene with a

computer, printing out pages and placing them in a fax machine. Answer the phone and make phone calls, receive a fax, and do other work.

4. Spring Cleaning. *Props: three chairs may represent a sofa, a stool or chair for a coffee table with newspapers and magazines, a chair for a side table with a lamp and bric-a-brac, imaginary windows upstage, window cleaner spray, cloth, dust cloth, mop, imaginary vacuum cleaner, carpet, and small rug.* You and another cleaning person dust a sofa, armchair, coffee table and side table, lamp and bric-a-brac. You vacuum the carpet and shake out a small rug. You move upstage to spray and wipe windows. Find other cleaning activities such as polishing the floor with imaginary wax and polisher, cleaning light fixtures, and polishing furniture.

IMAGINARY OBJECT AND COLOR EXERCISES

Transforming Real Props and Elements into Imaginary Objects and Characters through Mime

Imagine:

1. The floor is an ocean shore; you run into the waves and splash about. You see a small boat (stool or chair) tied to a nearby pier; you swim and climb into it. Row to the shore, get out, and pull the boat onto the shore.
2. You are imprisoned in a cell. Kneel behind a chair with bars. Press your face against the bars, anxiously looking to the right and left for a visiting family member or friend. Show your frustration by peering between the bars and pulling on them as if to break them.
3. Sit on a chair backward as though you are on a motorcycle speeding on a freeway, your body vibrating with the movement. Use the back of the chair as a wheel and move to the right and left to change lanes. Pass other cars. Lean back as the motorcycle races up a hill and forward as it descends. Create other action as you speed ahead or slow down.
4. Stand behind a desk or table that becomes an imaginary gas stove with four burners, and use desk props to fry an egg. Grab a ruler that becomes the handle of a frying pan. Use a letter opener or a pen for a knife to cut into a small paper tablet that represents a cube of butter; place the piece of butter in the pan. Use a pencil for a match you remove from an imaginary matchbox to light the gas under the pan. Use a box to remove an imaginary egg that you break on the imaginary pan's rim; empty the egg into the pan and return the imaginary eggshell to the box. Pick up a pen to represent a fork to scramble the egg. Shut off the gas and with the fork slide the scrambled egg onto a dish (sheet of paper).
5. In a garden, walk your imaginary dog with a rolled up newspaper that represents a leash; approach a standing lamp that becomes the trunk of an orange tree that your dog sniffs. Place your hand on the tree trunk and reach up for an orange (light bulb) that you pick, peel, and eat while your dog sniffs around the tree trunk.

6. Create action around other real objects changed into imaginary objects, such as a folded jacket or sweater to represent a baby in a blanket; a chair tipped and dragged backward to represent a cart; a plate that becomes a mirror; a rolled up piece of cardboard for a bottle from which you pour wine, and a shoe to represent a glass.

7. Create a scene with objects or props that become characters, interact, and are manipulated like puppets. For example, in a scene with a boy and a girl running from a detective who catches them and takes them to the police station, the following objects may be utilized: for the boy, a shirt gathered at the waist for his body, with a whiskbroom for his head and hair; for the girl, a rag tied around the handle of a feather duster for her dress, head, and hair; for the detective, a pair of black shoes and a scarf wrapped around a clothes hanger for his body, with dark glasses placed on the hook of the hanger to create eyes and a cap placed on the hook above the glasses to represent his head. (See the interview with Liebe Wetzel on puppetry in part III.)

8. Transform other real props and elements into imaginary objects and characters that interact in short scenes.

Imaginary Object Exercises without Real Props and Elements

Create the movements of each of the following imaginary objects to play these objects.

1. A feather flying into the air; a bicycle moving uphill; a bullet tearing through the air; a runaway wheelchair.
2. A tree swaying in the wind; a statue shaking in an earthquake.
3. A big rubber ball bouncing about; a ball racing along in a pinball machine; a newspaper rolling in the wind.
4. A rocking horse; a marching toy soldier; a waddling toy duck; other mechanical toys.
5. A leaf blowing in the wind, landing here and there and rolling about.
6. A tree, with your feet as the roots and your legs the trunk. Your arms are branches that bend in the wind, quiver in the rain, and sag under snow.
7. A puppet with each part of your body being moved by a puppeteer. You nod your head, bow, move forward, backward, dance, laugh, cry, and so on. (In appendix F, see the videography and DVD listings for puppetry titles *Charley Bowers*; *Brother Bread, Sister Puppet*; *Pinocchio*; *Puppetry as Creative Drama*; *Puppets for Theatre*; *Puppet Schmuppet*, and video clips on YouTube of the *Potter Puppet Pals, Kobe and Lebron, Rabbi Boing*, the *Puppet Art Theater Co.*, and other puppetry companies).
8. A cuckoo clock with a cuckoo jumping out; a grandfather clock with a pendulum swinging back and forth; an alarm clock that rings and vibrates.
9. A feather duster dusting; a broom sweeping; a washing machine washing clothes; other moving household objects.
10. (For two mimes.) Create interaction between a pan of boiling water splashing water on a frying pan frying an egg; between a waterfall splashing water on the branches of a tree blowing in the wind; a pencil writing and a

small eraser erasing what the pencil has written. Create interaction between other inanimate objects.

11. (For one or more mimes.) You are the sun shining down on the earth, water, and inhabitants, who respond to your bright beams with energetic movement such as swimming and other outdoor sports, gardening and outdoor activities.

12. (For one or more mimes.) You are the moon shining above the earth, trees, flowers, and inhabitants, who respond to your soft beams with gentle movements and relaxed recreational or other activity.

13. (For two mimes.) You are a radio or cell phone found by a jungle inhabitant who has never seen one and tries to figure it out. Reactions of the two as they interact.

14. (For one or several mimes.) You are a scarecrow with arms outstretched being attacked by crows who land on you and with their beaks pull at your skirt, blouse, and headscarf while you turn your head to the right and left to scare them away.

15. Create and play other imaginary objects.

Imaginary Color Exercises

Imagine you are the following colored objects and create the suggested images and feelings as well as other images and feelings for each:

1. *Black.* A nun's robe, a widow's veil, feelings of sadness and depression, and images or emotions you associate with black.
2. *Green.* Green ferns, tree leaves, grass, moss, and feelings of freshness and fertility.
3. *Brown.* Mountains, earth, wood, autumn leaves, and feelings of a solid, earthy quality.
4. *Red.* Anger, a bloody uprising by a crew on a ship, violence, and revolt.
5. *White.* A white baby bunny, snow, a bride's veil, purity, innocence.
6. *Yellow.* Sun, newborn chicks, brightness and warmth.
7. *Purple.* A king or queen, an archbishop, celebrants at a religious feast.
8. Create images and emotions evoked by other colors.

Imaginary Physical Images with Half Masks

The following are examples of scenes of imaginary physical images created at Charles Dullin's School of Dramatic Art in Paris. Utilized with a half mask, they help develop body expression without depending on facial expression, and although difficult and beyond everyday reality, the effort helps to liberate the imagination.

1. Imagine you are an enormous soap bubble with magnificent brilliant colors, rising lightly and slowly into the air.
2. Lying on the floor, your face covered with a half mask, relax and forget your body and its weight as much as possible. A light breeze touches your face

and your whole body. Open your eyes and discover the world, the sky, the earth, and the vegetation. According to your temperament, feel a sensation of plenitude, joy, power, or fear.

3. Stand with your legs heavily riveted to the earth. As the clouds pass in the sky, you want to reach for them, or you fear their mystery. You see a fountain that you approach; the water sends back your image which you want to seize; the water flows between your fingers. The sun appears and dazzles you.

4. The blood circulates in your veins; the life you feel in you provokes a violent physical reaction that makes you want to tear away the earth; you improvise a dance.

(Translated from the French from Charles Dullin, *Souvenirs et Notes de Travail d'Un Acteur*, 1946, p. 116.)

EVOKING MOVEMENT THROUGH
SOUND AND SOUND THROUGH MOVEMENT

The voice comprises tones and sounds that reveal inner feelings and give words their emotional meaning. The next exercises combining movement and sound may serve as an introduction to working with movement, text, and words, the text and words being considered an extension of movement. The exercises will help develop a range of vocal and other sounds allied to movement and gestures.

A. With a partner, create the following sounds with movement. Begin by taking a deep breath and allowing the sound to flow from your breath. Repeat several times and then allow the sound to evoke a corresponding movement. Expand on the movement for each sound by adding a brief dramatic action. For example, cough and then attempt to find a handkerchief in your pocket to stop a coughing spell while your partner tries to help you. Find other sounds that evoke movement to create a brief dramatic action with one or more partners.

1. Scream	7. Hum	13. Cough
2. Sneeze	8. Sing	14. Moan
3. Snore	9. Laugh	15. Grit your teeth
4. Blow your nose	10. Cry	16. Suck on a lollipop
5. Exclaim with joy	11. Whisper	17. Hiccup
6. Whistle	12. Hiss	18. Sniff

B. Create the following movements, and accompany each one with a sound that expresses an emotion.

1. Bump into a wall and bend over and vocalize your pain as you rub your leg.
2. Raise your arm to wave to someone in the distance and cry out to the person to catch his or her attention.
3. Clench your fist and snarl as you reprimand a person for closing a door in your face.

4. Pick up and pet a sick cat and make a soothing sound to show your pity.
5. Raise both arms and scream as a car suddenly drives by within inches of you.
6. Jump up and down and squeal for joy after winning a drama or other award.
7. Grimace and clench your teeth as you lift the lid of a hot, steaming pan of water.
8. Caress the head of a child who helps you carry your packages, and utter a thank you.
9. Open your mouth and exclaim in surprise as a person watering plants douses you.
10. Chew on a piece of fish and feel a bone in your throat that causes you to gasp loudly.

C. Create the following sounds and emotions, and accompany each one with the suggested or another movement.

1. Snort angrily and clench teeth and fists after being insulted by someone.
2. Giggle at a funny clown who makes your whole body shake.
3. Whine, crinkle your face, and rub your hurt arm after falling on it.
4. Gasp and jump up and down after hearing you have won the lottery.
5. Howl angrily and shrug your shoulders after another cyclist beats you in a bicycle race.
6. Exclaim impatiently as you run to pick up the phone while trying to quickly dress for an appointment.
7. Exclaim and throw your arms around a friend you have not seen for awhile.
8. Screech out as you fall into a pothole.
9. Inhale an audible deep breath and throw up your arms after passing a tough exam.
10. Scream and freeze as you feel an earthquake.
11. Inhale and exhale as you make a sound with your breathing and add a movement in the following opposing emotions: Inhale and move fearfully; exhale and move with confidence. Inhale and move angrily; exhale and move calmly. Inhale and move feeling elated; exhale and move feeling depressed. Inhale and move enthusiastically; exhale and move feeling bored.
12. Find other opposing emotions with which you inhale, vocalize your emotion, move, and then exhale, vocalize your emotion, and move.

D. Reacting Physically to Vowel Sounds. Select a vowel and as you take a deep breath and vocalize it, place your hand on the part of the body where it vibrates. For example, vocalize the vowel e (fee) on a high pitch and place your hand on top of your head to feel it vibrate; vocalize o (bo) on a low pitch and feel it vibrate on your abdomen; vocalize u (you) on a low pitch and feel it vibrate on your upper chest. Select and vocalize vowels on different pitches and feel their vibrations in the various parts of your body.

E. Combining Consonants and Vowels with Movement and Emotions. Combine consonants and vowels, finding a place in your body for the vibration of each sound to create a corresponding movement and emotion. For example, vocalize the consonant and vowel "blah" making it vibrate in your throat and move your hand to your throat as though swallowing a burning hot drink. Vocalize the consonant and vowel "clee" and feel it vibrate on your cheek, placing your hand on your cheek as you suddenly realize you made a serious blunder in your job.

F. Vocalize the following consonants and vowels and find a place in your body for the vibration of each consonant and vowel sound. Repeat, combining consonant and vowel sounds with movements and emotions. For example, for the sound "blo," open arms and hold mouth wide open to depict surprise. For "blay," lift hands and shrug shoulders as though questioning someone.

Vocalize the following sounds, exaggerating the pronunciation of the consonant sounds and follow through with the rest of the alphabet: blah, blay, blee, blo, blue; clah, clay, clee, clo, clue; dlah, dlay, dlee, dlo, dlue.

Repeat and combine vowels with other consonants along with movement and emotions.

This exercise may also be utilized as an excellent diction drill.

SLOW AND RAPID RHYTHM

1. Sweep a filthy floor with a broom, finding more and more dirt to sweep and pick up, which causes you to move at first slowly in discouragement and then faster to finish.
2. Dust and vacuum a living room with rapid, hurried movements before guests arrive.
3. After receiving a call that your boyfriend or girlfriend is not coming to dinner, sadly sit and on your own slowly eat the soup, salad, steak, vegetables, and dessert you prepared.
4. Jump into an icy cold lake and swim, moving your arms and legs rapidly. Jump out and run in the cold wind to find your towel, rub yourself vigorously, and quickly dress.
5. Slowly move about in a hot sauna; exit to jump up and down under a cold shower; return to the hot sauna and dress slowly.
6. Walk in place like a robot, slowly moving each foot and arm and performing other body movements. Continue with robotic movements to enter a living room, move about, and sit down.
7. Walk in place like a robot with rapid, jerky, abrupt movements. Rush along a sidewalk, stop at a corner, climb into a bus, and sit down, moving to the rhythm of the parting bus.
8. Create a scene in rapid motion, such as getting into a car, starting it, and driving erratically down a highway to see a friend in a hospital who has just had a car accident.
9. Move to the rhythm of a clock tick-tocking, a drill drilling a hole in the street, a kitchen blender blending fruit, a woodpecker pecking away on a tree, waves dashing against the shore, a motorcycle roaring up a hill, a thrashing waterfall, a horse on a merry-go-round, a slow dripping faucet.
10. Create other scenes in slow and rapid rhythm and move to the slow and fast rhythms of other objects.

CREATING PEOPLE, ANIMALS, INSECTS, AND OTHER CREATURES

These next exercises will help sharpen your reflexes and your sense of observation for future character and type study.

1. Standing or sitting in a line or a circle with a group, create a facial expression and tap the next person on the shoulder, who will re-create your facial expression and do the same with the next person, until everyone in the line or circle has done so. How much has the facial expression changed from the original one? Other group members then create facial expressions that the rest of the members re-create.
2. A couple faces each another, taking turns as one makes movements and the other reflects them as if looking into a mirror. Begin with slow movements and then augment the rhythm of the movements.

Create short scenes with the following persons interacting:

3. Persons you know entering a room, sitting down, and eating at the dinner table, conversing, and engaging in other activities such as playing cards or checkers.
4. Famous actors and actresses in a play or film.
5. Historical figures, such as Henry VIII, Cleopatra, Napoleon, and others.
6. Politicians and persons in the media.
7. Your favorite character in a novel or play.

Add bird, animal, or fish sounds and movement to the following:

8. A rooster strutting about, head high and toes pointed. Stop, flap wings, and pass by two chickens as though you are the king of the barnyard.
9. Poodle on a leash taking small quick steps to keep up with your owner. Stop to smell a bush and move to smell another bush. As a big dog approaches, run to your owner and stand behind him or her for protection.
10. A lion moving about with a majestic air. Lower your body to the ground and repose; keep head high as you gaze about; open and close your jaws and roar.
11. A giraffe taking long steps, holding its head high. Lower your head to the ground and raise it. Run across a field and stop; move your head slowly to the right and left.
12. A leaping frog, eyes bulging out of your head. Stop at the edge of a pond, slipping your tongue in and out of your mouth.
13. A bull, provoked by a bullfighter waving a red cloth. Rear back and rush forward. Run to the right, to the left, forward, back; drive your horns into the red cloth.
14. A pig, grunting, snorting, and brushing against other pigs looking for scraps of food. Find a scrap and push it into your mouth, swallow it, run around sniffing for more.

15. A sea lion swimming underwater and rising to frighten a passing swimmer. Follow the swimmer when she or he tries to swim away.
16. A butterfly flitting up and down from flower to flower. Slowly open and close your wings as you light on a flower.
17. A bat flapping its wings on a ledge and flying to another ledge when someone opens the attic door.
18. A deer prancing across a field, gracefully lifting your legs. Stop and chew on a leaf. See another deer, prance up to it, prance about with it.
19. A cow grazing on grass. Pull up the grass with your mouth and chew on it, from time to time looking up. Continue grazing as you shoo away a fly with your tail.
20. A fish caught on a hook. Struggle to unhook your mouth from the hook.
21. A bear entering a campsite. Trample over food and other camp supplies, swinging about and sniffing around for food.
22. An ant crawling rapidly and stopping before sugar covered with other ants. Crawl in other directions until you find an open jar of honey and climb into it.
23. A horse trotting, next galloping, and suddenly stopping and rearing back as a snake crosses your path. Turn around and gallop in the opposite direction.
24. A swan gliding along on a lake, dipping your beak into the water, turning, and continuing to glide along and dipping your beak into the water.
25. A canary hopping and flying about in a cage, chirping, bending your head up and down, to the right and left, and fluttering your wings.
26. Various birds such as parrot, hawk, hummingbird, and others.
27. Other animals, insects, birds, and fish.
28. Create situations in which animals, insects, birds, and fish interact with one another: a bear chasing a monkey, a lion trying with a big paw to crush an ant, a rabbit taking off with a dog's bone with the dog chasing after it.
29. Select several of the creatures in items 8 through 28 to show how people resemble them.

COSTUME AND STYLE EXERCISES

The next exercises, some of which may be done in groups, should be depicted in imaginary costumes that correspond to the characters or types portrayed. Build situations around them, and create other costume and style exercises.

1. A female or male model appearing in the newest style of evening gown or tuxedo; in beach clothes and swimsuits; in other fashionable clothes.
2. Enter a formal French seventeenth-century court in the period attire (woman's brocade robe with long, full skirt, tight bodice, and fan; man's tight-fitting trousers and long close-fitting jacket, shoes with heels and buckles). Bow to the king and queen. Interact with the noble men and women. Dance a formal dance with a young man or woman.

3. Walk through the ancient streets of Greece in a long flowing Grecian robe and sandals.
4. Sit on the floor in a kimono and eat Japanese food in Japanese traditional style.
5. Enter the ring in matador attire (close-fitting knee-length silk or satin trousers, short jacket, small ornate hat, long stockings and flat black slippers, red cape, and sword); nod and greet the spectators before fighting the bull.
6. A tribal chief wearing a feathered headpiece and surrounded by family and members of another tribe who are visiting.
7. A monk or a nun in Middle Ages robe, entering a church to pray.
8. A Chinese emperor or empress on a throne, being entertained at court.
9. A soldier in uniform; a general; a sailor; an admiral.
10. A caveman walking through a forest, drinking water from a stream and picking and eating berries on bushes.
11. A football player in football attire running onto the field.
12. A homeless person in rags, carrying a heavy bag over the shoulder and dragging feet in worn out shoes.
13. A Scotsman in a kilt, playing a bagpipe.
14. Enter as an archbishop in his robe and headpiece, blessing the public.
15. Dance as a tap dancer wearing a 1930s tap-dancing outfit.
16. A Roman soldier preparing for battle.
17. A Viking pirating on a seacoast.
18. Walk down the church aisle in a bride or groom's attire.
19. Dressed as an English gentleman or lady in late eighteenth-century attire, enter a cafe to drink tea. If you play a gentleman, remove your top hat when a lady passes, and make use of a cane, gloves, and snuffbox after you sit down. If you play a lady, sit down, pull your long skirt to one side, and rearrange your bustle; chat with elegant manners as you sip your tea and open your parasol when rising to leave.
20. A cowboy in boots and cowboy hat trying to lasso cattle.

CHARACTER AND TYPE EXERCISES

Build short scenes around the following characters or types.

1. An elderly couple trying to cross a very busy street.
2. A worried person pacing the floor while waiting for news of a partner who had a heart attack.
3. A pious priest visiting a sick person.
4. A nervous person trying to thread a needle, hammer a nail, or type out a page.
5. A woman or man dressing for the opera but interrupted by wrong number telephone calls.
6. A young husband waiting in a hospital as his wife delivers their first baby.
7. A lonely widow about to see her son returning from war.

8. A farm girl and boy being interviewed for jobs as a maid and gardener in a mansion.
9. A wealthy aristocrat ordering fancy dishes and expensive wines in a small bistro.
10. A sports announcer describing the end of a horse race.
11. A street person unsuccessfully trying to sell a newspaper to passersby.
12. A teacher trying to teach a mathematics problem to an inattentive class.
13. A hungry beggar finding scraps in a garbage bin and chewing on them.
14. A couple of longshoremen invited to take tea with high-society ladies.
15. An irritated judge calling a noisy court to order.
16. A flustered English butler opening the door to several guests who arrive at once, quickly taking the guests' coats and hats and conducting them into the living room.
17. An actor signing autographs before the flashing newspaper and TV cameras.
18. An exacting orchestra conductor conducting a symphony rehearsal.
19. An auctioneer rapidly taking bid after bid for a Picasso painting.
20. An older woman entering a beauty salon for a facial and massage. She leaves the salon feeling young, but after she looks into a mirror at home, she sees her wrinkles reappear.
21. A frugal man or woman bargaining to buy a diamond ring for less.
22. A salesperson ringing a doorbell and trying to sell products to the homeowner.
23. An elderly person sees a young couple holding hands and remembers when he or she was young, envisioning himself or herself as young again and walking arm in arm with a romantic partner. After the young couple leave, the older person's souvenirs vanish and old age returns.
24. Create situations with characters from mythology such as Mars vanquishing a foe; Jupiter snatching bags of gold; Apollo picking a flower for Venus; Venus graciously receiving a flower from Apollo; other mythological characters.
25. Create short scenes with characters and types you know, have observed, or read about.

FINDING THE BASIC PSYCHOLOGICAL GESTURE AND MOVEMENT TO CREATE A CHARACTER

Finding the basic gesture and movement to portray the essence of a character, as well as other gestures and movements that reveal a character's motivations, opens the door to the actor's psychological creativity. Once the basic gesture and movement and the motivating force of a character are discovered, the actor may, through improvisation or spontaneous additions, explore other gestures and movements to expand that characterization. This process of seeking a character's gestures and movements will reveal the character's inner workings and enrich the actor's interpretation.

Exercises for Basic Gesture and Movement

The next exercises for seeking a character's basic gesture are inspired by Michael Chekhov's *To the Actor: On the Technique of Acting* (see the bibliography in this book), concerning the actor's use of the psychological gesture to develop characterization.

1. Choose a character from a scene and find the basic gesture or movement and the motivating force that identifies that character. For example, play the pretentious Madelyn in Molière's *Ridiculous Ladies*, who holds an open fan in front of her face when describing to her father, Gorgibus, the unrefined manners of the suitors he has introduced to her and her cousin Bathos. The motivating force behind this gesture is her ambition to frequent only cultured aristocrats. Find other gestures and movements related to this basic gesture and motivating force, such as Madelyn's closing her eyelids and sighing, waving her fan with indignation, and turning her head away to show her disdain for her father's choice of suitors.

2. In the same scene, interpret the reaction of Madelyn's father, Gorgibus, hopelessly shrugging his shoulders and raising his eyebrows over the nonsensical remarks of his mannered daughter and niece. The motivating force behind his gesture is to marry his daughter and niece to solid, bourgeois husbands. Follow up with gestures such as narrowing his eyes, shaking a forefinger at his daughter and niece, and pounding his fists on a table as he tries to put sense into their heads.

3. Reproduce the basic gesture and movement that characterize a person you know or have observed. Add supplementary movements that complete the basic gesture and movement characterizing her or his personality. For example, if the person is carefree and happy-go-lucky, her or his basic gesture and movement may consist of a bouncing walk, arms swinging freely, with a smile on the face. Supplementary movements may consist of nodding the head and broadening the smile to happily greet everyone.

4. To broaden your creations of a character's basic gesture and movement, find the movement that characterizes an animal (dog, cat, monkey, or other animal), bird, fish, or insect. Add other movements when the creatures are frightened, hungry, or encounter another animal, bird, fish, or insect.

5. To continue broadening your creations of a character's basic gesture and movement, imagine the basic movement of a fallen leaf rolling about in a storm; raindrops tapping against a window; a palm tree waving in the wind; water slowly trickling out of a leaking faucet; the movements in other everyday occurrences.

Characters in Play Scenes

Find the basic gesture and movement of the characters in the following play scenes. Add other gestures and improvise a short scene for each. It is helpful to read these play scenes in advance.

1. Othello accusing Desdemona of betraying him with Cassio in Shakespeare's *Othello*.
2. Miss Julie's servant Jean seducing his neurotic, obsessive mistress into procuring money and running off with him in Strindberg's *Miss Julie*.
3. Shylock tormented by racial persecution in Shakespeare's *Merchant of Venice*.
4. Cyrano finally revealing his love for Roxane after fifteen years in *Cyrano de Bergerac*.
5. Ophelia rejected by a tortured Hamlet in Shakespeare's *Hamlet*.
6. Blanche in *A Streetcar Named Desire* being taken to a mental hospital, still believing a millionaire has come to take her to dinner.
7. The religious hypocrite Tartuffe seducing Orgon's wife in Molière's *Tartuffe*.
8. Lady Macbeth's guilt after she conspires in a murder in Shakespeare's *Macbeth*.
9. Phaedra describing her elicit feelings of love for her stepson Hippolytus to her companion Oenone in Racine's *Phaedra*.
10. The elderly *commedia* Pantalone suspicious of his servants robbing him.
11. Argan, the main character in Molière's *Imaginary Invalid*, devising a plan to marry his daughter to a doctor for his medical needs.
12. The cunning Harlequin tricking Pantalone into giving him gold coins.
13. The sorceress Medea, who is spurned by Jason and whose love has turned to hate and revenge, driving her to murder her children.
14. Joan of Arc hearing voices that reveal she can save her country.
15. The pompous *commedia* Dottore impressing others with his Latin phrases.
16. Find the basic gestures and movement of characters in Chekhov's *Cherry Orchard* and *Platonov*; Molière's *The Doctor in Spite of Himself* and *The Miser*; Ibsen's *Hedda Gabler* and *A Doll's House*; Tennessee Williams's *Rose Tatoo* and *The Glass Menagerie*; Jean Paul Sartre's *No Exit*; Ionesco's *The Lesson*; Jean Giraudoux's *Ondine*; Albee's *The American Dream*; characters in other plays.
17. Create the basic gestures and movement of characters in film, literature, history, mythology, or other resources.

SUBJECTS FOR IMPROVISATION, PANTOMIMES, NONVERBAL ACTING, PHYSICALIZING THE WORD, AND MIME AND TEXT

Chapter 5

Improvisation

Once we have mastered preparatory physical and related expressive exercises to gain body control, flexibility, and a freer physical expression, we are better prepared to engage in physical improvisation, pantomime, and mime and movement with or without a text. To improvise physically is to begin with enthusiasm to create spontaneously on a given theme or one discovered on the spur of the moment. It communicates ideas and feelings mainly through gestures, movements, body attitudes, and facial expression and with the use of few or no words. Improvisational exercises help relieve tension, exteriorize one's thoughts and feelings, develop original and spontaneous material, envisage a character in various situations, and provide an opportunity to interact with others.

The subjects for physical improvisation are vast. The improvisational exercises in this chapter revolve around the senses, physical sensations, emotions, descriptions, imaginary subjects, characters, and different stage styles. They are offered for students to follow through and eventually create their own subjects for improvisation. Suggestions are also given for impromptu situations built around an object, an emotion, or a subject with which the student may create the characters and action. If a text or words eventually accompany these exercises, more natural movement may be used (see Mime and Text, chapter 7) while pantomimic movement may be utilized in exercises based on silent and stylized communication of action. Yet in physical improvisation, the style, as exemplified in Jean-Louis Barrault's pantomimes in the film *Children of Paradise* and in Marceau's Bip pantomimes, needs to be derived from spontaneous creation rather than from a set piece of business.

When creating physical improvisations, one should develop the dramatic content of a theme and clearly communicate action through movements and gestures. Abstract themes should be made concrete and simplified until the student is more experienced in improvising. In stylized movement and pantomime, the order representing the action differs from that found in spoken sentences. For example, *The Capturing of a Cat* should be played as *The Cat Who Is Being Captured*, the cat first

121

being established as the main character through the player's catlike movements, followed by movements showing how it is being captured.

When improvising a scene from a play, become familiar with both the characters and the theme. After reading the entire play, determine the aim of a scene's action and the dramatic purpose and function of each of the characters. For example, before improvising on a scene from Molière's *The Miser*, it is important to establish as the central theme revolving around Harpagon that of a man who hoards money and all he possesses. He is mistrusting and believes that everyone is after his money. In love with young Mariane, whom his son also loves, he is jealous of every man who approaches her. He is a pitiful, miserly character confined to his mania.

Good sources for physical improvisation as well as pantomime subjects are play scenes containing physical action, such as Molière's and Shakespeare's comedies. In Molière's *Tartuffe*, Act III, scene 3, for example, Tartuffe makes advances to Madame Orgon while Monsieur Orgon is hidden under the table (see chapter 7). In Shakespeare's *Midsummer Night's Dream*, Act V, scene 1, the amateur players enact the tragedy of Pyramus and Thisbe in melodramatic pantomimic style.

Sections and episodes in children's stories, such as *Cinderella, Puss in Boots, Aladdin and the Magic Lamp,* and other favorite fairy tales; fables, such as *The Grasshopper and the Ant, The House Mouse,* and *The Country Mouse,* and other fables by Aesop and La Fontaine; mythology, such as *Orpheus and Eurydice, Dionysius, Hermes, the Mischievous God, Pandora's Box, Atalanta's Race;* historical events, such as *Pocahontas Saves Captain John Smith, Paul Revere's Midnight Ride, George Washington Chopping Down the Cherry Tree,* and scenes built around commedia dell'arte characters, such as Pantalone, Harlequin, Pierrot, and Colombine are excellent material for physical improvisation as well as for pantomime. In such scenarios, rather than translate the lines or words of the text into corresponding gestures, one should improvise and mime the main action.

In developing these improvisational subjects, one should be aware of the sense perceptions and emotions that are involved in each. Improvisation, like acting, requires seeing, hearing, smelling, touching, tasting, and feeling to express an action. Utilizing only the most essential movements will more effectively portray these sense perceptions and emotions.

The principal aim of improvisational work here is to free the body to discover and express itself fully. The exercises and solo and group improvisations need to be played spontaneously with no advanced blocking. In his book *Towards a Poor Theatre* (1968), Grotowski states, "improvisation must be completely unprepared, otherwise all naturalness will be destroyed."

In the suggestions in this chapter for improvisational subjects, any form of movement, or mixed forms, ranging from acting to mime, pantomime, *commedia,* clowning, physical theatre, or other kinds, may be utilized. The student players should be encouraged to create their own imaginative ideas to develop the themes suggested here without depending on teacher or popular stage and film star versions. They should work in a relaxed atmosphere that encourages imaginative game playing and complete freedom of physical expression. A spacious room with few if any props and costumes is recommended unless the students are rehearsing a play and improvising scenes that require utilizing props and costumes.

In group improvisations, it is important for the players to interact with one another and as an ensemble while each player retains freedom of expression. Students or other viewers should also be considered as an active audience that is part of the improvisational process of sharing the experience and helping to evaluate the student players' creativity.

Each improvisation calls for a basic instinctive structure, a flexible time limit, and a goal or object set by the teacher, group leader, or student players. The goal may be to improvise on a theme based on hearing sounds, smelling odors, a physical activity, a character or characters, or other subjects. If the student players lose sight of the goal or object during an improvisation, the teacher or group leader can guide them with minimal and positive side coaching. After the presentation of an improvisation, the discussion with student players, viewers, and the leader concerning the clear communication of the content of the improvisation is helpful.

The improvisational exercises range from elementary to more advanced. Some may be omitted and replaced by original work of a student, teacher, or group leader.

IMPROVISATIONAL GAMES

These improvisational games are intended to help players improvise in solos and in groups. In the following guessing games, a player volunteers or is designated to begin by creating a two- to three-minute improvisation for each question. The player, through body movements, interprets a character of his or her choice, such as someone fishing or a preacher, or a place, such as the seaside or a street. The teacher or group leader then asks who has understood who the character is or where the place is. And, without revealing the answer to the others, those who have guessed now join the first player and continue interacting with him or her on the same subject.

Guessing Games

1. Who am I?
2. Where am I?
3. How old am I?
4. What am I doing with what object?
5. What is my favorite pastime?
6. In what country am I? (For example, riding in a gondola in Venice, Italy, or fighting a bullfight in Spain, etc.)
7. Find other guessing games, such as "What am I cooking? eating? creating? building? seeing?"

Group Circle Games

1. Stand in a circle, each player facing the back of another. A designated first player turns around to face the player behind her or him and creates movements that this second player quickly mirrors and turns around to pass on to

the next player, who does the same until the circle is completed. How does the last player's interpretation differ from the original?

2. Stand in a circle, each player facing the back of another. A designated first player turns around to face the player behind her or him and creates movements that this second player responds to with other movements. The third player responds to the second player with other movements until the circle is completed. How does the last player's response differ from the first?

3. Standing in a circle, one player begins an action (e.g., eating a meal he or she dislikes, or meeting an imaginary former girlfriend or boyfriend) and chooses another player to continue or respond to the action. The second player continues or responds to the action with new movements and then designates the next player. The process continues until everyone in the circle participates.

4. Repeat item 3 adding a sound or verbal expression to the movements.

SOLO IMPROVISATION

Follow through on these short improvisational themes that offer an opportunity to develop a single character reacting to imaginary characters. For beginners, it may be less intimidating to have several students interpret these themes simultaneously. After improvising them, invent your own solo improvisations.

1. Follow, while attempting not to be seen, a person who has stolen a neighbor's bicycle.

2. Read a newspaper or magazine while waiting for the mail carrier to bring a letter from a company about hiring you for a job. You hear steps on your porch and run to the door to receive the letter and quickly open it.

3. A street person walks along the sidewalk, smells a freshly baked pie, and follows the scent to a windowsill where the pie is cooling.

4. Walk through a dark house at night. Suddenly hear footsteps.

5. Try to get rid of a person speaking to you on the telephone. Be bored, impatient, try to cut short the conversation, and find other ways of dealing with him or her.

6. You are home watching TV. The doorbell rings and you open the door to a sales person. The doorbell rings again and it is a neighbor. The doorbell rings a third time and it is a friend you have not seen for some time.

7. You are a politician running for office moving through a crowd to a stage to make a speech. Persuasively make promises of prosperity, lower taxes, and other issues.

8. You arrive on stage and prepare to sing. Your voice suddenly fails.

9. Open your closet door, fearful that a mouse is inside.

10. As you drive to work in heavy traffic, you run into stop signs, blocked intersections, a stalled car, and other problems. Do you finally park your car and take a bus or taxi?

11. Shower and dress for a dance. Scrub yourself, clean your ears, neck, the rest of your body, and wash your hair. Put on your clothes and look at yourself in the mirror. Decide to change your attire. Comb your hair. Put on makeup

and cologne or lotion. Decide whether to wear a jacket or a coat. Find a purse or wallet and place items in it. Check the time and quickly finish dressing so as not to be too late.

12. You have guests arriving and suddenly realize you need to tidy up the living room. Frantically vacuum, dust, and put everything in order before they ring the bell.
13. You suspect the landlord will be coming by soon to collect the rent and you are in despair because you forgot to go to the bank to get rent money.
14. Walk toward a store to buy a magazine but find you have no wallet. Did you drop it? Was it stolen? Did you have credit cards in it? Should you report it to the police? Should you run back along the street and look for it?

IMPROVISATION FOR TWO OR MORE CHARACTERS

1. A group of children discover an old trunk filled with various objects. The first is an old hat that does not create much interest; the second an old doll, quickly thrown aside; the third a belt that catches their attention; a string and a scarf fascinate everyone; an old-fashioned umbrella provokes general laughter as they use it to create old-time characters. Each article (pen, mask, shoe) produces different reactions. The children combine varied articles and actions, such as putting on a mask while riding a broom, or wearing a hat while writing with a pen. When they tire of playing, they put everything back in the trunk. (Mime class exercise taught by Etienne Decroux, teacher of Marcel Marceau, Paris, June 19, 1948.)
2. A suspicious person follows his or her spouse to a restaurant and reacts when the latter meets someone of the opposite sex.
3. A family arrives in a park to picnic. They put the baby on a little chair, spread out a blanket, unwrap food. Everyone happily begins to eat but then it starts to thunder and rain. Portray the family members' reactions.
4. A store vendor waits on a customer who suddenly turns the situation into a robbery.
5. A contractor rings the doorbell to tell you your roof will blow away with the next storm if you don't repair it immediately. You explain that you would like to think it over. How does the contractor react?
6. The bride and groom at a wedding greet each guest in a reception line. A clumsy person steps on the bride's foot; another shakes the groom's hand hard; another slaps the groom on the back. Create other characters' actions and the bride and groom's reactions.
7. Board a train, look for a seat, and sit down. The conductor arrives. You cannot find your ticket and do not have enough money to buy another ticket. Explanations and excuses. Are you told to get off the train? Other solutions?
8. Two painters carry a ladder, paint cans, and brushes. The first painter climbs the ladder and drops a paint can on the second painter, who is painting below. The angry second painter orders the first painter to descend and, when the latter ignores the order, the second painter climbs the ladder and throws the paint can at the first painter. Find other physical interaction between them.

9. Guests converse at dinner in a restaurant. Suddenly the waiter drops a plate of hot soup on the guest of honor, who is a famous opera singer. One guest puts a hand on his or her mouth to hold back laughter; another is angry at the waiter's clumsiness; another helps the singer wipe off her or his clothes. Follow through with others guests' reactions.

10. Three people get into a small boat. One rows the boat, another fishes, another goes for a swim and the water carries him or her out toward a roaring waterfall. What do the other two do?

11. A bartender serves drinks at a bar. A drunkard interacts with everyone as she or he drinks glass after glass of whiskey and falls to the floor. Reactions of the bartender and others?

12. Before guests arrive for your cocktail party, you arrange your living room and check the punchbowl, glasses, and dishes. The doorbell rings. Interact with each guest as he or she arrives and offer each one a drink. An uninvited guest arrives.

13. On a bus, some passengers are seated, others stand and hold onto overhead straps. As the bus moves, the passengers lean backward and sway. As the bus abruptly stops, the passengers are thrown forward. As it turns left, their bodies lean right, and as it turns right, they lean left. The bus collides with an automobile. Reaction of the passengers?

14. As the wait staff of a Paris restaurant take dinner orders, the cook suddenly runs in to announce that the kitchen lights have gone out. The lights in the dining room also go off. Reactions of the staff and customers?

SCENES BASED ON AN OBJECT, EMOTION, TOPIC, ELEMENT IN NATURE, OPPOSITE MOVEMENTS, AND A CHARACTER OR EVENT

The following lists of objects, emotions, topics, elements in nature, opposite movements, and characters and events are suggested as departure points for physical improvisation by single or group players. They should be done rapidly and spontaneously, without real props, allowing the body to freely discover movement. Create improvised action around each of the following suggested items.

An Object

1. Ring
2. Bottle of wine
3. Newspaper article
4. 100 dollar bill
5. Knife
6. Trapdoor
7. Buried treasure
8. Baby toy
9. Photo
10. Suitcase
11. Diary
12. Crystal ball
13. Pack of cards
14. Cane
15. Pair of broken eyeglasses
16. Bottle of pills
17. Box of chocolates
18. Suspicious package
19. Bouquet of flowers
20. Old broom
21. Sofa with three legs
22. Bloody handkerchief
23. Key
24. Antique violin
25. Lock of hair
26. Find other objects

An Emotion

1. Love
2. Hate
3. Jealousy
4. Shame
5. Greed
6. Surprise
7. Anger
8. Pity
9. Indifference
10. Pride
11. Desire
12. Suspicion
13. Anxiety
14. Temptation
15. Fear
16. Embarrassment
17. Desperation
18. Sadness
19. Disappointment
20. Find other emotions

A Topic

These topics may first be interpreted with concrete emotions and ideas that may involve one or more characters. After interpreting a theme concretely, create a more abstract version of it.

1. War
2. Adventure
3. Terrorism
4. Dictatorship
5. Hunger
6. Prejudice
7. Tyranny
8. Patriotism
9. Equality
10. Charity
11. Victory
12. Revolution
13. The fight for an ideal
14. Slavery
15. Injustice
16. Love of humankind
17. Material gain
18. Cruelty
19. Faith
20. Find other topics

Elements in Nature

1. Breeze
2. Earth
3. Sun
4. Water in a brook
5. Raindrops
6. Ice
7. Snowflakes
8. Ocean waves
9. Fog
10. Wind
11. Rock
12. Leaves
13. Waterfall
14. Thunder
15. Clouds

Opposite Movements

1. Push out, pull in
2. Open, shut
3. Jump up, squat
4. Sit, stand
5. Climb, descend
6. Lift, drop
7. Throw, catch
8. Reach up, fall down
9. Grab, offer
10. Run, crawl slowly
11. Take, give
12. Bend over, straighten up

Historical, Mythological, or Fabled Character or Events

1. Sinbad the Sailor
2. Rip Van Winkle
3. A Plymouth Pilgrim
4. Alexander Graham Bell's Telephone
5. King Midas
6. Cleopatra
7. The Two Pigeons (La Fontaine)
8. Richard the Lionhearted
9. King Solomon
10. The Juggler of Notre Dame
11. Jason and the Golden Fleece
12. Robinson Crusoe
13. Pan
14. The Wolf and the Lamb (La Fontaine)
15. Prometheus
16. Cupid and Psyche
17. The Sword of Damocles
18. Julius Caesar
19. Circe the Sorceress
20. Frankenstein

SUGGESTED SOURCES FOR IMPROVISATION SCENES AND CHARACTERS

Many of the expressive exercises for individual parts of the body in chapter 3 contain themes that may be utilized for improvisation. Also see the suggestions and exercises in chapter 3 for working with a mask and in chapter 4 for utilizing body movement to create a visual image. For additional resources for improvisation, see appendix B.

Traditional commedia dell'arte scenarios and characters may be found in Pierre Louis Duchartre, *The Italian Comedy* (New York: John Day, 1929); Thelma Niklaus, *Harlequin* (New York: George Braziller, 1956); Bari Rolfe, *Commedia dell'Arte: A Scene Study Book* (San Francisco: Persona Books, 1977) and *Farces, Italian Style* (Oakland, Calif.: Persona Books, 1981); Mel Gordon, ed., *Lazzi: The Comic Routines of the Commedia dell'Arte* (New York: PAJ Publications, 2001); Gustave Attinger, *L'Esprit de la Commedia dell'Arte dans le Théâtre Français* (Paris: Librarie Théâtrale, 1950, in French).

See appendix F of this book for helpful videos and DVDs, such as *Commedia dell'Arte*, *Commedia by Fava*, *A Commedia dell'Arte Hamlet*, and *Aspects of Commedia dell'Arte*. Also see video clips on YouTube, such as *Commedia dell'Arte Masks by Arnold Sandhaus* with *commedia* character interpretations.

Suggestions for pantomime themes may be found in R. J. Broadbent, *A History of Pantomime* (New York: Citadel, 1965) and in appendix B in this book. Pantomimes and scenes for nonverbal acting may be found in chapter 6 of this book.

Scenes for improvisation may also be found in T. Earl Pardoe, *Pantomimes for Stage and Study* (New York: Appleton, 1931). In Bari Rolfe's *Actions Speak Louder: A Workbook for Actors* (Berkeley: Persona Books, 1992), directed movement improvisation scenes and a few suggestions for improvisations are offered. Also see the themes and resources for improvisation in appendix B of this book.

Chapter 6

Pantomimes and Scenes
for Nonverbal Acting

These original pantomimes, created by the author, may also be adapted for use in silent movie or realistic silent stage style. They may serve for practice or class work as well as for public performances (please consult author for permission to utilize for public performances on stage or screen). They progress from elementary to more complex pantomimes regarding technique, expression, and staging. Although the general action of these pantomimes may be mimed as indicated, for class work they may be developed and interpreted with variations and additions in blocking and movement (please consult author for permission to make changes for public performance).

While the movement and gestures of silent acting are more realistic and natural, illusion pantomime should be magnified and stylized or conform to a conventional pantomimic style. If interpreted in an abstract and subjective mime style, they will need more preparation and work on clear projection.

Sets, blocking, and exits and entrances may be utilized according to need. Yet, as in directing plays with a text, once a choice has been made, individual and group movement and exits and entrances should be carefully blocked. Movement and gestures should be clear, concise, economical, and essential to the action. Through practice and the observation of other mimes and actors, pantomimic movement, gestures, and silent acting become easier to master.

Costume effects should not be overemphasized, and simple, flexible attire, such as tights and T-shirts, should be worn to render movement and gestures visible. Masks and whiteface are often utilized in *commedia* and pantomime (see appendices).

A minimum of stage setting should be used, and props, except in silent acting scenes, should be mimed as often as possible. In pantomime, a table, chair, elevator, and other objects may be mimed, and most often creating the illusion of these objects will provide the mime-actor with an opportunity to invent movement that challenges the imagination.

Music and sound effects, chosen at the discretion of the stage director and performers, enhance pantomime and mime. But they should serve the mime piece and suit the action and movement.

When creating one's own pantomimes, these should depict familiar subjects, be clearly set in a period, contain sufficient action, present a dramatic conflict and relationship between the characters, build progressively and rapidly to a climax, and reach a conclusive ending.

For additional information and examples, see appendix C on creating a mimodrama and appendix F for pantomime titles in the videography and DVD listings. You will also find clips of pantomimes on YouTube.

The stage directions indicated in the following pantomimes are similar to those utilized in the staging of a play:

Upstage right	Upstage center	Upstage left
Stage right	Center stage	Stage left
Downstage right	Downstage center	Downstage left
	Audience	

PANTOMIMES FOR ONE CHARACTER

Learning to Make French Fries

Set and props: a kitchen chair, an imaginary table center stage, imaginary cupboard, drawer, and sink stage right and gas burner on stove stage left.

Imaginary props: apron, bag of potatoes, cupboard, two potatoes, knife, drawer, paper towel roll, paper towel, dish, frying pan, bottle of oil, can of beans, can opener, faucet, fork, newspaper.

Length: 4 to 6 minutes. The rhythm of this pantomime is rapid.

The amateur cook puts on an apron, lifts a bag of potatoes out of the lower cupboard and a dish from the upper cupboard, places them on the table, opens the bag and removes a potato, takes a knife from a drawer, and begins to peel and slice the potato awkwardly.

Smiling, the cook proudly holds up a slice of the potato. After he or she puts the potato in the dish on the table and begins to peel and slice a second potato, the cook cuts his or her finger. The cook pulls off a piece of a paper towel from a paper towel roll to wrap around the cut.

The cook continues to peel and slice the potato very prudently, breathing a deep sigh after removing each peel.

The cook turns on a gas burner, moves a frying pan sitting on another burner onto the lit burner, pours oil from a bottle of oil into the frying pan, and jumps back as it sizzles. The cook picks up the dish of sliced potatoes, throws them into the frying pan, and jumps back a second time as they sizzle and burn his or her forearm. The cook reaches for the bottle of oil and pours and rubs some on the burned forearm. Keeping a safe distance, the cook shakes the pan so that the potatoes will not burn.

The potatoes appear to be frying well. The cook smiles and sits down to read a newspaper. Smelling something burning, the cook suddenly remembers the potatoes and jumps up, grabs the frying pan, throws the potatoes in the sink, turns on the faucet, and sadly watches the burned potatoes sizzle under the cold water.

Wiping his or her brow, the cook leans against the kitchen sink, picks up one potato, tastes it, grimaces because it is wet and burned, and throws it into the sink.

The cook opens the cupboard, removes a can of beans and a can opener, and opens the can. Removing a fork from the drawer, the cook sits down and grimaces as he or she eats the cold beans from the can while continuing to read the newspaper.

The Tightrope Walker

Set and props: a circus stage.

Imaginary props: ladder (or long rope), tightrope, parasol.

This pantomime may be more effective if drumbeats accompany the tightrope walker's feats and a group of spectators sitting below applaud and react to the performance.

Length: 4 to 7 minutes.

The tightrope walker enters, bows, and climbs a high ladder (or long rope) to the tightrope, indicating the height of the ladder by gradually lowering arms on the rungs of the ladder while progressing upward. When the tightrope walker reaches the top, she or he looks down, trying to hide fear of beginning the performance. As drumbeats announce the beginning of the act, the tightrope walker bows and forces a nervous smile.

The tightrope walker opens a parasol hanging from the wrist and holds it over her or his head. The other arm stretched out at the side, the performer begins to walk, knees slightly bent and body and smile tense.

The tightrope walker continues along the tightrope, bouncing slightly and leaning from side to side. Nearing the end of the rope, to a loud drumbeat, the tightrope walker jumps, turns, and lands on the rope, parasol in hand, facing the opposite direction. Turning to bow, the tightrope walker sways back and forth while forcing a smile to the applauding audience.

To a roll of drumbeats, the tightrope walker turns and begins to move along the rope backward, parasol in hand, as the applause increases.

Reaching the other end of the rope, the tightrope walker starts back to the other side, taking two steps forward and one back, parasol in hand, as the applause continues.

Head bent back, the tightrope walker now attempts to balance the parasol between the eyebrows and continues along the rope. Increased applause from the audience. Still balancing the parasol between the eyebrows, the tightrope walker runs to the end of the rope while the audience cheers.

The tightrope walker removes the parasol, closes it, hooks it onto her or his wrist, and descends the ladder (or slides down a long rope), progressively raising her or his arms on the rungs or rope to show the descent to the bottom.

The tightrope walker bows to the cheering audience and staggers off stage, wiping her or his forehead and heaving a sigh of relief while looking back up at the high tightrope.

The Juggler

Set and props: an area downstage center.
   Imaginary props: four juggling pins.
   Length 6 to 8 minutes.
   The juggler enters with four imaginary pins (or balls), sets them on the floor, and bows.
   The juggler picks up the two wooden pins and begins to juggle them, throwing the pin in the right hand up to the left and the pin in the left hand up to the right, catching the right hand pin in the left hand and the left hand pin in the right hand (showing the weight of the pin by nodding the head and slightly dropping the hand each time the pin falls in it). Repeat.
   The juggler throws both pins up to stage right and runs there to catch them, nodding and dropping both hands as the pins fall into them. Repeat stage left.
   The juggler throws the pin in the right hand upward under the right leg and the pin in the left hand upward under the left leg, nodding and dropping the hand with each catch. Repeat.
   Throwing both pins up into the air, the juggler whirls around once and catches them. Repeat throwing the pins up higher and whirling around twice.
   The juggler kneels on the right leg and quickly throws the pin in the right hand high up left and then kneels on left leg and quickly throws the pin in the left hand high up right, catching both pins while on both knees. Repeat.
   The juggler stands and throws the pin in the right hand behind and up to the left and the pin in the left hand behind and up to the right, stepping back and catching each pin. Repeat.
   The juggler juggles the pins very rapidly. He or she throws the pin in the right hand high up and the pin in the left hand high up and waits for both to descend. When the pins do not descend, the juggler walks around scratching his or her head and looking up for the pins.
   The juggler picks up two more pins and juggles them rapidly. As the juggler juggles the new pins, one of the first pair of pins that had disappeared falls on his or her head. The juggler swoons, continuing to juggle the pins in slow motion when the second pin that had disappeared falls on his or her head. The juggler dizzily throws the remaining pins over his or her shoulders and, with eyes half-closed, bows and dizzily zigzags off stage.

The Pleasures of Sea Travel

Set and props: an ocean liner's cabin; two chairs to represent a bunk bed center stage.
   Imaginary props: suitcase, book, pajamas, underwear, shirts, scarf, dresser drawer, closet, clothes hanger, jacket, sweater, cap, mirror, handkerchief, belt, shoes, bottle of pills, orange, porthole, lifejacket, water gushing into cabin.
   Length: 10 to 12 minutes.
   Smiling, the traveler enters the cabin, sets a heavy suitcase on the floor and opens it, removes a book, puts it on the bunk bed, and takes out pajamas, underwear, shirts, and a scarf and puts them in the dresser drawer. The traveler removes her or his jacket, hangs it on a clothes hanger in the closet, takes a sweater and cap from the valise, and puts them on, admiring herself or himself in a mirror.
   The traveler lies down on the bed, folding hands behind her or his head.

The traveler picks up the book, lies back, and begins to read. The ship sways. The traveler removes a handkerchief from a pocket and wipes her or his forehead. While reading, the traveler has a strange feeling in the stomach.

The ship's movement increases. The traveler closes the book and sways on the bed. The swaying increases still more. Feeling dizzy, the traveler throws the book down and holds onto the bunk bed with both hands.

The traveler removes sweater and shoes, loosens belt, and closes eyes. The traveler opens eyes and dizzily watches the shoes move from under the bed across the cabin.

The traveler gets down on all fours and tries to catch the shoes. Still on all fours, the traveler holds shoes with one hand and stomach with the other.

The traveler crawls over to the suitcase and takes out a bottle of pills. The traveler opens the lid, swallows a pill, and smiles hopefully. As the traveler sits beside the valise, the swaying increases. The traveler holds stomach, trying not to throw up.

The traveler takes another pill and then another and begins to feel drowsy.

The traveler tries to get up and falls onto the bunk bed. The traveler lays there, head over the side of the bed, breathing heavily.

The traveler remembers there is an orange in the suitcase (recommended for seasickness), crawls over to the suitcase, opens it, and removes the orange. Sitting on the floor, the traveler makes a hole in the orange and sucks it, still swaying with the ship's movement. Feeling sick, the traveler drops the orange, wipes forehead, and lies face down on the floor. Mouth tightly closed, the traveler digs fingernails into the floor, trying not to throw up.

The ship sways less. Still lying down, the traveler feels about on the floor to verify if the ship is still moving.

Trembling, the traveler stands up. The ship is hardly swaying. The traveler takes a few steps, climbs on the bunk bed, and opens the porthole (center stage right). As water gushes in, the traveler quickly closes the porthole. Is the ship sinking?

The traveler crawls under the bed to pull out a lifejacket, puts arms through the lifejacket, and ties the cords.

The traveler steps on the bunk bed and tries to climb out the porthole stage right. With the lifejacket on, she or he can't get through the porthole. Frantic, the traveler rips off the lifejacket.

Making the sign of the cross, the traveler begins squeezing through the porthole, falls out, and swims away (stage right) as the curtain falls.

Synopses of More Solo Pantomimes

Synopses of more solo pantomimes by the author follow. (For information about obtaining these and other pantomimes and plays, contact jeanlust@aol.com.) The length for each of these pantomimes may be increased or decreased according to need.

In the pantomime *A Ride on an Old Jalopy or Old-Style Dilapidated Car* (10 minutes), after the driver proudly walks around his or her car, cranks it up, and gets into it, he or she needs to keep getting out to crank it up. When the car finally starts up and moves, the driver discovers a flat tire. After changing the tire, the driver has still another mishap.

In *The One Man/Woman Orchestra* (8 to 10 minutes), the musician plays on a piano with one hand, a rubber horn with the other hand, then on a drum and a bugle, shifting hands from one to the other. As he or she frenetically moves from one instrument to another, the musician confuses one instrument with another and, exasperated, throws them all up into the air.

In *Homeless* (10 minutes), a homeless person sitting on the sidewalk holds out her or his hand but receives no money. A little dog passing by leads the homeless person to a surprise finding.

In *The Fountain of Youth* (10 to 12 minutes), an old blind person approaches a fountain and cups his or her hand under the water, drinks it, and splashes water on the face. The person sits down on a bench, leans with hands and face on his or her cane, and smiling, recalls the past, and then becomes an old blind person again.

PANTOMIMES FOR SEVERAL CHARACTERS

A number of these pantomimes for several characters or for groups may be used for silent acting scenes or transformed into scenes with both movement and dialogue for class work. However, for public performances, if you wish to alter the blocking or employ additional action, please consult the author at jeanlust@aol.com for permission to make changes.

The Disobedient Mirror

Scene: a room with an imaginary mirror.

Characters: two mimes, one looking into a mirror at his or her reflection.

Set and props: two chairs facing one another downstage center; one is the reflection of the other chair and other mime in the mirror.

The movements of the mime and the mime's reflection are simultaneous and should be synchronized precisely. As the lights go up, one mime is standing downstage center right a foot away from the front of a chair facing a mirror, profile to the audience, while the mime's reflection is standing center stage left in front of the other chair, profile to the audience.

Length: 5 to 7 minutes.

The mime at stage right looks into the mirror and smiles as the reflection smiles back.

Nod as the reflection nods.

Move back toward the chair as the reflection moves back.

Move forward as the reflection moves forward.

Throw a kiss to the mirror as the reflection throws back a kiss.

Throw another kiss as the reflection frowns.

Look perplexed as the reflection smiles.

Repeat throwing a kiss as the reflection frowns emphatically.

Repeat looking perplexed as the reflection smiles emphatically.

Open eyes wide as the reflection closes eyes.

Move back as the reflection moves forward.

Bend over as the reflection jumps up.

Jump up as the reflection bends over.

Kick left leg forward as the reflection kicks right leg backward.

Sit down on the chair as the reflection remains standing.

Stand as the reflection sits on the chair.

Sit down and place left elbow on left knee and head on left hand as the reflection does the same with left elbow and knee (*giving the impression they are using opposite elbows and knees*).

Repeat the above with right elbow, knee, and head action.

Shrugs shoulders as if to say "I don't understand" as the reflection repeats the same.

Walk off downstage right throwing arms up into the air as if to say "I give up!" as the reflection walks off downstage left doing the same.

Pulcinella the Doctor

Scene: a bare stage
   Characters: Pulcinella, three to six mimes
   Set and props: a large armchair.
   Imaginary props: a large trunk, flies, bottles of potion, spoons.
   Costumes: A dunce hat, black graduation robes to represent seventeenth-century doctors' robes.
   Length: 5 minutes.

In this pantomime, suitable for beginning students and created for an interval piece in a performance of Molière's *Imaginary Invalid*, Pulcinella and his friends parody doctors administering medicine to a patient in an initiation ceremony in which he becomes a new doctor.

The mimes push an imaginary trunk across the stage.

Pulcinella enters jumping, performing stunts, catching flies, and pulling off their wings.

The others show Pulcinella the trunk. All run to it, open it, and remove doctors' robes.

Each mime puts on a doctor's robe and they put a robe on Pulcinella.

They sit Pulcinella down in the armchair.

One mime removes a dunce hat from the trunk and places it on Pulcinella's head.

The others remove imaginary bottles of potion and spoons from the trunk.

Each gives him a spoonful of potion.

In between spoonfuls, Pulcinella prepares a short silent speech in Latin.

With each spoonful he swallows, Pulcinella feels fainter.

They set Pulcinella on his feet.

One of the mimes introduces him as the new doctor who will now make a speech.

Pulcinella bows and thanks the other doctors and then collapses into the armchair.

They stand Pulcinella up and push him forward to make his speech.

Pulcinella bows, opens his mouth and tries to speak, but faints in their arms. They carry Pulcinella off stage with great ceremony.

Wet Paint

Scene: the exterior of a building with two scaffolds.

Characters: three painters.

Set and props: a "Wet Paint" sign, a chair or table.

Imaginary props: long ladder, cans of paint, sticks to mix paint, paintbrushes, rope, scaffold, pocket knife.

Length: 10 minutes.

Three painters enter carrying a long ladder. They drop it downstage center and exit to carry in cans of paint, brushes, and a "Wet Paint" sign that they set up against the building.

They hoist up and attempt to balance the ladder, which falls from side to side, but they finally are able to set it up against the building downstage center.

The first painter puts a brush in his back pocket and climbs the ladder.

The second painter mixes paint in a can with a stick, ties the can to a rope attached to the scaffold, and pulls down the rope to hoist up the can to the first painter.

The first painter steps onto the top scaffold (table), unties the can, and begins to paint, holding onto the scaffold rope with one hand and painting with the other.

The second painter puts a paintbrush in his back pocket, climbs the ladder with a can of paint, and steps onto the scaffold (chair) below the first painter. *(The effect of a scaffold on two levels may be obtained by having the first painter climb onto a table while the second stands on a chair and third stands on the ground).*

The third painter climbs the ladder to join the second painter (second chair), bringing up a can of paint. The third painter mixes the paint with a stick, pours some of it into a can for the second painter, and then takes the other half and moves back down to the ground.

While the second painter is painting, paint spills down from above. The second painter angrily motions to the first painter to stop spilling paint.

The first painter ignores the second painter and continues to paint and spill paint on the second painter.

The second painter angrily shakes a fist at the first painter.

Still ignoring the second painter, the first painter continues to paint.

While the first painter mixes the paint, the third painter is also splashed with paint from above.

The second and third painters motion to the first painter to stop splashing paint.

The first painter ignores them and continues painting away.

The second and third painters wave their paintbrushes to attract the first painter's attention.

The first painter finally sees them, jumps back, and accidentally hits the paint can, tipping it over on the other painters.

The second and third painters shake their fists at the first painter, descend the ladder with their paint cans and brushes, and angrily remove the ladder and leave.

Dizzily clinging to the scaffold, the first painter waves for them to come back with the ladder. When they ignore her or him, the first painter prepares to slide down the rope used to hoist up the paint.

The second and third painters approach and the second painter cuts the rope with a pocketknife just as the first painter begins sliding down.

The first painter falls to the ground while the others laugh. Rubbing her or his backside, the first painter gets up and throws a can of paint at them.

As the second and third painters stand there dripping with paint, the first painter picks up the "Wet Paint" sign, places it on the others, and exits laughing.

The Fortune-Teller

Scene: outside the entrance of a circus tent.

Characters: fortune-teller, clown, circus owner, first female acrobat, second female acrobat, third female acrobat, fourth female acrobat.

Set and props:

Scene 1, three stools, a small table.

Imaginary props: crystal ball, 2 daisies, gardenia corsage, juggling balls, cane, top hat, moustache, coin.

Scene 2, same as scene 1, two imaginary fur coats, one imaginary gardenia corsage.

Scene 3, same as scenes 1 and 2, two imaginary fur coats, two imaginary gardenia corsages.

Length: 15 to 20 minutes.

Scene 1

The fortune-teller, seated on a stool at a table center stage in front of a tent, is gazing into a crystal ball.

The clown, seated on a stool center stage right, is pulling the petals off a daisy, nodding and shaking his head as he mumbles, "She loves me: she loves me not."

The first female acrobat exits from the tent. The clown's face lights up. Whistling, he begins to juggle balls he removes from his pockets.

Ignoring the clown, the first female acrobat approaches the fortune-teller and asks for a palm reading. The fortune-teller motions to her to sit on a stool at the table.

The fortune-teller looks at the acrobat's palm and describes two men who are in her life. The first is a good man but poor (she pulls out imaginary empty pockets from her dress and shrugs her shoulders). She gestures that the second has a moustache, a top hat, and a cane. He is rich (she rubs her hands and then her fingers together).

The owner of the circus exits from the tent, a gardenia corsage and cane in hand, greeting everyone by lifting his top hat, curling his moustache, and twirling his cane.

The first female acrobat gets up and takes his arm. He throws a coin to the fortune-teller, pins the corsage on the first female acrobat, and continues to curl up his moustache as they exit arm in arm stage right.

The clown, who has been watching them, drops his head into his hands. The fortune-teller moves over to the clown and pats him on the shoulder to console him.

Scene 2: Several weeks later

The first female acrobat exits from the tent wearing a fur coat and shows it to the fortune-teller seated at her table. The fortune-teller touches the fur and admires her fur coat.

The clown sitting on the stool near the tent looks very sad.

The circus owner comes out of the tent with the second female acrobat, who is wearing a fur coat and runs her hand over the beautiful fur. The circus owner pins a gardenia corsage on the second female acrobat, curls up his moustache, and twirls his cane as they pass by and exit stage right.

The first female acrobat watches them go off arm in arm. She takes off her fur coat, throws it on the ground, and angrily stamps on it.

The clown sadly watches the female acrobat burst out crying and exit stage left.

Scene 3: A month later

The clown and the first female acrobat exit from the tent and approach the fortune-teller seated at her table.

The circus owner and the third and fourth female acrobats, wearing fur coats, exit from the tent. They giggle and flirt with the circus owner. He pins gardenia corsages on both of them, curls up his moustache, and twirls his cane.

The clown and the first female acrobat watch them exit arm in arm stage right.

The clown pulls out his empty pockets. He has no money. He picks a daisy and gives it to the first female acrobat, who takes it and smiles.

The fortune-teller motions to them to approach and reads their palms. The lines of their palms correspond. The clown and the first female acrobat smile at one another while the fortune-teller predicts they will have many children (the fortune-teller indicates this by placing hands on different levels).

The clown and the first female acrobat exit stage left holding hands.

In the Park

Scene: a park

Characters: poor girl, artist, police officer, young man, nanny.

Set and props: scenes 1 and 2, a bench, a woman's new coat.

Imaginary props: baby buggy, wallet, money, easel, canvas, paints, paintbrush, sandwich, ring.

Length: 10 to 15 minutes.

This pantomime should be played in exaggerated older-movie style.

Scene 1: The park

The poor girl enters from stage left and sits down on the bench center stage.

A pretty nanny pushing a baby buggy enters from stage right.

A young man enters from stage left and smiles at the nanny, who ignores him and quickly exits stage right. The young man sits down beside the poor girl.

The poor girl is sobbing because she has walked all day and found no work. Her feet hurt and she is cold and hungry.

The young man tries to console her by giving her money from his wallet. She refuses the money.

A police officer enters from stage right and passes by. The young man quickly puts his wallet back into his pocket for fear of being misunderstood.

After the police officer exits stage right, the young man takes out his wallet and tries again to give the poor girl some money. The poor girl refuses and continues to cry. The young man has an idea. He exits stage right.

The young girl dozes off on the bench.

An artist arrives from stage left and sets up his easel and canvas near the poor girl, takes out his paintbrush and paint, and begins to paint her.

The poor girl awakens and is frightened. The artist begs her to let him continue.

The young man returns from stage right with a sandwich and a new coat for the poor girl. He sees the artist trying to persuade the poor girl to let him paint her. The young man gestures to the artist to go away. They argue.

The poor girl explains that the artist only wants to paint her.

As the artist paints the poor girl, the young man impatiently paces back and forth.

The painting is finished. To rid himself of the artist, the young man offers to buy it. The young man pays the artist and takes the painting from the artist, who thanks him, picks up his easel, canvas, and paints, and exits stage left.

The young man gives the sandwich to the girl and puts the coat on her. The poor girl thanks him and eats the sandwich.

The young man picks up the painting and they exit stage right.

Scene 2: The same park

The young man enters from stage left arm in arm with the poor girl in her new coat. He looks at her with admiration.

The pretty nanny enters from stage right and passes them with the baby buggy. She sees the young man take out a ring from his pocket and place it on the poor girl's finger. As she watches them walk by hand in hand and exit stage right, the nanny enviously sighs and pushes the baby buggy across the stage.

Pantaloon's Christmas Dinner: A Harlequinade

Scene: Pantaloon's living room stage left and adjoining dining room stage right with corresponding exits and entrances stage left and right.

Characters: Columbine; Pantaloon, an absent-minded professor, bearded and stooping; Harlequin, Pantaloon's assistant; Pierrot, a pale-faced, sad-looking poet; Clown, the happy servant; a fiddler, an older professor friend of Pantaloon.

Set and props: a table and five chairs center stage right (one chair upstage right).

Imaginary props: feather duster, living room furniture, Christmas tree in living room, box of ornaments, tablecloth, five plates, five knives, forks and spoons, napkins, a vase with flowers, five glasses, towel, two trays, two bottles of wine, apron, two big wrapped gifts, violin, bouquet of flowers, cane, four dishes of soup, small book of poems.

Costumes: if traditional commedia *costumes and masks are unavailable, simple costumes and masks may be fabricated (see masks section in appendix) or a few* commedia *costume items utilized to suggest each character. For example, to fabricate Harlequin's costume, sew or attach multicolored diamond-shaped patches on a pair of pajamas, place a rabbit's tail on a small felt hat, and use a rolling pin (covered with cloth or paper) or thick stick for Harlequin's club. Harlequin wears a black mask covering all or most of his face.*

For Columbine's costume, utilize a long full skirt (striped if possible and tucked up with a bow on one side) over two petticoats, a tight-fitting, low-necked, long-sleeved blouse with bows down the front, flat dance slippers with a bow on each slipper, and a round piece of matching skirt material, white or colored, affixed to the back of her head. Columbine does not wear a mask.

For Pierrot's costume, utilize wide-legged white pantaloons and a full long-sleeved (gathered, if possible, at the upper ends of the sleeves) tunic-shaped white top descending below the hips, with large black buttons down the front and a wide gathered high collar. Pierrot wears whiteface makeup and a beret placed behind his ears.

For Pantaloon's costume, utilize red or brightly colored close-fitting trousers, a matching shirt with a black belt or a jacket buttoned down the front, a loose-fitting black cape or over garment, a tight-fitting knitted red or colored cap, and a cane. Pantaloon's black half mask has a big nose, a moustache, and a beard made of absorbent cotton, wool, or other material.

Clown wears a traditional clown costume and whiteface makeup.

The fiddler may be dressed in nineteenth-century trousers and shirt or jacket.

The fiddler plays period music on his violin.

Length: 30 minutes.

Clown quickly dusts the furniture in both rooms for the Christmas dinner.

Columbine enters from stage right with a tablecloth and four plates that she places on the dining room table.

Clown exits stage right and reenters with four knives, forks, spoons, and napkins that he places them around each plate.

Columbine exits stage right and reenters with flowers in a vase that she places in the center of the dining room table.

The bell rings. Clown exits stage left and enters with Pierrot, who is writing a poem in a small book of poems for Columbine. Pierrot finishes writing the poem and, since Columbine is busy, slips the book in his back pocket. Pierrot greets Columbine, shakes her hand to wish her a Merry Christmas, and turns to leave.

Clown finds a way to retain Pierrot. Clown exits stage right and returns with a tray with four glasses and a towel. Winking, he gestures to Pierrot to help him wipe the glasses and place them on the table. Columbine smiles, glad to have Pierrot help.

Pierrot happily wipes and sets each glass at a place on the table.

Columbine exits stage right and brings in a box of ornaments, removes one, hangs it on the Christmas tree stage left, and gives the box to Clown and Pierrot to hang the other ornaments.

The bell rings. Clown exits stage left and reenters with Harlequin carrying two large gifts.

Columbine runs over to greet Harlequin, who gives her the two gifts for Pantaloon and herself. Columbine kisses Harlequin on both cheeks and places the gifts under the tree.

Columbine excuses herself to check the places on the dining room table.

Pierrot feels his back pocket. He only has the small book of poems for Columbine's Christmas gift. As he nervously hangs an ornament on the tree, he drops and breaks it.

Harlequin laughs at Pierrot's clumsiness.

Clown quickly passes another ornament to Pierrot to place on the tree, picks up the broken ornament, and slips it into his pocket.

The bell rings. Clown exits stage left and brings in the fiddler, who stands in a corner upstage left, tuning his violin.

Harlequin takes hold of Columbine and twirls her around to the fiddler's music as Pierrot, still hanging ornaments on the tree, sadly watches them.

The bell rings. Clown exits stage left and brings in an old professor friend of Pantaloon, who gives a bouquet of flowers to Columbine. Columbine thanks him and adds them to the flowers on the table stage right.

Enter Pantaloon from stage right with a cane, greeting everyone.

Clown announces that dinner is served in the dining room stage right.

Everyone moves to the dining table. Pantaloon sits at the head of the table and the old professor friend sits next to Pantaloon. Harlequin pulls out a chair for Columbine at the other end of the table and places himself next to her.

Pierrot is about to leave when Clown has an idea. He takes off his apron and places it on Pierrot, pushing him into the kitchen stage right.

Clown and Pierrot return carrying trays with plates of soup they serve to each guest.

Clown and Pierrot exit and return with wine they pour into each guest's glass.

As Pierrot sees Harlequin flirting with Columbine, he accidently spills some wine on Harlequin. As Harlequin reprimands him, Pierrot quickly wipes it up with a towel.

As the guest professor stands to propose a toast to Pantaloon, he suddenly loses his voice. All look at one another. Who will make the toast in his place?

Clown has an idea. He draws Pierrot to one side and points to the little book in Pierrot's back pocket. Pierrot can read one of his poems as a toast. Intimidated, Pierrot shakes his head.

There is an embarrassing silence. Seeing that Columbine is disturbed, Pierrot takes the book out of his back pocket, opens it, and reads one of his poems (an original poem may be read aloud or mimed).

All applaud and lift their glasses in a toast to both Pantaloon and Pierrot.

Columbine asks to see Pierrot's book and invites him to sit down beside her. Pierrot gives Columbine the book and then fetches a chair upstage right and sits down beside her.

Clown places a glass, plate, knife, fork, spoon, and napkin at Pierrot's place.

Pierrot is content to be beside Columbine while Harlequin's face drops.

Clown pours wine into everyone's glass as they all happily eat and drink.

Synopses of Pantomimes for Several Characters

Synopses follow of more group pantomimes by the author.

The Toy Shop (15 to 20 minutes, with 11 characters) takes place in a toy shop in which the toys come to life after the Toy Maker leaves the shop. The jealous Chinese Doll trips the Ballerina, who injures her leg, which is repaired by the Tin Soldier. All the toys perform for the Ballerina as they rejoice over her recovery.

The Robot's Revenge (20 minutes, with 4 characters) is set in the engineer's home, where the engineer creates a female robot with which he becomes enamored. In order to get rid of the robot, his jealous wife invites her husband's company president to see the robot in order to buy it. After the pleased company president gives the engineer a check for his invention, the robot turns the engineer, his wife, and the company president into robots.

The Love Affair of the Frying Pan and the Coffee Pot (12 to 15 minutes, with 3 characters) depicts the Frying Pan and the Coffee Pot who, despite their love for one another, spit water and oil on each other when they are together on the stove. But when they are separated, they no longer boil Cook's water or fry her eggs. Back together on the stove, they function well and Cook is happy.

Bella and Busy Peter (30 to 40 minutes, with 10 to 20 characters) has four scenes in a garden with a beehive. It portrays the love story of Busy Peter, a yellow jacket who loves Bella, a bee. They attend a honey festivity in the beehive, where a moth Prince flirts with Bella and steals away with her. The next day, Busy Peter finds Bella's torn wing in the garden.

SUGGESTED SOURCES FOR OTHER PANTOMIMES

For information about obtaining these and other pantomimes and plays, please contact jeanlust@aol.com. For additional resources for mime plays and pantomimes, see appendix B. For information on constructing a mime piece or mimodrama and utilizing whiteface, see appendix C.

Pantomimes for one character may be found in T. Earl Pardoe, *Pantomimes for Stage and Study* (New York: Appleton, 1931). Also see appendix B for more current titles.

Group pantomimes and mime plays may be found in Pardoe's *Pantomimes for Stage and Study* and in Isabel Chisman and Gladys Wiles, *Mimes and Miming* (London: Thomas Nelson, 1934); Winifred Jones, *Nine Mime Plays* (London: Methuen, (1940); Dieter Mehl, *The Elizabeth Dumb Show* (Cambridge, Mass.: Harvard University Press, 1966); and Rose Bruford, *Teaching Mime* (Southampton: Camelot, 1969). Also see appendix B for more current titles.

Chapter 7

Physicalizing the Word

The choice of a movement style will depend on the purpose for which the movements and gestures will be used. For example, pantomime differs from movements and gestures that eventually accompany a spoken text. When combined with a text, pantomimic gestures and movements tend to be overly expressive and artificial. As the mime Séverin wrote in *l'Homme Blanc* (1929):

> Actors in regular theatre could never use the gestures of pantomime when speaking for two reasons; these gestures would not be the habitual gestures of life; the artist who makes use of them would have the air of an exuberant articulated puppet. For the generality of actors of regular theatre the gestures and facial expression must be, I believe, only those that are taught by the attentive observation of everyday life; they are the gestures and facial expression of conversation and not those of pantomime. [Translation by author]

To differentiate between pantomime and a more natural form of movement in acting, Séverin gives an example of Taillade in the principal role of *The Old Corporal* by Dumasnoir and Ennery, who, in a silent scene, conveyed through gestures as follows:

> After having been prisoner for fifteen years in the forts of Russia, the corporal escaped and went to a village to render to his general's daughter a heritage that a dishonest individual had sequestered. To rid himself of the intruder and of the evidence he brought with him, this dishonest individual slipped a purse into the old soldier's satchel and accused him of robbery. With the discovery of the purse, which was proof of his guilt, the brave soldier, victim of an attack, fell and when he returned to consciousness had lost the use of his tongue. Taillade mimes this scene with all the principles of stylized pantomime or sign language reenacting in detail the entire battle, the death of the general, how he had been wounded and taken into captivity, the cold, the sufferings he had endured, finally his evasion in killing the guard. One wonders how a brave corporal who had been a laborer, a soldier, and a prisoner in Siberia for many long years could suddenly perform pantomime like a Pierrot. Where would he have learned this art? [Translation by author]

Here Séverin suggests that the use of silent acting rather than a sign language substituting gestures for words in which the actor indicates more than he acts would better harmonize with the character, the situation, and the action.

The gestures, movements, and facial expressions that accompany a text vary from natural to more stylized. Most modern plays require natural movement, while classical tragedy requires more stylized or formal movement. Yet the modern use of diverse movement styles may heighten the form of a dramatic work. While in tragedy movement can elevate the nobility of a text, in comedy it can accentuate the comic elements.

As in the themes suggested in preceding chapters for improvisation and pantomime, children's stories, fairy tales, fables, mythology, and historical events may also be utilized for miming to a narration or the dramatization of a text.

The next set of exercises and scenes, although based on a spoken text, may be acted with or without words. If a spoken text or words are incorporated into the movement, the text should be an extension of body expression. Rather than translate corresponding gestures and movements from words, the text should result from gestures and movement. Whenever gestures and movements are combined with a spoken text, these gestures and movements should precede speech by a single breath's time and, if desired, continue during the speech. In acting with a text, the movement should thus be used with discretion and fuse with the spoken word rather than illustrate it. And since gestures and movement convey a subtext, sometimes feelings that are opposite to what one is saying are expressed by the use of conflicting movement.

Whether movement and gestures are the sole form of communication or are accompanied by a spoken text, precise and clear movement should be utilized. The following suggestions for short improvisations should be rendered first through movement and then repeated with words.

Begin by giving physical and emotional interpretations to each of the following, and then add the verbal equivalent:

I don't believe you!
Here is the letter I found under the bed!
Will you please help me?
I hate you!
Have you seen my baby?
It can't be helped!
You scared me!
Are you really leaving?
Quickly, where is the nearest phone?
How is she, Doctor?
You fool!
Repeat what you just said!
Who are you?
I don't care!
You don't say!
I'm all worn out!
That's not possible!
Let me out!
How awful!

Don't look!
Come here immediately!
Run after him!
Is that person really honest?
I don't know!
I quit!
Where did I put my wallet?
I love her.
I found him!
Who's to blame?
What a pity!
It's so beautiful.
Watch out!
Don't make fun of me!
Where have you been?
I lost my job!
What do you mean?
Hypocrite!
I'm starving!

I will never return!
I'm so happy!
I'm not surprised!
Don't stare at me like that!
Don't go there!
It's too late!
Don't worry about it!
Bless you!
I don't have a penny left!

Help!
I give up!
I can't breathe!
My little boy ran away!
Where is everyone?
No, I won't!
It's so dark here!
That's not fair!
He was my best friend!

ETIENNE DECROUX MIMO-VERB CLASS

The next exercise is an example of a text and its various interpretations for a character's movements that were utilized in Etienne Decroux's improvisation class in "Mimo-Verb" at Charles Dullin's school in Paris in March 1951. The a, b, c, d examples show several movement interpretations that the teacher and students found to portray the description of a sincere person.

The text is as follows:
"He is a sincere man!"

a. "It is this sincerity which I guarantee and which reinforces my desire to live honestly," says the actor as he extends a hand toward a partner, seizing the latter's arm firmly to be more convincing.

b. The calm authority of a person who appreciates certain qualities on the part of a collaborator while the person he addresses does not agree. The right arm moves slightly away from the body while the hand opens several times energetically and impatiently, implying, "I am not insisting on showing you this person's value. It is evident. But why try to persuade you since you do not appreciate him!"

c. Fatigued defense of a person who reproaches another of injustice toward a third. The elbows draw slightly away from the body; the forearms rise abruptly; the hands remain open; the head inclines languidly toward the right. This shows the lassitude and the despaired attitude of the former toward a partner. He is saying: "Your injustice toward him overcomes me. You cannot shake my conviction that he is for me a man of value!"

d. A mocking evil humorist epilogues on the qualities of famous men. When the latter speaks of this person, he says condescendingly, "He is an honest person." For example, having boasted about Rembrandt, Mallarmé, and Valéry, the actor says about Victor Hugo, "He is a good republican!"

A possible gesture would be that of shrugging the shoulders, inclining the head feebly to the right and returning it to its place. The sarcastic tone implies an air of according the qualification of "honesty." But in so doing the latter finds no pleasure and his/her esteem is limited.

The final interpretation of a text should be the one closest to the author's intention, with the spoken words corresponding to the gestures employed.

EXAMPLES OF A CHARACTER'S BASIC PSYCHOLOGICAL GESTURE AND ATTITUDE IN A TEXT

To "physicalize" or bring movement into a text, the actor should start by examining the text to find the basic body attitude and gesture derived from the motivating force that characterize the role. Next find additional attitudes and gestures in another of the character's scenes. In Molière's *The Doctor in Spite of Himself*, for example, Sganarelle's wife, Martine, is a hard-working peasant resentful of her lazy husband, who has beaten her for nagging him. Her basic body attitude suggests an energetic and solid gait, shoulders compact and strong from hard work, while her head leading the rest of her body indicates her aggressiveness motivated by her husband's treatment of her. Sganarelle is slow moving, his feet dragging because he is lazy and believes his wife should do all the work. In the scene in which Martine meets two young men looking for a doctor, Martine's head leads when she suddenly finds a way to revenge herself on her husband. Her whole body moves forward in a determined manner as she lies to the two young men, telling them that her husband reposing under a tree nearby is a doctor who will only admit to it if they beat him. When the two men approach Sganarelle, his body movements contract as he slowly stands, backs away, and denies he is a doctor. As they hold up their canes to beat him, the center of his cowering body pulls in, his head is lowered, and his arms and hands are raised to protect himself from the blows.

Another approach to physicalizing a text that is utilized for play rehearsals is that of temporarily discarding the verbal text to reinterpret it by means of improvised movement and in one's own words. This method of improvisation can help discover the emotions and meaning in the subtext to bring new life to a text. See Molière's *The Doctor in Spite of Himself* in the section on *Medieval, Classical and Modern Scenes for Improvisation and Movement Interpretation* further on.

A careful study of the actor's character and motivations in the play's text and between the lines will reveal the character's movements and gestures. This, along with the use of physical metaphoric imagery or symbolic physical images, such as that which Jean-Louis Barrault evokes in the following scenes, help dramatize the emotional quality of the play's motifs and strengthen the actor's physical characterization. Metaphoric imagery will not only help the actor grow into the role and energize it, but it will render the performance whole as it marries lyrical physical movement to the poetry of the playwright's words.

JEAN-LOUIS BARRAULT'S USE OF METAPHORIC PHYSICAL IMAGERY IN SPEAKING THEATRE

The use of metaphoric physical imagery in speaking theatre and the relationship between movement and voice are exemplified in the theatre of Jean-Louis Barrault, who also performed in Decroux-style mime and in whiteface pantomime earlier in his career. Barrault's metaphoric physical imagery varies according to the kind of play, the text requirements, characterization, and the use of stylized or natural movement.

For Barrault, movement is as essential to acting as is voice and is as intricate technically as the use of voice. Just as voice is composed of three principal moments (inhaling, exhaling, and a moment of breath retention), gesture also has three plastic moments, "pulling, pushing, and contracting," or what Barrault describes in his 1947 essay "Propos sur la pantomime" as "receiving, giving, and maintaining."

Each gesture is considered a "mime sentence" in which the subject depicts the physical "attitude" or the emotional and mental intention of the person who is about to act or have someone act. The actor's "movement" is the "verb" of the "mime sentence," and the "indication" or completion of this movement is the "object" of the sentence.

Hamlet

In Barrault's discussion in "Propos sur la pantomime," his comparison of gesture to a mime sentence is exemplified in Hamlet's encounter with his father's ghost. When Hamlet meets his father's ghost, who asks him to follow him, his "attitude" is that of a person simultaneously obedient and terrorized. The body, though tense with fright, is bent forward, ready to execute his father's order. As he obeys his father's call, his movement toward the ghost is the "verb" or the "putting into action" of Hamlet's reaction. The "object" or "indication" is Hamlet's completion of these reactions after he moves toward his father's ghost. By visualizing gesture as a mime sentence the movements implied in this text find their exterior form.

Phèdre

Barrault's stage production of *Phèdre*, which he describes in his book *Mise-en-Scène et Commentaire sur Phèdre* (1946), is an example of the use of metaphoric physical imagery to uncover the dramatic and psychological elements of a play and its characters. In *Phèdre*, metaphoric physical images are used to describe the bodily appearance of the characters that express their motivations and emotional feelings. The young Hippolyte, with whom Phèdre is passionately in love, is portrayed in the first scene as a wounded athlete with a strong and harmonious physique. Phèdre's confidante, Oenone, enters resembling "a great bird batting its wings and bumping to the right and left between the partitions of a long hallway" while Phèdre follows "feeling the wall like a blind person." When Phèdre's husband, Thésée, returns with everyone still believing he is dead, Phèdre is as bewildered as "a bird bumping into the bars of its cage," and then is like "a broken puppet or a sick person who has just been given a shot of morphine."

In some scenes, immobility (considered as contained movement) may express intense emotion. For example, when Oenone asks Phèdre if she loves Hippolyte, the note indicates "general immobility." Petrified by this question, Phèdre closes herself up and shuts her eyes. When Thésée learns that his wife loves Hippolyte, he has "a somber flow of speech, a fixed look, and a maximum of plastic immobility."

Ever present is Barrault's concern for unity of movement and rhythm in relation to the emotions underlying each scene. The entire performance is compared to a symphony and the five acts to four musical movements. In the first act, in which the atmosphere is compared to a "luminous, warm, clammy, heavy summer's day," this first movement is conducted with reserve and careful attention. In the second act, in which the sun is at its zenith, the temperature is scorching and "the flames begin to gush forth," the second movement is temperate and discreet so as not to encroach upon the orchestral power of the following one. In Acts III and IV, which comprise the third movement, as the climax approaches, the flames grow stronger in an atmosphere of delirium. "The wind intensifies the fire." The fourth movement, Act V, played with force as in the incessant tremolo of a double bass, describes an atmosphere of combustion. In this act, everything crumbles with Thésée's maledictions, leaving only "ashes of Phèdre."

According to the action and the underlying emotion, each scene corresponds to specific motifs that are also described in terms of physical images. For example, in the scene in which Phèdre learns from Oenone that Hippolyte loves Aricie, she plunges her fist into her stomach, her right knee touching the ground. According to Barrault, "She has voluntarily crushed herself."

Later, when Phèdre evokes the image of her father and is asking herself what he would say about her conduct, "she is taken by a trembling, a very rapid and brief oscillation. She is like an electric chair. Her blood leaves her. Her teeth chatter."

While the actor's individual movements, linked to voice, rhythm, and breath control, express the secret desires and innermost thoughts of each character, they also complete or intensify the words of the text. For example, regarding Hippolyte's words "If I hated her, I would not flee from her," the director's note is: "It is Hippolyte's first avowal. He says it in a very low voice, turning his back to Théramène and moving a step or two away from him." At the end of the play, the dying Phèdre takes Hippolyte's defense, "bellowing like a wounded stag."

Barrault's indications for movement, which result from the actor's and the stage director's findings, serve as an example of how movement can bring out, enhance, and deepen the text's meaning. His use of metaphorical physical imagery helps to convey the inner feelings of each character, strengthening the actor's characterization and acting interpretation, as well as establishing the underlying dramatic motifs of each scene.

USING METAPHORICAL PHYSICAL IMAGES IN PLAY SCENES

In these exercises, use metaphorical physical images to interpret the main conflict and motivating force in the characterizations in each scene. If a verbal interpretation will be added, improvise the scene in your own words and then utilize the original play text.

1. In Arthur Miller's *A View from the Bridge*, Eddie and Catherine play a game of ping-pong in which Eddie aggressively hits the ball back to Catherine with whom he is in love and wants to keep close to him. A disappointed Catherine weakly returns the ball as Eddie vehemently declares his disapproval of her taking the job that would separate them.
2. In John Guare's *House of Blue Leaves*, Artie plays a game of checkers with his wife, Bananas, removing all of her checkers one by one as he slowly reveals his plan to leave her, defeating her with the final blow that he will be going to California with Bunny and that she will be placed in a mental institution.
3. In *Othello*, Iago plays a game of poker with Othello in which he cheats by receiving signals from a third party standing behind Othello. Observing his victim's every move during the game, Iago lies and torments Othello about Desdemona's infidelity.

4. In the final scene of Shakespeare's *Othello*, as Othello prepares to choke Desdemona, the action evokes the image of a cat slowly circling around a mouse before it pounces on and devours it.
5. At the end of Eugene O'Neill's *Moon for the Misbegotten*, Josie's unrequited love for farm owner and wasted drunkard James is similar to her spading sand at the edge of the ocean waves that only returns to its initial state with each spadeful.
6. In Jean-Paul Sartre's *No Exit*, Inez, a lesbian, Estelle, a flirt, and Garcin, tormented by being a coward, play a game of tag with one another. Inez is attempting to attract Estelle; Estelle is flirting with Garcin; Garcin is fleeing from them both to find reasons about his cowardice.
7. In the last act of Molière's *Misanthrope*, when Célimène's fiancé, Alceste, discovers she is being courted by a younger suitor, Oronte, the two suitors confront one another before her in a tug of war in which they pull a rope back and forth to force her to choose between them.
8. In Shakespeare's *The Taming of the Shrew*, Petruchio's relationship with Kate is like a duel between the two. Smiling, he forces Kate against the wall with his sword whenever she screams and rages. After their wedding, he withdraws his sword, sweeps her up, and carries her to his home where, still smiling, he throws her about and deprives her of dinner and sleep.
9. Find metaphoric physical images for the interpretation of other scenes.

PLAY SCENES FOR IMPROVISATION AND MOVEMENT INTERPRETATION

In the scene summaries and descriptions, find and interpret the basic psychological gesture and movement and the motivating force of each character. Interpret the character's basic psychological gesture and movement, adding, if pertinent, other related gestures and movement that best sum up the character and scene's action. It is helpful to devise a step-by-step list of a character's gestures and movements. Suggestions for each character's gestures and movements are included in the following scenes.

Repeat the movement interpretation first with your own words and eventually, if desired, with those in the original play text.

Choose and interpret other scenes in the plays suggested here, and find and interpret the characters' basic and other related gestures and movements in them. Select scenes in other plays to interpret the character's basic and other related gestures and movements.

As much as possible, the props used in these scene exercises should be mimed.

MEDIEVAL AND CLASSICAL PLAY SCENES

The Farce of the Washtub

Characters: Jaquinot and Jeannette

In the anonymous French medieval *Farce of the Washtub*, a giant washtub, (which if imaginary will provide an opportunity for more expressive acting movement) stands center stage. Before Jeannette beckons to husband Jaquinot to help wring out the sheets in the washtub, the presence of the imaginary washtub must be established through the actors' movements.

Jeannette approaches the washtub and walks around it, grabbing the imaginary edges of the tub and dipping her fingers into the hot water to feel the temperature. She then gestures to Jaquinot sitting nearby to help her. They each take one end of an imaginary wet sheet, draw it up from inside the tub, and begin to wring it out over the tub. At one point, Jeannette signals to Jaquinot to pull harder, and he pulls so hard that Jeannette loses her balance and falls into the tub. Jeannette throws up her arms and cries out to Jaquinot that she is drowning. Jaquinot removes a parchment hanging on the wall on which Jeanette has written a list of his duties. He reads out his duties, illustrating each of them with gestures (putting wood in the stove, feeding the baby, sweeping the house, cooking the dinner, washing the dishes, wringing out the wash). Jaquinot shakes his head as he finishes reading the list, stating that pulling his wife out of the washtub is not on his list!

The Tragedy of Gorboduc, **Thomas Norton and Thomas Sackville**

The Dumb Show Preceding Act I
Characters: Six Wild Men

To the music of violins, six Wild Men, who appear to be a united group, enter clothed in leaves. The first carries a bundle of small sticks. One takes a stick from the first one's bundle and breaks it; the others follow suit and break all the sticks. They begin to fight with one another. They exit still quarreling. This dumb show symbolizes a unified state that is strong until it is divided because some envy the possessions of others. Duke Gorboduc, in dividing his land between his sons Ferrex and Porrex, caused dissention that brought about a civil war.

The Dumb Show Preceding Act II
Characters: King, Old Man, Young Gentleman, two Court Members

To the music of cornets, enter a King accompanied by his court. After he sits on his throne, an Old Man kneels and offers him a cup of wine he pours from a bottle that the King refuses. A Young Gentleman kneels and with gestures of flattery presents the King with a gold cup filled with wine that he pours from a bottle into which, while no one is looking, he adds poison from a small container. After the King unknowingly accepts and drinks the cup of wine, he falls dead on the stage and is carried away by two Court Members. This dumb show demonstrates how Ferrex and Porrex refused advice from good counselors and instead accepted flattery, symbolized by the gold cup with poisoned wine that brings them destruction and death.

Dumb shows likewise precede Acts III, IV, and V of *The Tragedy of Gorboduc.* For other dumb show scenes of this period, see Dieter Mehl, *The Elizabethan Dumb Show* (Cambridge, Mass., Harvard University Press, 1966).

A Midsummer Night's Dream, **Shakespeare**

Act II, Scene 1
Characters: Demetrius, Helena

Helena, in love with Demetrius, who spurns her, follows him into the woods as he searches for Hermia, who has stolen away with Lysander. Annoyed with Helena, Demetrius tries to push her away, but Helena clings to him like a "spaniel" and runs after him everywhere.

Act II, Scene 2
Characters: Puck, Helena, Demetrius, Lysander, Hermia

After Puck has placed the juice of wild thyme on the eyes of Lysander instead of Demetrius, enter Helena running after Demetrius. She finds the sleeping Lysander, who awakens to express his love for Helena rather than for Hermia. Helena thinks Lysander, who scorns the sleeping Hermia in order to follow Helena, is mocking her. When Hermia awakens to find Lysander gone, she runs off into the forest to look for him.

Act V, Scene 1
Characters: Pyramus, Thisbe, Wall, Moonshine, Lion

In the dumb show of "Pyramus and Thisbe," Pyramus and Thisbe meet and kiss one another through a hole in the Wall. Enter Lion and Moonshine, holding a lantern. Enter Thisbe, whose mantle is torn off by Lion. Exit Lion. Enter Pyramus, who, seeing Thisbe's mantle stained with blood, stabs himself. Exit Moonshine. Enter Thisbe, who finds Pyramus dead and then stabs herself.

Macbeth, **Shakespeare**

Act V, Scene 1
Characters: Lady Macbeth, Doctor, Servant

While the doctor and servant look on, Lady Macbeth enters sleepwalking and rubbing blood from her hands. Repulsed by the sight and smell of blood on her hands, she continues rubbing them frantically. When she hears a knock on the door, she rushes out.

Romeo and Juliet, **Shakespeare**

Act II, Scene 2
Characters: Romeo, Juliet

Juliet appears on her balcony while Romeo, hiding in the orchard below, calls to her. Romeo declares his love for her. When the nurse calls Juliet from within, she goes inside and then sneaks back out to declare her love to Romeo, accepting to marry him. The nurse calls Juliet again. After agreeing to join Romeo the next day, Juliet goes inside only to reappear and to quickly bid Romeo goodnight, throwing him a kiss. Romeo lingers, bidding Juliet goodnight and throwing her kisses.

Hamlet. **Shakespeare**

Act III, Scene 2
Characters: Hamlet, King, Queen, the Players: Duke, Duchess, Poisoner, one or two actors (optional Ophelia, Polonius, Rosencrantz, Guildenstern)

Hamlet has arranged for the Players to perform the *Murder of Gonzago* before the King and Queen, to move the conscience of the King, who murdered his father. The silent scene, which precedes the scene played with dialogue in the original version, includes the departure of the King after the poisoning of the Duke.

The Players begin by performing a silent scene in which a Duke and Duchess enter, caress, and kiss one another. The Duke places his head lovingly on the shoulder of the Duchess and then lies down on a bed of flowers. After he falls asleep, the Duchess exits. The Poisoner arrives, kisses the Duke, pours poison in his ear, and exits. (At this point the King watching the play is disturbed and departs rapidly with the Queen, who is baffled over his behavior while Hamlet feigns surprise over the King's action). In the Players' scene, the Duchess returns, finds the Duke dead, and bursts out crying. The Poisoner returns with one or two actors to lament the Duke's death. They carry the Duke out. The Poisoner then courts the Duchess with gifts that she at first refuses but then she finally offers him her hand. The Players then bow and exit.

The Doctor in Spite of Himself, **Molière**

Act I, Scenes 1, 2, 3, 4, 5
Characters: Martine, Sganarelle, Monsieur Robert, Lucas, Valère

Martine and Sganarelle enter, Martine shaking her finger at her husband and accusing him of being a lazy drunkard. As he begins to beat her, she struggles to free herself from him. Monsieur Robert, a neighbor, enters and tries to help Martine, who turns on him. Monsieur Robert leaves bowing and apologizing.

As Sganarelle attempts to make up with Martine, she mutters she will be revenged. Lucas and Valère enter looking for a doctor for a young girl named Lucinde. Martine pulls them aside and points to her husband, who is sitting under a tree drinking. But, she explains, for him to admit he is a doctor they need to beat him. When they approach Sganarelle and call him doctor, he shakes his head and denies it. They beat him until he admits he is a doctor. They go off with Sganarelle to find Lucinde.

The Miser, **Molière**

Act I, Scene 3
Characters: Harpagnon, La Flèche

A suspicious Harpagnon confronts his valet, La Flèche, to see if he has stolen money from him. He searches La Flèche's pockets, feels along his breeches, and makes La Flèche show him his empty waistcoat pocket. Harpagnon lets him go, but his facial expression and movements show he is still suspicious.

Act IV, Scene 7
Characters: Harpagnon

Discovering he has been robbed of his money, Harpagnon does not know whom to accuse. Looking around and feeling about for the robber, he takes hold of his own arm but soon realizes the arm belongs to him. He madly waves his arms about. He will seek justice even if it means hanging his whole family, the entire world, and himself.

Tartuffe, **Molière**

Act IV, Scenes 4, 5, 6, 7
Characters: Elmire, Orgon, Tartuffe

Elmire pushes Orgon under a table behind a tablecloth to witness that Tartuffe has been making advances to her. Tartuffe enters and flirts with Elmire. Elmire coughs to warn Orgon each time Tartuffe approaches. To get more of Orgon's attention, she leans back against the table and proceeds to kick Orgon. When Tartuffe gets too close to her, she sends him to the door to see if her husband is coming. Orgon then comes out from under the table, and before Tartuffe returns, Elmire pushes Orgon behind her. When Tartuffe is about to embrace her, she steps aside. Orgon angrily tries to throw Tartuffe out, but Tartuffe reminds Orgon that he has made Tartuffe legal owner of the house.

The Ridiculous Ladies, **Molière**

Act I, Scenes 12, 13, 14, 15, 16, 17
Characters: Jodelet, Mascarille, Cathos, Magdelon, Du Croisy, La Grange, Gorgibus

Jodelet, Mascarille, Cathos, and Magdelon are flirting and dancing when, to the astonishment of Magdelon and Cathos, Du Croisy and La Grange enter and begin to beat Mascarille and Jodelet and remove their ribbons and feathers, revealing them to be their cook and valet. Magdelon and Cathos are humiliated as their father, Gorgibus, enters, reprimanding them and shaking his cane at his two foolish daughters for falling for a cook and a valet.

The Bear, **Anton Chekhov**

Characters: Popova, Luka, Smirnov

This short one-act farce may be condensed into the following action. Popova has been mourning her dead husband for a year, and her old male servant, Luka, is trying to persuade her to go out or receive people, which she refuses to do. Smirnov, a landowner, forces his way in to claim money that her deceased husband owed him. Popova refuses to give him the money immediately, and Smirnov refuses to leave until he gets it. A fight between Smirnov and Popova ensues but ends with Smirnov falling in love with and kissing Popova.

A Marriage Proposal, **Anton Chekhov**

Characters: Natalya Stepanova, Lomov, Chubukov

Midway through this short farce, Natalya Stepanova begins arguing heatedly with Lomov, a neighbor, about land between them that each claims to own. The argument renders Lomov, who already has a lame foot, ill. After she throws Lomov out, Natalya's father, Chubukov, shakes his head and informs his daughter that the neighbor actually came to propose to her. Natalya, who does not want to miss this chance to marry, begs her father to bring Lomov back.

Lomov returns, but the two, along with the father, begin to argue again, each one criticizing the other's dog. They argue so ferociously that first Lomov and then the father fall fainting into an armchair. Natalya tugs at Lomov's sleeve, blaming him for killing her father.

When the father and the neighbor come to, the father urges Lomov to conclude the proposal and kiss his daughter. Lomov proposes, and Natalya accepts. As they resume arguing that each one has the better dog, the father brings in the champagne to celebrate their wedding.

The Jubilee, Anton Chekhov

Characters: Bank chairman Shipuchin, bank clerk Khirin, Shipuchin's wife Tatyana, old Mrs. Merchutkina, Bank Delegate, several delegation members

When Chairman Shipuchin's talkative wife, Tatyana, enters to disrupt the shareholders' jubilee he is preparing with his clerk Khirin, they try to rid themselves of her.

Mrs. Merchutkina arrives to beg the Chairman not to fire her husband. Shipuchin tries to convince her that her husband never worked for the bank but for a medical office. To rid himself of her, he gives her money. Mrs. Merchutkina insists, while Shipuchin, harassed by his wife's babbling and Mrs. Merchutkina's pleas, orders Khirin to throw the latter out. Misunderstanding, Khirin chases after the Chairman's wife, and when told he is throwing out the wrong woman, goes after Mrs. Merchutkina, threatening to kill her.

The Bank Delegate arrives with several other delegates and begins his formal speech honoring and thanking the Chairman. But when he sees Tatyana lying on the divan moaning and Mrs. Merchutkina, who has fainted in Shipuchin's arms, he backs away, mumbling that it might be better to return at a later time to give his speech.

MODERN PLAY SCENES

Thieves' Carnival, Jean Anouilh

Act I
Characters: Hector, Town Crier, Chair Woman

Wearing a wig and moustache, Hector, a thief, steals the Town Crier's watch and purse during the latter's proclamation. After the crowd leaves, Hector sits down in the public gardens.

The Chair Woman approaches to collect money for his seat, and as he looks for his money, she steals his wallet and then the watch and purse he has stolen from the Town Crier. On her next move into his pockets, Hector seizes her hand. As she tries to free herself, she loses her wig. He removes his wig and moustache. They are thief friends.

Act III
Characters: Gustave, Two Figures

Gustave moves about in the dark drawing room with a flashlight, examining each object. He hears a noise and switches off the flashlight. Two Figures suddenly appear and turn their flashlights on Gustave, who points a revolver at them while they laugh, thinking he is only a person wearing a thief's costume.

Act without Words I, **Samuel Beckett**

Characters: Player

The Player in this short pantomime repeatedly attempts to reach a carafe of water hanging from the ceiling. Frustrated, the Player examines his failed hands.

The Time of Your Life, **William Saroyan**

Act III

Characters: Kitty, Tom, Joe

Kitty Duval is seated on the bed of her hotel room, tying a ribbon in her hair. After looking in a hand mirror, she sees the change in herself and pulls off the ribbon, angry and hurt. She picks up a book, tries to read, and begins to sob again. She picks up an old photo of herself and then falls on the bed and buries her face, sobbing.

There is a knock on the door and Tom enters with Joe and a large toy carousel. Tom puts the toy carousel at the foot of Kitty's bed and bends over to console her as she continues to sob.

Chips with Everything, **Arnold Wesker**

Act I, Scene 10

Characters: Guard, Whitney, Wilfe, Pip, Dodger, Andy, Dickey, Cannibal

The airmen in the Royal Air Force who are out of coke (fuel derived from coal) decide to raid the coke yard. A guard passes back and forth, patrolling a fence, while the airmen wait in the shadows for him to leave.

Whitney dashes to the fence, where he puts down a chair.

From a running start, Pip uses the chair to leap up over the top of the fence.

Wilfe hands a second chair over the fence to Pip, who throws himself to the ground. Dodger dashes up and takes the chair.

The guard passes.

Wilfe runs back with the chair.

Andy enters with two buckets and hands them over the fence to Pip.

Pip fills one bucket and hands it over the fence to Wilfe.

Pip lies low, holding the other bucket under him.

Dickey runs by, removing the first chair.

The guard passes.

Dodger runs on with the first chair again while Pip fills the second bucket.

Andy arrives and Pip hands him the second bucket.

Cannibal takes away the first chair.

Pip, using the second chair, jumps back over the fence.

The guard passes.

Dodger runs on and leaves a stool by the fence.

Dickey steps up on the stool.

Whitney runs up and is helped to the top of the fence by Dickey as Andy runs on.

Whitney fishes up the chair, dropping it to Andy, and then gets down and exits.

Wilfe runs in and removes the stool.

The guard passes.

Ah, Wilderness, **Eugene O'Neill**

End of Act I
Characters: Richard's Father, Richard, Richard's Mother, Richard's Aunt

Richard's Father gives Richard a letter from his girlfriend, Muriel, whose father has forced her to write to Richard that she will never see him again. As Richard takes the letter, his expression changes from uncertainty to dread.

After his Father leaves the room, Richard continues to stare at the letter until he finally has the courage to open it. He reads it quickly, forces back tears, and then becomes angry with Muriel. Hearing voices in the parlor, he shoves the letter into his pocket and pretends to be indifferent, whistling "Waiting at the Church." When his Mother and Aunt appear, he pretends to be sick and exits, indignant and miserable.

Dylan, **Sidney Michaels**

End of Act II
Characters: Dylan

Dylan is about to die. He spins and snatches the top drink off the pyramid of drinks and tosses it down. He drinks another and then another drink. He leans on the table to support himself. He gasps for breath, the tears running down his face. The lights fade.

Barefoot in the Park, **Neil Simon**

Act II, Scene 2
Characters: Corie and Paul

After being married for six blissful weeks, Corie and Paul have their first argument as they return home after dining with Corie's mother on a blind date with the flamboyant neighbor Mr. Velasco.

As Paul tries to go to bed because he has an early court case in the morning, Corie begins to undress and insists that Paul stay up and discuss their marriage problem and a divorce. Paul takes out a pen and legal pad from his attaché case to make notes on what grounds she wants a divorce.

Corie goes into the bedroom and throws out a blanket, sheet, and pillow for Paul to sleep on the couch. As he hears Corie sobbing in the bedroom, Paul prepares to sleep on the sofa, mumbling to himself about their illogical argument.

The Lesson, **Ionesco**

Characters: Maid, Pupil, Professor, Second Pupil

At the beginning of the play, the Professor's Maid, age forty-five to fifty, opens the door for the new Pupil, offers her a seat, and exits to call the Professor. The smiling Pupil sits down, draws together her legs, holds her satchel on her lap close to her, looks around the room, takes out her notebook from her satchel, and writes the date on a page as she waits for the Professor.

The Professor enters wearing a pince-nez (eyeglasses clipped to the nose). The Pupil rises to shake his hand. After an introductory explanation about her reason for taking lessons with him, they sit down facing one another at a table and the Pupil removes books from her satchel. The excessively polite Professor rubs his hands together before beginning the lesson, a lewd gleam in his eye.

The Maid enters to look for a plate, which annoys the Professor. She signals to him to remain calm, which irritates him still more.

The Maid leaves and the Professor begins an arithmetic lesson by asking questions, lecturing, and writing on an imaginary blackboard while the student writes down answers, which he checks from time to time. He grows more dogmatic and exasperated as he tests her knowledge of arithmetic.

The Pupil becomes increasingly terrified, holding her hand on her jaw and repeating that she has a toothache that grows more painful as the lesson continues.

At the play's end, the exasperated Professor stands over the seated Pupil during the language lesson, screaming at her and brandishing an imaginary knife as she holds her painful jaw. The Pupil squirms in her seat, feeling pain all over her body, as the Professor, circling around her in a mad scalp dance, makes her pronounce the word "knife." As the Pupil languidly stands, the Professor stabs her. After the Pupil flops onto a chair, the Professor stabs her a second time, has a convulsion, and falls exhausted into a chair. The Professor rises to call the Maid, makes excuses, and unsuccessfully attempts to knife the student again. The Maid enters, orders him to put the knife away, and puts an armband with a Nazi swastika around his arm to make his act acceptable. They carry out the body of the young girl and exit stage left.

The doorbell rings and the Maid enters to open the door stage right, smiling as she greets the Second Pupil.

The New Tenant, Eugene Ionesco

Characters: Tenant, Landlady, Two Movers

The new Tenant arrives while the Landlady is looking out of the window of the empty room. The Tenant signals to her to close the window and puts his case and overcoat on the floor. Annoyed over her presence, the Tenant finally rids himself of the Landlady, who exits.

Two Movers place a chair in the middle of the room, upon which the new Tenant sits. Carrying the light pieces with effort and the heavy ones with ease, they place furniture and screens around the new Tenant until he is blocked off from view. Climbing a ladder, the Movers hand the new Tenant his hat and a bouquet of flowers. The Movers turn off the lights and exit.

The Human Voice, Jean Cocteau

Act I

Characters: The Woman

The Woman is seated at the telephone, impatiently trying to reach the other party without success. When she reaches him, she asks if he has tried to call her. Pretending not to be concerned, she adds that she has been out all day. When she asks where he has been and he lies about having been at work and adds he will now remain at home, she overlooks his lie.

She hangs onto the phone for fear they will be cut off. She offers him the letters they have written one another. It is not his fault that they are separating. She has nothing to reproach him. She is the one who wanted this crazy sort of happiness. He asks if she has found his gloves. She sets down the telephone and returns holding the gloves against her cheek and says she has not found them.

She sobs softly as she asks him to keep a shell box she has given him in memory of her. She denies she is crying, pretending she is only blowing her nose. Looking into a mirror above the telephone, she tells herself that he still loves her even if she looks like an old woman. She then hides her face in her hands.

They are cut off. She dials his home number. He is not there. She realizes he has lied about being at home.

She paces up and down. She has been waiting for him all this time, waiting for she does not know what . . . just waiting . . . waiting . . . waiting.

The phone finally rings and she answers it. She tells him he is right to leave her. When he asks if she is still listening to him, although she is about to break down, she replies that she is.

The Killing of Sister George, **Frank Marcus**

Act II, Scene 2
Characters: June, Alice

In this parody of Laurel and Hardy, June and Alice enter from the bedroom, dressed as Laurel and Hardy for a fancy dress ball. As they practice a comical dance, Alice jabs June and June retaliates. Alice borrows June's hat, spits into it slowly, puts the hat on June's head, and gives it a little tap. June remains passive. Alice then indicates she wants June's hat, and June gives it to her. June points upward, and when Alice looks up, June grabs a bottle of soda and squirts soda water from a siphon into Alice's hat. She then puts the hat on Alice and the water spills all over Alice. Alice hits June and they continue other farcical pantomime business.

Vieux Carré, **Tennessee Williams**

Scene 9
Characters: Jane, Tye

Jane has taken in Tye, a handsome, brutish addict and barker at a strip-show joint. She is getting weaker from her leukemia and cannot count on him for financial support.

Tye is in bed while she is packing his clothes to rid herself of him. Jane angrily points to the needle mark on Tye's arm that proves he has broken his promise not to shoot drugs. He tries to get her back in bed, and she throws his shirt and pants at him. He must leave because she has an appointment with a Brazilian fashion illustrator at her studio.

He stumbles out of bed, pours coffee from the coffee pot into a cup, drinks the coffee, and as she screams No! No! and he screams Yes! Yes! he pulls her into the bed.

Ondine, Jean Giraudoux

Act II, Scene 4
Characters: Hans, Bertha

Earlier in the play, while riding through the enchanted forest to prove his bravery and win Princess Bertha's hand, the handsome knight Hans passed a peasant hut where he saw Ondine, a sea nymph, and fell in love with her. After he brings Ondine back to the court to marry her, Bertha tries to win him back.

In Act II, scene 4, Bertha and Hans collide as they chase after an escaped bird that Bertha catches. Hans apologizes for his clumsiness, and Bertha spurns him for marrying a peasant. He tells her that when she next meets a man she loves, she should pocket her pride and show him that she loves him. Bertha throws her arms around him, kisses him, and is about to run off.

Hans angrily squeezes the hand in which she holds the bird, killing it. Hans removes the dead bird and asks for forgiveness. She bids him farewell, saying she wants nothing more of him.

Come Back, Little Sheba, William Inge

Act II, Scene 3
Lola, Doc

Lola and Doc have been married for twenty years. After abandoning his medical studies to marry the pregnant Lola, Doc became a chiropractor and an alcoholic. When recently their eighteen-year-old boarder, Marie, engaged to Bruce, flirted with someone else, Doc was furious because his shallow wife encourages Marie to have a good time while she is young.

In this scene, it is 5:30 a.m. The previous evening, Lola prepared dinner for Marie, Bruce, and Doc, but Doc did not come home all night. Lola now calls Doc's friend, Mr. Anderson, to ask him to come help her. After hanging up, she goes to the kitchen for a cup of coffee, trying to put her thoughts in order and jumping at the least sound.

Doc enters through the kitchen back door on his tiptoes with a bottle of whiskey that he leaves in the pantry. He hangs up his overcoat and places his coat on the back of a chair.

As Lola turns around to see if it is Doc, he staggers toward her. Lola reproaches him for not coming home for dinner last night and he accuses her of not cleaning the house nor using the china his mother gave them, among other things. He pulls the tablecloth off the table, causing the china to fall to the floor. As Lola cries out, Doc goes to the kitchen for a drink.

While Lola phones Mr. Anderson, Doc looks for the kitchen knife in the kitchen cabinet, which he cannot find. He grabs a hatchet in another drawer and accuses Lola of being a fat slut. She denies it and he lunges at her and they struggle. Frenzied, she clutches him around the neck and holds his arm with the ax at his side. She reminds him how pretty he used to find her. Remembering this, he collapses and passes out. Lola stands there in a trance.

A Raisin in the Sun, Lorraine Hansberry

Act II, Scene 1
Characters: Ruth, Beneatha, Walter
   As Ruth is ironing, she is astounded as Beneatha enters in a Nigerian costume and headdress and dances a Nigerian dance. Beneatha's brother Walter enters drunk and jumps up on the table to mock his sister by imitating an African warrior spearing his enemies.

M. Butterfly, David Henry Hwang

Scenes 3, 5
Characters: Gallimard, Marc
   French diplomat Gallimard, in prison, interprets the perfect woman with his friend Marc by playing the roles of Butterfly and Pinkerton the sailor, who seduces Butterfly and betrays her, to the music of Puccini's opera *Madame Butterfly*. In scene 5, Gallimard pulls out pornographic magazines from a crate in his cell, from which a pin-up girl appears and seductively removes her clothes piece by piece.

Other Sources for Play Scenes

A number of the above scenes containing movement selected for mimed interpretation may be found in *Great Scenes and Monologues for Actors*, edited by Michael Schulman (New York: Avon, 1998) and other play collections listed in appendix B, section 3. Mime in actor training technique and scenes from plays that may be utilized for miming may be found in T. Earl Pardoe, *Pantomimes for Stage and Study* (New York: Appleton, 1931); Bari Rolfe, *Actions Speak Louder Than Words: A Workbook for Actors* (Berkeley, Persona Books, 1992); and in appendix B.

   Also see the plays of Alan Ayckbourn, Edward Albee, Sherwood Anderson, Thomas Babe, Joseph A. Fields and Jerome Chodorov, Athol Fugard, Griselda Gambaro, Paul Green, Lady Gregory, Eugene Ionesco, Marsha Norman, David Parker, David Rimmer, Neil Simon, August Strindberg, and Tennessee Williams.

ADAPTING STAGE ACTING TO SCREEN ACTING

After interpreting the characters' basic stage gestures and movements in the above modern plays, try the same scenes using film-acting techniques. Imagine you are playing to a camera rather than to an audience, with the actors performing closer together and utilizing less expansive and smaller, more natural movement and voice projection. Compare and find the differences between these two styles.

MIME AND FABLES

In the following fables, a narrator stands downstage, reading or reciting the text acted out by one or more performers. Timing is important so as not to break the rhythmic flow of the poem. The movements should be carefully worked out line by line in relation to the original text and coincide with the oral and poetic rhythm of the poem. The following La Fontaine's fables, which contain lively dramatic and narrative content, were mimed and narrated at a French Honor Society event at Dominican University of California.

The Grasshopper and the Ant, La Fontaine

Scene: a forest.

Characters: Grasshopper, Ant (one actor/mime may play both the Grasshopper and the Ant), Narrator.

  Set and props: an imaginary shovel.

  Costumes: the grasshopper may wear green or brown tights with wings (optional) and the ant black tights.

The suggested movement and blocking may be utilized or modified and may be performed simultaneously with the narration or before or after it, according to the performers' or director's choice. The narrator's spoken lines are indicated by italics.

The grasshopper singing
All summer long
Now found winter stinging
And ceased in his song.
Not a morsel or crumb in his cupboard
So he shivered and ceased in his song.

The actor/mime playing the grasshopper enters from upstage right and moves to downstage left, happily hopping about, jetting out his legs and arms and hands with claw-like fingers. As the winter wind begins to blow, he shivers and moves about, looking for something to eat. The ant is downstage right on all fours, shoveling up dirt and storing food in a hole.

Miss Ant was his neighbor
To her he went.
"Oh you're rich from labor
And I've not a cent.
Lend me food and I vow I'll return it
Though at present I have not a cent."

The grasshopper, still shivering from the cold, hops on one leg to stage right and holds out his hand to the ant. When the ant does not respond, the grasshopper takes the ant's hand and kisses it. The ant, annoyed, withdraws her hand and keeps on shoveling food into a hole.

The ant's not a lender
I must confess.
Her heart's far from tender
To one in distress
So she said: "Pray, how passed you the summer
That in winter you come to distress?"

The ant puts her hands on her hips and asks the grasshopper what he did all summer long.

"I sang through the summer,"
Grasshopper said.

"But now I am glummer
Because I've no bread."
"So you sang?" sneered the ant. "How very nice!
Now it's winter, go dance for your bread!"

The grasshopper moves downstage center and does an arabesque (a ballet posture in which the body is bent forward from the hip on one leg with the arm extended forward and the other leg and arm extended backward), first on one foot and then on the other while singing to the audience. The ant imitates the grasshopper's movements and words and says that since he sang all summer and now starves in the winter, he can dance for his food. The ant then picks up her shovel and chases him off.

The Raven and the Fox, La Fontaine

Scene: a forest.
Characters: Raven, Fox, Narrator.
   Props: a chair or stool, a morsel of cheese (optional).
The suggested movement and blocking may be utilized according to the performers' and director's choices. The narrator's spoken lines are indicated by italics.

   Mr. Raven was perched upon a limb
   And Reynard the Fox looked up at him
   For the Raven held in his great big beak
   A morsel the Fox would go far to seek.

Raven stands on a chair or stool upstage right, perched on his limb, happily flapping his wings with a morsel of cheese in his mouth. Fox enters downstage left, smelling the cheese and rubbing his hands together as he winks at the audience.

   Said the Fox, in admiring tones: "My word!
   Sir Raven, you are a handsome bird.
   Such feathers! If you would only sing
   The birds of these woods would call you King!"

The Fox approaches the Raven upstage right and bows as he admires his fine feathers and lovely voice and gets down on his knees to beg him to sing.

   The Raven, who did not see the joke,
   Forgot that his voice was just a croak.
   He opened his beak, in his foolish pride,
   And down fell the morsel the Fox had spied.

The Raven flaps his wings, proudly expands his chest, and opens his beak wide to sing, causing the cheese to fall to the ground. The Raven trembles as he watches the morsel fall.

   "Ha, Ha!" said the Fox. "And now you see
   You should not listen to flattery.
   Vanity, Sir, is a horrid vice.
   I'm sure the lesson is worth the price!"

Fox grabs the cheese, tosses it in the air, and catches it in his mouth as he exits downstage left while the Raven angrily flaps his wings at the Fox.

Other La Fontaine Fables

Several other La Fontaine fables are summarized below. The original fables should be consulted for oral and mimed interpretation.

The Drunkard and His Wife: To teach him a lesson, a drunkard is locked up in a tomb-like cellar by his wife and awakens to find himself draped in a white sheet, a candle burning at his side. The drunkard believes he is dead and that his wife is a widow. His wife enters disguised as one of the Furies to make him believe he is a citizen of Hell. "Who are you?" he asks her as she presents him with a hot plate of soup. "The Keeper of the keys of Satan's Kingdom," she replies. "And I am bringing you something to eat." The husband responds, "And you bring me nothing to drink?"

The Miller, His Son, and the Donkey: A miller and his young son carry their donkey through the village. As several villagers mock them, the miller sets the donkey on its feet and has his son ride it. Other villagers mock them for allowing the boy instead of the old man to ride the donkey. When the miller rides the donkey, they are again mocked. Why is the son not also riding the donkey instead of following along behind? Both ride the donkey, only to be mocked again for tiring the poor animal. The miller shrugs his shoulders and decides that since it is impossible to content everyone, in the future he will transport his donkey as he pleases.

The Frog Who Wanted to Be as Big as the Ox: A frog sees an ox and envies his size. She tries to stretch and blow herself up to be as big as the ox. "Am I big enough yet?" she asks the ox. "Still not big enough? Still not?" She keeps on blowing herself up until she finally bursts.

The Oak and the Reed: The oak brags to the reed about how strong he is and how weak the reed is, how he can brave any tempest while she will succumb, and how unjust nature has been to the reed. "Wait and see the end," replies the reed. "I can bend but do not break!" After the reed speaks, the north wind blows so hard that it uproots and throws over the oak while the reed bends and resists.

MIME AND POETRY

Some poems and sonnets suitable for miming and improvisation follow.

Sonnet 61, Michael Drayton

> Since there's no help, come, let us kiss and part;
> Nay, I have done, you get no more of me;
> And I am glad, yea, glad with all my heart
> That thus so cleanly I myself can free.
> Shake hands forever, cancel all our vows,
> And, when we meet at any time again,
> Be it not seen in either of our brows
> That we one jot of former love retain
> Now at the last gasp of Love's latest breath,
> When, his pulse failing, Passion speechless lies,
> When Faith is kneeling by his bed of death,
> And Innocence is closing up his eyes

Now if thou wouldst, when all have given him over,
From death to life thou might'st him yet recover.

Suggested mime or dumb show to accompany Sonnet 61 by Michael Drayton:

In the foreground, the couple are ending a love affair. Upstage is a dumb show in which Love (Cupid) is dying with his attendant, Passion, at his side. Faith kneels to give the dying Cupid comfort. Innocence waits to do the last offices for Cupid.

The last two lines revealing hope for the woman in the couple, who is given the power to re-create life through their dying love, may be read and interpreted with subtle and minimal movement and gestures as she kneels beside Cupid.

Find other sonnets by Drayton that may be interpreted with mime or dumb show.

The Highwayman, Alfred Noyes

This description of the poem's content is given to help create the movement and blocking of the action (see original poem for details).

Part 1

The Highwayman comes riding up to the old inn door and taps his whip on the shutter, behind which Bess, the landlord's daughter, braiding a red love knot into her hair, waits for him. Tim, the Hostler, is in the stable seething with jealousy as the Highwayman kisses Bess and promises to return the next day by moonlight.

Part 2

The next day, King George's men arrive at the inn and, after drinking the landlord's ale, gag his daughter and tie her with a musket beside her. Bess twists her hands until the tip of one of her fingers touches the trigger of the musket. As she hears the Highwayman approaching in the moonlight, she warns him by firing the musket, and the bullet shatters her breast.

The Highwayman turns and flees. At dawn, he hears how Bess saved him. Cursing, he returns, riding like a madman to seek revenge, but he is shot.

Still on certain winter nights, the Highwayman returns. Riding up to the inn, he taps with his whip on the shutters while Bess is waiting there, braiding a dark red love knot into her long black hair.

Other Sources for Poems

Many ballads and narrative poems may be simultaneously mimed and recited. Ballad collections, such as *The Ballad Book*, edited by MacEdward Leach (New York: Harper Bros., 1955), contain ballads suitable for miming. These include *Fair Margaret and Sweet William, Lord Thomas and Fair Anet, The Farmer's Curst Wife, The Wife Wrapt in Wether's Skin,* and others. Other ballads and poems that contain action that may be mimed along with the narration are the following:

- *Frankie and Johnnie*
- *Casey Jones*
- *Thomas the Rhymer*
- *Cupid and the Nymph*

- *Childe Maurice*
- *Father Grumble*
- *Get Up and Bar the Door*
- *Jesse James*, William Rose Benet
- *The Fear*, Robert Frost
- *The Witch of Coos*, from *The Two Witches*, Robert Frost
- *Roan Stallion*, Robinson Jeffers
- *The Death of the Craneman*, Alfred Hayes
- *Simon Legree, A Negro Sermon*, Vachel Lindsay
- *The Daniel Jazz*, Vachel Lindsay
- *Snowbound*, John Greenleaf Whittier (parts may be mimed)
- *The Vision of Sir Launfal*, James Russell Lowell (parts may be mimed)
- *Richard Cory*, Edwin Arlington Robinson
- *Flood's Party*, Edwin Arlington Robinson
- *Captain, My Captain*, Walt Whitman
- *I hear America Singing*, Walt Whitman
- *Come Up from the Fields, Father*, Walt Whitman
- *Sally in Our Alley*, Henry Carey
- *The Song of the Shirt*, Thomas Hood
- *The Raven*, Edgar Allan Poe
- *Eldorado*, Edgar Allan Poe
- *The Lady of Shalott*, Tennyson
- *Two Lovers*, George Eliot
- *The Farmer's Bride*, Charlotte Mew
- *The Owl and the Pussy Cat*, Edward Lear

Examples of poetic passages in Shakespeare's plays suitable for miming along with the verbal interpretation are:

- *As You Like It*, Act II, scene 7: "All the World's a Stage."
- *Romeo and Juliet*, Act I, scene 4: Mercutio's description of Queen Mab. "She is the fairies midwife and she comes / In shape no bigger than an agate stone . . ."
- *Love's Labor's Lost*, Act V, scene 2: Winter's speech at the end of the play. "When icicles hang by the wall / And Dick the Shepherd blows his nail . . . "

For more resources for ballads, ballad plays, and a list of songs and sonnets that may be mimed or improvised, see appendix B.

MIME AND PROSE

While adaptations of short stories and novels may be seen less on stage than on the screen, there are companies that stage such adaptations. Among them are Word for Word Theatre Company in San Francisco, California, and Book It in Seattle, Washington, from which Word for Word originated. Their productions utilize expressive movement along with dialogue and prose narration to interpret the original texts of short stories, novels, and poetry.

Passages in novels and short stories may be utilized for miming or physical improvisation with or without dialogue or narration. The following prose passages have been selected for their dramatic content and action that may be communicated through movement and gestures along with dialogue and prose narration. The original text of these selections should be consulted before miming or improvising them.

Nathanial Hawthorne, *The Scarlet Letter*

The Revelation of the Scarlet Letter
   The minister ends his speech at the marketplace and is applauded by all. Feeble and pale, he walks toward the scaffold where Hester and Pearl are standing and gives his arm to Hester, who supports him as he ascends the scaffold, holding little Pearl's hand. The minister reveals the scarlet letter (the same worn by Hester) on his breast before he dies. This scene recalls the dumb show scenes in Morality Plays. (New York: Dodd Mead, 1900, 358–71)

James Baldwin, *Go Tell It on the Mountain*

Part Three: The Threshing Floor
   John falls in a faint on the threshing floor before the altar, fighting with his inner self to rise as his family looks on. But his struggle only thrusts him downward, symbol of his conflict between salvation and sin. (New York: Dial, 1963, 219)

Richard Wright, *Native Son*

Bigger carries Mary, who is drunk, to her room and puts her to bed. Hearing her mother entering in the dark, Bigger puts his hand over Mary's mouth to quiet her, suffocating her to death. Bigger then carries Mary's body to the basement furnace to burn it. (New York: Harper, 1940, 72–80)

Richard Wright, *The Outsider*

Cross gets out of bed and takes the handkerchief full of blood out of his pants pocket and stuffs it into his bathrobe pocket. He moves down the hallway into the kitchen, pausing and listening for sounds before turning the knob. Inside the kitchen, he throws the handkerchief into the gas stove, and as he turns to go to his room, Hilton flicks on the light. (New York: Harper, 1953, 237)
   Cross reaches Hilton's hotel room, and while the maid is cleaning it, he steps inside and hides in the closet. After she leaves, he looks into the drawers where he finds the handkerchief he threw into the stove. He sits down and listens to the radio. When Hilton returns and sees Cross, he begins to look for his gun in his dresser drawer that Cross now aims at him (269).

William Faulkner, *Sanctuary*

Popeye, the man who fetched the jug, and the stranger are seated at the table. The woman enters with a platter, surveys the table, moves to an open case in a corner, and removes a knife and fork that she places on the table. Goodwin enters leading the old blind deaf man to the table. After regurgitating into a filthy rag, the old man sucks on a piece of meat. The woman raps his knuckles, cuts up his meat into small pieces, and pours sorghum over them. (New York: Modern Library, 1931, 11)

After running back into her room, Temple hears Miss Reba's steps in the hallway. When they are gone, she removes her hat and hurls it into a corner of the room, flings herself down on the bed, and gets up and throws one of Popeye's black suits lying across a chair into the corner with her hat. She tears down the dresses hanging in her closet and flings them along with a row of hats and another of Popeye's suits into the corner. She takes a pistol out from a holster and hides it under the pillow and gathers up jars of perfume, brushes, and flasks that she hurls into a corner. She then returns to the bed and lies there (269).

Temple walks through the Luxembourg gardens with her father, and after paying the old woman attendant for two chairs, they sit down. Temple yawns and removes her compact to look at her sullen, discontented face. Her father sits there with his hands crossed on his walking stick. She closes her compact and listens to the music with her eyes fixed on the grey sky that "lies prone and vanquished in the embrace of the season of rain and death" (298–99).

Hans Christian Andersen, *The Mermaid*

Characters: Mermaid, Prince, Young Girl (later Bride), Sea Witch, two Mermaid Sisters, Mermaid Grandmother, dancing sailors who are later dancing slaves (optional).

Scene 1

The mermaid rises above the seawaters and through the porthole of a large ship sees a handsome young prince and sailors dancing on deck to celebrate his birthday. As a storm arises, she sees the torn-up ship drop to one side and the prince fall into the sea. She looks for the prince and finds him almost drowning. She holds his head above water and pulls him to shore. From the sea, she sees a young girl find the prince lying there and call for help.

Scene 2

From the sea, the mermaid watches the prince on his palace balcony as he looks up at the moon, not knowing she is watching him. The mermaid returns home to ask her grandmother how she can become a mortal with an immortal soul. Her grandmother replies that this can happen only by a mortal man's love for her.

The mermaid visits the sea witch for help. Surrounded by sea snakes and feeding on a toad, the sea witch laughs at her for wanting to rid herself of her tail and have legs that are painful to bear just to enchant the prince. In return, the mermaid must cut off her tongue to give her beautiful voice to the sea witch. After the sea witch cuts off the mermaid's tongue, the mermaid blows kisses to her family and rises up through the blue sea to the prince's palace.

Scene 3

The mermaid enters the prince's palace feeling such sharp pain in her legs as she tries to walk that she faints. When she awakens, the prince is standing beside her and takes her by the hand into his palace. There she is given clothes for her naked body covered only by her long hair. Slaves dance around her and sing, but she cannot sing with them because she has lost her voice.

The prince, who has the mermaid accompany him on horseback and climb mountains with him, becomes attached to her. Not knowing it was she who saved him, he tells her she reminds him of a young girl on the shore who once saved his life. The mermaid, who cannot speak, shows her affection for him through her eyes.

The prince is unhappy because he must visit the daughter of a king in a neighboring land his parents have chosen for his bride. He does not believe he can love her because he is still thinking of the girl who once saved him and of whom the mermaid reminds him.

They mount a ship that takes them to the neighboring land where the prince's intended bride, who is very beautiful, appears. The happy prince believes she is the girl who saved his life and wants the mermaid to be happy for him. The mermaid kisses the prince's hand and is sad since the prince will no longer be giving her his love to bring her an immortal soul before her death when she will be changed into foam on the sea.

Scene 4

After the wedding, the happy bride and groom board a ship and there is great rejoicing. The mermaid tries to rejoice but is very unhappy. When the bride and groom go to rest behind the curtain of a tent and the mermaid is alone, her mermaid sisters appear with a knife they give her to thrust into the heart of the prince. When the blood from his heart falls on her feet, they will grow together into a fishtail and she will be a mermaid again. With the knife in hand, the mermaid pulls back the curtain of the tent and approaches the sleeping prince and his bride lying on his chest. The knife trembling in her hand, the mermaid kisses the prince's brow and looks at the sharp knife and then at the prince. She flings the knife into the sea, takes one last look at the prince, and throws herself into the sea, where she dissolves into foam.

The mermaid rises out of the foam to become a daughter of the air and accomplish good deeds to acquire an immortal soul and float into paradise. The mermaid lifts her eyes filled with tears toward the sun. She sees the prince and his bride on the ship, who are looking sadly at the sea foam, believing she has thrown herself into the waves. The mermaid moves toward them and invisibly kisses the bride's forehead and fans the prince. The mermaid mounts on a rosy cloud passing through the ether to do good deeds and to one day float into paradise.

Joseph Barry Gurdin, *Border of Lilies and Maples*

The reader is drawn into the story through a variety of intriguing characters that Henry meets and historical events he experiences. On his way to Périgord to his professor's archeological dig where he will work, Henry encounters his first of a series of conflicts based on differing cultural expectations that lend to humorous dramatizations provided here by the author.

A young Alexandrian, Adel, stirs Henry from his reading to warn him that an adolescent from Quebec, Francine, is arguing with a middle-aged woman from France over Henry's backpack outside their train compartment. The older woman is trying to toss Henry's backpack that she finds dirty, because for her all backpacks are dirty, from its place on the cabin's rack. Rebuking the older French woman that she has no right to displace another passenger's baggage, Francine grabs Henry's backpack from the older woman, commenting that the older woman "is probably a reactionary who hates all young people because they wear their hair long. Mon Dieu!" After Henry thanks Francine for saving his backpack, he assures the older woman that his backpack is most sanitary and invites her to join them in the compartment, but instead, she huffs away. Meanwhile, Adel flirts with Francine, but she politely and adroitly outmaneuvers his advances. (Baltimore, Md.: Publish America, 2005, 58)

Gurdin suggests that the above scene may also be interpreted by four hand puppets. The puppets should roughly follow the novel's descriptions of the characters. For example, Francine is described as the "jovial, fresh-looking maiden from Quebec" whose "rosy rounded cheeks complemented her full breasts half-covered by a light cotton pullover." One or up to two actors and two actresses could dramatize the plot through the movement of the puppets playing the characters interacting in various locations on the train. For example, the puppet representing Francine could be pulling on the backpack in the direction of the storage rack, declaring, "You have no right to take another passenger's baggage," while the puppet playing the "middle-age French lady" could be pulling it in another direction, saying, "Backpacks are filthy!" Henry's speech could be limited to an irritated "What is going on here?" as he enters the corridor, where he is thrust toward the face of the older woman. The resolution of the conflict would be Francine placing Henry's backpack back on the overhead rack while the older woman exits huffing. In the denouement of the scene, the puppets representing Adel, Henry, and Francine could be seated in the train compartment with Adel and Henry sitting on one side of the cushioned benches and Francine on the other. The Adel puppet should be manipulated in such a way as to convey that he is looking into Francine's eyes, while the hand of the Francine puppet could be placing the hand of the Adel puppet back in his own lap as Henry stares outside the window.

WORD FOR WORD COMPANY'S USE OF MOVEMENT TO DRAMATIZE NOVELS AND SHORT STORIES

While preserving the author's language and literary intent, Word for Word's Performing Arts Company acts out short stories in their entirety. In their stagings of prose selections, company members as well as their workshop students animate these prose selections through expressive physical movement and vocal theatricalization.

In their production of Guy de Maupassant's short story "The Necklace" (*Epiphanies*, 2005), for example, the use of physical expression enlivens the prose narration of the main character's feelings. After the socially ambitious Mathilde has lost a necklace she borrowed to attend the Ministry Ball, she and her husband move to a smaller apartment in order to purchase an expensive necklace to replace it. In a scene in which the actress playing Mathilde is doing the dishes and taking out the trash, she encounters some sleazy, idle men who ogle her as she works outside her building. While climbing up and down the back stairs of her building, she transforms into an aged and haggard woman, the repetition of the blocking creating a simulation of many years passing.

The company actors utilize movement not only to express emotions and feelings but also to convey props and objects on sparse stage sets. In Tobias Wolff's "In the Garden of the North American Martyrs" (*Stories by Tobias Wolff*, 2002), the actors portray the movements of power plant machinery. In "The Ride," chapter 1 of Upton Sinclair's *Oil* (staged in 2003), the actors mime road signs, an engine, a speedometer, motorcycles, and wheat fields as well as interpret human characters. The actors in their production *Three Blooms: Three Stories by Amy Bloom* (2004) animate puppets and objects, such as a car door that represents an automobile and a sheet that they fluctuate to convey water in a swimming pool. In Daniel Handler's *4 Adverbs* (2006), the actors interpret inanimate objects such as wine bottles, donuts, and earrings.

Among other works, the company has dramatized Edna Ferber's "The Kitchen Side of the Door," Langston Hughes's "The Blues I'm Playing," Rudyard Kipling's "The Elephant's Child," Bernard Malamud's "The Jewbird," Alice Munro's "Friend of My Youth," Dorothy Parker's "The Standard of Living," Grace Paley's "Goodbye and Good Luck" and "The Loudest Voice," Virginia Woolf's "Mrs. Dalloway's Party," Gertrude Stein's "Miss Furr and Miss Skeene," Tennessee Williams's "Two on a Party," stories by Tobias Wolff, and James Baldwin's "Sonny's Blues."

Word for Word is an example of how literature can be revitalized on stage through a dynamic use of body movement along with vocal dramatization. In this company, actors and storytellers take on the challenge of marrying the poetry of the written and spoken word to the poetry of movement.

Interview with JoAnne Winter

Word for Word co-founder JoAnne Winter reveals how the company theatricalizes literature physically.

Could you give a short description of Word for Word and your role in it?

Winter: Susan Harloe and I founded the company in 1993 and have been the co-artistic directors since that time. Word for Word is a professional theatre company that stages short stories, performing every word the author has written. Our goals are to excite people about the written word, to inspire them to read more, to create new audiences for the theatre, and to share the world's diverse cultures and stories. Our program annually employs more than 100 Bay Area theatre professionals while attracting more than 20,000 people each year to public performances. As one of our company members says: "It's like being read to and then some. While it's fully literary in content, it's completely theatrical in form." After seeing Word for Word perform three of his stories, Tobias Wolff said: "Their brilliant inventiveness in performance, choreography, and staging has created a new art form and a deeply affecting experience."

How is movement utilized in your work?

Winter: When we stage a short story, or a chapter from a novel, we set about to theatricalize or activate every word of the text, including the narrative and the attributives (she said, he said). In doing so, we create many theatrical challenges for ourselves that we hope will ultimately become exciting theatrical moments on stage. Hearing this, one might think of a narrator reading the story or of several actors simply reading the text aloud while actors "act out" what is being read. However, we strive to create a performance where all the characters in the story are telling the story as it is happening, so that there is no identifiable narrator, or that everyone and sometimes everything becomes the narrator. As our focus is the language of the story, we keep our production values very simple and let the actors use the words, with the aid of lighting, sound, and limited props and sets, to create the images of the play. This form is an exciting challenge for actors who must bring their best vocal and physical skills to the task.

Could you give examples of how you incorporate movement into your work?

Winter: The Word for Word style often yields very physically stylized or choreographed movement. For example, in our production of Dorothy Parker's "The Standard of Living," directed by Amy Freed, two young shop girls share a game of "What would you do if you had a million dollars?" as they promenade down Park Avenue in 1930s New York. Freed stylized the girls' walk past tony shops by having the actors walk in place shoulder to shoulder, facing the audience, or pace from stage left to stage right, taking turns passing each other so that neither was ever blocked for long from view while simulating their movement down the street.

In Barbara Kingsolver's "Rose-Johnny," directed by Sandra Crews, a young girl looks up a mysterious word in the dictionary of her one-room schoolhouse. As the discovery of the definition of this word is an important moment, the director highlighted it by having an actor become the dictionary stand by rolling onto his back with his legs extended up and feet flexed to hold the dictionary. When the girl finds the word, the actor playing the dictionary stand reads the definition so that in effect, the dictionary speaks the definition to the girl.

The narrative in Sherwood Anderson's *Winesburg, Ohio* was especially challenging to stage. An omniscient narrator told the characters' stories. In order to physicalize this narrator, director Delia MacDougall chose to embody him in the collective community of the Winesburg townspeople and view the main characters through their eyes. The director and cast, with the guidance of a choreographer and vocal coach, created a movement and vocal vocabulary for the townspeople of Winesburg. This ensemble narration manifested as a sound scope, eliciting the mood or opinions of the town, and also created the physical world of the scenes.

"The Fall River Axe Murders" by Angela Carter, an exploration of the Lizzie Borden murder case, is an atypical short story, not following a linear storyline. It is an examination of what might drive someone to such a brutal crime. To embody the narrative, again a physical and vocal stylization was employed, created with the ensemble by co-directors Amy Freed and Jeffrey Bihr. Three actors portrayed Lizzie, her father, and mother, while an ensemble of eight other actors became ghost observers, who occasionally entered the action as "real" characters from the Bordens' story (Lizzie's friend, the Bordens' maid, etc.). At one point Lizzie's pet pigeons are described and part of the ensemble, women dressed in period dresses, become the pigeons, sitting in two rows of benches in their "coop."

"Bullet in the Brain" by Tobias Wolff presented what at first seemed like an impossible challenge. Halfway through the story, the protagonist is shot in the head by a bank robber and the balance of the story is a detailed description of the bullet's journey through his brain and his last thoughts: "The bullet smashed Anders' skull, ploughed through his brain and exited behind his right ear, scattering shards of bone into the cerebral cortex, the corpus callosum, back toward the basal ganglia, and down into the thalamus. But before all this occurred, the first appearance of the bullet in the cerebrum set off a crackling chain of ion transports and neurotransmissions."

Director Stephanie Hunt chose to illustrate this sequence with an actor portraying the bullet wearing a bullet-shaped bicycle helmet (in the previous scene this actor portrayed another bank customer standing in line holding her bike helmet) while the rest of the ensemble became the brain, using a parachute and a baseball (later in the story the protagonist's last memory is of a childhood baseball game). In a tightly choreographed moment, the actors use the parachute (along with lighting and sound effects) to create a living, breathing human brain, and toss the baseball between them, simulating the "crackling chain of ion transports and neurotransmissions."

These are just a few examples of how we in the Word for Word Company use movement in our "fiction as theatre" form.

What poetry programs have you staged?

Winter: In 1997, we staged Dylan Thomas's *A Child's Christmas in Wales*. In December 2001, we created a show with director/composer Jeffrey Bihr called *Scattering Poems All through the Night*. It was a family holiday show in which the ensemble performed forty-five different poems. We devised a basic story line (without words) of a young boy getting ready for bed, falling asleep, dreaming, and waking. The boy was visited by an ensemble of fantasy characters that brought him into the world of the poems and performed them for and with him.

Could you describe the workshops you offer.

Winter: In our Literature as Theatre Workshops, students from grades 3–12 and up take a theatrical ride through a short story or poem. Using our unique style of theatricalizing narrative, the students go deeply into a text through language and theatre games. Guided by Word for Word artist/teachers, students participate in deciding "Who says what?" and learning "How can you use your body/voice to act out the feeling of that word?" Students will learn to inhabit the characters of a story just as actors do, mining the story for themes, metaphors, and imagery and discovering the physical power and nuance of language. By the end of the workshop, the students bring the story to life on stage as an ensemble, experiencing it from the inside out, and taking with them a way into books that they will never forget.

(For more information about Word for Word, call 415-626-0453, ext. 126, or e-mail jwinter@zspace.org and visit www.zspace.org.)

Laurence Ballard, Peter Silbert, and Mark Petrakis in Waiting for Godot. *Berkeley Repertory Theatre.* Photo by Ken Friedman

Joan Mankin, Victor Talmadge, and Lizzie Calogero in Mrs. Bob Cratchit's Wild Christmas Binge. *SF Playhouse.* Photo by Zabrina Tipton

Joan Mankin and Arthur Keng in Mrs. Bob Cratchit's Wild Christmas Binge *SF Playhouse.*
Photo by Zabrina Tipton

Cathleen Riddley, Bill English, and Louis Parnell in Man of La Mancha *SF Playhouse.* Photo by Zabrina Tipton

Donald Forrest and Joan Schirle in Performance Anxiety. *Dell'Arte Players Co.* Photo by Michael K. Rothman

Michael McGuigan, Joanna Sherman, and Sima Wolf in Werk. *Bond Street Theatre.* Photo by Gabriella Simon

Homer Avila and Andrea Flores in Pas. Phoenix Dance film by Karina Epperlein. Photo by Gina Leibrech

Ilka Schönbein in Chair de Ma Chair. *Théâtre Meschugge.* Photo by Marinette Delanné

Compagnie Ilka Schönbein. Theatre Meschugge. Photo by Marinette Delanné

Compagnie Ilka Schönbein. Theatre Meschugge. Photo by Marinette Delanné

Cast of Word for Word Company in Rose-Johnny. Photo by Jaime Kibben

Cast of Word for Word for Word Company in Mrs. Dalloway's Party. Photo by Jaime Kibben

John Flannagan and Laura Lowry in Angel Face *Word for Word.* Photo by Clayton Lord

Liz Burritt, Marit Brook-Kothlow, Marc Morozumi, and Barrueto-Cabello. Joe Goode Performance Group. Photo by R. J. Muna

Vong Phrommala and Jennifer Cook in Folk. *Joe Goode Performance Group.* Photo by R. J. Muna

Lynn-Audrey Tijerina in Blithe Spirit. *Ross Valley Players.* Photo by Kim Taylor

Lunatique Fantastique Company in Executive Order. Photo by Liebe Wetzel

Lunatique Fantastique Company in Attack. Photo by Liebe Wetzel

Bill Irwin in Fool Moon. Photo by Ken Friedman

Gaetana Caldwell-Smith in Sôkaku-Reibo (Cranes in an Empty Sky). Photo by John Hendrickson

Françoise Faucher in La Célestine. *Mime Omnibus Theatre Company.* Photo by Robert Etcheverry

Jeff Raz, Circus Center Clown, Performing at San Francisco Jewish Center with young audience member. Photo by Larry Rosenberg

Mumenschantz Company. Photo by Pia Zanetti

Geoff Hoyle in Act without Words. Berkeley Repertory Theatre, 1993–1994 Season. Photo by Ken Friedman

Engrenage Company, Street Mime, Mimos Festival '07, Périgueux, France. Photo by Arnaud Delon

S'il Vous Plaît, *Street Mime, Mimos Festival '07, Périgueux, France.* Photo by Arnaud Delon

Passage Desemboîté, *Les Apostrophés Company, Street Mime, Mimos Festival '07, Périgueux, France.* Photo by Arnaud Delon

Eisa Davis and Daniel Breaker in Passing Strange. *Berkeley Repertory Theatre.* Photo by Kevin Berne

Stephen Epp in Théâtre de la Jeune Lune's The Miser. *Berkeley Repertory Theatre.* Photo by Kevin Berne

Carson Elrod in Neil Bartlett's adaptation of Charles Dicken's Oliver Twist. *Berkeley Repertory Theatre.* Photo by Kevin Berne

Ivonne Coll (top) and Katie Huard in Lisa Peterson's production of Mother Courage. Berkeley Repertory Theatre. Photo by Kevin Berne

Agnew in Théâtre de la Jeune Lune's Miser
by Molière at Berkeley Repertory Theatre.
Photo by Kevin Berne.

Charlie Chaplin, 1916

Easy Street (Charlie Chaplin and Cast), 1917

Part III

INTERVIEWS AND ESSAYS

The following interviews and essays were written at the author's request for *Bringing the Body to Stage and Screen*.

Chapter 8

A Conversation with Bill Irwin on Mime and Acting

One of America's leading clown-mimes, actors, and directors, Bill Irwin studied acting at the University of California in Los Angeles, worked in theatre with Herbert Blau of the Kraken Theatre Co., and trained at the Ringling Bros and Barnum and Bailey Clown College before entering the Pickle Family Circus and performing in the Oberlin Dance Collective. In 1981, Irwin staged his Obie-winning *The Regard of Flight*. He played in the 1984 Broadway production of Dario Fo's *Accidental Death of an Anarchist*, and in 1985 he appeared in Brecht's *A Man's a Man* and in Chekhov's *The Seagull* at the La Jolla Playhouse. In 1989, Irwin's *Largely New York* became a Broadway hit, and from 1993 on he performed his clown show *Fool Moon* with David Shiner and the Red Clay Ramblers. Irwin continued to act in such plays as Beckett's *Texts for Nothing*, adapted and directed by Joseph Chaikin, and directed *A Flea in Her Ear* for the Roundabout Theatre Co. Irwin has fused the actor's art with that of the clown and the slapstick, silent film comedian, vaudevillian, and music-hall entertainer, creating a dynamic, postmodern clown art.

In the following interview, Irwin reveals how he developed his mime-clown and acting talents and expresses his views on the importance of physical expression in the actor's art.

Did the preparation for your career in theatre begin in acting classes in the UCLA Drama Department?

Bill Irwin: I hope it began earlier than that. Watching people, figuring out what you admire, what you want to emulate—that starts early. Sometimes those of us who are drawn to acting observe other actors (good and bad ones), when watching in the street or animals—primary research—would actually help us more in creating something original. One teacher at UCLA often said, "Shakespeare asks the actor to hold the mirror up to nature, not to Marlon Brando."

Before I went to the university I had done theatre in high school and junior high and during the summer in drama workshop programs. For better or worse, I entered the university fancying myself a thespian. Fortunately I had teachers all along the way who said, "No, let's start from the beginning. Watch out for habits."

Who were your masters in acting, mime, and clowning who influenced you in your career as an actor, mime, and clown?

Irwin: I've grown leery of the word "mime," but in the 1960s and '70s, in the heyday of a "mime revival," Marcel Marceau was a great hero (still is, though I don't find it as valuable to separate "mime" from the rest of the craft of performing as did Mr. Marceau). I watched Jackie Gleason and Art Carney on TV—great masters, brilliant—and Red Skelton, Phil Silvers, and Burns and Allen. Later I watched Chaplin and Keaton and really studied them when I was in college and after (our great American heritage, baseball, jazz music, and the silent film comics). There are many people I've worked with and seen in the profession: Geoff Hoyle and Larry Pisoni of the early Pickle Family Circus. I learned a lot from them. George Carl was an American physical comic who worked a lot in Europe. David Shiner, who I worked with in *Fool Moon*—he's a genius. Actually I'd take anyone for a master, anyone I can learn from or steal from.

I believe some critics consider you to be one of the most avant-garde of the New Vaudevillians. What skills make you an avant-garde Vaudevillian?

Irwin: I'll beg off that question because I don't find the term New Vaudeville very useful. It was maybe useful once, but I think it has become a period term. And "avant-garde" is one of those terms one has to be careful of. As Mike Nichols often says, "everything changes but the avant-garde." So I'll stay away from both of those terms.

You have skillfully fused the art of the actor with that of the clown and the slapstick silent film comedian, which includes vaudevillian and music-hall elements, to create a dynamic postmodern clown art. Could you comment on how this fusion came about in your postmodern clown art?

Irwin: Ninety percent of my use of the word postmodern was always with my tongue firmly in my cheek. It was an attempt to get a laugh, especially before dance audiences before which I was playing. There was a kind of modishness of performance vocabulary liberally scattered with the word postmodern. So I used the term satirically. But interestingly and ironically enough, while I was pursuing whatever I was pursuing, my shows did come to embody a postmodern ethos, an ethos that appropriates elements from different styles and eras and puts them into a kind of cafeteria or smorgasbord arrangement, taking what you like and using it. I am a product of my time, and yet I was not trying to find a postmodern clown but rather a funny clown for today that was not created in a museum style but would work for audiences I was trying to make laugh.

How do the mime and clown arts differ from that of the actor?

Irwin: That's a tricky question. I think it's important to see the performer's job as reaching the audience, no matter how you go about it. The crafts of the speaking actor and the actor whose language is exclusively the language of the body are different, but only in approach. Sometimes I think seeing them as separate can be counterproductive. Mime or clown festivals, for instance, can be wonderful but can sometimes leave one uncomfortable if it feels that jargon barriers are being put up that people then feel forced to defend. That sort of "mime nationalism" sometimes gets a little precious.

But there are differences in craft. For one thing, you have to make sure you're seen. If your storytelling is visual, you have to make sure the audience-eye is receiving what you want it to receive. How's the light? Are there visual distractions? Is what you're doing compelling to the eye?

One of the big differences is the relationship to the audience. If the convention is that the audience members are secret onlookers, as in a realistic play, then you have to help preserve that. If someone sneezes loudly, you have to continue telling the story in a way that brings the audience back. You may have to guide the audience (and maybe yourselves on stage) back to the world of the play. But in a lot of clown work, the audience's presence is a part of the world of the play. Sometimes—though not always—the most important reaction you can give, the truest action you can play as a clown, is to acknowledge a sound from the audience, to react to it and make it part of the story (certainly my partner David Shiner would never miss a chance, if it were appropriate). The most important thing is to know what it is you want to be telling the audience, and what the right relationship with the audience is for the work you're doing. Experience and instinct are usually your key.

Could you speak about the expressivity of the actor's body on stage? Do you believe as Stanislavsky states in his book Creating a Role *that the physical actions of the character he is interpreting are the first steps to entering into a role and creating his character?*

Irwin: Yes, I do, although lately I have realized that we American actors sometimes make a fetish of that and make that first entry a stopping point rather than an entry. And the responsibility to interpret the author's words, whether it is Shakespeare or Beckett or something you have written yourself, is to make the words heard. And yes, I agree with Stanislavsky that the first step is to find the physical life of the character that will help you discover how to best say those words.

Do you feel as Stanislavsky that the physical approach to a part can act as a kind of storage battery for creative feeling and that the two merge with each other?

Irwin: Yup! I need to know how a character stands, listens, and speaks before I know how to speak his words. But it is important for those who have done physical theatre, and maybe Americans in particular, not to make that a stopping place rather than a first step. If we feel that what we are doing physically is more important than the words, then we have "bad soup." And the audience will be unhappy or angry and stop listening.

Is physical expression also important in highly verbal theatre?

Irwin: At a certain point I don't think physical and verbal expression can be separated. It may sound like a glib cliché, but they are basically the same thing. There are different techniques and muscles involved, but the same function of needing to reach the audience is inherent in both. So, in a word, yes.

Do you believe as Marcel Marceau believed that the acting ability of such mimes as himself and Chaplin is essential to their movement art?

Irwin: Yes, anyone interesting to watch is also a good actor. Performers who are "technically proficient in movement" or have lots of "movement training" but no sense of acting or storytelling will not be very interesting to watch. I am often grateful that some of my early training was as an actor. I wish as a younger kid I had more actively studied dance and acrobatics. But at the same time, I'm glad that my first systematic training was as an actor with the Stanislavsky texts and good acting teachers because that gives you a sense of how to approach a scene and analyze a text to tell a story.

Do you feel that movement skills are likewise essential to the actor's art whether he performs on stage or on screen? In short, may miming, if used appropriately, also enrich acting? And how may the actor harmonize words with movement?

Irwin: Again the actor's art is telling a story to people witnessing, whether it is three people on a street corner or fifteen hundred people in a theatre or millions of people via a camera. His job is to tell a story in a way that spectators find meaningful, whether it is with words or with his body. These are in a sense all different styles or a variety of approaches to the same job, but it's the same job.

What have been your biggest challenges in movement theatre or in speaking theatre?

Irwin: My challenges have been pushing myself to get better, to be clear and listen to audiences, and to keep training. You need strength and flexibility. The gymnast and the actor have these same concerns. So when your knees are old, you need strength in your muscles to do the things you want to do and have finally learned in middle age. Also you need metaphoric flexibility, nimbleness in your mind in order to leap to try new things and not get stuck in one approach. You need strength and flexibility in both the literal and figurative sense.

Who is your stage director for your solo pieces? Or are you mostly your own director?

Irwin: Usually I am and have often been my own director for better or worse. But I am reexamining that notion. There is certain efficiency and also certain inefficiency to directing yourself. It's a tough one.

What are your plans for the future? More solo shows? Speaking theatre?

Irwin: All of the above, I would like to hope, and some good paychecks, too.

Chapter 9

Interview with Bernie Schürch and Floriana Frassetto of the Swiss Mummenschanz Company

Bernie Schürch, Floriana Frassetto, and Andres Bossard founded the internationally renowned Swiss mime, mask, and puppetry Mummenschanz Company that began incorporating dance, theatre, and visual arts in its creations in 1972. After Bossard passed away in 1992, American mime-actor John Charles Murphy assisted the company in 1995 in their retrospective program *Parade*. In 2000, they invited Danish sculptor, painter, and mask maker Jakob Bentsen and dancer-choreographer Raffaella Mattioli to perform in their creation *Next*.

In this interview, Floriana Frassetto and Bernie Schürch talk about the use of movement in the work of Mummenschanz.

What role does movement play in your company?

Frassetto: Although we come from a school of mime training, we are not basically mimes. Still we operate facial masks with our hands and we express emotions with the solar plexus and the chest. In fact, our entire body manipulates the shapes we create. In our work, sometimes the butt becomes the head, the head becomes the tail, and the feet become the arms.

Schürch: We are foremost a theatre based on movement.

Do you feel that the use of movement is important in verbal theatre?

Frassetto: Yes, for example, in Beckett the text is so condensed that movement is a strong counterpart to speech. In Shakespeare, movement is also important. But, of course, it is different for each play. For both speech and movement, it is important that there is feeling and a balance between all components.

Schürch: Movement is extremely important in theatre presently because we live in a very visual world today. This is greatly due to the role of TV.

What kind of training in movement, mime, mask work, puppetry, clowning, dance, drawing, or other visual arts have your company members had?

Frassetto: I studied mime with Roy Bosier in Rome, where I met Andres and Bernie, who were invited to perform there. I then met them again in Paris, where they were performing in a small café-theatre called *La Vieille Grille*, and we began to work together to develop our transformable mask language. Andres and Bernie's teacher Jacques Lecoq knew how to bring out the creator in them, and even if I did not have the same knowledge, I quickly progressed with their wonderful teachings. And so we joined creatively like three frustrated children who had not played enough and sought a way to pull out the playful innocent quality in us.

Schürch: I studied with Jacques Lecoq in Paris and in a traditional acting school in Switzerland.

Why did you call your company Mummenschanz?

Frassetto: Andres and Bernie had seen an exhibit of the Bauhaus, including most of the experimental stage work of Oskar Schlemmer. In one of his statistics, they discovered the name Mummenschanz, an early form of theatrical expression. Andres and Bernie identified with that name, and when they suggested it to me, I thought it would be an appropriate name.

Schürch: We needed to find a name to distinguish our visual theater from whiteface mime. It is an old German name that is related to carnivals and masks.

Why do you associate Mummenschanz with the word masquerade?

Frassetto: It is related to *mummen* meaning mask and *schanz* meaning chance. So it means the chance to mask or transform yourself.

Schürch: It is derived from the carnival and the use of the mask.

Your pieces appear to be constantly gravitating from mask, puppetry, mime, clowning, and cartoon drawing to dance, without being limited to one art form or another. Could you comment on this?

Frassetto: Because it is important that through these different art forms, once we find the object or the shape we wish to utilize, that we research how we can bring in emotions and communicate with our audiences. This combination of art forms offers a freedom to express ourselves. Of course, this depends on the reactions of the audience. Thus it is never played the same way twice.

Schürch: It is because of this blend of theatrical forms that Mummenschanz is so unique.

How does the content of your pieces originate? Through company collaboration? From Swiss folklore? Other sources?

Frassetto: There is an unconscious influence of Swiss folklore and medieval carnivals. Today the carnivals in Basel and Zurich, for example, contain political messages that are emphasized with masks. Even though some of our sketches could be interpreted politically, we are more concerned with communication and emotions. For example, in one sketch in which Bernie and I wore a half mask made of pie dough, we began by tasting one another and then eating each other's face. This sketch signified an encounter of seduction in which greed for power took over and one of us was left eating himself. Somehow this was a symbolic resemblance of what is happening in our world today.

Schürch: The content of our pieces is derived mostly from collaborative work.

How much improvisation do you engage in while creating your pieces and performing?

Frassetto: All of our sketches begin with weeks of improvisation until we find the basic choreography and we then bring it before the audience, and that's when the fine-tuning begins. Bernie and I bring our ideas to this collaborative process and they eventually mesh into one idea.

Schürch: All of our sketches are the result of improvisation especially done to keep our work fresh and to avoid repetition.

How has the content of your work changed or evolved within the past years?

Frassetto: The major change was the loss of Andres Bossard several years ago. After working twenty years together with Andres in Zurich, we moved to Lugano and continued touring with John for the next four years. The first show dealt with the initial experimentation of what we call whole body masks. In the first half, we evoked the evolution from the amoeba through Monkey man and woman encounters. In the second show, we dealt with this theme but with a more intricate expression of evolution. The creatures in the first half were almost from a different planet but with recognizable human conflicts, and in the second half we dealt with a man losing his head due to miscommunication. In our show *Next*, there is a very playful way of evoking life's problems.

Schürch: Although the content dealing with human evolution may be the same, the masks and materials have changed.

You appear to be more children oriented now than in your earlier work. Do you feel this is true?

Frassetto: I don't think we aim for that. We try to awaken the child in adults.

Schürch: We have always attempted to appeal to children. We try to play like kids. We want to tickle the audience's stomach and use the stage like a huge playground where we play our characters.

Your pieces are like drawings come to life on stage. To what is their visual power due?

Frassetto: We love what we do. We have worked together for many years and are also friends who have fun working with one another. A critic once wrote that we "were doing analysis at our own expense." We find it to be a wonderful tool to communicate with people, to awaken in them the child, and to discover that when they find their childlike spirit, how much they resemble one another universally.

Schürch: Our visual power is due to the simplicity of the raw materials we transform into essential shapes and expressions that communicate the pure emotions with which we confront our audiences.

Is this the reason for the unique originality of Mummenschanz?

Frassetto: Yes, it is because we evoke basic emotions with the use of inanimate materials to which we give life and emotions.

Schürch: It is due to the out-of-the-ordinary, down to the essence, inventive way in which we explore the use of masks and puppetry.

How do you feel your company will evolve in the next few years?

Frassetto: We still have many dreams. We will see what the future brings!

Schürch: We expect to continue evolving and play our findings of the human condition to audiences all over the world.

Chapter 10

Interview with Geoff Hoyle on the Mime-Clown-Actor's Art

Geoff Hoyle began studying acting at Birmingham University in England and then trained in corporeal mime with Etienne Decroux and at the Gymnase du Cirque in Paris. He joined San Francisco's Pickle Family Circus in 1975 to play Mr. Sniff and later created his one-man shows *Boomer* (1986), *Feast of Fools* (1990, 1993), *The Convict's Return* (1992), and *The First Hundred Years* (with daughter Kailey, 1999).

In 1982, Hoyle won a Bay Area Theatre Critics Circle Award, along with comedian percussionist Keith Terry, for *Geoff Hoyle Meets Slap Happy*. Hoyle has played in Amlin Gray's *Ubu Unchained* (1982), Dario Fo's *Accidental Death of an Anarchist* (1984), *Archangels Don't Play Pinball* (1987), Ben Jonson's *Volpone* (1993), *The Alchemist* (2000), the Broadway production of *The Lion King* (1998), Ionesco's *The Chairs* (2001), in his own original play *Geni(us)* (1994), and in *For Better or for Worse* (2005) in his adaptation and translation of George Feydeau's plays. In 1991 and in 2007, he performed in the Cirque du Soleil and in 2000 with the Circus Flora. Hoyle's talents range from clowning, slapstick, and stand-up comedy to corporeal mime, pantomime, mimicry, commedia dell'arte, and absurdist comedy.

After beginning as an actor at Birmingham University, why did you train with Etienne Decroux in corporeal mime and what did that training bring to your career?

Hoyle: I already had an interest and ability in mime at Birmingham University, England, where I graduated in drama and English literature in 1967. Clive Barker, my mentor and teacher, suggested the next step, "go to the master: Decroux." I auditioned at the French Consulate in London for a French government state scholarship and was awarded a nine-month stipend to study in Paris. Later, to support myself, I became a lecteur in English at the Sorbonne. For two years I absorbed Decroux's rigorous techniques of "mime corporel." I acquired a specialty skill and then began to develop the mimetic approach that underpins all my performance work.

Did you train and perform elsewhere in movement theatre earlier?

Hoyle: Long before studying acrobatics with Tudor Bono at the Gymnase du Cirque, I learned clown and comedy techniques by imitating the vaudeville and music hall comics I saw and heard onstage or on TV and radio while I was growing up. I got laughs in the living room by copying them. Later, after Paris, I did street theatre for several years and learned how to play to a noncaptive audience.

Where else did one train in clowning beside the Gymnase du Cirque in Paris?

Hoyle: Lecoq's was "the other school" when I was in Paris.

Could you comment on the value of the Lecoq school of movement theatre? The Grotowski school? Anne Bogart's method? Other methods?

Hoyle: Lecoq's modern drama school setting involved actor training in "personal clown" scene-work and movement-based acting for the contemporary stage. Decroux, on the other hand, was formed in the crucible of the Théâtre du Vieux-Colombier and the theatrical experiments of Jacques Copeau (ironically, Decroux, the master of modern mime, had wanted to become an orator). With Suzanne Bing, he had worked on mask theatre and became involved in mime and silent expression. His school, out near the Renault factory, was more isolated physically and spiritually (he was fond of ironically comparing it to the first Christian catacombs only half-joking when quoting Christ's "Whenever two or three are gathered together in my name . . . ") and focused more on a systematic analysis of abstract body movement and the acquisition of the nuts and bolts of physical expression. Lecoq gave you the moves. Decroux gave you movement.

When Grotowski's *Towards a Poor Theatre* came out, it impressed many theatre practitioners. The concept of "via negativa," stripping away, is useful but in the wrong hands can be abusive, arrogant, and destructive. I saw this happen when I worked briefly with a Grotowski trainee who led workshops in Paris. I saw Grotowski's troupe perform *Apocalypsis cum Figuris* with Cieslak at Avignon in the late 1960s. I remember being very impressed but thinking that to do this kind of work it was better to be Polish, Catholic, and underfed.

I am not familiar with Anne Bogart's work. I think all "methods" have limitations, however, since they are products of a particular historical context and can never be absolute. Besides Decroux, I draw on several "methods" in my work, including Brecht, Stanislavski, and Laban, and several popular comedy traditions, including music hall, silent film, and the historically subversive antics of the Fool. The point is to make the method work for you somehow and not become a slave to the method.

Do you consider yourself equally a mime, clown, and actor?

Hoyle: I perform as a clown, mime, and an actor, though not always at the same time. I tell students, "When I'm acting, I'm not always clowning, but when I'm clowning, I'm always acting."

In what kinds of movement theatre have you performed? Pantomime? Clown shows? Verbal theatre with movement? Other kinds?

Hoyle: All of them. Often within the same show.

How essential is expressive movement in verbal theatre? In film? In other theatre forms?

Hoyle: Actors have two tools: body and voice. A successful actor articulates these tools using imaginative impulses to re-create credible imitations of human behavior. A great actor hides the process completely. In film (unless you're Buster Keaton), these articulations are usually weighted toward the expressive and imitative skills of the voice. Body expression is miniaturized almost, but it's very much there. All good actors can move. It's part of their expressive arsenal in depicting character and telling a story. John Wayne once told a fellow actor seeking advice, "Watch the way I walk."

What are some of the stage plays in which your movement training has played an important role?

Hoyle: All of the plays mentioned in my bio above.

Have you taught movement theatre to actors, clowns, or mimes? Of what does this training consist?

Hoyle: I occasionally teach classes in comedy acting and physical comedy, using clown archetypes (duos and trios), clown scripts, music-hall routines, commedia dell'arte, and character masks. I consult with working performers, helping shape acts, sharpen comic logic, and clarify acting intentions.

What would you advise an actor in theatre or film concerning the need for movement theatre training?

Hoyle: I would say seek out any movement training that increases range, flexibility, and precision. Ballet, mime, circus skills, modern dance, ballroom dance, martial arts—they're all of use. And learn to play a musical instrument.

If you believe that mime enriches the art of the actor, dancer, clown, puppeteer, juggler or acrobat, how does it do so?

Hoyle: To me, mime doesn't enrich the art; it is part of the art.

How do you feel movement theatre has changed or evolved in the last thirty years?

Hoyle: I feel uncomfortable with the concept of "movement theatre." A presenter once told me, "The '70s was the decade of dance. The '80s are the decade of movement theatre." It's a convenient label, like "New Vaudeville" (I'm a "neo-Old Vaudevillian"), but I'm not sure what that tells us. All theatre is, or should be, movement theatre. The job is to get movement back to its rightful place as a fundamental tool of theatrical expression—in plays, film, and live performance—as it was with the ancient Greeks, with commedia dell'arte, with Shakespeare, and with Chinese Opera.

As theatre gets more and more expensive to produce, movement might help reestablish the primacy of the actor. The actor is the theatre. Theatre can be done without scripts, lights, costumes, sound, and décor but not without actors. One model is the *pantomimus* meaning literally "imitator of everything." I'm thinking of Dario Fo and Lily Tomlin as much as Marcel Marceau.

What do you feel you have contributed to movement theatre?

Hoyle: In my solo work, I have used physical comedy to reinvent popular movement-based characters through historical research (e.g., the Fool, Harlequin, Pantalone, music-hall clowns). As part of my creation of comic characters in classic plays, I have attempted to balance the verbal text with an equally strong movement component, aiming to excite the audience's eye as well as its ear, and expose the truly physical basis of eloquent, dramatic writing.

What are your plans for future movement theatre performances?

Hoyle: I am currently revisiting my original show *Feast of Fools*, in which not a word is spoken, and adapting Feydeau farces in which there are many words.

Chapter 11

Etienne Decroux and the Contemporary Theatre: Decroux Corporeal Mime

Robert Fleshman

From 1957 to 1959, Robert Fleshman studied corporeal mime with Etienne De-croux, worked under Drid Williams in ideokinesis, and later in human move-ment anthropology, and trained with J. L. Moreno in psychodrama. In 1968, he began teaching mime and drama therapy at Loyola University (New Orleans) in one of the few undergraduate programs of its kind in the United States. Flesh-man's mime and movement therapy research includes the publication of *Vid-eotherapy in Mental Health* (1980) and *The Arts in Therapy* (1981), both with Jerry Fryrear, and the editing of a multicultural movement study, *Theatrical Movement: A Bibliographical Anthology* (1986).

Corporeal mime. This is the formal and official term for the work of Etienne De-croux. Another term, widely used in the mid-twentieth century, is pure mime. The most direct term, my favorite, was and remains simply Decroux mime.

If we think of the popular, realistic, commercial theatre of today, the idea that Etienne Decroux has little or no place in theatre seems quite apt. However, in relation to this book of acting exercises, it demands further examination. First, numerous honored theatre professionals who passed through Decroux's school recognize his influence. Secondly, Decroux's presence is in his absence. Like Hamlet's father, he is a ghost that walks in the shadows of old and creaky stages, reminding us of what theater still is not.

The Stanislavsky method and Decroux corporeal mime are in most ways directly opposed. This is true in spite of the shared sponsorship of Decroux in NYC by the Actors Studio, a Stanislavsky center, and the Dramatic Workshop, originally oriented in epic theatre. Taken together, these opposite approaches of Stanislavsky and Decroux may represent two basic areas in the develop-ment of acting in Western theatre. Decroux's work is approached in a ritualistic manner, with each element programmed to specific aesthetic principles. While always starting with improvised movement, the ideal is the complete control of the body, achieved through physical discipline and mental concentration. Stan-islavsky's work is largely based on improvisation, acting and reacting in the mo-ment, and rooted in the senses and emotional energy. Obviously I have overly simplified this description, but it does suggest the rocky ride for the directors when working with both approaches by the same performer or performers in the same production.

Of course, all this should not and does not keep many actors from studying with different teachers in various approaches, perhaps especially in America, where the sense of authority is less deeply rooted. The individual actor can in this way pick and choose training methods according to chance offerings and discover how he or she understands his or her artistic and professional needs. Finally, since much of general acting fits somewhere between the two extremes, for better or for worse, it will finally meld into some sort of personal style. Also, for some it may be comforting to know that the general audience like the general actor is less concerned about artistic principles than about the actual theatrical experience.

Contemporary theatre has opened up all sorts and manners, kinds, and styles of production. It is in the area of nonrealistic theatre that problems most often occur in dealing with acting styles. One Off-Off Broadway theatre had as its main goal to produce the complete plays of Strindberg, both naturalistic and nonrealistic. For the latter, it was difficult to find actors who could adjust to the demands of the poetic drama, who understood the nature of poetry and how to perform it on stage. Almost invariably they struggled not to speak the poetry but to make the poetry into vernacular rhythms and the characterization into everyday realistic portrayals. Such problems continuously arise within nonrealistic productions, from the classics to the most recent experimental pieces. I do not wish to present the work of Etienne Decroux as the main solution to such problems. However, his contribution is generally overlooked in contemporary theatre.

The seed of Decroux mime was planted in the period prior to World War I. Keeping in step with the spirit of a new century, there was a rejection of the old romantic theatre, the well-made play, and the star-dominated performance. First, Constantin Stanislavsky formed the Moscow Art Theatre, built upon the principles of naturalistic production, acting based upon real emotions of the actor, and with an imagined fourth wall between performance and audience. Second, Edward Gordon Craig led a search in the opposite direction, toward an art of pure theatre based upon the elements of physical acting rather than the written drama and character acting. It would grow out of the actor as instrument, moving in silence through theatrical space.

Each had found his special approach within the renewed interest in the Italian commedia dell'arte: Stanislavsky in the dynamic energy of improvisation; Craig in its physicality of acting and meaningful movement of the human body. Both of these aspects influenced Jacques Copeau in his Paris theatre and school, the Vieux Colombier. It was there that Decroux started his career in mime.

The two approaches continued with some difficulty through the two world wars, and with peace it continued afresh. With a special American panache, the Stanislavsky approach to acting was further developed by the NYC Actors Studio, led by Lee Strasberg with Marlon Brando as its special show-person. It now carried a verbal banner: "The Method." Gordon Craig, on the other hand, removed himself from active experimentation, using the book form to promote his theories. It was in that period that Etienne Decroux became the active leader of the work toward, within, and then beyond Gordon Craig's broad vision of theatre.

The early work in mime was shared with his partner-in-mime and first student, Jean-Louis Barrault. Mime of the early period seems to have been somewhat more free and athletic than it was later.

One day in the NYC classes, Decroux surprised the students. "It is a good thing," he said, "that Barrault did not remain in the mime." He then explained that Barrault was extremely talented, mastering the work quickly and easily, almost on his own. If the mime form was to continue, he realized that a solid training system had to be created. Somewhat later, Decroux withdrew from teaching for two years to dedicate himself to rethinking, reshaping, and in certain ways re-creating the art of the mime. In the process, he designed a didactic system for mime training. The nature of Decroux's work was firmly established and later its verbal flag was raised as "corporeal mime."

Barrault held a somewhat similar position as had been held by Brando at the NYC Actor's Studio and became a show-person for Decroux's mime. Even after the break in their relationship, Barrault continued to represent the mime of Decroux. Within his career as actor, director, and producer in French theatre (one can almost say he was the French Theatre), he spoke of the vision of Gordon Craig, but it was generally understood that his work with Decroux was central to the special quality in acting.

The film *Children of Paradise*, with Decroux's role as the older mime and father to Barrault's role of Deburau, the popular nineteenth-century mime, has become part of the lore surrounding Decroux's mime. This film holds the two mimes together in the mind of the theatre.

In Decroux's NYC studio, after a series of the one-a-week lectures on the nature of the mime, the students were introduced to and suffered through two exercise series, "Erase the Blackboard" and "Physical Culture." These were designed to rid the body of bad habits and to replace them with uncomfortable new ones, and of course to prepare the body for the work ahead. Much later, after some students had dropped out, those remaining recognized that the way we think of the body, the way we use the body, and eventually but still unrealized by the body, how to think within and through the body—all this had been reshaped and the mime process had begun.

On the first day of technique class, Decroux presented the project: place a plate before a person seated at the dinner table. Few students volunteered. After more problems than solutions, Decroux stepped forward to demonstrate and elaborate. It would be a long time before the students were able to graciously serve the unseen guest of the mime.

The real meaning of the exercise was revealed: the manner of the mime as servant, in action and stillness, to meet the needs of the audience and the meaning of theatre. This leads into a concept of attitude in mime. While the term is usually understood to mean a mental or psychological state, it also means the physical arrangement of parts of the body, or posture. When blended together, they become the starting point toward understanding the nature of mime as a unique state of mind-body.

All movement forms have a system of training exercises built upon the particular demands of the individual form. In this book, the author has listed and described systems from various sources and approaches, including the Decroux scales. The term "scales" comes from music. Decroux considered music to be the most important and purist of the art forms, and which he used as one of his main models in constructing the mime, perhaps the most important one. "The scales" are usually understood as a system composed of a series of related and developing exercises or "scales." They deal with the human body, its structure, articulations, dynamics, and movement potential. They are sometimes referred to as "didactic exercises" or "mime gymnastics," but in class they were called simply "technique exercises." They are related to "isolations," and in this book are referred to as "disassociations." The confusion of terminology is caused by differences in translation and the particular period of study. Perhaps this can be corrected in the future.

Throughout the early training, the mime student is promised that if the scales series is accomplished, then all mime movement is possible. Likewise, if all of the movement in mime should disappear except the scales, then it would be all right: "The mime will survive." However, for many young mimes, it is something to be learned as soon as possible and to get on to the real thing, on a real stage, with the true nature of the scales overlooked.

The system of the scales was developed to meet the needs of the art of mime, and in that process it became the center of Decroux's link to other movement forms. These exercises must not be considered as a simple system akin to aerobatics, but rather approached with a sense of protocol, with certain formality, almost as ritual. It is presented here in belief that it has significance for the physical actor as well as the mime performer.

The short section entitled "Disassociation of Mime Exercises" describes many of the exercises. The most basic scales are given in several early how-to books on modern mime, namely in David Albert, *Pantomime: Elements and Exercises* (1971) and *Talking about Mime: An Illustrated Guide* (1994); Claude Kipnis, *The Mime Book* (1974); and Richmond Shepard, *Mime: The Technique of Silence* (1971).

The study of the form of Decroux mime starts with a concept of the perpendicular. This is realized as a vertical line in the center of the body, based upon the line of gravity. It is not the downward pull of gravity that is of interest at this point, but its centrality, the "centeredness" of the line.

Along and around this centerline are various areas of the human body, referred to as "organs," forming an inventory for the body of the mime. While there are internal connections of muscles, sinews, and ligaments, the organs are basically shaped by the skeletal structure and viewed by an audience as separate and independent units.

The inventory consists of the head, neck, chest, waist, pelvis, semi-total (the head through the thighs) and Total, plus Feet. The mime is mainly concerned with the trunk of the body, chest through pelvis, as the main agent of communication. The head is considered a key unit because it holds the all-important brain. The face is held in a neutral state, keeping the attention on the trunk. The appendicular organs are forward. All is ready for action.

Along this centerline, where the body is divided into units, the two primary scales are located: the composed organs and the acquired organs. For the composed organs, the individual organs are combined together and moved as a single unit: head; head and neck; head through chest; head through waist; head through pelvis; head through upper legs (thighs); and total, head to feet. For the acquired organs, the head leads, taking with it, one unit at a time, the organs below, all following the design of the head: head, and neck, and chest, and waist, and pelvis, and total. The feet can be used as needed, flat on the floor, a very low lift, or a modest en pointe.

The units of these two scales can be moved in three ways: inclination, rotation, and translation (moving in a straight, level line, as if on a shelf: sometimes designated as "Slide" and in this book called "Separation"). They may be accomplished in a variety of directions, speeds, and dynamics. These two scales, along with their natural development and variations, are the base study of the mime, and as they are extended outward into mime space, the whole complex of the form of mime opens up.

When considering all possible movements with variations of the mime exercises, it is quite impressive: 2 scales: with 3 types of movement: in 4 directions (front, back, right and left), and 4 secondary directions (midpoints between the main directions): in 3 speeds (slow, medium, fast): in 3 dynamics (soft, medium, hard); add to this the variation of the base (modified ballet position of feet), and then add to that the direction taken for the figure (top to bottom or bottom up), and, as the saying goes: do the math for yourself. It all adds up to an amazing mime potential.

In the mime lectures that preceded actual workshop classes, Decroux explained with his unique logic that of the four mime personages briefly introduced, one of them is more beautiful and the most difficult. Therefore, the class would start with the Man of the Drawing Room and retrogress to the others.

The Man of the Drawing Room is the figural representation of the idealized Western man. A general technical description for this area of mime includes a sense of the solidarity of the figure and a sound alignment. Movement is in straight lines with precise corners. It provides a base for the geometric structure that lies within each mime figure. Everything is very much one-thing-at-a-time. Action is limited to the top portion of the body (head, neck, chest, and "a little bit" of the waist). Many exercises of the Man of the Drawing Room, walks and simple actions, accompanied those of the scales. The world of the Man of the Drawing Room is further discussed, along with his companions later in this essay. I think of the Man of the Drawing Room as Mr. Perpendicular itself, moving in a world of personification.

For both the physical actor and the mime performer, these scales help to develop a number of important qualities: body alignment and articulation, balance, a feel for body shape, and a sense of direction. As the training continues, there is a growing surety of self in space and a more solid stage presence. For both the actor and the mime performer, instead of a slippery thing so often lost, confused, or forgotten, movement becomes a tangible reality.

The exercises of the scales lead directly into the center of the area of Configuration or Mime Figures. A figure, in a long view, might be thought of as the structuring of the units of the body, in relationship to each other, through time and space, and in accordance with some specific design, arriving in conclusion with a sense of completeness and meaning. However, not all figures are equal. The simple ones may be rest stops along the way. Others may be quite meaningful, pulling both mime and viewer together in a unique experience.

Starting with the simplest and most direct description of the process, the following of one unit after another throughout the body can be thought of as a geometric figure or even as a pure figure. By adding variations of time or energy, the use of designed arms, and so forth, a meaningful figure can be built. A good example is the shaping of the Backward Arch. From the opening movement, there is an attraction of interest, because a backward movement is less often used and is more difficult than a forward one. By adding arm work in progress and a strong "special ending," an important mime figure will have been created.

The actual "Call" of the figure is quite important. It gives the timing and dynamics for the figure as it moves in process. Also, it is the important instrument for teaching the process of Shock-and-Resonance that is one of the keys of Decroux's movement system. A sensitive Caller, the time, the rhythm, volume, etc. will inform the students in subtle ways about the nature and meaning of the figure.

The Basic Figure: in the Acquired Scale, an extended backward arch, with arms added in progress, from the sides of the body into a wide overhead "V" design.

The Neutral is adjusted to a Zero with weight forward, to better reveal the backward movement.

In the Call regarding the Backward Inclination: (1) Head, (2) Neck, (3) Chest, and a little bit of the arms, (4) Waist, and a little bit of the arms, (5) Pelvis, and a little bit of the arms, (6) Hold figure-in-process in short pause, (7) Arms continue with own energy, (8) Arms lock in with the chest at a certain point and continue into a backward arch. (9) An extremely nice figure, in a somewhat longer hold. (10) With figure frozen, a small sudden collapse (a "let-go" of knees and quick fall-catch, with pelvis up and forward, and on balls of feet, holding figure steady). (11) The final figure, the Sun Worshipper (then a simple return).

There is an interesting side note to the sun-worship figure. At one evening class, with Decroux leading this figure, he said that there are two ways to work in mime: one, with the didactic system, and the other, using the senses. He suggested the use of the warmth of the sun on the body as the figure opens. This is the only time I remember Decroux taking such an approach. However, it opens a small crack in the door separating the Stanislavsky method and the Decroux mime.

The training in Mime takes an important turn with the introduction of the Triples, a design resulting in a combination of three types of movements: inclination, rotation, and translation, one following the other, in any chosen order. The creation of the Triples resulted from cracking the secret of the Curve. Besides indicating the nature of a particular curve, it gives a means of designing movement with greater precision. It always seems somewhat magical to watch a mime figure evolve, almost a blossoming, from a Triple.

This early basic part of mime training is layered with purpose. The first and most obvious is that it gives a basic understructure for mime training and performance. The structure has a vocabulary, words with which to explain or talk about the nature of mime. Besides the skeletal structure of a figure, there is a protocol of how to approach and accomplish the figure that sharpens the very subtle relationships between the personal self, the form of the art, and needs of the audience. Furthermore, these early figures can be quite beautiful within themselves, forming something like an abstract art.

The mime training is also a means of movement analysis. As such, some feel it is on par with that of Rudolf Laban, and even perhaps in one way more practical with its inside-body simplicity, and that it can be carried along inside both mind and body, and even during performance.

The thrust of the work so far has dealt with the training of the body and learning key mime figures. Their same work, although perhaps unnoticed, has given the internal sense for the tricky business of mime improvisation.

It is obvious that the process of mime improvisation is quite different from that for method acting. They are located in different parts of the mind. Beyond the meaning of the act itself, it is the kinesthetic sense and the manner of the movement that are basic to the act of mime. After many hours of work with the scales, a good internal map has engraved itself upon the mind that the performer can follow.

In the midst of improvisation, when an important figure has been created but not clearly understood, the mime can break down the figure to make the figure repeatable and to improve upon it. The basic designs of the scales remain in the back of the mind and inside the skeletal structure of the mime body. Finally, when involved in improvisation, the body itself knows what it is doing and how to go about doing it, but keeping in touch by the oldest device, the technology of the trained human mind.

With all the talk about movement in mime, there is still much to be said about "mime stillness." First, of course, is the fact that movement in mime grows out of the stillness of the Neutral and returns to it for the conclusion. It is also found in various states of purposeful pauses. The term "mime stillness" seems to imply something more, an "active nonmovement." According to Decroux lore, reported by Thomas Leabhart, the art of mime began at the exact moment when some Decroux student assistant, calling the scales, said, "Head without the Neck." This not only gave the movement for the head; it also indicated a nonmovement for the neck. As it is natural for the neck to tag along behind the movement of the head, a conscious physical effort is required to hold it in place. This creates a tension, one that is registered as a "dramatic tension." This happens in many body locations. At times, for artistic needs, it is necessary to cover over the tensions, and at others to artificially create such tensions. Likewise, intensified relaxation becomes part of the repertoire of the mime actor. Most of all, there is a sense of silent stillness, very much like a Neutral, that mime carries, even during performance, in the deep center of the body. It is there that the artist lives.

The elements of movement structure can be seen and understood, both in art and life. Images of the scales, lodged securely in the mind and body, guide the mime through the work, allowing him or her to follow the changes and developing images of the creative mind. And at the same time, the body in movement may lead the mind into new spaces.

As the students advance in their study, they move into another very important area of mime, "Les Hommes." This is divided into four units: (1) Man of the Drawing Room, or civilized Western man; (2) Man of Sport, or man of action; (3) Moving Statuary (follows the mind); and (4) Dream Mime (free of gravity). While these may sometimes be thought of as "personages" to be used as a guide toward physical character acting, they are much more. Each has a separate theoretical base and technical physical structure. They may be thought of as prototypes, or perhaps archetypes, of human movement as revealed in mime.

The Man of the Drawing Room was briefly discussed earlier, mainly in regard to its physical presentation. The theory behind this personage is that humankind somehow created a concept of a perfect world for itself, where there is no struggle, within or without, only the love of humankind giving the energy and reason for being.

He lives in his special space, a drawing room, where unseen servants meet all his needs. He is allowed acts of small generosities, for example, to accept an orange from his left and hand it to his right front oblique. At times he takes himself out on a walk to survey and enjoy his special world. As he walks, his body moves evenly on a level ground. His legs carry him with the trunk of his body much like riding a well-bred horse. In fact, the logo of the Man of the Drawing Room is the Horse.

Side note: Quite in spite of his own personal perfection, he has one possible foible: he can too easily overdo his perfection and beautiful manner. When he does so, it creates the one kind of comedy that Decroux approves of in this incomplete state of the art of mime. Traditionally, in the public mind, mime is and probably always has been a form of comic entertainment. Marcel Marceau was known as a comic mime. This was reinforced by his great popularity.

The Man of Sport is the personage, unlike the Man of the Drawing Room, that lives in the enjoyment of an open world. The word "sport" is misleading. It refers to something more than athletic competition. He enjoys expressing himself in physical action from play to work. He has an ease and freedom of movement. He is strong and confident of his body and can express himself by pushing and pulling objects of various shapes and weights. The exercise series for the Man of Sport is called he Counterweights. In this, the body is used as an opposing force to that of an object.

The concept of "center" must be adjusted for this area of mime. While the vertical centerline remains as a strong frame of reference, the finding of the body center for the whole body, somewhere along that line, is something the performer must do for himself. Meeting different weights requires adjusting that center point.

The logo for the Man of Sport is the Cat, because it uses its whole body in movement.

These two personages, Man of the Drawing Room and Man of Sport, are based upon two opposite concepts of life, and as such they can be used in moderation for characterization in the theatre.

Moving Statuary: this term is somewhat confusing. There is a long tradition of statues that refuse to stand frozen and come to life. One of Decroux's main mime works has this theme. Because of the relationship between sculpture and mime, one automatically links them together. However, that is not quite the case.

Moving Statuary is the elongation and amplification of the Acquired Organs, with the addition of a freedom of the body to follow the lead of the head in the designs of the thinking process, with the rhythm and timing of thoughts in action.

The term "Moving Statuary" becomes alive (so to speak) within the continuing movement, one beautiful figure leading into another one and still on into others. It is as simple as that and as difficult. The logo for Moving Statuary is the Eel.

The Man of Dreams is built on a singular, rather simple technical design. Instead of the perpendicular held in gravity, dreams are not rooted in logic, but rather float through the space of the mind in off-center obliques, rotating into new and other obliques as needed. It seemed to me at first to be a rather forced concept. Decroux would sometimes illustrate a point with a short mime, perhaps on the spur of the moment, with an explanation or narration. These were wonderful learning experiences.

On one occasion, his example for dream mime was an elderly man who meets by chance a lady from his past—they had been lovers when young, but they had parted—they walk along together—there is a bench in the park, and they sit down—he takes her hand—their heads touch (and they dream of yesterday). All this was on various obliques. This was done with the artistic distance of Decroux mime, without undue sentimentality. Now, in my memory of that short, simple mime piece, as I get less young every year, I am still touched.

In Western culture, particular meanings have been placed on the human body, its various parts, and its movements. Experimental studies based on that cultural concept were part of the movement training in Jacques Copeau's school that accompanied his theatre, the Vieux Colombier, in Paris. One such concept assumes that the various parts of the body represent or hold within themselves the meaning associated with the special function of the particular organ (i.e., head; the brain within, the mind, to think, etc.). By applying those meanings to the body units of the scales and animating them with the primary movement impulse of attraction-repulsion, we create a simple base for modern mime.

Undoubtedly there are a number of psychological processes within mime performance. One seems especially significant: the very human mechanism of empathy. We all have experienced that in life. We also have known the process on an artistic level, especially in theatrical performance, but also in visual arts and literature through the imagination that is mental imaging.

There is a closely related process of the physical body. It is a kinesthetic empathy whereby one body automatically reacts to the movement of another body. The various elements of movement can be composed in specific ways to artistically affect the viewer, thereby giving meaning to the work. This happens as the viewer's body is in empathy with the mover's body, reenacting the movement deep inside the bone and muscle systems, mostly under the conscious level. I usually refer to this mechanism as the "understructure of movement," and for mime performance, the "inner-structure."

The theoretic work of Gordon Craig included the theater of silence and movement, and the controversial concept of the ubermarionette. While Decroux kept a certain distance from Craig's ideas, Craig himself recognized that Decroux had created the A-B-C's of the super-marionette (or super-puppet, or perhaps super-actor), having an objective rather than a personal nature: he is the perfect instrument for the theater artist, and is the model for Decroux's mime actor.

The wholeness of a mime work includes three elements: the mind-creator, the mind-performer, and the objective, responding body. The first two are often the same person in two roles, sometimes positive, sometimes less so. In a group-improvised work, the process of course is much more complex, falling into a model of the music ensemble.

All this may sound dry and mechanical. For many that seems to be one of the chief characteristics of the work of Etienne Decroux. Certainly there is an objective quality developed from a systematized approach, and a withdrawal of outward individual personality. In contemporary theatre, which is dominated by Stanislavsky's method acting, the work of Decroux must seem strange to many people, where the meaning is not built on the outside personality. It is quite subtle, like classical music; special attention and sensitivity are necessary to bring forth the meaning of the work in performance, for the audience as well as the mime actor.

Thomas Leabhart, Decroux's last and very important student assistant, has taken a certain leadership in the world of mime and has published generously on Etienne Decroux and other areas of Decroux mime. See the special Decroux issues of *Mime Journal*, published by Pomona College, and Leabhart's books *Etienne Decroux* (2007) and *The Decroux Sourcebook* (2008), both published by Routledge Performance Practitioners.

When considering all this, I think back on two related ideas from Decroux's classes. (1) Two mimes, no matter how much they might try, will never execute a movement exactly alike. No two bodies are the same; therefore the movement of each will be different. Even with identical twins, there are subtle differences that establish the uniqueness of each. (2) The art of mime is not about the action, nor even about the movement itself. Finally, it is about the manner of the movement. This is a very mysterious thing, Decroux explained, coming from the energy source deep within the individual. This is true in life situations as well as in mime.

My study of Decroux mime was in the mid-twentieth century. That was a very exciting period for the arts and especially the theatre. This was captured by Eric Bentley, perhaps the most important theatre critic of the period, not merely of particular productions but of the nature of the theatre itself. See Eric Bentley's "The Purism of Etienne Decroux" in *In Search of Theatre* (1953).

American theatre had discovered the work of Etienne Decroux through two sources, the first mentioned earlier in this article, the film *Children of Paradise*, and in Eric Bentley's article that discusses in faithful detail Decroux's concept of theatre, and almost as important, the most interesting veracity of the personality of Etienne Decroux.

Remember, like Hamlet's father, Decroux is a ghost that walks in the shadows of old and creaky stages, reminding us of what theater still is not. And so, in the darkness of the theatre, there is a "to be or not to be" ghost awaiting an answer.

Chapter 12

Interview with Joanna Sherman and Michael McGuigan on the Bond Street Theatre

Founded in 1976 by Patrick Sciarratta and Joanna Sherman, the Bond Street Theatre is one of the foremost American political theatres. The company has played in New York City and throughout the United States, Europe, Brazil, Colombia, Venezuela, Afghanistan, Pakistan, Israel, Japan, Indonesia, China, Kosovo, Bosnia, and throughout the Balkans. Under the artistic direction of Joanna Sherman and management of Michael McGuigan, the company is composed of actors, acrobats, dancers, musicians, and multiskilled physical artists. It has developed a program of physical theatre studies that includes mime, dance, circus arts, martial arts, clowning, mask work, commedia dell'arte, and the physical performing arts of many traditions.

When and how did the Bond Street Theatre originate and why is it called Bond Street Theatre?

Sherman: Actually we originated at the Avignon Theatre Festival, where Patrick and I had brought a short piece that had a bit of mime, acrobatics, some masks, and a little story with a surreal, happy ending that we performed successfully in the Off section. At that time, we decided to create a physical theatre company that would address current issues and be accessible to a wide audience.

But why Bond Street?

Sherman: Because we lived on Bond Street. So when we returned from Avignon, enthusiastic about our success, we went to Ellen Stewart of La Mama Theatre to ask her to help us create a new physical theatre. We thought it was new but really it was quite like the commedia dell'arte updated to reflect a modern context. Ellen Stewart accepted us in residence at La Mama Theatre, where we worked for two or three years.

Is that where you got your training?

Sherman: I had had dance training and later worked in acrobatics. André Serban and others of the 297 School, who combined acrobatics with theatre, further inspired me. Patrick had worked in traditional theatre until he traveled to Sweden to study with Ingemar Lindh, a colleague of Grotowski and Decroux. And so we initiated Bond Street Theatre in 1978.

215

How do you describe your form of physical theatre? Is it more commedia influenced or is it a mime and clown theatre?

Sherman: It is eclectic. In the beginning, we were much like the San Francisco Mime Troupe that was also based in the commedia dell'arte tradition with updated characters, such as Pantalone, who might be represented by the politician, and Capitano by the military man. Like the Mime Troupe, we were politically engaged with current local issues. Then we began to address national issues and later international issues. After that, the Odin Theatre with its abstracted content and disciplined and precise movement style strongly influenced us.

Since our work has moved toward symbolic images and actions, we have had to be aware of how our symbolism relates to different audiences. And since we are now more international in reach, we need to look at what our body language and gestures mean to international audiences. That has led us into other areas of physical study, but we still retain the use of masks and clownesque characters such as the Trickster, a character who has relatives around the world: the Monkey King in China and the comic characters of the Native Americans. Almost every culture has a kind of a Trickster character. We have also found that everywhere in the world there is some form of circus skills because everyone is subject to and enjoys playing with gravity: for example, throwing objects as in sports and juggling, or people aloft as in gymnastics and stilt walking.

McGuigan: Today there are a lot of little circuses that are theatre oriented or what we could call "circus theatre" that evoke the physical theatre ensembles of the old days. Then there were animators like Grotowski who also used some of these circus techniques and yoga in his new physical theatre language. Bond Street Theatre has followed all of these steps in its search for a universal physical language, an ongoing, ever-expanding process. To enrich our work, in our travels we have studied European theatre, Brazilian and African dance, martial arts, puppetry, Peking Opera, Baharata Natyam, and physical techniques from cultures all over the world.

What renders your physical theatre unique?

Sherman: In the United States, we are unique because there is not that much theatre that incorporates the variety of physical styles that we use and addresses meaningful issues nonverbally. We also apply our techniques in an artistic-humanitarian context performing in refugee camps and post-conflict zones. This is quite unique.

How do you differ from the San Francisco Mime Troupe and the Dell'Arte Players?

Sherman: They have remained in the *commedia* style with its use of burlesque elements and direct rapport with the audience.

McGuigan: We used a *commedia* structure in the past, but our work is more multicultural now, and we have worked with guest directors from many parts of the world who have influenced us. We also ran an artist colony from 1984 to 1995. Its artists, writers, musicians, and performing artists greatly influenced us just as we inspired them with our work. Our company has not remained with one aesthetic but has been quite eclectic.

Sherman: In working in other countries, we have learned that art helps us communicate with others. I believe that artists can be the leaders who, through their art, cross bridges between nations better than the politicians who rely on language. Artists have always been problem solvers and good communicators. It's the essence of creativity.

So the need to communicate is at the basis of your vision of physical theatre?

Sherman: Yes, we would like to communicate with the broadest range of audiences.

McGuigan: We describe ourselves in short as "a physical theatre company with a social consciousness, a global view, and a sense of humor."

Is the need to reach a broad number of people also part of your political aim?

Sherman: Yes. When we performed in Pakistan and Afghanistan, the fact that we were Americans playing in these countries was a political statement. The same was true when we performed in Kosovo and Serbia. We represent another aspect of America beside the military point of view. We represent the aspect of America that wants to reach out to people. In Afghanistan and Pakistan, they thanked us for coming. In the refugee camps where we performed, aid workers told us that what we were doing was as valuable as providing food and shelter. We were lifting the spirits of those in the camps who had nothing to do but sit around and worry about what was happening at home.

How is the content of your pieces developed?

Sherman: One of our company members will initiate an idea concerning a current topic. For example, *Werk* was my idea and it addressed issues regarding women and those who live off of garbage. Michael came up with the idea of *Cozmic Jazz* that is based on creation myths combined with our own satirical look at humanity. It starts with a Trickster, who represents our physical nature, and a Bird representing our higher nature. Together they create humans. The humans evolve and become civilized, and the play ends with a catastrophe that leaves just the Bird and the Trickster once again.

McGuigan: The piece also includes acrobatics, mask work, music, stilt dancing, and other physical skills.

What is the central theme of Cozmic Jazz?

Sherman: We are pointing out that, as much as humans think they are the center of the universe, really we are just a tiny glitch in time and could easily destroy ourselves. The universe will continue on without us. The theme is timely and we present it in a way that is not too preachy. We also want to stimulate audiences to perceive more in our theme than what we directly convey.

What is the message of Cozmic Jazz *that is a satirical history of the universe?*

McGuigan: Human beings in their pursuit of happiness want to survive. Yet humanity as a whole is egotistical and involves itself in the pursuit of money, power, and other temporary or transitory activities that are no more than an illusionary quest for happiness. In our story, once human beings discovered fire and later gunfire, it became a question of who has the control of the gunfire. But this control has never signified true power or happiness.

Is your piece Romeo and Juliet *based on understanding and accepting others despite family, ethnic, and various differences?*

Sherman: Yes, and it also relates to the issue facing many young men today: the choice of joining the gang, the KLA, rather than staying home with family and loved ones. The way the play was staged, Juliet remains on stage at her wedding during the entire sequence of the fights and deaths. This powerful visual idea moved women spectators watching Juliet patiently waiting at home while battles were fought. It directly relates to many women's experience during war, waiting for a husband, a father, or a brother to come home.

Do you make much use of a text?

Sherman: For the last fifteen years, we have used little dialogue since we have been traveling so frequently to non-English-speaking countries. We may some-day go back to using more text.

What role does improvisation play in your work?

Sherman: Our shows take many months to develop and actually come out of the process of improvisation. From an idea we create a scenario—the schematic for the physical creation of the show—and then begin improvising on each scene that eventually develops into the entire play. During the show, we may also have moments that are improvised on the spot.

Of what does your training program for your company members consist?

Sherman: We do physical, vocal, and musical training all year round to keep everyone in shape, and we consistently bring in and study new forms. For ex-ample, one member may study Japanese dance and we will all share what that member has learned. We frequently collaborate with theatre companies in other countries, Bulgaria and Afghanistan, for example, and we have incorporated new techniques gathered from these exchanges.

McGuigan: We also offer training for young performers in the schools and have programs that are adapted to the school curriculum. One is called "Travels with Tricksters," for elementary schoolchildren, in which we present Trickster charac-ters around the world with a big map of the world as backdrop. We illustrate how a Trickster character is performed in the traditions of a particular country, such as the Monkey King in China, the African Caribbean stilt-walking Moko Jumbie, and other traditions. We likewise offer workshops to the general public.

With what masters have your company members been trained?

Sherman: Some of our people come from Lecoq training and some from De-croux and Grotowski. I have had Decroux and Lecoq training through their train-ees, plus direct study with Ingemar Lindh, the Odin Theatre, dance training from childhood, and acrobatics training from an old vaudevillian, Joe Price, among others.

McGuigan: I come from more of a circus background through my college train-ing. And some of the ensemble members have worked with the Ringling Brothers Circus and Dell'Arte.

Sherman: We also include our musicians in our physical training so that they can participate as actors in our shows. But we generally look for artists who have had some physical training already so that we can train them more easily.

What are your plans for your theatre company in the future? Will you return to areas of conflict to perform?

Sherman: Yes, we will go back to Afghanistan and Pakistan and work with the-atre groups there. Many of the actors that worked underground during the Tali-ban are really excellent. We learn as much from them as they do from our physical techniques, although women are still conspicuously absent from the stage.

How important do you feel physical expression and expressive movement training are for stage and screen actors and for clowns and other stage performers?

Sherman: First of all, being able to express yourself physically is important not only for actors but for everyone, artists or nonartists, nationally or internationally, for example, people on the performing stage of politics or studying international relations or law. I was invited to teach communication skills and expression in a workshop in the Balkans for young leaders. I have some good ensemble exercises that I teach to people who will be leading groups, and for those who need to learn how to acquire good communication skills for public speaking. These skills are especially important if you want to communicate with people who don't speak your language.

Secondly, to answer your question, you have to ask: what is the job of an actor? For any performer, their job is to communicate an idea, an emotion, a character.

And how will the performer communicate that idea?

Sherman: You have your body and your voice. You need to train your entire instrument in order to communicate. You need a finely tuned, well-trained body and an awareness of every part of it so that you know exactly how and what you are communicating in order to transmit a clear rather than a contradictory message. Otherwise the voice may say one thing, the body another, and the text still another. Good physical training and expressive movement is necessary for all stage performers.

I feel that the study of mime is the most basic training for clarity of gesture. It helps you learn awareness of every part of your body right down to your little finger, which can actually make a very big statement. I train actors to look for the message in different postures and try to eliminate unnecessary and amateurish gestures. I teach neutrality and how to identify your own personal gestural habits.

And what else do you teach them?

Sherman: The next important training, I feel, is breathing. Your breath supports both your actions and voice. I usually combine breath awareness along with movement so that the two elements are working together. Also, learning breath control fills you with confidence and gives your body life and energy.

McGuigan: There is another aspect to teaching physical theatre. As much as actors want to be natural in the context of a play, they are physically on a stage with other performers and before an audience. They need to project this energy. Besides animating props and objects and giving life to the body, actors must also give life to the negative space of the stage and animate the entire playing space.

Does this also apply to the kind of theatre you do internationally?

Sherman: Even the verbal theatre that we do, if the spectators do not understand English, is still more communicative than normal English-speaking theatre because of our strong physical components. This physicality supports and enhances the words. So in a marriage of the physical and the verbal, the words are intensified through the physical elements, just as the words heighten the physical impact of the work.

Chapter 13

On Movement Training for the Actor

Joan Schirle

Joan Schirle is founding artistic director of Dell'Arte International, a center for the exploration, development, training, and performance of the actor as creator. As performer, director, playwright, and teacher, she is a principal collaborator in the original works of the Dell'Arte Players, and director of training at the Dell'Arte International School of Physical Training. Her directing credits include her circus production of Charles Dickens's *A Christmas Carol*, Steve Martin's *Picasso at the Lapin Agile*, and Samuel Beckett's *Waiting for Godot* at San Diego Rep, Bloomsburg Ensemble, the Alley Theatre in Houston, A Traveling Jewish Theatre in San Francisco, Touchstone Theatre, and Dell'Arte. Since 2001, she has performed her solo work, *Second Skin*, at theatres and festivals in the United States, Canada, Europe, and Scandinavia. In 2006, she was recognized for distinguished acting work with a Fox Foundation/TCG Resident Actor Fellowship. She is a senior teacher of the FM Alexander technique, as well as of movement, mask, and physical acting.

Our first education—sensory, kinesthetic, and spatial—precedes the acquisition of language and formal schooling. In a network of stimuli that includes things, people, sounds, elements, and invisible forces, our universal human "original instructions" include survival lessons about falling, about distance, comfort, even gestural codes—so that the opening of the arms means "come toward"; the stillness of a raised hand implies a slap.

It is the work of the actor to *link* us to the first education, to establish a visceral connection to the audience through the deepest shared ground of human experience. Invoked in great theatre is the fullness of life, the size and excitement of great characters arising from the actor's ability to reveal to the audience what it means to "fall" in love, to be "moved" by an experience, to be "crushed" by defeat, or to be "thrown" off balance. The actor in the live theatre exists not only in relation to the individuals who witness his performance, but also in relation to the collective ancestral body of the audience. The universal shared ground of human experience is deeper than any psychology and permeates narrative and abstract forms, figurative and nonfigurative movement.

As we grow up, we forget our first "school." We may not even realize how much we know "in our bones"; we take for granted how well our movement and spatial education serves us—after all, we've survived and we function in the world without having to think too much about how to walk down a flight of steps or close a door or take a breath. Except perhaps in progressive systems of childhood education, the education of our kinesthetic sense ceases once we begin our formal schooling. We acquire skills like swimming or playing ball, but we aren't taught to look at how we do these things. Our physical intelligence gradually becomes separated from our verbal, mathematical, and other intelligences. We learn to mask the play of emotion across the face, to control the physical manifestation of our feelings. Habits can develop that interfere with the actor's flexibility and ease at one level and with his availability and responsiveness at the level of invention.

"The freest use of the most intelligent body" (thank you, Isadora Duncan) requires an integrated training in which player and instrument are educated as one. The eye, the muscles, and the imagination must all be trained as a unity. We cannot think only about improving the actor's "instrument," as though there were an instrument (the body or voice) "controlled" or "played" by the mind of the actor, and that the instrument required a different kind of training than the "player" of that instrument. Separating instrument from player, even as a casual frame of reference, disorganizes body, mind, and spirit, leading to a disembodied practice for the actor—a practice in which the body does not have to be intelligent or conscious, only obedient. And so actor training that does not embrace the whole of dynamic play leads to productions in which bodies are not available to be moved by feelings, passions, and wants, or in which the actors have trained voices and trained bodies but the two do not function as an organic whole.

At the Dell'Arte International School of Physical Theatre, our study is movement as related to the theatre and to the work of the actor. A high level of theatrical play puts the body at a higher tension level than that of daily life, so we train to achieve an extra-daily, heightened state of tone that can be adjusted in large or small increments to the demands of the work. The performing body differs from the athletic body in that it is available to play in the world of illusion, and the imagination, especially the physical imagination, must also be cultivated. We study the nature of play and the dynamic presence of the actor in the empty space. We embrace the vital paradoxes—we train to be strong and flexible; we train to play with economy and abandon; we train to be easeful at a high level of tension; we train to be both analytic and intuitive; we train to have a wakeful internal eye as well as to see and hear fully our partners, our audience, our space, our props. The training is always in the context of how a piece of theatre is developed, rehearsed, and performed in ensemble.

As I reflect back on when I started exploring stage movement three decades ago, the idea that the study of dance or fencing is adequate preparation for a stage career now seems quaint. Most serious conservatory or university MFA acting programs and many undergraduate programs now include "Movement for Actors" classes based on Laban, Lecoq, Grotowski, Meyerhold, Suzuki, Viewpoints, the FM Alexander technique, Feldenkrais, yoga, martial arts, combat, and others; the number of job postings for movement specialists grows yearly. There is a branch of ATHE (Association for Theatre in Higher Education) that is devoted to movement: ATME (Association of Theatre Movement Educators). Advances in sports, psycho-physical education, dance, and medicine have given us amazing information about the human body, allowing actors to demand more of themselves with greater range, safety, and endurance.

So, what needs to happen next? There are arguably few directors or teachers of acting who would not advocate the importance of movement training for the actor. However, many of them haven't a clue how to carry movement training into script work, rehearsal, and production. Directors like Anne Bogart, Julie Taymor, Ariane Mnouchkine, and Simon McBurney have showed us full-bodied theatre that is rich in ideas as well as images, performed by actors who create in time and space, word and deed. We have an extraordinary legacy from the work of earlier twentieth-century pioneers like Copeau, Lecoq, Decroux, Laban, Grotowski, and others. The evolution of movement training in our time, and indeed of theatre itself, will come not solely through educating actors, but requires that we inspire directors, designers, playwrights, and theatre makers to explore and benefit from this great legacy.

Chapter 14

Dance and the Female Body

Ilka Schönbein

From Darmstadt, Germany, Ilka Schönbein trained in Rudolph Steiner's eurythmic dance based on the alliance of harmonious body movements with the expression of the soul rather than on technique. She then studied marionettes with Albrecht Roser in Stuttgart and toured for ten years with other theatre companies before presenting her own solos. Among her pieces are *Metamorphosis: The Frog King* (1998), a children's piece, and *The Winter Voyage* (2003). She has performed in numerous international theatre, mime, and marionette festivals and in cultural centers and theatres throughout Europe and Canada.

As in my preceding creations, my scenes of *Winter Voyage* illustrate subjects that have a primal importance in the life of a woman: childhood, love, birth, old age, and the fear of death.

What more? The theme, which already appeared in my piece *Metamorphosis* and penetrates my conscience with more and more acuity, is the dance of the human being, the embryo in the body of its mother, the dance of the ecstasy of love, the dance that fills the soul when the body suffers from anguish, the dance against and with death.

I read a marvelous story, alas I do not remember where. During a glacial winter, with the morning roll call, a young man half-naked, completely frozen, and near death heard behind him the voice of a Jew. "Dance! Dance if you are a true Hassid! You need to dance now! Dance!" And the young man tore his feet from the earth, the skin glued to the snow, and danced with his bloody feet and saved his life!

Powerful words! Oh if I could dance like that! A dance that liberates our fear of being alive for nothing, oh mortals!

With my piece *Metamorphosis*, I have become engaged in a path that I must pursue. No big surprise like the first time when everything was new. But I continue to search how to extract characters from my own body; beings that end up burning alive and will one day in the far future teach me why they were born.

This seems to be a very feminine way to create. Women often allow themselves to be guided by their bodies; that fills them and allows them to understand the meaning and content of their existence.

Chapter 15

Interview with Liebe Wetzel on Movement in Puppetry

After hauling around props and juggling equipment as a street and county fair mime-clown-stiltwalker, in 1997 in San Francisco Liebe Wetzel began her *Lunatique Fantastique* puppetry company by animating these physical theatre articles along with everyday objects. In *Snake in the Basement*, Wetzel stages the true story of pedophile Presbyterian pastor Bill Pruitt by breathing life into newspapers, napkins, and fabric. In *Brace Yourself*, a leg brace, cane, and wheel move about to depict Wetzel's father's struggle with polio. *My Dinner with Lunatique Fantastique* features a French waiter, created out of bread rolls, a napkin, white gloves, and a menu, who chastises his helper Jo Jo (made of a cup and a napkin) for stealing bread rolls and who interacts with other characters created from vegetables, citrus fruits, leafy greens, mops, brooms, and kitchen utensils. In still another piece, two armies of toilet paper rolls displacing a ruler and bombing one another with a plunger and wads of paper represent the Middle Eastern boundary disputes. As she packs precisely choreographed movement and meaningful substance into her creations that give birth to these inanimate objects, Wetzel challenges our imagination and awakens our reactions to current social, political, and human issues.

Among other achievements, Liebe Wetzel received the Goldie Award in 2000 for outstanding local discovery on stage. *Brace Yourself* was the Best of the S.F. Fringe 2001 and Top Box Office Hit of S.F. Fringe 2001. In 2004, she received the Barbara Bladen Porter Award from the S.F. Bay Area Critics Circle for her community theatre activity. The company has received grants from the Zellerbach Family Fund, the Jim Henson Foundation, and Theatre Bay Area's CA$H Grant.

How is movement connected to puppetry?

Wetzel: Movement is the essence of puppetry. Without movement, the objects remain sculptures, whether one is using highly sculpted doll-like marionettes or simple everyday objects such as a hat and a trench coat. The juxtaposition of dramatically motivated movement and stillness merely sets the story for the audience. However, without movement, the objects would be devoid of life. For example, in the opening of *The Wrapping Paper Caper*, the protagonist is born from a trench coat and hat left on the table by his owner, and it is through manipulation as they are assembled into a bumbling detective with a large magnifying glass that the hat and coat come to life. At one point a box lid attacks the detective, who fights it off, and after it flies off and hovers above his head, he is able to discover it before it squishes him. In another scene, five toilet paper rolls are simply toilet paper until they are assembled into a short person with stubby arms and legs. And the Japanese tea set that becomes a mother and two children (her head is the inverted tea pot and her body the tablecloth, while her children have inverted tea cup heads and napkins for bodies) are soon endowed with meaning through movement.

What is mime for you and what role does it play in your work?

Wetzel: Mime is anything that supports theatre. Mime begins when the actor walks onto the stage. How fast he is walking, what he does before he begins to talk, the attitude of his body when he is talking, all of these myriad physical, visual clues tell us more about what is happening on stage than language that becomes superfluous. I feel the actor should only speak when actions and gestures can no longer adequately tell us what he is thinking. In the work of *Lunatique Fantastique*, what the audience sees is vastly more important than any text. I create a piece using image phrases. These are similar to dance phrases expressed by a simple gesture of compassion, such as the mother teapot holding her hurt child's head that is reminiscent of the *Pieta*.

What type of acting and movement training did you have?

Wetzel: I first discovered theatre when I took a drama class from a wonderful actress in Seattle named Tawnya Pettiford Wates, who had trained as a dancer and studied theatre at Carnegie Mellon. She used movement as a means to discover and enhance character. We walked as the character, leading with different parts of our bodies. She taught us how to create emotion in characters by using the body. How do we move when we are afraid or angry or sad? How does the architecture of the spine differ with each emotion? Tawnya directed me to Cornish, where I enrolled in the actors training program and studied the Lecoq mime technique with Diane Schenker, a graduate of the Lecoq school in Paris. She introduced me to mask as a form of physical theatre. The neutral masks were reddish brown, and the female ones had a softer look, while the male ones had more prominent cheekbones. They were made of gauze and covered the entire face with almond-shaped eye holes and holes in the nose for breath. As they lay on a table on the side of the classroom, you approached them with conventions of respect. You touched the mask around the edges and could not speak while wearing the mask or make any noise whatsoever. The mask was to be placed on the face with our backs to the spectators so that they never saw an uninhabited character. Since these first masks were neutral, we explored very simple themes. I was actually not good at mask work and was quite frustrated because I knew it held something for me.

It has only been through my study of puppetry that I have begun to understand what the mask is really about. For a puppet is merely a mask that is attached to the end of your arm. The eyes of the mask tell us where it is looking and the body tells the audience what it is feeling. Where mask and puppetry meet is in the immediacy of the mask, especially with neutral and character masks that cover the full face. In the absence of language, action becomes the driving dramatic force as well as communicates what the character feels. This applies to our work in *Lunatique Fantastique*.

I moved to the Bay Area to study mime with Decroux-trained mimes Leonard Pitt, Bert Houle, and Vera Wiboux. I enjoyed the physical precision of mime so much that I remained in the Bay Area to continue this study. I landed in a clown class and broadened my studies to include movement and improvisational dance. I ultimately ended up at the Dell'Arte School of Physical Theatre in Blue Lake, California.

At the Dell'Arte School, I was allowed to indulge my love of mask. Our mask instructor Ralph was also a graduate of the Lecoq school. He had us work with larval or naive masks that were very specific large white character masks. You could only do one character when you put on the mask that demanded a huge physical commitment. Your body would be in a very awkward position that looked ridiculous when you took off the mask but worked well when you inhabited it. We also studied mask construction with Christine Cook of Green Fools.

At Dell'Arte, I had three moments when I felt that the mask is something like being possessed. During those moments you release the creature that wants to come out and then watch him run around.

After Dell'Arte, I spent eight years as a walk-around clown at fairs and festivals. I learned things on the street about performing. In short, people will watch anything. But your character must deal with what is happening at the time. If a dog walks through your show, bark at it. If a person walks through, try to engage him in the show. If you are having fun, your audience probably is as well. Your audience members are smart. Respect them and make them look good. Thus, in the work of *Lunatique Fantastique*, I rely on the intelligence of my spectators, who help us puppeteers create the characters and fill in the gaps between the objects.

In 1996, while I was working as a clown, I took a workshop in London with Stephen Mottram in which we worked with simple principles of breath, stillness, and gesture. I remember that magic moment when I learned that an object could breathe and come to life with the simplest movements in the chest area.

What made you want to work with puppets?

Wetzel: I saw a wonderful one-woman show by Ilka Schönbein that made me breathless and opened my soul to inspire me to do something like what she did. In her vignettes, she was wrapped in the costume of a giant rat, manipulating the head of the rat with one hand and playing herself opposite this creature that she was enticing to sweep. He refused to sweep and the vignette became a movement dialogue about broom usage. It was after I saw Schönbein's work that I began to experiment with puppets. Since I had had no formal puppetry training, I applied what I knew about mime and mask, thinking that the principles used in those mediums would work with puppets, and they did.

After a minimal success with creating a piece using a broom and wearing a pair of sunglasses and a suit, I studied with Avner Eisenberg (Avner the Eccentric), another graduate of the Lecoq school. I spent two weeks trying to be funny but to no avail. Finally in despair, I grabbed a puppet and everyone laughed. I worked on a routine where I was asleep and the puppet woke me up and took over my body, using my legs to walk off stage. Avner took me aside and told me I was not a clown but that my puppets were. I began to play with puppets more and more and in 1997 wrote *First Aid for the Soul*, in which a woman is awakened by a puppet and explores a world where everything she touches comes to life. At that time, I formed *Lunatique Fantastique, Beyond Puppetry*.

In 1997, I explored body-based puppets, creating puppets that were the heels of my feet and using my knee as well as my gloved hands as puppets. By the end of 1998, in addition to fabricated puppets, I had begun to explore some of the inanimate objects around me. However, I was spending more time building a puppet than working on discovering its dramatic story. So I decided to spend 1999 creating puppets that could be made rapidly in front of the audience from ordinary objects such as newspaper, strips of foam, and a sweatshirt. Suddenly the world opened up and I began to write pieces for multiple pairs of hands. In September 1999, *Lunatique Fantastique* premiered *Objects in Predicaments* at the S.F. Fringe Festival and it was a hit. I have been using found objects ever since.

I have been blessed by being able to study with students of the masters of twentieth-century mime, Etienne Decroux and Jacques Lecoq. From Decroux, I inherited the desire to be meticulous about breaking down a gesture into movement phrases. For example, when the detective in *Attack of the Wrapping Paper Caper* looks through his magnifying glass, his arm extends holding the glass, next his head rotates on its axis and then inclines toward the glass, and lastly his head slides toward the glass. From Lecoq, I learned about the importance of immediacy in dramatic action. The trench coat is simply a trench coat until it becomes a character brought into the action of trying to pull the lid off the box or searching for a clue with his magnifying glass.

For what purposes was Lunatique Fantastique founded?

Wetzel: After years as a performance artist, mime, stiltwalker, clown, and puppeteer, when I had become infatuated with the theatrical possibilities of ordinary objects that generated a new kind of puppet theatre in 1997 and made discoveries in this new form, the work of my company took on the following threefold purpose.

(1) To explore object theatre and the expressive, dramatic, and narrative power of everyday objects. In our work, everyday objects evoke traditional, crafted realistic, or fantasy figures. A napkin may represent a little girl; a box becomes a pulpit, a cup a head. Because they are free of an imposed identity or personality, mundane objects activate the imagination and creative intelligence of puppeteer and audience, and the imagination of puppeteer and audience meet at the object. Because there is no precedent for this kind of nonverbal object-based puppet theatre, the company is simultaneously discovering and inventing an untried form.

(2) To foster the growth of artists in association with *Lunatique Fantastique*. The company provides to puppeteers in the cast a forum for their own creative expression through *Lunatique Fantastique* performances. The company also seeks and welcomes collaborative work with artists in other fields, such as the visual artist who illustrated our program covers and the composer who created the musical score for *Snake in the Basement*.

(3) To educate audiences about the versatility of puppetry as a medium not only for children but also for adults, and to make this expressive vehicle available to everyone. *Lunatique Fantastique* meets this goal through public performances and

workshops that teach puppet manipulation and performance and that foster the expression of stories within the human heart.

What are some of your company's accomplishments?

Wetzel: We can claim several kinds of accomplishments.

(1) Performance. We have performed a series of works in our found object medium, received very good reviews, and had quite a few sold-out performances.

(2) Creative Innovation. We are continuously inventing and discovering new means of expression. In a piece in 2003, for example, we incorporated food, and a manipulator's bare head became a penguin's belly.

(3) Fostering Individual Artists. We curate late-night puppet slams once a month at the Marsh Mock Cafe, where puppeteers, including members of our company, can perform emerging works.

(4) Artistic Collaboration. We work with a flexible, creative, and collaborative process with some pieces originating from the artistic director's ideas and others from objects introduced by members of the ensemble.

(5) Introducing Audiences to Found Object Puppet Theatre. Many of our performances conclude with a question/discussion period with audiences investigating and manipulating our object-puppets. I have taught in the San Francisco Public Schools Arts Education program, at the San Francisco School of Circus Arts, and the California Shakespeare Summer Camp.

Chapter 16

Images and
Body Expression in Film

Karina Epperlein

Karina Epperlein has worked as a filmmaker, teacher, and theatre artist in Europe and the United States for over thirty years. A native of Germany, she came to the United States in 1981 as a dancer, choreographer, and actress with the avant-garde theatre company SOON 3. She then developed her own poetic vision of theatre, directing and performing several original pieces. Haunted by her country's past, she created her one-woman show *Deutschland* (1987–1993) dealing with the aftermath of the Holocaust.

Karina's work is always looking into dark corners, finding the light, addressing the themes of transformation and healing. Her earlier video pieces *Labyrinthian* (1984) and *Deutschland* (1988) were followed by the documentaries *Voices from Inside* (1996, women in prison and their children), *Women's Rites* (2000, Anna Halperin's Expressive Art Therapy), *I Will Not Be Sad in This World* (2001, a portrait of a ninety-four-year-old Armenian woman surviving genocide), *We Are Here Together* (2003, charter high school experiment and the young people's growth), and *Phoenix Dance* (2006, Homer Avila's return to the stage as a one-legged dancer in a pas de deux by Alonzo King). *Phoenix Dance* has been screening in more than fifty festivals and theatres all over the world. It was short-listed for the 2006 Oscar nomination for Short Documentary and it won several awards, including a Golden Gate Award from the San Francisco International Film Festival.

"Gift of the Gods."

It's been true all my life: moving my body puts me easily into an ecstatic state. For me, movement is like water—like a river, moving with gravity. Movement is music, melody, rhythm, breath, and life. It flows, nourishes, connects, and tells stories. As a child, I wanted to be a dancer. No money for classes, I could though indulge in roller-skating, running, climbing trees and fences, playing badminton, ping-pong, and tennis. People kept saying: "You move so beautifully!" It was not my doing—it was grace, a blessing. Movement made me feel sublimely alive. The child knows the gift of the gods.

Later I did become a dancer. Then I moved on to theatre, music, directing, teaching, and filmmaking. I proudly became more than a dancer. Now with the days of my stage activities behind me, I accept that at heart I am a dancer. Movement informs my relationship with the world, my daily life, and all my work. It's the place my soul can express itself most easily. It's home.

Images and physical memories return: playing the cello, I dance with it on stage; teaching Tai Chi, sound and breath, I dance with the students; doing handheld camera work, I dance with my subjects. I am connected. For me, this is heaven on earth.

I am working with the women prisoners on freeing their voices and bodies, which makes them extremely powerful in their presence on stage and on the screen. Audiences wonder. Freedom through movement and poetic expression, something we all yearn for.

Following ninety-four-year-old Zaroohe around her garden—she, shovel in hand, me, camera in hand—we dance and harmonize. My being and eye revel in the beauty of her authentic and natural presence, not an iota of self-consciousness. Under her abundant grapefruit tree, I (and later the audience) recognize her with the wave of her hand: universal grandmother, earth mother. It's direct communication.

As a documentary filmmaker, I am interested in the emotional story or information of movement. The deeper I connect, the more I disappear and become the witness rather than the observer. This intimate dance starts with the first meeting, the set-up and preparation, and continues in the long hours in the edit room.

My camera in both hands, I am running, sinking, rising with one-legged Homer, his pas de deux partner Andrea and choreographer Alonzo in rehearsal. Homer gets off the floor for the twenty-fourth time (all this without crutches) to practice another take of the "strength-building" scene. In awe, we recognize utter determination and will. He is the quintessential dancer. It does not matter if he has one or two legs, three or none, we see his spirit communicating through his body more eloquently than words could do.

Audiences are viscerally affected and linked to those images and body expressions. The connection is inspiring and nourishing. We are in the river of life. When I construct and edit my films, it's this river that I pay attention to: the outer visible river of body expression but also the inner river of emotional movement. Both intertwine, and their flow transports us into realms we otherwise might avoid, have forgotten, or simply don't know. Movement is the crucial element in my work; I use it as a bridge for the audience. "It moves me, it touches you."

Scanning life for the inner and outer dance, including the stillness, pauses, and silences, looking for beauty, I'll find it every day: in a disabled man walking down the airport hall with his severely uneven, elegant gait; in the child spinning, waiting, then throwing herself into the grass; in the old, old woman picking her dimes and pennies from her wallet before the supermarket cashier. For me, as witness and artist, beauty abounds, the world becomes the gods' stage and screen, pulsing with tragedy and comedy, with mystery and meaning. How could I refuse to dance with it?

Chapter 17

Theatrical Dance

Joe Goode

Joe Goode is a choreographer, writer, and director whose first concern as an artist is to provide a "deeply felt, profoundly human experience in the theater." He is widely known as an innovator in the field of dance for his willingness to collide movement with spoken word, song, and visual imagery. Joe Goode was the recipient of a John Simon Guggenheim Foundation Fellowship in Choreography for 2007–2008. His work has been recognized with numerous awards and prizes, including a New York Dance and Performance Award ("Bessie") and several Isadora Duncan Dance Awards ("Izzies"). In 2003, Goode was commissioned by the Magic Theatre in San Francisco to write and direct a play, *The Body Familiar*. Formed in 1986, Joe Goode's Performance Group has toured throughout the United States, Canada, Europe, South America, the Middle East, and Africa. A master teacher, he has attracted participants from around the world to his summer workshops in "felt performance." As a professor at the University of California, Berkeley, he teaches choreography and interdisciplinary performance in the Department of Theater, Dance, and Performance Studies.

When you tell people you are a dancer, you can just see their eyes glaze over with images of dancing princes and flowers that come to life. Not that these very whimsical visions are bad in any way, but it is distressing that most people define dance in such narrow terms. I think of dancers as people who have trained their bodies for the purpose of having a supple and expressive instrument, one that can reveal the psychological dimension of a character or the raw ragged impulses that overtake us in everyday life.

But how does one train for that? Aside from the obvious necessities of strength, flexibility, and an ability to articulate parts of the body separately, I like to stress that a movement artist must sensitize his/her instrument. In other words, there needs to be a mind/body connection so that a mover can respond to information without stopping to think or plan. For instance, in practicing the various placements of the shoulders, in order to discover all of the different emotional states they contain, if the shoulders are up and tense, the body becomes breathless, the lungs don't work properly, there is a feeling of defensiveness. This can be very useful information for a particular type of character or mood. My hypothesis is that we don't just act these states, but rather that they are all stored in the body like a complex computer. By familiarizing ourselves with the subtleties and variations of these body configurations, we are accessing real memory and creating real experience.

Is contemporary dance about real experience for the performer? Well, that is my contention. It's a fairly renegade stance, I know. But I think the only way we can provide real experience for the viewer is to be going through it ourselves. I also train my dancers to use their voices as part of their stage equipment.

The mute dancer has never really made sense to me. As much as I admire the work of some of my colleagues who use movement as a silent art form, I seem to have no capacity for it. I'm trying to create a theatrical experience that acknowledges the frail, fallible aspects of being human. For that task, I need a flesh and blood dancer, one with human skin and human voice. I guess I want to get dancers down off that pedestal of the ethereal, other worldly plane, and let them be real.

Chapter 18

The Clown Conservatory Teaching of Professional Clowns in the Twenty-first Century

Jeff Raz

For the last thirty years, Jeff Raz has performed nationally and internationally with circuses and theatres including the Pickle Circus, Lincoln Center Theater, Vaudeville Nouveau, Dell'Arte Players, Berkeley Repertory Theatre, Marin and San Francisco Shakespeare Festivals, Theatre Works, and Marin Theater Company. He has written ten plays, directed many more, and taught physical theatre and circus arts around the country. His TV work includes *Live from Lincoln Center*, Disney's *The New Vaudevillians*, and commercials for Ford, First Union Bank, Frulatte, and others. Jeff worked for seven years with the Artist Diversity Residency Program at the University of Nebraska, Lincoln. He has been director of the Clown Conservatory, stage director of Yosemite Park's Bracebridge Dinner, and a lead teaching artist at the Julia Morgan Center for the Arts. In the following essay, he describes the training program at the Clown Conservatory.

The Clown Conservatory trains adults to work as professional circus clowns. The students take eighteen hours of classes per week, including acrobatics, Alexander technique (to survive the acrobatics), dance, mime, circus skills (juggling, stilts, unicycle, etc.), and core clowning. The students offer monthly in-house performances and tour schools, senior centers, and medical facilities at the end of the school year.

I often hear that clowning cannot be taught, that a clown is born funny or learns only by performing. Many who teach clowning start with character, which seems obvious, since character is what we remember about a clown, along with his makeup, costume, how he moves, and how he makes us laugh or cry. Although I do address character, my main focus is on structure and skills (acrobatics, mime, etc.). These are teachable clowning elements that are important if not essential for a professional clown. My students' characters emerge slowly over the course of their schooling (and their careers). I find that rich characters take time and often come from performing good material with good people over and over again. Many young clowns have trouble building a character, learning clown skills, and creating good material at the same time. Giving students classic routines, at least at first, allows them to concentrate on the performing aspects without having to also be a playwright. Within a classic gag, a student can experiment with different skills, walks, weight, and other physical characteristics. For classic material, we teach everything from *commedia* lazzi to simple silent bits, to 1930s European clown entrees, to Beijing Opera scenes. In approaching these structures, Dominique Jando has the best advice: "Make the most vulnerable choice naturally." I ask the students to approach these routines as themselves, to be natural, and to tell the story as simply as possible, bringing their own sense of humor to each strange new set of rules. Often students who have acting training struggle at this point, trying to find their way to a character. In clowning, the character begins with oneself, or possibly a slice of oneself, and usually a slice that the world has never seen. Being oneself does not mean abandoning all the tools that have helped clowns for hundreds of years.

We emphasize basic concepts such as making comedy in beats of three, status play between characters, contrast in size and energy, and so on. Using these age-old clown tools in their own unique ways, students can begin to put together material that is good enough to take before an audience. They then have opportunities to perform and build their characters as well as their skills.

When it comes time to explore the playwriting side of clowning, I start by offering a unit in storytelling. We arrange the audience in an old-time circle around a campfire (without the fire). If a clown student can tell a simple story to a circle of folks, as humans have been doing for time immemorial, they have a good chance of being able to put together a clown routine that is, as Geoff Hoyle says, logical and simple.

Because clowns have the most immediate, intimate, and complex relationship with an audience of any performing artist, they must constantly be with audiences in order to grow. When students have good material to work with, they can focus on this relationship with the audience when they perform, as well as on their partnerships with their fellow clowns and with their props. If a clown is tuned into his or her audience, his or her character, timing and structure will become richer and funnier.

The adjustments they make between shows, the refinements of timing and character, the honing of the skills is when they start to become clowns. Clowns do learn by performing, and they need to know their history and craft first, before the audience will welcome them into the ring.

Chapter 19

Movement for Puppeteers

Jo Tomalin

Jo Tomalin is a professor of theatre arts at San Francisco State University, where she teaches movement, acting, voice, and storytelling with puppetry. She trained in physical theatre at Ecole Jacques Lecoq in Paris, and her experiences with mask work led her to develop and perform a one-person puppet show. Tomalin has given movement, voice, and character development workshops to puppeteers at several Puppeteers of America national festivals. She has also acted in many plays and directed physical theatre performances in the San Francisco Bay Area.

If the art of puppetry is defined as breathing life into an inanimate object, then a puppet's life relies on the imagination, manipulation techniques, acting, and movement skills of the puppeteer.

Movement in puppetry is intrinsic to every aspect of bringing puppets to life. Puppeteers need to understand physical acting and body language techniques to project nuances of physicality to their characters for authenticity, emotional depth, and to draw empathy from the audience. For example, a delicate tilt of a puppet's head, a long look to the audience, or an arm gesture can each create a meaningful reaction in the puppet whose facial features are otherwise fixed and unable to change expression.

Physical skills such as balance, coordination, and strength are also vital for a puppeteer. Space behind a puppet theatre is often cramped, and puppeteers have to maneuver over and around props, puppets, and other puppeteers with cat-like stealth in the dark. Physical coordination is required not only to manipulate several different puppets during a performance but also to press foot pedals to operate lights or music cues in rapid fire. Balance, coordination, and strength are required all at the same time for puppeteers who choose to perform a puppet show without a puppet theatre—and where the puppeteer must make physical choices to support and not detract from the performance. An example of physical choices that enhance a puppet performance in front of the audience is Ilka Schönbein's *Metamorphosis*, where she brings her newborn puppet to life with sustained movement choices and a dancer's grace.

Puppeteers develop a love for the art form from all walks of life. They may have had a fascination with puppets from childhood or an interest as an adult developing out of experience with a related art form such as masks, storytelling, dance, or theatre. Puppeteers usually start creating puppetry performances by making or buying puppets and then applying prior performance skills to develop characters and stories that reflect their own sensibility and interests. The puppeteer's self-expression through the puppet is very important to develop a unique quality based on a chosen puppet style.

There are many puppet styles, such as glove, rod, shadow, table, bunraku, string marionette, and object puppets, which all make different demands on the puppeteer physically, artistically, and vocally. For example, regarding movement skills, simple glove puppets cover the puppeteer's hand, and the fingers are used to move the puppet's arms and head. A puppeteer may have a glove puppet on each hand, which requires specialized movement and coordination of the arms, wrists, and each finger to make the puppets act and react to each other and face out to the audience.

Rod puppets require the puppeteer to hold the puppet up by a central rod while using one or both hands to manipulate rods attached to each of the puppet's arms. Balinese shadow puppets are flat rod puppets made of hide and are performed behind a white back-lit screen using similar manipulation techniques as used for rod puppets. The puppeteer's placement of the flat, thin shadow puppets behind the screen and the movement of the rods holding the arms for the puppet's gestures require an exacting awareness of space to animate them for the audience to see the characters act and react with each other.

An example of puppet manipulation requiring advanced movement techniques is Japanese bunraku puppetry. Bunraku puppets have a wooden structure, carved wooden head and hands, fabric arms and legs, traditional Japanese clothes, and are usually a little more than half the size of a human. Two or three puppeteers who have apprenticed in bunraku techniques for many years have the honor of bringing one bunraku puppet to life. Each of the main bunraku characters in the performance requires three specialist puppeteers to animate them. The more experienced puppeteer manipulates the body, head, right arm and hand, while the second puppeteer animates the left arm and hand, and the newest puppeteer works the feet. These puppeteers need to move in a traditional Japanese way with precise movement and physical coordination to make each character walk smoothly and emote effectively.

Puppetry is an international art form encompassing traditional stories and styles, such as Turkish Karagöz shadow puppets, British Punch and Judy shows, and Balinese rod puppets, and companies performing original stories with creative puppetry styles, such as Green Ginger in England and Phillippe Genty, France.

Chapter 20

Too Much Geniality: Notes and Quotes on a Reappraisal: Stage versus Screen Acting

Ken Bullock

Ken Bullock has been affiliated with Theatre of Yugen in San Francisco since 1980. He is a freelance performing arts critic and a member of the San Francisco Bay Area Theatre Critics Circle. His reviews have appeared frequently in the *Berkeley Daily Planet* and *Commuter Times*. A different and expanded form of this essay may be found on the website http://alegorias3.blogspot.com.

Classically, performers learned their art by imitation—watching a teacher, following along. The old theater schools of Asia still follow this practice, rehearsing set pieces, like the *shimai* of Japan's Noh Theatre, short character dances from plays in the repertory.

In Europe, ballet began as a Baroque theatrical interlude, quickly incorporating mirrors (themselves a favorite conceit of Baroque poets and painters) as an aid in teaching études. Dramatist Heinrich von Kleist would later use the student's glance at his own reflection as the image of a performer's self-consciousness in his parable of naturalness and artificiality in performance, "On the Marionette Theater."

From its earliest days, film has been used for studying movement and behavior as much as for entertainment. Muybridge's photographic motion studies serve as an immediate predecessor to cinema, and the short proto-documentaries of the Lumière Brothers were both research into documenting the nuances of everyday life and popular entertainment.

Paired off against the stylized performances of stage magician Méliès, the Lumières' films exemplified one end of the spectrum of the filmmaker's art from the beginning, showing what Walter Benjamin later characterized: "A different nature opens itself to the camera than opens itself to the naked eye—if only because an unconsciously penetrated space is substituted for a space consciously explored by man. . . . The act of reaching for a lighter or a spoon is familiar routine, yet we hardly know what really goes on between hand and metal, not to mention how this fluctuates with our moods. . . . The camera introduces us to unconscious optics as psychoanalysis does to unconscious impulses."

This phenomenon of filmed behavior, emphasized by the selective process of editing and the expanded image on the big screen, helped give rise to the comparison of acting in film and on stage to the depiction of thinking (film) versus the projection of feeling (stage)—eventually worn down to the cliché: overacting (stage) versus underacting (film).

Orson Welles, familiar with being on either side of the camera as well as on both sides of the footlights, sidestepped the dichotomy to emphasize the actor's focus: "[James Cagney] came on in the movies like he was playing to the gallery of an opera house. . . . Cagney was *focused*, Christ, like a laser beam!"

"Cooper was a movie actor—the classic case. You'd see him working on set, and you'd think, 'My God, they're going to have to retake that one!' He almost didn't seem to *be there*. And then you'd see the rushes and he'd fill the screen. Why does the camera seem to diminish Laurence Olivier with all his technique? And enlarge Gary Cooper, who knew nothing of technique at all?"

Another actor, from a stage background, embodied this paradox: Bertolt Brecht's favorite, Peter Lorre, whose stage name meant "parrot," but whose abilities exceeded mere mimicry. "Some subtlety of expression was seen by the camera and recorded by the microphone that the naked eye and ear did not get," commented director John Huston.

Regardless of the particular screen presence of one professional actor versus another, the results of cinematic research pointed to another factor in the audience's reception of a performance on screen. Pudovkin's famous experiment (an inspiration for Hitchcock's *Rear Window*) in which a close-up of a man gazing with a neutral expression was spliced together with different images, resulting in spectators attributing different emotions to the same recycled close-up, is perhaps the most famous of these.

Following the lead of documentary film, and of theater, of Russian public spectacles and of French and Italian folk and popular festivities, filmmakers began casting more and more amateurs and nonprofessionals for their onscreen qualities of naturalness and authenticity. Jean Renoir's *Toni* marked a watershed. Then, at the time when Stanislavskian-inspired method acting began to make inroads on New York stages and in Hollywood film studios, neo-realist cinema, associated with the Second World War partisans of the Resistance in Italy and postwar popular social movements, put "nonacting" and improvisation on a new pedestal, creating a new relationship between actor and director.

There was resistance among actors, too. On the set of *Viaggio Italia*, an iconic film for the *Nouvelle Vague* and a touchstone for *Cahiers du Cinema*'s "*politique des auteurs*," George Sanders reportedly wept when director Roberto Rosselini fed him his lines only just before the shot, later claiming he couldn't even recognize himself on screen.

"The actor is one of the elements of the image. A modification of his pose or gestures is a modification of the image itself. The film actor need not understand, simply be." Michelangelo Antonioni's remarks reflect the attitude of many directors who came from the experience of neo-realism. Another, Pier Paolo Pasolini, who paired professional actors with amateurs in his "mythic" films, said, "real life is full of nuances, and actors like to be able to reproduce them. An actor's great ambition is to start out weeping, and then move very gradually through all the different stages of emotion to laughing. I hate nuances and I hate naturalism, so an actor inevitably feels a bit disappointed working with me because I remove some of the basic elements of his craft—indeed the *basic element*, miming naturalness."

In Robert Bresson's words, "The actor is double. The alternate presence of him and of the *other* is what the public has been schooled to cherish . . . forcing the public to look for talent on his face, instead of the enigma peculiar to each living creature." Bresson, who only cast amateurs in his films from *Journal d'un Curé de Campagne* (1950) and never more than in a single film for each one, called his actors "models," whose reality ("his way of being inward, unique, inimitable") he contrasted with the professional actor, on whose "expressive face . . . the slightest crease, controlled by him and magnified by the lens, suggests the exaggerations of the Kabuki"—contrasting what he called "the cinematographic" to "the cinema—filmed theater."

As with neo-realism and its offshoots, Bresson's innovations proved widely influential, admired from the start even in Hollywood circles. One admirer was Russian director Andrei Tarkovsky, interested in Pasolini's work as well as Bresson's austere stylization.

Actor Erland Josephson recalled a set-up during the shooting of Tarkovsky's first film shot in the West, *Nostalgia*. After days of the director's injunctions to suppress gesture and overt expression, Josephson found himself alone in a field for an extreme long shot. Experiencing a sudden sense of freedom, he decided he could do "a little acting," and lifted his hands a few inches from his sides—only to hear Tarkovsky yell "Cut!" and then call to him, "Erlando, Erlando, fratello mio! Troppo agitato! Troppa genieàlita!" ("Brother Erland! Too much movement! Too much cleverness!").

With the rise of composite styles of film performance—different combinations of approaches that go back to the Lumière Méliès dichotomy—the paradoxical opportunity arises for film to realize the sublime theatrical insights of modern stage visionaries like Antonin Artaud (Theatre of Cruelty, in the Nietzchean sense of the word) and V. S. Meyerhold ("The Grotesque is the triumph of Form over Content")—what Roland Barthes called "The Obtuse," in his essay on examining stills from (Meyerhold follower) Sergei Eisenstein's films.

Or, put a different way by filmmaker Raùl Ruiz (who has expressed an interest in "the grimace" of silent film actors), when asked about realism in film, the verity of film reproducing reality, Ruiz replied that there are those who doubt the existence of what they see on film—even natural phenomena—simply because they've seen it on film! "So the suspension of disbelief itself has become an element of the fantastic."

Chapter 21

The Body of Theater
Mark Jackson

Mark Jackson is a theatre director, playwright, performer, and teacher based in San Francisco. His work has been produced at a number of Bay Area theatres, as well as in Washington, D.C., the United Kingdom, and Germany. Jackson was the founding artistic director of Art Street Theatre, San Francisco, from 1995 to 2004, during which time he wrote, directed, and performed in numerous productions for the company. He is a 2004 German Chancellor Fellow of the Alexander von Humboldt Foundation, which took him to Berlin, Germany, for the 2004–2005 season to work with Mime Centrum Berlin, a practical research center for physical theatre. Jackson has led workshops for actors at theatres and schools, and served on the faculties of universities in both California and Berlin. In addition to his work as a freelance theatre maker, he continues to teach theatre courses at San Francisco State University, the American Conservatory Theater, and other organizations. He can be found digitally at www.artstreettheatre.org.

As a theatre maker interested in the visceral nature of the theatrical experience, I have found that critics of my work often slot me in the "Movement" box. As if all theatre were not physical! Even Shakespeare, our most famous language-centric playwright, scripted physical events in time and space. Speaking is a physical, not just intellectual act. It takes breath and muscle as well as thought. This is obvious. So strange then that we often try to compartmentalize the theatre into definite categories. Does this really help us understand the experience of the work better in the moment we are experiencing it? Aren't these compartments merely distractions that close off possibilities in our perceptions and awareness?

For myself, I can say that I have never been concerned about what compartment a given piece I work on fits into. I just make the work. I am fascinated by history and by the classic forms of world theatre. I've studied and even practiced some of these things. But when it comes time to make work, the question becomes very simple, "How?" And the very general answer is, "Whatever works." The process of exploring this question and answer is a physical, intellectual, and emotional one, in other words a full-body process.

My significant training is in Stanislavky, Meyerhold, Viewpoints, and the Suzuki method of actor training. But other considerable influences carry me along as well—Steven Berkoff, Bob Fosse, Ariane Mnouchkine and Théâtre du Soleil, modern dance, Buto, Kabuki, Vaudeville, *The Bugs Bunny Road Runner Hour*, American films from the 1920s to 1940s. Being a magpie of sorts, I'm not concerned about identifying myself with any particular philosophy. I make theatre. That's it.

That said, there are a few philosophies I lean on with consistency. I believe that language in the theatre must be as physical as any other movement. I believe that, to be of any use, the theatre must be a place of possibility on multiple levels—ethical, aesthetic, thematic, the purpose it serves in local, national, and international communities. I believe that although different cultures speak different languages and even feature certain unique physical gestures and signs, all people have a body, and so the body is the most efficient means by which the theatre can get to what it is to be human. The live body in time and space is the basic fact of the theatre, regardless of style, genre, et cetera. So if something can be done just as well or better on a screen, then I say do it there instead. Theater is live flesh, blood, breath, time, and space. As such, it is too high-stakes a medium to waste on anything that isn't driven by a *need* to be expressed through it.

As World Theater continues to evolve, die, and be reborn, I hope it will always remember its *raison d'être*, the human body—all it contains, all it connotes, and the many possibilities of all it can be.

Chapter 22

How Charlie Chaplin Spun Stagecraft into Cinematic Gold

Dan Kamin

While Dan Kamin is primarily a performer, he occasionally coaches individuals in physical alignment (using a system called Structural Awareness, derived from Ida Rolf's "rolfing" system of Structural Integration). He has also created physical comedy sequences for movies, including *Chaplin* and *Benny and Joon*, and he trained Robert Downey Jr. and Johnny Depp for their performances in those films. Kamin does movement workshops, usually during residencies associated with his theatrical performances and engagements as a guest artist with symphony orchestras. He has written two books on Charlie Chaplin, *Charlie Chaplin's One-Man Show* (1984) and *The Comedy of Charlie Chaplin: Artistry in Motion* (2008). The latter has an article about how Kamin trained Downey for the *Chaplin* film. Both books deal in depth with Chaplin's transition from stage to screen, a subject Kamin also covers in his live presentation *Funny Bones: The Comic Body Language of Charlie Chaplin*.

For information on Dan Kamin's work, see www.dankamin.com.

Years before he made any of the films we would call classics, Charlie Chaplin became world famous. He made his first film appearance in 1914, and within two years he had become the highest paid actor in history. He did it by transforming the physical acting techniques he learned on stage into a new style of film acting and literally mesmerizing the entire world with his movement.

By the time Chaplin first stepped before a camera at age twenty-four, he was already a seasoned stage veteran, with thirteen years of professional touring experience behind him. He began in a clog dancing troupe, worked in legitimate theatre for a couple of years, then learned his comedy craft as a member of Fred Karno's Speechless Comedians, the premier sketch comedy company in the world. It was while touring the American vaudeville circuits between 1910 and 1913 that Chaplin was discovered by Hollywood.

Chaplin modified his stage technique in a variety of ways once he could watch himself performing on screen. He reduced his tendency to mug and exaggerate his facial expressions, seen in his earliest Keystone films. In those first films, he seemed to be imitating Ford Sterling, the hammy Keystone actor he was hired to replace. However, when he saw how effective his body language was, he developed a marked preference for letting his body, rather than his face, talk for him. Faced with the visual possibilities of a screen that was much more silent than the silent stage, he investigated the comic possibilities of virtually everything he did on screen. He turned commonplace actions such as tipping his hat, shrugging his shoulders, and walking—especially walking—into trademark comic gestures that people everywhere found funny and imitated.

About three months into his film career, as he took control of the directing process, he also began experimenting with camera placement, formulating his lifelong method of shooting himself in mid-range or long shots rather than close-ups, which are extremely rare in his films. At the same time, when he realized the effect that speeding up the film had on his performances, he started moving more slowly (in real time) so that he could create more intricate fight and physical comedy sequences. He knew that when seen speeded up, these sequences would take on a geometrical precision that was both satisfying and highly amusing to watch. His physical precision, which helped him suggest the "gentleman" aspect of his Tramp character, was at the heart of his comedy.

Chaplin also exploited the speed-up in hundreds of gags in which his body and the bodies of others are treated as though they're inanimate objects, allowing him to make the extreme violence of his films seem funny rather than painful. He also discovered a corollary gag in which bodies become machine-like. The most celebrated example is when Charlie goes nuts from his repetitive nut-tightening factory job in *Modern Times* and wreaks choreographed chaos on the factory.

The factory gags are based on rhythm, one of the fundamental elements of stage movement. Chaplin's signal achievement as a comedian who made the transition from stage to screen is that he figured out how to conjure comedy from all the fundamental physical laws of movement. This is a paradoxical achievement, in that film tends to contradict the very physical laws that make stage performances interesting to watch. For example, one must cut within sequences to avoid static shots, yet cutting negates the spatial continuity that provides the background for all stage performances. This is one of the reasons why it's so difficult to film dance and theatre performances effectively. Chaplin, though, learned how to use the medium's very contradiction of reality to his advantage. For example, when Charlie spins through a revolving door in *The Cure*, the speeded-up action allows him to create an exhilarating illusion that he's "falling" upstairs, an amusing exaggeration of the law of momentum that would be impossible to achieve on the stage. Similarly, when he roller-skates in *Modern Times*, blindfolded and perilously close to the edge of an unfinished department store floor, he accomplishes the thrilling comedy sequence with an overlapping series of filmic illusions, including speed-up, reverse-action, and other forms of trick photography. But because he always merges film technology with his spectacular physical skills, and because of the brilliance of his choreographic style of directing, Chaplin's movement, rather than film trickery, remains the focus of viewers. In other words, Chaplin, like Fred Astaire after him, learned how to celebrate highly theatrical movement in a notoriously nontheatrical medium.

While Chaplin's sound films necessarily became less movement centered, he remained true to his silent (and stage) roots in subtle and surprising ways. For example, in 1940 he released *The Great Dictator*, a no-holds-barred comic assault on the pernicious ideas and pretensions of Adolf Hitler. The film capitalizes on the bizarre fact that Hitler appropriated Chaplin's mustache, and features Chaplin's lampoon of Hitler as a gibberish-spouting buffoon. But Chaplin also fills the film with sneaky moments of speeded-up physical comedy action, and it contains several brilliant comedy sequences in which he continues his play with those laws of movement. For example, early in the film, Chaplin, as a German soldier during World War I, is unaware that the plane he's piloting has flipped over; he's baffled by the strange anti-gravity behavior of his watch floating in front of his face and water flowing upwards from his canteen. It's a hilarious image of a world gone topsy-turvy, one of many understated metaphors in the film that depicts the madness of war.

Two celebrated physical comedy set pieces define the double roles Chaplin plays in the film. As Hitler, he dances with a globe of the Earth that turns out to be a giant balloon, reducing Hitler's desire for world domination to infantile megalomania. And as the look-alike soldier, who turns out to be a Jewish barber, he shaves a customer while moving to the tempo of music he hears on the radio, Brahms's Hungarian Dance Number Five. The humor derives from the barber's sticking to the frenetic tempo and rhythm of the music despite his customer's alarm and discomfort. It's silent comedy for the sound era—Chaplin couldn't have done a sequence that depended on synchronized sound in a silent film.

All of Chaplin's sound films contain similar clever blends of physical skills and cinematic technique, and Chaplin agonized throughout the rest of his career with the problem of how to integrate physical and sound comedy. Of necessity, he toned down many of the more presentational aspects of his silent performing style—for example, his habit of frequently looking directly into the camera, as though addressing a stage audience with a glance or a classical theatre aside. His gestures also became less exaggerated. Most significantly, in dialogue scenes, he had to move at the actual speed of life for the first time in his career. Inevitably, this made him look slower, older, and more sluggish than the sprite he played in his silent films. Appropriately, he solved the problem in his last American film, 1952's *Limelight*, by returning to his roots and playing a music-hall comedian. In this film, his theatrical acting style is particularly effective.

Chaplin's highly physical acting style remained firmly rooted in his stage technique throughout his film career, and the core of that technique was his deep understanding of how to use movement to communicate ideas and emotions in arresting and novel ways. Chaplin seemed to be thought incarnate, expressing his every thought with his entire body. This led him to develop a form of screen acting that was quite stylized. Yet one of his greatest achievements is that he's so persuasive, we seldom catch him at it.

Since the 1930s, when former stage performers like W. C. Fields and Laurel and Hardy successfully made the transition from stage to screen, and effectively blended silent and sound comedy, very few performers have succeeded in accomplishing either of these feats. Jacques Tati is the sole filmmaker of the second half of the twentieth century with a comic vision comparable to that of the great silent comedians. Like the earlier greats, he managed to create a unique acting style based upon his years of work as a stage mime artist, infusing his stage technique with a totally original cinematic vision. Since Tati, physical comedy has largely languished on film. Although there have been many good visual gags in films like *There's Something about Mary* and *Meet the Parents,* these gags are mostly directorial conceits that have little to do with the physical skill and performing finesse of the actors.

The audience is waiting . . .

Epilogue

The purpose of this book has been to aid artists, actors, teachers, students, and all who aspire to work in theatre, film, mime, dance, clown art, and all the stage and screen arts and beyond become familiar with varied movement forms to better understand themselves and their talents and engage in artistic choices accordingly. The program also has aimed to render participants physically attuned and vital to awaken their imagination and spur them on to higher levels of creative expressivity. The achievement of higher levels of creative expressivity is based on the belief that the body's potential for creative expressivity is limitless. It is also based on the belief that the practice of physical movement releases feelings and emotions, and the development of a solid technique can lead to the discovery and expansion of expressive movement.

I also hope that the suggestions for the use of movement in the improvisational exercises, pantomimes, and mime and text are broad and flexible enough to spark that creative process in artists involved in all of the stage and screen arts and other realms of communication and beyond. May they serve as a springboard for those utilizing them to create their own expressive exercises for the various parts of the body, to devise their own improvisations, pantomimes, and mimed scenes, to animate the silent movement or spoken words they interpret as well as other artistic means they utilize, and to thus bring new life to their creations.

May this approach addressing artists, teachers, students, and all who have participated in this program have achieved its purpose to accord a revitalized body its proper place in their work and lifestyle. By the same token, may the training here serve those seeking personal enrichment help them free the body from programmed and conventional physical movement to rediscover the body's potential for a more lively, natural, and integrated mobility and spontaneous corporal expression.

Last of all, I hope this program and the testimonies of international artists will help future stage and screen artists more fully integrate movement with voice, dance, clowning, or other arts. May bringing the body to their art weave together and empower their creations with a totality and wholeness of imaginative dramatic expression.

For as the movement of the body liberates creativity and gives birth to expressivity, the gestures of the body evolve in silence or between words or musical notes. And so are born the lyricism of the body and the poetry of movement.

Creating a Movement Training Program: Ten Sample Lessons

(For possible updated information of each appendix, consult www.AnnetteLust. com.)

These ten sample lessons are intended for those who seek guidance in setting up a movement training program. They are based on the exercises in chapters 3 and 4 of the book and progress from basic simple and elementary to more challenging physical and creative expressive exercises for each part of the body. The exercises increase in number as they progress and the students become more adept.

The number of preliminary physical exercises in each lesson may be reduced but should not be entirely omitted unless replaced by comparable body training exercises. The physical exercises for each part of the body alternate with the expressive ones in order to connect the physical and the expressive aspects of movement and incite participants to explore and create expressive movement from basic physical exercises.

The exercises in the sample lessons may be taught in a class by a teacher or practiced in a group with a designated leader or practiced on one's own. The exercises comprise a variety of movement training forms, from stage and screen acting to pantomime and corporeal mime, that may be selected and utilized as needed. Participants who presently have basic movement training in another program may wish to omit or replace some of the physical exercises with the expressive movement exercises or begin work in part II of the book in physical improvisation, pantomime, movement for acting, and mime and text.

The ten sample lessons are ideally based on a minimum of four hours for training sessions (with short breaks) once a week to complete one lesson, or two hours twice a week to complete half a lesson at each session. This is only approximate since it is difficult to set a time limit for meetings that depend on the number and ages of the group members, the participants' previous physical training and experience, and on how much time is allotted to repeat and complete the exercises. If not enough time is allotted, the teacher, coach, or participant may select a limited number of warm-ups and physical and expressive exercises for class and demonstrate others to practice at home, reduce the length of the discussions and demonstrations, and assign some of the background information on mime and movement as reading material. However, whether the number of exercises suggested for each session is reduced or increased according to need or time allotted, it is important to master the exercises begun before moving on to new ones.

Depending on the size of the classroom, a group of fifteen or less will allow students to practice exercises more comfortably and receive individual attention from a coach or teacher. To gain time and provide individual attention when working with larger groups, the coach or teacher may engage an advanced student to move around the room to observe the physical, expressive, improvised, and other exercises practiced by the students. To sustain a solid training sequence, the relaxation, body alignment, breathing, body center, basic, and related expressive exercises for each part of the body should be practiced regularly and reviewed in class and at home. Besides reviewing these suggested exercises, the students should be encouraged to create related exercises.

For the remaining meetings of a fifteen-week semester, the coach, teacher, or student may create variations of those exercises that have been mastered in chapters 3 and 4 and begin to select other exercises in part II. During these remaining meetings (or earlier if the students are prepared), if teachers and participants wish to concentrate on physical improvisations, pantomime, movement for acting, or mime and text, the meetings should still be preceded by selected relaxation, body alignment, breathing, body center, and individual parts of the body exercises. These may be repeated as needed or others created by the participants or the teacher. If a group or individual can work out twice a week with additional hours, the second weekly meeting may be devoted to improvisations, pantomime, movement for acting, and mime and text. If a second semester of movement training is offered, the improvisation, pantomime, movement for acting, and mime and text exercises in part II may be more thoroughly explored. This program attempts to introduce students to a variety of movement methods to offer a broader training foundation, but if training in some movement forms (e.g., pantomime or corporeal mime) are of less need or interest, they may be allotted less time or omitted.

Depending on whether the class is from two hours to four hours long, the length of each lesson may range from twenty to thirty minutes for warm-ups, one hour to two hours for basic physical and expressive exercises, and forty minutes to one hour thirty minutes for discussions and demonstrations. Since it is important to be engaged in actively moving rather than in discussing how to move, time should be allotted to repeat and improve each exercise. The basic physical exercises involving each part of the body should be repeated slowly (e.g., a minimum of five times) with concentration on improving the movement and how it may be eventually used expressively. They should never be practiced mechanically but reworked for improvement. More time may then be utilized to develop the expressive exercises related to the basic physical exercises in chapter 3 as well as the exercises in chapters 4 through 7. The teacher and students may also utilize the expressive physical exercises in chapter 3 to develop material for improvisations, pantomimes, movement for acting, and scenes with mime and text in part II.

Whenever possible, the expressive exercises, improvisations, creative mime work, and pantomimes (with the exception of solo creations) may be interpreted by students in pairs or groups.

The improvisations, pantomimes, and mime and text sections may serve for class or school performances. To stage the author's original solo and group pantomimes for public performance, please contact the author for permission to perform.

INTRODUCTORY DESCRIPTION OF ALL CLASSES

1. What will each class be doing? What is the topic for each class?
   Practicing and developing the physical, expressive and creative aspects of utilizing the body in mime, physical theatre, acting, and stage and screen arts as well as for educational or personal benefits.
2. Purpose of Classes (see Introduction: Goals and Objectives for Learning to Move Expressively).
   (a) Understanding and utilizing different forms of movement theatre.
   (b) Learning to breathe, relax, and relieve tension.
   (c) Exercising the individual parts of the body to better express emotions and ideas.
   (d) Creating dramatic movement, characterization, improvising and inventing spontaneously with the body.
3. Clothing and materials for classes.
   * Loose, comfortable clothing that allows for free and safe movement: for example, tracksuit pants, T-shirt, flexible flat-soled shoes, sneakers, or no shoes. Remove jewelry and watches.
   * No props are needed for most exercises.
   * Masks may be used for some exercises and scenes and whiteface makeup mainly for pantomime or clown performances and for the *commedia* character Pierrot.

LESSON 1

Goal

Begin practicing Relaxation, Alignment, Breathing, Body Center Warm-ups, Physical Trunk, Shoulders, Arms, Hands, Wrists, Fingers, Toes, Feet, Legs, Hips, and Evoking the Illusion of Movement Exercises.

Introduce meaning of miming and importance of training the body to express physically.

Class Content

1. Warm-up Exercises (see Basic Physical Exercises, chapter 3)
   * Explain need for Relaxation, Aligning the Body, Breathing, Body Centering, and Basic Physical Exercises before expressing with the body.
   * State the need to visualize each physical exercise before beginning it.
   * Relaxation Exercises 1, 2
   * Aligning the Body 1–7

- Breathing 1, 2 (standing)
- Body Center 1, 2

2. Basic Physical and Sense Perception Exercises
   - Trunk, Shoulders, Arms 1, 2
   - Hands, Wrists, Fingers 1
   - Toes, Feet, Legs, Hips 1, 2
   - Evoking the Illusion of Movement 1, 2, 3 (chapter 4)

3. Discussion

   Class discussion of what miming is, for example, expressing ideas and emotions with the body often without words and the various forms it may take on. If time permits, show photos or a short film or video, for example, of Chaplin, Marcel Marceau, Decroux, and scenes of actors utilizing expressive movement in both stage and screen acting.

   To view pantomime artists, see video clips on YouTube of Marcel Marceau; Charlie Chaplin; Buster Keaton (*The General* and *Hard Luck*); Jean-Louis Barrault and Arletty in *Les Enfants du Paradis* (*Children of Paradise*, 1945); Classic Pantomime, Metacafe; Cset English-Genres of Theatre, Pantomime, Metacafe; International Pantomime Artists (Link: Bodecker Neander and click on Artists). To view corporeal mime artists, see video clips on YouTube of Mime Corporel (Hippocampe, Charlotte Irvoas); Corporeal Mime; Etienne Decroux; and www.corporealmime.com (click on Giuseppe Condello, Théâtre de l'Ange Fou, Moveo).

   For clown mime, see video clips on YouTube of *Bill Irwin Clowns Around*, *The Clown Bagatelles*, and *Bill Irwin Regard of Flight*. To see mime and ballet combined in Suman Mime in Kolkata, India, visit www.Sumanmime.net and click on Suman Mukherjee's "Ballet Meets Mime" from Kolkata India.

   For these and other movement forms and artists, consult the Videography and DVD sections in appendix F.

4. Homework

   Review Lesson 1, Basic Physical Exercises, and create two original Evoking the Illusion of Movement Exercises to show at next class.

LESSON 2

Goal

Practice Warm-ups, Physical Trunk, Shoulders, Arms, Hands, Wrists, Fingers, Toes, Feet, Legs, Hips, and Sense Perception Exercises.

Continue discussing definitions and give examples of stage and screen movement forms where the movement is generally more magnified for stage and minimalized for screen.

Class Content

1. Warm-up Exercises
   - Relaxation 1, 2
   - Expressive Relaxation 1, 2

- Aligning the Body 1–7
- Breathing 1, 2 (standing)
- Expressive Breathing 1, 2
- Body Center 3
- Expressive Body Center 1

2. Basic Physical and Sense Perception Exercises
   - Trunk, Shoulders, Arms 1, 3
   - Hands, Wrists, Fingers 2
   - Toes, Feet, Legs, Hips 3, 4
   - Sense Perception 1, 2, 3
   - View and comment on students' Evoking the Illusion of Movement Exercises for homework based on the previous lesson.

3. Discussion

   Continue class discussion of definitions and introduce differences between mime, pantomime, and improvisation (see definitions in chapter 1; choosing a movement style in chapter 2; and chapters 5–7).

   Continue showing photos and videos of Marcel Marceau, Chaplin, Decroux, or other pantomime, film, and stage artists utilizing expressive movement and mime.

4. Homework

   Review Lesson 2, Basic Physical Exercises, and create two original Sense Perception Exercises to show at next class.

LESSON 3

Goal

Practice Warm-ups, Physical and Expressive Trunk, Shoulders, Arms, Hands, Wrists, Fingers, Toes, Feet, Legs, Hips, Head, Neck, and Physical Sensation Exercises.

Review movement theatre definitions and differences and begin short history of mime.

Class Content

1. Warm-up Exercises
   - Relaxation 1, 3
   - Expressive Relaxation 3, 4
   - Aligning the Body 1–7
   - Breathing 2, 3 (standing)
   - Expressive Breathing 3, 4
   - Body Center 3
   - Expressive Body Center 2, 3

2. Basic Physical and Expressive Exercises
   - Trunk, Shoulders, Arms 4
   - Expressive Trunk, Shoulders, Arms 1, 2, 3
   - Hands, Wrists, Fingers 3, 4

- Toes, Feet, Legs, Hips 5, 6
- Head, Neck 1, 2
- Physical Sensation Exercises 1, 2, 3
- View and comment on students' Sense Perception Exercises for homework.

3. Discussion
   Briefly review definitions and differences between mime, pantomime, and improvisation. Begin short history of mime. (See Preface in this book; and Annette Lust, *The Development and Art of Mime*, www.mime.info/history-lust.html. Also see Annette Lust, *From the Greek Mimes to Marcel Marceau and Beyond*. Lanham, Md.: Scarecrow, 2003.)

4. Homework
   Review Lesson 3, Basic Physical Exercises, and create two original Physical Sensation Exercises to show at next class.

LESSON 4

Goal

Practice Warm-ups, Physical and Expressive Trunk, Shoulders, Arms, Hands, Wrists, Fingers, Illusion Pantomime for Hands, Wrists, Fingers, Toes, Feet, Legs, Hips, Walking, and Physical Sensation Exercises.

Have students give examples they have seen of stage and screen movement where the movement is generally more magnified for stage and minimalized for screen in scenes without a text or words and with a text or words.

Class Content

1. Warm-up Exercises
   - Relaxation 1, 3, 5
   - Expressive Relaxation 5, 6
   - Aligning the Body 1–7
   - Expressive Aligning the Body 1, 2
   - Breathing 1, 4, 5 (standing)
   - Expressive Breathing 1, 5
   - Body Center 4
   - Expressive Body Center 4

2. Basic Physical and Expressive Exercises
   - Trunk, Shoulders, Arms 5, 6
   - Expressive Trunk, Shoulders, Arms 4, 5
   - Hands, Wrists, Fingers 5, 6
   - Illusion Pantomime for Hands, Wrists, Fingers 1, 2
   - Toes, Feet, Legs, Hips 7, 8
   - Walking 1, 2
   - Expressive Toes, Feet, Legs, Hips: Walking 1, 2
   - Introduce several Physical Sensation Exercises 1–18

  • View and comment on student Physical Sensation Exercises for homework.

3. Discussion/Demonstration

    Discussion and student participation in the use of movement in acting without a text or with few words (see chapter 7). Give examples with students of play scenes that require movement with few or no words, such as Lady Macbeth in *Macbeth* rubbing the blood from her hands after Macbeth murders the king, or Orgon in *Tartuffe* hiding under the table while his wife proves to him that Tartuffe is making advances to her (Act IV, scenes 5–6). Next, have students give examples of play scenes requiring movement related to a text. Continue history of mime or assign as reading homework.

4. Homework

    Review Lesson 4, Basic Physical Exercises, and create two original Physical Sensation Exercises to show at next class. Give more examples of stage and screen scenes requiring movement with and without a text.

LESSON 5

Goal

Practice Warm-ups, Physical and Expressive Trunk, Shoulders, and Arms, Illusion Pantomime for Trunk, Shoulders, and Arms, Toes, Feet, Legs, Hips, Walking, Static Attitude, Weight, Volume, Space, and Time, Descriptive and Occupational Exercises.

   Have students continue to experiment with movement in acting without a text and with a text.

Class Content

1. Warm-up Exercises
   • Relaxation 1, 3, 6
   • Expressive Relaxation 7, 8
   • Aligning the Body 1–7
   • Expressive Aligning the Body 3, 4
   • Breathing 1, 6 (standing)
   • Expressive Breathing 6, 7
   • Body Center 5
   • Expressive Body Center 5
2. Basic Physical and Expressive Exercises
   • Trunk, Shoulders, Arms 7, 8
   • Expressive Trunk, Shoulders, and Arms 6, 7
   • Illusion Pantomime for Trunk, Shoulders, Arms 1, 2, 3
   • Toes, Feet, Legs, Hips 9
   • Expressive Toes, Feet, Legs: Walking 3, 4
   • Body Expression through Static Attitude 1, 2, 3
   • Introduce Weight, Volume 1, 2, and Space and Time 1, 2 (chapter 4)

- Introduce Descriptive and Occupational Exercises 1, 2, 3 (chapter 4)
- View and comment on students' Physical Sensation Exercises for homework.

3. Discussion/Demonstration
Continue discussion and student demonstrations of use of movement in acting without and with a text, utilizing examples of scenes that students were assigned to bring to class in Lesson 4. If time permits, review, improvise, and add words to Sense Perception, Descriptive, or other exercises, such as exclaiming while bumping into various objects in a dark room or crying out while running about to locate a burning smell (chapter 7). Discuss Jean-Louis Barrault's use of mime in speaking theatre (see section on "Jean-Louis Barrault's Use of Metaphoric Imagery in Theatre" in chapter 7).

4. Homework
Review Lesson 5, Basic Physical Exercises, and create one original Weight, Volume, Space, and Time and one Descriptive and Occupational Exercise to show at next class.

LESSON 6

Goal

Practice Warm-ups, Physical and Expressive, Toes, Feet, Legs, Hips, Walking, Static Attitude, Head, Face, Neck, Eye Movements, and Imaginary Object Exercises.

Have students create scenes to demonstrate mime and movement for acting without and with a text.

Class Content

1. Warm-up Exercises
   - Relaxation 1, 3, 7
   - Expressive Relaxation 9
   - Aligning the Body 1–7
   - Expressive Aligning the Body 5, 6
   - Breathing 1 (lying)
   - Expressive Breathing 8
   - Body Center 6
   - Expressive Body Center 6
2. Basic Physical and Expressive Exercises
   - Toes, Feet, Legs, Hips 10
   - Expressive Toes, Feet, Legs, Hips: Expressive Walking 5, 6
   - Static Attitude 4, 5, 6
   - Head, Neck, Face 1, 2, 3, 4
   - Expressive Head, Neck, Face 1, 2, 3, 4
   - Eye movements 1, 2, 3, 4
   - Expressive Eye Movements 1, 2, 3
   - Introduce two or three Imaginary Object Exercises (chapter 4)

- View and comment on students' Weight, Volume, Space, and Time and Descriptive and Occupational Exercises for homework.

3. Discussion/Demonstration

Improvise a short scene, for example, based on a review of Physical Sensation Exercises such as plodding through deep snow, jumping under a cold shower, or making your way through flames, to continue demonstrations in previous lessons of mime and movement in acting without and with a text or words. (See chapter 5, Improvisation.)

4. Homework

Review Lesson 6, Basic Physical Exercises, and create two original Imaginary Object Exercises to show at next class.

Choose a portion of a scene with a text and utilize movement to interpret in class.

LESSON 7

Goal

Practice Warm-ups, Physical and Expressive Toes, Feet, Legs, Hips, Walking, Head, Face, Neck, Eye Movements, Imaginary Object, and Movement through Sound Exercises.

Have students continue to create scenes to demonstrate mime and movement in acting without and with a text.

Class Content

1. Warm-up Exercises
   - Relaxation 1, 3, 8
   - Expressive Relaxation 10, 11
   - Aligning the Body 1–7
   - Expressive Aligning the Body 7
   - Breathing 1, 2 (lying)
   - Expressive Breathing 9
   - Body Center 7
   - Expressive Body Center 7
2. Basic Physical and Expressive Exercises
   - Toes, Feet, Legs, Hips 11, 12
   - Expressive Toes, Feet, Legs, Hips: Expressive Walking 7, 8
   - Head, Neck, Face 5, 6, 7
   - Expressive Head, Neck, Face 5, 6, 7
   - Eye Movements 5, 6, 7
   - Expressive Eye Movements 4, 5, 6
   - Introduce two or three Imaginary Object Exercises 1–8 (chapter 4)
   - Movement through Sound 1–5 (chapter 4)
   - View and comment on students' Imaginary Object Exercises and scenes with a text and movement for homework.

3. Discussion/Demonstration

   Improvise a short scene, for example, based on a review of Descriptive and Occupational Exercises, such as sitting down to dinner and eating different kinds of food, or giving a friend a haircut. Review and have students continue to create examples begun in previous lessons of movement in acting without and with a text or words and mime.

4. Homework

   Review Lesson 7, Basic Physical Exercises, and create two Imaginary Object Exercises to show at next class.

LESSON 8

Goal

Practice Warm-ups, Physical and Expressive Walking, Head, Face, Neck, Eye, Mouth, Jaws, Lips, Tongue Movements, Basic Facial Expression, Disassociation of Movement, and Evoking Movement through Sound Exercises.

Have students continue to create scenes to demonstrate mime and movement in acting without and with a text.

Class Content

1. Warm-up Exercises
   - Relaxation 1, 3, 9
   - Expressive Relaxation 1, 2
   - Aligning the Body 1–7
   - Expressive Aligning the Body 8
   - Breathing 1, 3 (lying)
   - Expressive Breathing 10
   - Body Center 7
   - Expressive Body Center 8

2. Basic Physical and Expressive Exercises
   - Walking 1, 2
   - Walking in Place 1
   - Head, Neck, Face 8, 9, 10
   - Expressive Head, Neck, Face 8, 9, 10
   - Eye Movements 8, 9
   - Expressive Eye Movements 7, 8
   - Mouth, Jaws, Lips, Tongue 1, 2
   - Expressive Mouth, Jaws, Lips, Tongue 1, 2, 3
   - Basic Facial Expression 1, 2, 3
   - Disassociation of Movement Exercises, Inclination 1, Rotation 1
   - Introduce one or two Evoking Movement through Sound exercises (chapter 4)
   - View and comment on students' Imaginary Object Exercises for homework.

3. Discussion/Demonstration

Improvise a short scene, for example, based on a review of Weight, Volume, and Space Exercises, such as disengaging a heavy canvas that has fallen on you, or carrying glasses of wine on a tray and serving them, to demonstrate mime and movement in acting with and without a text. (Review definitions of stage and screen mime in chapter 1, and choosing a movement style in chapter 2.)

4. Homework

Review Lesson 8, Basic Physical Exercises, and create an Evoking Movement through Sound Exercise to show at next class.

LESSON 9

Goal

Practice Warm-ups, Physical and Expressive Walking, Eye Movements, Mouth, Jaws, Lips, Tongue, Basic Facial Movements, Corporeal Mime and Disassociation of Movement, Slow and Rapid Rhythm Exercises.

Have students create scenes to demonstrate differences between mime and pantomime and movement without and with a text.

Class Content

1. Warm-up Exercises
   - Relaxation 1, 3, 10
   - Expressive Relaxation 1, 3
   - Aligning the Body 1–7
   - Expressive Aligning the body 9
   - Breathing 1, 4 (lying)
   - Expressive Breathing 11
   - Body Center 7
   - Expressive Body Center 9
2. Basic Physical and Expressive Exercises
   - Walking 3, 4,
   - Walking in Place 2
   - Eye Movements 1, 10
   - Expressive Eye Movements 9
   - Mouth, Jaws, Lips, Tongue 1, 3, 4
   - Expressive Mouth, Jaws, Lips, Tongue 4, 5, 6
   - Basic Facial Expression 4, 5
   - Corporeal Mime, Disassociation of Movement, Inclination 2, Rotation 2, Undulation 1
   - Expressive Disassociation of Movement 1, 2
   - Introduce two or three Slow and Rapid Rhythm Exercises (chapter 4)
   - View and comment on students' Evoking Movement through Sound homework exercises.

3. Discussion/Demonstration

Improvise short pantomime scenes based on a review of Imaginary Object Exercises, such as imagining that you are standing on an ocean shore and you run in and out of the waves and get into a small boat and row. Or imagine that you are in a prison cell, peering between the bars and pacing back and forth as you wait for your family to visit you. Repeat this exercise utilizing stage and screen movement where the movement is generally more magnified for stage and minimalized for screen without and with a text.

4. Homework

Review Lesson 9, Basic Physical Exercises, and create three Slow and Rapid Rhythm Exercises to show at next class.

LESSON 10

Goal

Practice Warm-ups, Physical and Expressive Walking in Place, Climbing and Descending Pantomime, Basic Facial Exercises, Head, Neck, and Face Scenes for Improvisation, Corporeal Mime and Disassociation of Movement, and Solo Improvisation.

Have students continue to create short scenes to demonstrate movement for stage acting without and with a text, and differences between stage and screen movement and pantomime.

Class Content

1. Warm-up Exercises
   - Relaxation 1, 4, 11
   - Expressive Relaxation 1, 4
   - Aligning the Body 1–7
   - Expressive Aligning the Body 10
   - Breathing 1, 5 (lying)
   - Expressive Breathing 12
   - Body Center 7
   - Expressive Body Center 10
2. Basic Physical and Expressive Exercises
   - Walking in Place Pantomime 1, 2, 3
   - Climbing and Descending 1
   - Basic Facial Exercises 6, 7, 8
   - Head, Neck, and Face 11
   - Disassociation of Movement: Undulation 2, 3; Separation 1, 2
   - Expressive Head, Neck, and Face 11
   - Expressive Disassociation of Movement 3, 4
   - Create a short scene based on Disassociation of Movement
   - View and comment on students' Slow and Rapid Rhythm Exercises.

3. Discussion/Demonstration

   Improvise short pantomime scenes utilizing walking in place and climbing and descending based on character and type exercises, such as an elderly couple hearing and seeing poorly as they cross the street to go to the drugstore for pills. Or improvise a pantomime about a worried person pacing the floor while waiting for news of his or her friend who has had a car accident and then climbing down stairs to rush to the hospital to see the friend. Repeat this exercise utilizing stage and screen movement where the movement is generally more magnified for stage and minimalized for screen.

4. Homework

   Review Lesson 10, Basic Physical Exercises, and improvise a Pantomime to show at next class.

During the course of the next meetings, other warm-ups and physical and expressive exercises in the main section of this program may be chosen according to group or individual needs. Or the exercises in the sample lesson plan may be repeated and improved and new related ones created. The class or participants may continue to alternate with solo and group improvisations or impromptu scenes based on an object, emotion, or subject and eventually devote more time to creating pantomimes and scenes with movement for acting without or with a text.

When the students are prepared to move on to longer creative physical improvisations, solo and group pantomimes, movement for acting, and mime and text in part II, it would be helpful to review the differences between these forms (see definitions in chapter 1, and chapters 5–7).

Improvisation is an important skill not only for solo pantomime artists but also for collaborative group work. Students should also benefit from training in illusion and whiteface pantomime before learning abstract or corporeal mime. Abstract or corporeal mime requires more advanced training and conveys ideas and emotions in a nonliteral and non-anecdotal manner (see chapter 1). Although the exercises included here are for the most part concrete, some could be selected as a basis for creating abstract or corporeal mime.

Reading material on the historical background, contemporary mime, and mime related to the various stage arts may be assigned during the course. If time permits, more films and videos on mime or physical acting may be shown (see the bibliography in this book, and the videography and DVD listings in appendix F).

Resources for Mime Plays, Pantomimes, Themes for Improvisation, and Scenes with and without Words

MIME PLAYS AND PANTOMIMES

Barlanghy, Istvan. *Mime: Training and Exercises*. Trans. Hugo Kerey, ed. Cyril Beaumont. London: Imperial Society of Teachers of Dancing. New Rochelle, N.Y.: Sportshelf, 1967. Limited number of mime scenes.

Beckett, Samuel. *Endgame and Act without Words*. New York: Grove Press, 1958. *Act without Words I and II* are two pantomimes and *Endgame* contains minimal dialogue.

Bruford, Rose. *Teaching Mime*. London: Methuen, 1958. Exercises, solos, and mime plays.

Champfleury, Gautier, Nodier, and Anonymes. *Pantomimes*. Ed. Isabelle Baugé, Paris: Cicero, 1995. In French. Original nineteenth-century pantomimes performed by Deburau at the Théâtre des Funambules.

Chisman, Isabel, and Gladys Wiles. *Mimes and Miming*. London: Thomas Nelson, 1934. Mime training and mime plays.

——. *Mime for Schools*. London: Thomas Nelson, 2009. Originally published in 1938.

Feder, Happy Jack. *Mime Time: Forty-five Complete Routines for Everyone*. Colorado Springs: Meriwether, 1992.

Gherardi. *Recueil Général du Théâtre Italien de Gherardi*. Paris: Cusson et Witte, 1700. In French. General collection of Gherardi's *commedia* theatre.

Goby, Emile, ed. *Pantomimes de Gaspard et Charles Deburau*. Paris: E. Dentu, 1889. In French. Original Gaspard Deburau pantomimes.

Gordon, Mel. *Lazzi: The Comic Routines of the Commedia dell'Arte*. New York: PAJ, 1983. Over 250 *commedia* comic routines that may be mimed.

——. "Lazzi: The Comic Routines of the Commedia dell'Arte." In *Physical Theatres: A Critical Reader*, ed. John Keefe and Simon Murray. New York: Routledge, 2007. Contains a list of *commedia* lazzi scenes.

Gousseff, James W. *Pantomimes 101*. Woodstock, Ill.: Dramatic Publishing, 1974. 101 pantomimes and how to produce a pantomime.

——. *Pantomimes 102*. Woodstock, Ill.: Dramatic Publishing, 1981. 102 new pantomimes and how to produce a pantomime.

——. *Street Mime*. Woodstock, Ill.: Dramatic Publishing, 1993. Pantomime scripts.

Hamblin, Kay. *Mime: A Playbook of Silent Fantasy*. New York: Doubleday, Dolphin, 1978. Introductory mime games and exercises with illustrations.

Harris, Paul. *The Pantomime Book*. Chester, Pa.: Dufour, 2001. Pantomime sketches and gaga.

Jones, Winifred. *Nine Mime Plays*. London: Methuen, 1940.

Keysell, Pat. *Mimes, Themes, and Motifs*. Boston: Plays Inc., 1980.

Lawson, Joan. *Mime: The Theory and Practice of Expressive Gesture with a Description of Its Historical Development*. New York: Dance Horizons, 1973. Suggestions of mime-plays relating to dance.

Lazy Bee Scripts. 2 Wood Road, Ashurst, Southampton, SO4O 7BD, UK; www.lazy-beescripts.co.uk. Short and long new English-style pantomime and play scripts for all ages that are a form of mime with words.

Leabhart, Thomas. *Etienne Decroux*. New York: Routledge Performance Practitioners, 2007. Contains Decroux's mime pieces *The Carpenter* and *The Washerwoman*.

Mawer, Irene. *The Art of Mime*. London: Methuen, 1960.

Mehl, Dieter *The Elizabeth Dumb Show*. Cambridge, Mass.: Harvard University Press, 1966.

Mitchell, Theresa. *Movement from Person to Actor to Character*. Lanham, Md.: Scarecrow, 1998. Character improvisation exercises related to acting and scenes for case study.

Pardoe, T. Earl. *Pantomimes for Stage and Study*. New York: Appleton, 1931.

Rémy, Tristan. *Clown Scenes*. Trans. Bernard Sahlins. Chicago: Ivan R. Dee, 1997. Classic clown routines for class or performance.

Rice, Elmer. *Three Plays without Words*. New York: Samuel French, 1934.

Rolfe, Bari. *Actions Speak Louder than Words: A Workbook for Actors*. Berkeley, Calif.: Persona Books, 1992. Introductory workshop with movement exercises, play scenes, and improvisations.

———. *Commedia dell'Arte: A Scene Study Book*. San Francisco: Persona Books, 1977. Scenes and *lazzi* for class and other purposes with some dialogue.

———. *Farces, Italian Style*. Oakland, Calif.: Persona Books, 1981. Short plays for class and performance. *Commedia* plays adapted from French versions.

———, ed. *Mime Directory/Bibliography*. Vol. 2, International Mimes and Pantomimists. Madison: University of Wisconsin Press, 1978. Contains an extensive list of mime scripts.

———. *Mimespeak and Mime Bibliography*. Ed. Bari Rolfe and Annette Thornton. Lewiston, N.Y.: Edwin Mellen, 2008. Includes all of the original references plus updates of Rolfe's *Mime Directory/Bibliography*, with titles of books, scripts, films, and reference works on mime.

Rovine, Harvey. *Silence in Shakespeare: Drama, Power, and Gender*. Ann Arbor, Mich.: UMI Research Press, 1987. Examples of silent scenes and characters in Shakespeare.

Stolzenberg, Mark. *Exploring Mime*. New York: Sterling, 1979. Illustrated exercises, short mime pieces, and makeup for mime.

Storey, Robert. *Pierrots on the Stage of Desire: Nineteenth-Century French Literary Artists and the Comic Pantomime*. Princeton, N.J.: Princeton University Press, 1985. Pierrot's role in romantic and modern literature. An extensive list of nineteenth-century pantomime scenarios in Paris libraries.

Toomey, Susie Kelly. *Mime Ministry*. Colorado Springs: Meriwether, 1986. Ideas for miming religious songs, scripture skits, and mime skits with a message.

THEMES FOR IMPROVISATION

Andrews, Richard, trans. *The Commedia dell'Arte of Flaminio Scala*. Lanham, Md.: Scarecrow, 2009. Translation and analysis of thirty scenarios.

Barlanghy, Istvan. *Mime: Training and Exercises*. Trans. Hugo Kerey, ed. Cyril Beaumont. London: Imperial Society of Teachers of Dancing, 1967. A limited number of improvisations.

Callery, Dymphna. *Through the Body: A Practical Guide to Physical Theatre.* New York: Routledge, 2001. Exercises and themes for improvisations.

Dennis, Anne. *The Articulate Body: The Physical Training of the Actor.* New York: Drama Book Publishers, 1995. Exercises including improvisational themes for individual and group actor bodywork, and mask and comedy workshops.

Gordon, Mel. *Lazzi: The Comic Routines of the Commedia dell'Arte.* New York: PAJ, 2001. Over 250 *commedia* comic routines.

———. "Lazzi: The Comic Routines of the Commedia dell'Arte." In *Physical Theatres: A Critical Reader*, ed. John Keefe and Simon Murray. New York: Routledge, 2007. Contains a list of *commedia* lazzi scenes.

Gwinn, Peter, and Charna Halpern. *Group Improvisation: The Manual of Ensemble Improv Games.* Colorado Springs: Meriwether, 2003.

Johnstone, Keith. *Impro: Improvisation and the Theatre.* London: Methuen Drama, 1992. Johnstone's invaluable guide to improvisation and mask work.

Keller, Betty. *Improvisations in Creative Drama: A Program of Workshops and Dramatic Sketches for Students.* Colorado Springs: Meriwether, 1988.

Lugering, Michael. *The Expressive Actor.* Portsmouth, N.H.: Heinemann, 2007. Body and voice exercises and improvisational studies.

Mawer, Irene. *The Art of Mime.* London: Methuen, 1960. Mime and impromptu scenes.

Mitchell, Theresa. *Movement from Person to Actor to Character.* Lanham, Md.: Scarecrow, 1998. Character improvisation exercises related to acting and scenes for case study.

Rolfe, Bari. *Actions Speak Louder than Words: A Workbook for Actors.* Berkeley, Calif.: Persona Books, 1992. Introductory workshop exercises and improvisations.

———. *Commedia dell'Arte: A Scene Study Book.* San Francisco: Persona Books, 1977. Scenes and *lazzi* for the classroom and other purposes.

Spolin, Viola. *Improvisation for the Theatre: A Handbook of Teaching and Directing Techniques.* Evanston, Ill.: Northwestern University Press, 1999. Exercises, games, and scenes for adults and children.

Zaporah, Ruth. *Action Theater: The Improvisation of Presence.* Berkeley, Calif.: North Atlantic Books, 1995. A twenty-day program of improvisation exercises to find one's own themes.

Also see video clips on YouTube of *Commedia dell'Arte Masks* by Arnold Sandhaus, including *commedia* character interpretations and other commedia dell'arte scenes.

SELECTED PLAY SCENES CONTAINING MOVEMENT

The following play scenes require movement in silent sections as well as in scenes containing dialogue. They may at first be acted out silently or mimed and then played with an improvised dialogue and eventually with movement integrated with the dialogue of the original scene.

Alan Ayckbourn. *Bedroom Farce.*

Act I (Malcolm, Kate)

While Malcolm and Kate are dressing for their housewarming party, they hide each other's shoes in the bedroom. Malcolm enters with one of Kate's shoes that he tucks into the bottom of the unmade bed and then sits looking innocent in a chair. Kate enters with one shoe accusing Malcolm of taking the other one. After

Malcolm exits to get his shirt, Kate finds her shoe and hides Malcolm's shoes in one of the pillowcases. When Malcolm returns to put on his shirt and look for his shoes, Kate leaves. He then hides Kate's shoes in the bed. Kate enters brandishing the brush he threw into her bath. After Kate exits, Malcolm laughs.

Edward Albee. *Everything in the Garden.*

Act I, Scene 1 (Mrs. Toothe, Jenny)

Mrs. Toothe, who runs a house of prostitution for suburban housewives, has heard that Jenny and her husband need money to keep up with their affluent neighbors. She visits Jenny and places an envelope with one thousand dollars on the table. When Jenny refuses the money, Mrs. Toothe throws the bills in the fireplace. As Jenny asks her to leave, she removes another bundle of money from her purse and pretends to throw it into the fireplace when Jenny holds out her hand. Mrs.Toothe hands her the money as Jenny inquires what kind of a job she is being offered. When Jenny understands, she tries to return the money. And when Mrs. Toothe does not take the money, Jenny throws it back on the table and angrily asks Mrs. Toothe to leave. After Mrs. Toothe hands her card to Jenny, who refuses it, she places it on the table and exits. Jenny picks up the card, reads it, tears it in half, and disgustingly drops it in the wastebasket. She returns to the table, stares at the money, picks it up and is at first uncertain what to do with it, then puts it in a desk drawer, locks the drawer, removes the key, walks toward the window, glances back at the locked drawer, and looks out of the window.

Sherwood Anderson. *The Triumph of the Egg.*

Short one-act with scenes containing movement, one in which the Father, a restaurant owner, to draw customers, overwhelms Joe Kane with an overly friendly greeting, and in a second scene entertains him with outrageous egg tricks.
(Father, Joe Kane, Mother)

When he sees rich Joe Kane in his restaurant, Father removes his dirty apron, puts on a clean one, tidies his hair and moustache, and places a clean towel over his arm. As Joe Kane reads a newspaper, Father approaches him from behind smiling, raises his hand, hesitates, and then gives Joe a forceful, cordial slap on the back. Joe drops his paper and falls forward along with his chair, the newspaper, and Father's pipe. Father picks up the chair, paper, and pipe and hands them to a dazed Joe. Father apologizes, gets Joe a glass of water, offers him a cup of coffee and a cigar, and looks for his pipe that Joe has been holding. Joe swallows the coffee and makes a face. Father lights Joe's cigar that Joe smokes with great difficulty while Father sits down beside him with a cup of coffee. While bragging about how well his restaurant is doing, he picks up Joe's glass of water to drink it just as Joe reaches for it.

At the play's end, Father shows Joe an egg trick by making it stand on its end without breaking. He takes an egg from a plate on the counter, rolls it in his hands as he paces back and forth, and stands it on the counter several times. Each time he gets the egg to stand, Joe is reading the paper and only sees it when it falls. Father then shows Joe a trick by removing an egg from a pan of vinegar with a spoon and attempting to push the egg through the neck of a bottle. As the egg enters the bottle, it breaks and spurts all over the frustrated Father. Laughing, Joe gets up and exits. Father gets another egg and tries to throw it at Joe, who has left. Looking at the egg, Father places it on the table and sobbing throws himself into a chair, his head in his hands. Mother enters and puts her arms tenderly around Father.

Thomas Babe. *A Prayer for My Daughter.*

Act I (Sergeant Kelly, Jimmy, a murder suspect)

As Sergeant Kelly interrogates murder suspect Jimmy, he receives a call from his daughter threatening to kill herself because her problems with her husband have come to a head. Kelly hangs up and puts a trace on her phone call to send a squad car before she kills herself. He takes a drink and expresses his feelings for his daughter, whom he calls a friend for life. From time to time Jimmy, who overhears him, giggles.

Joseph A. Fields and Jerome Chodorov. *My Sister Eileen.*

Act I, Scene 1 (Ruth, Eileen)

Aspiring actresses Ruth and Eileen are shocked by the dinginess of their tiny apartment on their first night in New York. After the landlord talks them into taking the apartment, Ruth goes to the window and, seeing a woman stopping with her dog at a lamppost behind their apartment, motions to her to go away. Ruth puts her hat and purse on the mantel while Eileen opens her overnight bag on the bed. Ruth draws a curtain, looks into the kitchenette, closes her eyes in disgust, and pulls back the curtain. She throws open the bathroom door and looks in repulsed. Ruth begins to undress and, noticing the window that exposes her, runs to the bathroom. Eileen removes the bedcover and folds it back.

As they talk about leaving the apartment in a month and about Eileen's former boyfriend, whom she left in Columbus, Eileen goes to the bathroom while Ruth crosses to the wall and bumps her behind violently against it. They decide to call their parents, but when Ruth lifts the receiver, the phone does not work. Ruth puts her stockings under her pillow and turns out the lights. Eileen comes out of the bathroom and they realize that their room is still light from the lamppost outside their window. Ruth goes to the window to pull down a shade to find there is none.

After they go to bed, Ruth kicks her feet up and pulls the sheet out from the bottom of the bed. Disgusted, she pulls it back in place and puts her arm over her face to keep out the light so that she can sleep. A moment later, they both sit up in fright as they hear a kid running a stick across iron bars that resounds like a machine gun.

Athol Fugard. *Coming Home.*

(Grandfather's ghost)

At the play's end, the Grandfather's ghost comes out to look at his garden and up into the trees where the birds are chirping. He joyfully throws up his arms and, imitating their movement and chirps, cries out: "They are chirping Work hard! Work hard!"

Griselda Gambaro, *Personal Effects.*

(Artist)

In the opening stage movement directions and throughout the entire short play, the artist mimes how his personal suitcases and effects that he moves about and sits on at a train station burden him.

Paul Green. *Quare Medicine.*

(Old Man Jernigan, Dr. Immanuel, Jernigan's son Henry, Henry's wife Mattie)

An action-packed one-act in which Dr. Immanuel, a patent-medicine vendor, sells a bottle of medicine to Henry Jernigan that everyone believes poisons him but which actually helps him tame his shrewish wife and her religious lady friends.

After Jernigan and his son Henry discuss the ladies' religious meetings and Henry's nagging wife, Mattie, the doctor arrives with his medicine case, opens it, removes, shakes, and examines bottle after bottle. After selling a bottle to Old Jernigan, he tries to sell them a magic stone that cures bites and poisons that they turn down. He then points a finger at Henry, indicating that he can make a man of him and soften his wife's ways. Henry shakes his head, but as the doctor picks up his case to leave, Henry gives in. The doctor opens his case and removes two bottles. Henry gulps one bottle down just as his wife appears, screams as though poisoned, chases the doctor around the room and out, and forces Mattie to drink the other bottle. A subdued Mattie throws her arms around Henry as he pretends to bark like a mad dog, scaring away the approaching religious ladies. Henry is proud that he is finally boss in his house.

Lady Gregory. *The Rising of the Moon.*

(A Ragged Man, Sergeant, Policeman X, and Policeman B)

The police are posting a £100 reward sign for a prisoner who escaped from prison and who now tries to slip by the Sergeant. In the last scene, after conversing with the Sergeant about the missing prisoner, smoking a pipe with him, and suggesting that he should be on the side of the people rather than the law, the Ragged Man removes his hat and wig and admits he is the man they are looking for. As the Sergeant seizes his hat and wig and refuses to let the prisoner go, they hear a whistle. The Ragged Man slips behind a barrel, asking the Sergeant not to betray him. The Sergeant puts the hat and wig behind his back as Policeman X and Policeman B arrive to ask if the Sergeant has seen anyone. The Sergeant pauses and says no. After they leave, the Ragged Man comes out from behind the barrel, asks for his hat and wig, and thanks the Sergeant, adding that one day they will all change places at the Rising of the Moon. He waves as he disappears. The Sergeant scratches his head over the reward he lost and asks himself if he is as great a fool as he thinks he is.

Eugene Ionesco. *The Bald Soprano.*

(Mr. Martin, Mrs. Martin, Mary, Mr. Smith, Mrs. Smith)

At the play's beginning, after a scene in which the Smiths speak about themselves and their friends, Mary leads the Martins into an adjoining parlor. Mr. and Mrs. Martin sit facing one another as if they have never met. They smile timidly and attempt to speak. Little by little they realize that they are married to each other. The Smiths enter to greet the Martins. Embarrassed silence, coughing, hesitation, and more silences before and during their absurdist conversation.

Eugene Ionesco. *The Chairs.*

(Old Man, Old Woman, Orator).

After a scene in which the Old Man and Old Woman talk about their life together and on the island where they live, they exit and bring in invisible chair after chair to receive and react to an invisible woman, an invisible colonel, an Emperor, and other invisible guests who attend a lecture by the Orator. After the Orator arrives, he mounts a platform, signs autographs, rejects signing others, and after the Old Woman and the Old Man throw themselves out of the window, he makes signs like a deaf mute, writes on a blackboard, points to what he has written, bows, descends, bows again to the rows of invisible people, and exits.

Marsha Norman. *'Night, Mother.*

(Jessie Cates, Thelma Cates or "Mama")

At the play's end, Mama struggles with Jessie to stop her from running into her bedroom to shoot herself. Jessie gets away and locks her door. Mama pounds on her door and screams to stop her. Mama, breathless, puts her ear to the door to hear nothing. She stands up straight and screams again. There is a shot and Mama collapses against the door, tears streaming down her face.

David Parker. *The Collector.*

Act III, Scene 2 (Miranda, Clegg)

Clegg has kidnapped Miranda and is holding her prisoner in the cellar of a lonely country house. Miranda has just hit Clegg with a table leg and will now offer him her body in order to escape.

(Miranda) In the first silent scene preceding the dialogue, Miranda soaks her bloodstained dress in a bowl of water and then goes to the dressing table and studies her face in the mirror. She opens one of the dressing-table drawers and carefully selects a black bra and stockings to seduce Clegg.

(Clegg) In the second scene, entering cautiously, Clegg listens and, after he hears Miranda cough, creeps toward the dressing room. He peers through a gap in the plastic door and returns to the main door, slides the bolts forward, and slams them open. Smiling, he knocks on the door, and after Miranda speaks, he locks the door and straightens the rug.

David Rimmer. *Album.*

Act I, Scene 3 (Trish)

When sixteen-year-old Trish, who is listening to the Beatles on her blaring radio in her room, is asked by her parents to turn it down, she grudgingly does so and walks around the room frustrated. After she hears them leave, she pulls out a pack of cigarettes and an ashtray from under her bed, defiantly lights up a cigarette, is disturbed by the smoke, turns her radio up very loud, and kisses a picture of John Lennon. As she hears a car pull into the driveway, thinking it is her parents, she quickly fans the air, hides the cigarettes under the bed, and runs to the window to see her best friend Peggy arriving from summer camp.

Neil Simon. *The Prisoner of Second Avenue.*

Act I, Scene 2 (Mel, Edna)

Mel, who lost his job four days ago, returns home after Edna has just come back from the supermarket to find her apartment ransacked. After realizing what has happened, trembling, Edna phones the police. Next, in a silent scene in which she looks for her liquor bottles and does not find them, she runs to the bedroom for a Valium. Mel enters and reacts to the sight.

August Strindberg. *Miss Julie.*

(Kristine the Cook)

A mime scene in which Kristine the Cook is alone, humming to a Scottish round dance as she clears the table, washes the dishes, dries them, and puts them away. She removes her apron, takes a small mirror out of a drawer, and places it against a vase with lilacs on the table. After lighting a candle to heat a hairpin that she uses to curl a lock on her forehead, she moves to the door, listens, and returns. She finds Miss Julie's handkerchief and smells it, spreads it out, smoothes it, and folds it into quarters.

Tennessee Williams. *Vieux Carré.*

Scene 9 (Jane and Tye)

Jane is trying to wake up Tye, her drug addict lover, from his narcotic sleep with a wet towel that she slaps on his face. She throws his shorts, pants, and a sport shirt on the bed so that they can vacate the place and she can rid herself of him. Tye puts on his shorts, stumbles over to the table to take a gulp of coffee, grasps Jane's arm, and pulls her back into bed.

Tennessee Williams. *The Strangest Kind of Romance.*

Scene 4 (Little Man, Boxer, Landlady)

The Little Man has returned to his former room in the boarding house to look for his cat. He pushes the door open to find the Boxer seated on the bed paring his corns with a penknife. He enters looking dazed as he calls his cat. The Boxer tells him he has come to the wrong room. He asks if the Boxer has seen his cat. The indifferent Boxer has not seen his cat. The Little Man trembles as the Boxer stares at him and then begins to laugh. The Little Man tries to laugh with him but then begins to sob. The Boxer grunts and goes to the door to call the Landlady.

A number of the above and other scenes from contemporary plays that were adapted here for mimed dramatization may be found in *The Actor's Scenebook* edited by Michael Schulman and Eva Mekler (New York: Bantam, 1990). For more play and film scenes, see Michael Schulman, ed., *Great Scenes and Monologues for Actors* (New York: Avon, 1998); Eric Lane and Nina Shengold, eds., *The Actor's Book of Scenes from New Plays* (New York: Penguin, 1988); Angela Nicholas, *99 Film Scenes for Actors* (New York: Avon, 1999).

BALLADS AND BALLAD PLAYS, SONGS, AND SONNETS

Many ballads, folk songs, and sonnets contain dramatic material for miming and acting. The following ballads and sonnets may be both acted out or mimed and narrated by a narrator or acted out with a dialogue spoken by performers along with sections narrated by a narrator.

Ballads and Ballad Plays

See *Ballad and Ballad Plays*, ed. John Hampden (New York: Thomas Nelson, 1937). Listed below are several of the ballad mimes, plays, and ballads in *Ballad and Ballad Plays* that are suitable for miming and acting, some of which may be found on the website under the ballad title "Green Broom Ballad."

Green Broom. A mime play with narration arranged by Marion Welham (Lady, Maid, Old Man, Johnny, Johnny's Bride, Clergyman, Chorus or Narrator).
The Bailiff's Daughter of Islington. A ballad mime arranged by Daisy Dykes (Bailiff's Daughter, Squire's Son, two Friends, Village Maidens, Chorus or Narrator).
Hynd Etin. A lyrical ballad in play form (Minstrel, Lady Margaret, Hynd Etin, Eldest Son, two Brothers, Earl, Earl's Minstrel, two Rangers, Porters, Maids, Attendants).
Robin Hood and the Potter. (Minstrel, Robin Hood, Little John, Will Scarlock, Potter, Sheriff, Sheriff's Wife, two Retainers, three Wives, Citizen, Outlaws, Sheriff's Maid, Citizens.)
Hynd Horn. Short mime play (Minstrel, Chorus, King, Hynd Horn, Lady Jean, Beggar, Porter, Bridegroom, Wedding Guests, Courtiers).
Tam Lin. A fairy play (Tam Lin, Janet, four Maidens, three Spirits, Fairies).
The Three Kings. A nativity play (Minstrel, Melchior, Balthazar, Kaspar, Herod, Angel, and unseen Choir or two Narrators).

Other ballads in this collection suitable for acting and miming are:

- *Sir Eglamore* (Knight and Dragon).
- *Parsley, Sage, Rosemary, and Thyme* (one Male, one Female).
- *The Old Market Woman* (Old Woman, Peddler, Little Dog).
- *Robin Hood and the Widow's Sons* (Robin Hood, Old woman, Old Man, Sheriff, Robin Hood's Men).

- *Get Up and Bar the Door* (Wife, Husband, two Men).
- *Lochinvar* (Lochinvar, Bride, Bride's Father and Mother, Bridegroom, Guests and Family at the wedding).

Also see *American Ballads and Songs*, ed. Louise Pound (New York: Scribner's, 1922; reprinted in 1972). The following ballads are suitable for miming and acting.

- *Lord Thomas* (Lord Thomas, Fair Ellen, the Brown Girl, Narrator).
- *Father Grumble* (Father and Mother Grumble, Narrator).
- *William Reilly's Courtship* (William Reilly, Coolen Bawn, Coolen Bawn's Father, Narrator).
- *Young Charlotte* (Charlotte, Charlotte's Mother and Father, Young Charles, Narrator).
- *Johnny Sands* (Johnny Sands, Betty Hague, Narrator).

Among the dialogue, nursery, and game songs in this collection are:

- *The Quaker's Courtship* (Quaker, Girl).
- *Dutchman, Dutchman, Won't You Marry Me?* (Dutchman, Girl).
- *What Will You Give Me If I Get Up?* (Mother, Daughter).
- *Paper of Pins* (Boy, Girl).
- *The Milkmaid* (Gentleman, Girl).
- *Billy Boy* (Billy Boy, Interrogator).
- *Poor Robin* (Narrator, Old Woman, Robin).
- *Let's Go to the Woods* (Richard, Robin, Bobin, Johnny).

Titles of more ballads may be found on the website under *Ballad Indopedia* (Famous Ballads), *A Collection of Ballads* by Andrew Lang. Also see *The English and Scottish Popular Ballads*, ed. Francis James Child (Northfield, Minn.: Loomis House, 2001). Examples of the ballads in *English and Scottish Popular Ballads* may be found online under *The Child's Ballad Index of English and Popular Ballads*. The Early Modern Center of the English Department at the University of California, Santa Barbara, provides information on the Pepys Ballad Collection. See http//ebba.english.ucsb.edu/, and click on Collections and then on Pepys.

Songs

The following old-time songs with music were found in a local library in *Weep Some More My Lady* collected by Sigmund Spaeth (Garden City, N.Y.: Doubleday, Page, 1927). These songs may be recited as well as sung. In *The Old Arm Chair* (narrator, lawyer, brother, sister), suitable for both adults and children, the text may be mimed along with the singing or recitation.

My grandmother she, at the age of eighty-three, one day was taken ill and died.
And after she was dead, the will of course was read by a lawyer as we all stood by his side.

To my brother, it was found, she had left a hundred pound, the same unto my sister, I declare.

But when it came to me, the lawyer said, "I see, she has left to you her old arm chair."
Chorus
How they titter'd, how they chaff'd
How my brother and sister laugh'd
When they heard the lawyer declare
Granny had only left to me her old arm chair!

I thought it hardly fair; still I did not care,
And in the evening took the chair away;
The neighbors they me chaffed,
My brother at me laughed
And said, "It will be useful, John, some day.
When you settle down in life, find some girl to be your wife
You'll find it very handy, I declare;
On a cold and frosty night, when the fire is burning bright,
You can sit in your old arm chair."
One night the chair fell down, when I picked it up I found
The seat had fallen out upon the floor,
And there, to my surprise, I saw before my eyes
A lot of notes! Two thousand pounds or more!
When my brother heard of this, the fellow, I confess,
Went nearly mad with rage, and tore his hair;
But I only laughed at him, and slyly whispered,
"Jim, Don't you wish you had the old arm chair?"

Two other songs in this collection suitable for adults with dramatic action and characterization for miming are *Pierre De Bon Bon* (Pierre and Rosalie), a caricature of a Frenchman, and *The Bashful Young Lady* (Young Lady, Mama, two males).

In *The Weavers' Song Book* (New York: HarperCollins, 1960), *The Devil and the Farmer's Wife*, a Southern version of the old Scottish ballad, lends itself to dramatic action and miming indicated in the ballad that may be interpreted for adults and older children. In this charming comical ballad, the characters are a devil, old farmer, farmer's old wife, farmer's son, and three to nine small devils.

When the devil arrives at the farmer's house to take one of the members of his family to hell, the farmer pleads with him to take his wife rather than his son, whom he needs to work on the farm. But once the devil arrives in hell with the old wife, she "tears up hell" to such an extent that the devil drags her back to the farmer, declaring that even if he was a devil all his life, he never was in hell until he met the farmer's wife.

In the same collection, *You Old Fool* (a male and female) is a comical song about a drunken husband who comes home and sees another horse in the stable, a hat on the hat rack, a pair of pants, and another head on his pillow. The wife replies that the horse is a milk cow her mother sent to her, the hat is a chamber pot, the pants are a dishrag, and the head a melon her mother sent her. Her husband's reactions to these responses are still more comical as he ends up saying, "It's a good thing I'm not of a suspicious nature."

In *The Ring of Words: An Anthology of Song Texts*, selected and translated by Philip L. Miller (New York: Norton, 1973), among the many international action-filled art songs in the collection is Paul Verlaine's *Sentimental Colloquy*, in which a male and a female ghost recall their past love.

In Harold Courlander's *Negro Folk Music* (New York: Columbia University Press, 1963), there are ballads and songs such as *Frankie and Albert* (also known as *Frankie and Johnny*), *The Ballad of Casey Jones*, and *John Henry*, some of which are accompanied by music that could be sung or recited to a mimed dramatization.

Pennsylvania Songs and Legends, ed. George Korson (Baltimore: Johns Hopkins University Press, 1949), contains British, German, Amish, and other ethnic group songs, many of which depict the lives of the working class, of lumberjacks, rafters, coal miners, and industrial workers.

Sonnets

Among Shakespeare's sonnets, the following may be considered for movement interpretations and improvisations.

Sonnet 18 "Shall I compare thee to a summer's day?" Praise of the youth and beauty of the person he addresses that shall never fade in the poet's verses.

Sonnet 19 "Devouring time, blunt thou the lion's paws." The poet appeals to time to keep his lover young and beautiful. And if not, his verses will keep his love young.

Sonnet 22 "My glass shall not persuade me I am old." The poet believes he may remain young as long as his lover's heart that he gave to the poet remains youthful.

Sonnet 23 "As an unperfect actor on the stage." The poet is like a bad actor unable to express his love and begs his beloved to understand his silent love through his books and hear it through his eyes.

Sonnet 27 "Weary with toil, I haste me to my bed." Fatigued, the poet goes to bed but cannot rest because his mind is on his beloved.

Sonnet 29 "When in disgrace with fortune and men's eyes." The poet bemoans his loss of friends and fortune, but when he thinks of his love for his beloved, he would not exchange with kings.

Sonnet 34 "Why didst thou promise such a beauteous day?" Your shame for promising me a beautiful day is poor relief for my disappointment. Yet your loving repentance makes up for your ill deed.

Sonnet 66 "Tired with all these, for restful death I cry." The poet gives all the reasons why he is disappointed with life and wants to die, but then he would have to leave his love alone.

Sonnet 147 "My love is as of a fever, longing still." I am like a madman because I thought my beloved was moral and found the contrary.

Sonnet 149 "Canst thou, O cruel! Say I love thee not." The poet defends his love for his beloved and cites all he has done to prove his love. But since he cannot understand her complaint, he tells her to go on hating him for he is blind.

MYTHS, LEGENDS, AND ADVENTURE STORIES

Greek and Roman myths such as Arachne, who was turned into a spider for boasting she could weave better than the Goddess Athena, and the myth of Persephone, the daughter of Zeus kidnapped by Pluto, lend to dramatization with movement, dialogue, and narration. Colorful legends and historical incidents such as *The Wooden Horse of Troy* or *Ali Baba and the Forty Thieves* may serve as interesting subject matter for the physical interpretation of historical events.

The following is a selected list of myths, legends, and adventure stories.

Colum, Padraic. *The Adventures of Odysseus and the Tale of Troy.* New York: Simon and Schuster, 2004.

———. *Nordic Gods and Heroes.* Mineola, N.Y.: Dover, 1996.

Coolidge, Olivia. *Greek Myths.* Boston: Houghton Mifflin, 1976. *The Trojan War.* Boston: Houghton Mifflin, 2001.

Osborne, Mary Pope. *Tales from the Odyssey Series.* New York: Hyperion Books for Children, 2002, 2003. *Tales from Homer's Odyssey* contains lots of action in, for example, *The One-Eyed Giant* (Bk. 1), *The Land of the Dead* where Odysseus and his fleet meet up with giant cannibals and a witch (Bk. 2), *Sirens and Sea Monsters* in which they encounter a six-headed monster and a deadly whirlpool monster (Bk. 3), *The Grey-Eyed Goddess* in which Odysseus' son Telemachus wards off the man who tries to marry his mother, Penelope (Bk. 4).

Pyle, Howard. *The Story of King Arthur and His Knights.* Mineola, N.Y.: Dover, 1965. Provides physical action adventures such as King Arthur's battle with the Sable Knight and his acquiring of the sword Excalibur. Also see such stories as *The Enchanted Island* in Pyle's *Twilight Land* (Project Gutenberg, 1999) and Pyle's *The Merry Adventures of Robin Hood* (Project Gutenberg, 1997).

Constructing a Mime Piece or Mimodrama

Mime pieces and mimodramas should not be lengthy and may depict subjects drawn from personal experiences, literature, plays, poetry, the Bible, legends, and fairy tales of different periods and countries, historical or current political figures and events, or commedia dell'arte and Pierrot themes and characters.

The mime piece or mimodrama may spring from improvising on a particular subject or theme developed through selection and notation of movement, with exits and entrances, blocking, and stage directions worked out during the improvisational process.

A second method, as in playwriting, is to first write out in detail the mime piece or play's structure, scenes, action in dialogue, characters, exits and entrances, blocking, and stage directions. Rehearsed in silence, movement may be added and deleted during rehearsals. If music is utilized, it should be clearly indicated when and where it will be utilized in the piece and how it will be interpreted to support the mime piece or mimodrama.

Like a verbal play, the mime piece or mimodrama must have dramatic content and form, with the difference that it is mimed or acted out silently. It should have an introduction, the development of a dramatic conflict, a dramatic climax, and an ending. The movement or gestures need to be visually and dramatically interesting and should be clearly, concisely, and economically expressed. If it is a period piece, period gestures and movement as well as music and costumes may be utilized.

If applicable, clown white makeup and masks may be used appropriately (see the sections on makeup and masks below).

WHEN AND WHERE TO STAGE A MIME PIECE OR MIMODRAMA

Besides being performed on stage in a program of its own, in outdoor and indoor mime festivals, or accompanying verbal theatre productions and dance and clown shows, mime, pantomime, and physical and improvisational theatre pieces may be utilized in school programs for educational and artistic purposes as well as in student talent and other kinds of student shows. They may be useful in the classroom to dramatize subjects like history, religion, literature, science, mathematics, social studies, geography, and other studies. They may also be included to benefit physical education, dance, performing arts, and clown classes.

If authorized, mime shows may be more easily staged than other kinds of theatre or dance performances in restaurants, cafes, hotel and other lobbies, stores, shopping malls, public parks, and on street corners and public squares. They may be performed in private dwellings for birthdays, anniversaries, and other occasions as well as in schools, libraries, churches, auditoriums and assemblies, in youth clubs, at fund-raising events, and for religious, political, historical, national, and other events. They may also be presented in hospitals, children's detention homes, prisons, senior citizens centers, nursing homes, in psychiatric wards, and programs for the physically challenged.

Information about where one may stage a mime piece may be obtained from a local Chamber of Commerce or phone directory for a list of libraries, restaurants, churches, clubs, or other public places.

HOW TO APPLY WHITEFACE MAKEUP

The following steps for applying whiteface are simple for beginners. Artists or performers who are more experienced with applying whiteface may wish to utilize their own face designs and shapes.

1. After washing your face and splashing cold water on it to close pores, cover it with moistener, cold cream, or facial oil.
2. Although white flour may be used, as did the mimes of ancient Rome, clown white or mime white in cream or pancake form is easier to apply smoothly from the hairline to the chin, including the eyebrows.
3. Next pat white powder or cornstarch over face and brush away excess powder or cornstarch with a face brush on lips, eyebrows, and eyes.
4. If desired, with a black eyebrow pencil or liner, draw the extremities of your facemask from your chin around to sides and above your forehead.
5. With a black pencil, outline your eyes and draw small upward lines at far ends.
6. Draw eyebrows one-half to one inch above eyebrows.
7. Draw elongated triangles one to two inches long starting from above and below the center outside each eye that end in a point like an elongated V (the point on the triangle pointing upward above the eyes and downward below the eyes) and blackened inside.
8. Pencil out and color lips with bright red lipstick (slightly turned up at the ends if desired). If needed, lightly apply powder or cornstarch over face again.
9. To remove makeup, use cold cream and tissues followed by soap and water.

MASKS

Masks may be used either for *commedia*, ancient Greek, or other types of performances and for characters such as Pierrot in illusion pantomime. Neutral or expressionless noncharacter masks are helpful as a rehearsal technique to aid performers express more fully with their entire bodies. They alleviate stage fright and permit one to perform more freely. They help the performer focus, utilize only essential movements, and incite creativity and a sense of discovery.

Simple masks may be made of papier-mâché, cardboard, plaster of Paris, cloth, and other materials such as a nylon stocking or a veil or semitransparent material pulled over the head. For the actor or performer speaking or singing a text, a half mask is easier to use. A simple mask for children may be made out of a paper bag or a paper plate with eye and mouth holes and tied behind the head with a string or elastic. To create a Pierrot mask, whiten the face and make it up in classic whiteface as in illusion pantomime (see whiteface makeup above).

Commedia Masks of Burlap for Commedia or Other Purposes

Items to make the mask:
A piece of burlap that will cover the face, starch, water, old newspapers, hair dryer, glue, knife, scissors, paint, needle and thread, stapler.
Directions:

1. Dilute the starch with water into a thick liquid.
2. Make pleats in the burlap to indicate the nose, lips, eyebrows, and other parts of the face.
3. Crush the newspapers into a ball as a base to hold the mask.
4. Dip the burlap into the starch and affix it on the newspaper ball. Mold the facial traits (nose, lips, eyebrows) by more detailed pleating of the desired facial features, and staple each pleat together.
5. Pull out sections of the burlap into threads to use for hair or a beard. Use burlap threads for eyebrows or a moustache.
6. Wipe burlap and dry with a hair dryer.
7. Cut the borders of the burlap into small strips in several places and turn the strips under the mask and staple them together to give the mask volume.
8. Dry the mask for several days at warm or room temperature and keep it stuffed with the newspaper to retain its form.
9. After the mask is dry, place pieces of paper on mouth and eye sections and with a knife cut out these sections and glue around the edges of cut-out areas to avoid raveling. Instead of cutting out large holes for eyes, you may make slits and paint eyes or sew buttons on the burlap above them.

Masks of Plastic Strips or Gauze Tape

Items to make the mask:
Long plastic strips or gauze tape (may be purchased in a pharmacy), Vaseline, water, scissors, and stain to apply on mask.

Directions:

1. If your strips are very wide, cut them down to two inches wide. Strips should be long enough to cover the face across and from ear to ear and from the top of the forehead to the bottom of the chin.
2. After placing a cap over the hair and covering the actor's or performer's face with Vaseline (or apply on a hat block or wig holder), wet the strips and apply them one by one horizontally across the face, leaving the nostrils and eyes open.
3. Apply a second layer of plaster strips.
4. Dry for a half-hour.
5. Remove the mask by gently lifting the sides while carefully pressing down on the plastic strips.
6. Dry for several days.
7. Stain with walnut stain or another color.

Paper Masks

Directions:

1. With a basic mask (neutral plastic mask or face mold), create a mold or frame in plaster or clay covered with Vaseline.
2. Tear paper into strips and dip them in a mixture of glue and water; apply them to the mold in seven layers, and allow to dry in the sun or heat.
3. Cut out holes for the eyes and mouth and cut away rough edges. Add hair, beard, other features, and color.
4. To create a demimask, cut across the mask from above the mouth.
5. To keep masks in place, use strings or elastic strips affixed to each side of the mask.

Adapted from "*Commedia* Masks" in *Commedia dell'Arte* by Madeleine Moget-Renault (Collection BT2, PEMF. In French).

For information on how to make a leather mask, see John Rudlin, *Commedia dell'Arte: An Actor's Handbook* (New York: Routledge, 2000).

For information on performing and working with masks, see Toby Wilsher, *The Mask Handbook: A Practical Guide* (New York: Routledge, 2007); Bari Rolfe, *Behind the Mask* (Oakland, Calif.: Persona Books, 1982); and Keith Johnstone, *Impro: Improvisation and the Theatre* (London: Methuen Drama, 2007). Also see Jonathan Kipp Becker's website, www.theater-masks.com/about_commedia_dell_arte, for resources on commedia dell'arte, and the website Making Masks, www.commedia-dell-arte.com/makem.htm.

MASK MAKERS

To obtain masks for classes or performances, contact the following mask makers.

Jonathan Becker Masks
3101 West Petty Road, Muncie, IN 47304
401-954-1768
jonathan@theater-masks.com
www.theater-masks.com
   Full character masks, headpieces, *commedia*, half masks, neutral masks for training, and quarter masks. For information on commedia dell'arte resources and actor training with masks, see www.theater-masks.com/about_commedia_dell_arte.

Michael Chase, The Mask Studio
The Glasshouse, Wolleston Road, Amblecote, Stourbridge, West Midlands DY8 4HF, Great Britain
mask.studio@virgin.net
www.mask-studio.co.uk

Dark Side Masks International
P.O. Box 3305 Hamilton D.C., NSW 2303, Australia
+61 406 578 244
Enquiries@darksidemasks.co.nz
www.darksidemasks.co.nz
   Latex rubber commedia dell'arte masks and fiberglass. Basel masks and basel mask teaching kit.

Libby Marcus Masks
40 Seeley Ave., Portland, ME 04103
207-772-9924
Libby@libbymarcus.com
www.libbymarcus.com

Willy Richardson Masks
1 West 24th St., Baltimore, MD 21218
410-243-0010
fax 410-467-9886
maskman@verizon.net
   See masks online: http://mysite.verizon.net/vzert0c5/masksbywillyrichardson2/.
   See video clip on YouTube of Masks by Willy Richardson MPT.

Stanley Allan Sherman, Mask Arts Company
203 West 14th St., Studio 5F, New York, NY 10011-7138
212-243-4039
Stanley@maskarts.com
www.maskarts.com and www.commediau.com
   Leather and neoprene commedia dell'arte masks, custom leather masks. Commedia dell'arte workshops at Roving Classical Commedia University (unaccredited).

For more mask makers see www.theater-masks.com/meet-the-suppliers and www.mask-studio.co.uk. Also see video clip on YouTube of *Commedia dell'Arte Masks* by Arnold Sandhaus.

WHEN TO WEAR WHITEFACE MAKEUP, MASKS, AND COSTUMES

Modern actors and dancers who mime do not necessarily wear costumes or traditional masks and mime makeup, and mimes and clowns often perform in tights or in clothing that allows for free body movement. However, depending on the kind of performance or stage or film piece they are performing, some clowns, mimes, and *commedia* actors may wear traditional costumes. For example, nineteenth-century Pierrot pantomime may be staged in Pierrot costumes consisting of tights, loose blouse, and whiteface, and *commedia* plays are presented in traditional *commedia* costumes and masks. Neutral masks, worn mainly for training purposes to develop actor confidence, creativity, and sense of body and space, are sometimes utilized for abstract themes of pieces. Jacques Copeau first developed the neutral mask for actor training at the Théâtre du Vieux Colombier in Paris. Based on the masks created by the Italian sculptor Amleto Sartori, it is used at the Jacques Lecoq school in Paris and in a number of movement training programs.

For books and articles on masks, see Masks in the Association of Theatre Movement Educators, http://atmeweb.org/movement/mask.shtml.

USE OF MUSIC

This section is by Dr. Evelyne Luest, concert pianist and teacher, soloist and chamber musician, and pianist with Contrasts Quartet.

Although mimes and movement theatre performers should learn to move in silence, music may help interpret mime pieces, pantomimes, and improvisations. Music may also serve to accompany the expressive movement exercises in this text or inspire new ones. The choice of music for mime pieces, pantomimes, and improvisational work depends on one's needs and taste. If utilized, it is important that the movement not be dependent on the music, but that the music is used as an accompaniment to the movement. Among the many musical pieces that are available, the following suggested titles are categorized according to theme, subject matter, and mood.

Waking Music

"Prelude: Morning Mood" from *Peer Gynt*—Edvard Grieg
Here Comes the Sun—Beatles

Exuberance

"Alla Hornpipe" from *Water Music*—George Frideric Handel
"Allegro" from *Eine Kleine Nachtmusik*—Wolfgang Amadeus Mozart
"Allegro" from *Mandolin Concerto*—Antonio Vivaldi

1st and 3rd Movements from *Brandenburg Concerto No. 6*—Johann Sebastian Bach
"Russian Dance" from the *Nutcracker Suite*—Peter Ilyich Tchaikovsky

Triumphant

Theme from *Star Wars*—John Williams
"Prelude" to *Die Meistersinger*—Richard Wagner
Ride of the Valkyries—Richard Wagner

Meditation and Reverie

Air on the G String—Johann Sebastian Bach
Jesu, Joy of Man's Desiring—Johann Sebastian Bach
"Clair de Lune" from *Suite Bergamasque*—Claude Debussy
Gymnopedie No. 2—Eric Satie
"Reverie" ("Traumerei") from *Scenes from Childhood*—Robert Schumann
"Aase's Death" from *Peer Gynt*—Edvard Grieg
Fratres—Arvo Pärt
Musica Celestis—Aaron Jay Kernis

Music of Excitement

The Flight of the Bumblebee—Nikolai Rimsky-Korsakov
"The Aquarium" from *Carnival of the Animals*—Camille Saint-Saëns
4th Movement of *7th Symphony*—Ludwig van Beethoven
4th Movement of *4th Symphony*—Peter Ilyich Tchaikovsky
"Fêtes" from *Nocturnes*—Claude Debussy

Doom

3rd Movement "Marche Funebre" from *Sonata in B-flat Minor for piano*—Frederic Chopin
1st Movement "Trauermarsch" from *5th Symphony*—Gustav Mahler
3rd Movement from *1st Symphony*—Gustav Mahler

Anxiety

1st movement from *5 Movements for String Quartet*—Anton Webern
1st movement from *3 Pieces for Orchestra*—Alban Berg
1st movement from *Pierrot Lunaire*—Arnold Schoenberg
Ballet Mécanique—George Antheil

Nostalgia

Nocturne in D-Flat Major—Frederic Chopin
"Meditation" from *Thais*—Jules Massenet
Helpless—Crosby, Stills, Nash, and Young
Let It Be; *Imagine*—Beatles

The Sound of Silence—Simon and Garfunkel
Without You—Mariah Carey

Humor and Gaiety

"The Elephant" from *Carnival of the Animals*—Camille Saint-Saëns
"Spring" (1st movement) from *The Four Seasons*—Antonio Vivaldi
"Rondo" from *Horn Concerto in E-flat Major*—Wolfgang Amadeus Mozart
Golliwog's Cakewalk—Claude Debussy
"March" from *The Love for Three Oranges*—Sergei Prokofiev

Deep Emotion, Passion

"Intermezzo" from *Cavalleria Rusticana*—Pietro Mascagni
"Variation 18" from *Rhapsody on a Theme of Paganini*—Sergei Rachmaninov
"Nimrod" from *Enigma Variations*—Edward Elgar
Adagio for Strings—Samuel Barber
Cantus in Memoriam Benjamin Britten—Arvo Pärt

Falling Asleep

"Child Falling Asleep" ("Kind im Einschlummern") from *Scenes from Childhood*—Robert Schumann
Lullaby (Waltz)—Johannes Brahms

Battle Scene

"Battle on the Ice" from *Alexander Nevsky*—Sergei Prokofiev
1812 Overture—Peter Ilyich Tchaikovsky
Wellington's Victory—Ludwig van Beethoven

Love Scenes

Love theme from *Romeo and Juliet*—Peter Ilyich Tchaikovsky
Famous love themes from movies (e.g., *Titanic*, *Casablanca*) or musicals (e.g., *West Side Story* by Leonard Bernstein)

Upbeat

Help—Beatles
Ohio—Crosby, Stills, Nash, and Young
Heart of Gold—Neil Young
Brown Sugar—Rolling Stones
Hang Up—Madonna

Seductive Contemporary Beat

Overprotected—Britney Spears
Turn It Up—Paris Hilton

Appendix D

Schools and Movement Training Centers

The following information was current at the time of publication. Permission has been given for providing direct links to the websites and e-mail addresses.

UNITED STATES

National Schools and Training Centers

The Academy of the Sword
587 Lisbon Street, San Francisco, CA 94112
(415) 239-6650
(415) 239-4604 fax
Richard@academyofthesword.org
www.academyofthesword.org

AcroSports
639 Frederick St., San Francisco, CA 94117
(415) 665-2276
(415) 566-0102 fax
info@acrosports.org
www.acrosports.org
   AcroSports is a non-profit school for physical, performing and circus arts.
   Training is offered in a wide variety of physical disciplines for beginners through advanced students ages ranging from 18 months to adults.

Action Theater
P.O. Box 23002, Santa Fe, NM 87502
(505) 988-2676
Zap@.actiontheater.com
www.actiontheater.com

Ruth Zaporah, master teacher of Action Theater, has developed a physical theater training process that unites the body, imagination and wisdom into crafting
the expression of present experience.

Action Theater
CRS Studios, 123 Fourth Ave., New York, NY 10003
(212) 677-8621
(415) 250-7228 cell
hharpham@earthlink.net
www.actiontheater.com
   Ongoing physical theater and improvisation training with Heather Harpham
designed to expand expressive range and build ensemble skills.

The Actor's Biomechanics Lab
1019 Lisbon Street, Coral Gables, FL 33134
(305) 903-9250
Bruce@actorsbiolab.com
http://actorsbiolab.com
   A revolutionary physical assessment system designed specifically for theatre
movement educators. The ABL is a computer, video-based, cutting-edge technology that gives you and your students the ability to assess specific physical habits
both before, during, and after classroom work. This system will help students turn
physical habit into choice—providing them with motivation for change regarding
their posture, use of energy, habitual movement patterns, and areas of tension
from both a front and side view. The ABL is an invaluable tool to "fast-track" a
student's understanding of physical habitual behavior and assist the body's desire
for the balance, coordination, and release.

Actors Movement Studio Conservatory
302 West 37th St., 6th floor, New York, NY 10018
(212) 736-3309
ams@actorsmovementstudio.com
www.actorsmovementstudio.com
   Actors Movement Studio Conservatory has been training actors in NYC for
over thirty years in physical methods for the Actor, specializing in teaching the
Willamson Physical Technique and Michael Chekhov Technique for the Actor,
the Edwardian, Baroque, and Elizabethan period styles, Viewpoints and Composition, Laban, Feldenkrais, Rasa Boxes, Mask, and Mime. Classes are in fall and
spring, in a Summer Theater Institute in Physical Theater Methods and Training,
and in a Teen Summer Program.

A Laboratory for Actor Training Experimental Theatre Company
1561 Union Street (#4), Brooklyn, NY 11213
(718) 773-6803
vernice.alat@gmail.com
www.alatetc.org

Classes and workshops frequently offered: Working with Text, Physical Actor Training, Voice, Integrating the Actor, Directing and our signature workshop, The Sacred Actor, a journey designed to integrate the scientific with the spiritual.

The American Mime Theatre
Paul Curtis, Director
61 Fourth St., New York, NY 10003-5204
(212) 777-1710
mime@americanmime.org
www.americanmime.org
  Classes in American Mime that develop professional proficiency in mime training, acting, directing, playwriting, designing, and the use of theatrical equipment.

Letitia Bartlett
4075 24th St., San Francisco, CA 94114
(415) 647-0722
tishmick@aol.com
  Dynamic movement for the stage and screen, expressive physicality, mime, masks, commedia dell'arte, clowning, contemporary archetypes, and yoga.

Marcia Berry, Ph.D.
Communication Studies Department, Azusa Pacific University
901 E. Alosta Ave., P.O. Box 7000, Azusa, CA 91702-7000
(626) 815-6000 ext. 3503
(626) 815-2045 fax (attention Marcia Berry)
mberry@apu.edu
  Consultation, lecture-demo on creating whiteface pantomime focusing on beats and transitions.

Bond Street Theatre
2 Bond St., New York, NY 10012
(212) 254-4614
(212) 460-9378 fax
info@bondst.org
www.bondst.org
  Training in a wide variety of physical and gestural arts and in physical comedy and related techniques for the actor; world theatre workshops in physical theatre and dance styles.

Bill Bowers, Mime and Actor
339 E. 10th St. 3w, New York, NY 10009
(212) 353-8309
Bill@Bill-Bowers.com
www.Bill-Bowers.com
  Workshops and master classes in mime and movement improvisation.

Broward Community College
Deborah A. Kondelik
Central Campus, 3501 SW Davie Road, Ft. Lauderdale, FL 33314, Building 4/Room 180
(954) 201-6842
(954) 261-2712 cell
(954) 201-6605 fax
dkondelik@broward.edu
   "Movement for the Actor" at Broward Community College in Ft. Lauderdale, Florida is based on the Laban System of Movement and the Michael Chekhov techniques of physical acting. It includes mask work as a tool for transformation (neutral, beginning character, animal, complex character). The Meisner Technique is also incorporated into the classes.

Marti Cate—The Magic of Mime
850 Bolinas Road, Fairfax, CA 94930
(415) 459-0141
(415) 459-0142 fax
marti@unexpectedcompany.net
www.unexpectedcompany.net
   Decroux technique, Chinese animal chi gung, Kathak (Indian storytelling dance), contemporary dance styles, physical theatre, and exploration of the body in all its expressive potential.

Celebration Barn Theater Summer Workshops
190 Stock Farm Road, South Paris, ME 04281
(207) 743-8452
info@celebrationbarn.com
www.celebrationbarn.com
   Workshops in commedia dell'arte, the Montanaro Method, physical comedy, improvisation, storytelling, eccentric performing, comedy writing, young performers workshop and more by renowned teachers from June to September.

Le Centre du Silence Mime School
Samuel Avital, Director/Founder
P.O. Box 1015, Boulder, CO 80306-1015
(303) 661-9271
savital@concentric.net
www.bodyspeak.com

Circus Center
755 Frederick Street, San Francisco, CA 94117
(415) 759-8123 ext. 814
peggy@circuscenter.org
www.circuscenter.org or www.jeffraz.com
   Comprehensive professional clown training that in the first year includes acrobatics, circus skills, mime, physical theater, dance, Alexander technique, circus

and clown history, classic clown routines, makeup, character development, and clowns in community. The second year offers individual coaching on a professional act, continued training, and ensemble performance.

Joya Cory Improvisation and Solo Performance Workshops
1586 27th Ave., San Francisco, CA 94122
(415) 564-4115
joya.cory@aol.com
www.joyacory.com

Classes in full spectrum physical improvisation and the development of scripted solo performance pieces.

Dell'Arte International School of Physical Theatre
P.O. Box 816, Blue Lake, CA 95525-0816
(707) 668-5663
(707) 668-5665 fax
Info@dellarte.com
www.dellarte.com

The training of actor-creators in an intensive one-year program, summer workshops, or a two-and-a-half-year MFA program comprised of classes in movement, mask, mime, tai-chi, Alexander Technique, voice, and exploration of dramatic territories (melodrama, *commedia*/grotesque, clown) that are the basis for a full-bodied contemporary ensemble-based theatre. Accredited by the National Association of Schools of Theatre (NAST). Approved for vets and foreign students.

Fight Action Associates
P. O. Box 34115, San Francisco, CA 94134
(415) 341-5427
sffightdirector@att.net
Fight direction, stage combat, armoring, stunts.

Flying Actor Studio
40 First St., 3rd Floor, San Francisco, CA 94105
(415) 512-4388
flyingactorstudio@gmail.com
www.flyingactorstudio.com

Physical Theater training. Movement, mask, neo-classic mime and clown, circus arts, improvisation, voice, new performance. Core faculty Leonard Pitt and James Donlan.

Nancy Gold
Workshops, Coach, Director
250 Redhawk Road, Novato, CA 94949
(415) 382-1800
(415) 522-0550 cell
(415) 382-7980 fax
www.findingyourfunnybone.com

Training to become a more powerful, energized, and spontaneous actor/performer with Nancy Gold's techniques in her book *Finding Your Funny Bone! The Actor's Guide to Physical Comedy and Characters*. From children to adults, Nancy's training focuses on acting, mime, masks, movement, and clowning.

Geoff Hoyle
1708 Sanchez St., San Francisco, CA 94131-2741
(415) 826-8593
geoffhoyle@yahoo.com
Physical comedy, comic acting, mask, mime, private teaching, workshops, consultations.

Jef (Jef the Mime)
P.O. Box 3331, Lumberton, NC 28359
(910) 738-8179
woole@mindspring.com
Master classes and 8-week residencies on mime techniques, body language, improvisation, mime composition, physical exercises, ensemble work, and circus techniques. Teacher training in these subjects, integrating mime into a curriculum, and analysis of nonverbal communication.

Laban/Bartenieff Institute of Movement Studies
520 Eighth Ave., Suite 304, New York, NY 10018
(212) 643-8888
(212) 643-8388 fax
limsnyc@aol.com
www.limsonline.org
Laban-based movement and certificate training workshops. Accredited by U.S. Department of Education for postgraduate study.

Joan Mankin
423 Peninsula Ave., San Francisco, CA 94134
(415) 794-4460
queeniemoon@sbcglobal.net
Teaching skills: clowning, physical theater, and comedy routines.

Margolis Method Center
P.O. Box 6, Barryville, NY 12719
(845) 468-4340
(612) 791-7287
info@margolismethod.org
www.margolismethod.org
Workshops in dramatic movement, technique, theory, and structured improvisation with exercises incorporating the Decroux technique. Full time and intensive training in New York and intensive workshops in Minneapolis.

Mimeistry Europe (Innovo Physical Theatre)
The Coach House
Woodhill, Congresbury, North Somerset BS49 5AF, England
+44(0) 1934 833652
+44(0) 1934 833652 fax
uk@innovotheatre.com
http://www.innovotheatre.com/
  Mimeistry has two distinct programs: a three-year degree (BMA, Bachelors of Ministering Arts) in "Mime and Christian Ministry" at Mimeistry School of the Ministering Arts, or an international certificate program offering certificates in "Mime Apprenticeship" or "Journeymanship" from Mimeistry International (for main offices in Europe, America, and New Zealand contact theo@mimeistry .com). Both programs involve multiple styles of mime (Marceau, Decroux, and Mimeistry) with experience in practical performance/tours and studies that include dance, drama, physical theatre, fencing, arts theology/philosophy and theology . Mimeistry's instructional materials for mime may be purchased online at www .mimeistry.com or info@mimeistry.com

Mimeistry International (Innovo Physical Theatre)
1605 E. Elizabeth St., Pasadena, CA 91104
(626) 475-0103
info@innovoheatre.com
www.innovotheatre.com

Mime Theatre Studio
Lorin Eric Salm, Director
Los Angeles, CA
(310) 494-MIME
(818) 300-7473
info@MimeTheatreStudio.com
www.MimeTheatreStudio.com
  Year-round workshops and classes, private coaching and consulting in mime and movement for theatre, film, TV, animation, and digital media. Marcel Marceau technique, Corporeal Mime (Decroux technique), and other mime styles combined in a study useful to mime artists, actors, dancers, and all interested in physical expression.

National Theatre of the Deaf
139 North Main St., West Hartford, CT 06107
(860) 236-4193 tel
(860) 607-1334 videophone
Info@NTD.org
www.NTD.org
  A professional theatre school training program and summer workshops for Deaf, hard-of-hearing, and signing artists that examines the key elements of theatre including acting techniques, script analysis, improvisation, dance and movement, stage combat, and playwriting.

Pomona College Dept. of Theatre and Dance
Thomas Leabhart, Professor of Theatre and Resident Artist
300 East Bonita Ave., Claremont, CA 91711-6349
(909) 621-8186
   Tleabhart@pomona.edu. Home Page: http://research.pomona.edu/thomas-leabhart/Corporeal mime training.

Lorin Eric Salm
Movement Coach
Los Angeles, CA
(310) 494-6463
(818) 300-7473
Lorin@Lorin.info
www.movement-coach.com
   Movement coaching for theatre, film, TV, animation, motion capture, music videos, and digital media. When actors, animatronic figures, or animated characters require mime or specialized movement, Mime and Movement Coach Lorin Eric Salm consults on movement research and creation, and trains or coaches talent in performing required movement.

The School for Mime Theatre
At Kenyon College in Gambier, Ohio
Theatrical Mime Theatre
2657 E. Sylvia St., Tucson, AZ 85716-2113
(520) 990-7425
www.theatricamimetheatre.org
   A center for physical theatre, new choreography, expanding physical acting range, and developing body articulation and performance techniques.

Henry M. Shreibman-Everyman
P.O. Box 5278, Novato, CA 94948-5278
(415) 948-6659
HMS@midot7.com
   Pantomime in the classical tradition. Performances (school/theatre), individual and master classes, private lessons, body isolations, improvisation, stage combat. Adapt to your art form in dance, opera, performance arts, comedy, theater, and teacher training.

The Society of American Fight Directors
1350 East Flamingo Road, #25, Las Vegas, NV 89119
www.safd.org
   For stage combat training contact: Linda McCollum, University of Nevada, Las Vegas.
(702) 895-3662. Mccollum@cc.mail.nevada.edu

Daniel Stein
Brown University/Trinity Rep.
201 Washington St., Providence, RI 02903
(401) 521-1100 ext. 184
DStein@TrinityRep.com
www.DanielStein.org
   Movement for actors, Decroux mime, partnering, devising solo and ensemble work, pantomime, consultations, workshops, private teaching.

Strike Anywhere Performance Ensemble
P.O. Box 2396, Times Square Station, New York, NY 10108
(212) 875-7476
office@strikeanywhere.info
www.strikeanywhere.info
Master classes in physical theatre.

Studio Bob Fleshman
1000 Joliet St., New Orleans, LA 70118
(504) 865-1522
fleshmanre@aol.com
   Private classes in movement theatre, body orientation, and movement therapy. Physical training based on Decroux technique and improvisational work. Puppetry and physical theatre master classes.

Studio of the Moving Dock Theatre Company
Fine Arts Building, 410 S. Michigan Ave., Suite 720, Chicago, IL 60605
(312) 427-5490
contact@movingdock.org
www.movingdock.org
   Michael Chekhov Acting Technique offered in eight-week sessions throughout the year as well as weekend intensives (fall, winter, and spring) and longer summer intensives. Master teacher Dawn Arnold bridges the Chekhov training with the needs of professional performing and offers workshops and residencies to schools and theatre companies.

Jo Tomalin Ph.D.
Professor Theatre Arts Department
San Francisco State University, 1600 Holloway Ave., San Francisco, CA 94132
(415) 338-1036
jtomalin@sfsu.edu
www.theatre.sfsu.edu/faculty/92/jo-tomalin
   Class Titles: ThA 125 Movement I Skills, ThA 425 Movement II Styles. Movement classes that incorporate Lecoq and Laban movement techniques and free the actor for physical expression through mask work, movement analysis, and improvisation.

Touchstone Theatre
321 E. 4th St., Bethlehem, PA 18015
(610) 867-1689
www.touchstone.org
   Focus is on utilizing movement to build a physical vocabulary as a foundation for original theatrical work. Training influences include Paul Baker, Paul Curtis, and Jacques Lecoq. In the apprenticeship program for early career or transitioning actors, in addition to performing in Touchstone productions, apprentices participate in investigation of movement as a basis for playwriting, group work, projects, and programs providing opportunities for people in diverse community settings, and applying the principles of the actor-creator to devise and perform their own new theatre work.

Towson University Theatre Department
8000 York Road, Baltimore, MD 21252-0001
(410) 704-2792
(410) 704-3914 fax
theatre@towson.edu
www.towson.edu/theatre
   Graduate Program: The MFA in Theatre at Towson University supports the artist in creating original, adapted, and devised works. As part of their training the students are exposed to a variety of movement-based workshops, residencies and externships. Past trainings have included Alexander Technique, Impulse Improvisation, Laban Movement, Lecoq Training, Suzuki, Viewpoints, Puppeteering, Object Theatre, Contact Improvisation, Clown, Kabuki, Noh, and Butoh. The three-year program, rich in guest artists, offers these classes during that cycle.
   Undergraduate Program: Performance track students are required to take a Laban-based class and an Impulse Improvisation class. They may also take Alexander Technique, Mime & Movement Theatre, Advanced Study in Movement Styles, Asian Movement for Western Actors, Suzuki/Viewpoints, *commedia*, and physical comedy. All classes in the major program stress physical awareness and expressivity and movement-based performances are part of the matrix. It is a four-year program and classes are usually offered at least once during that cycle.

University of Central Florida Conservatory Theatre
P.O. Box 162372, Orlando, FL 32816-2372
(407) 823-2862
theatre@mail.ucf.edu
www.theatre.ucf.edu
   The program offers BFA and MFA degrees in acting and a BA in performance studies. Graduate students take daily movement class from Professor Christopher Niess guiding them through body awareness and alignment, use of physical impulse and energy, characterization and the physical connection to emotion. Movement training exercises from various training techniques are used where applicable and include those connected with Lecoq, Laban, Alexander, Grotowski, Boal, Chekov, and Bogart. Supplemental instruction and exploration is given in

mask work, circus arts, stage combat, and dramatic territories (period styles). BFA candidates take two semesters of movement, a semester of period movement styles, a semester of combat, and a semester of theatre dance (Jazz or Modern).

University of Miami Department of Theatre Arts

P.O. Box 248273, Coral Gables, FL. 33124
(305) 284-4474
(305) 284-5702 fax
blecure@miami.edu
theatredepartment@miami.edu
www.as.miami.edu/theatrearts/

An intense Conservatory-style training program with a liberal arts requirement culminating in a undergraduate BFA degree (Musical Theatre or Acting). Movement coursework includes physical self-use analysis, methods of physical characterization, period style training, mask work, unarmed combat as well as training in weapons. Combat work culminates in a skills test through the Society of American Fight Directors. All Conservatory classes focus on the importance and integration of the acting process into specific skill work. Program focuses on small class sizes and individual attention in a private school environment.

Tom Vasiliades

Alexander Technique Center for Performance and Development
19 West 34th St., Suite 1013, New York, NY 10001
(212) 564-5472
info@atcpd.com
tvasiliades@nyc.rr.com
www.atcpd.com

Individual lessons and group classes for actors.

Wakka Wakka Puppet Productions

(347) 535-1005
info@wakkawakka.org
www.wakkawakka.org

Workshops in puppetry with hand and rod puppets, object theatre and physical theatre. Also bookings for touring puppet shows.

INTERNATIONAL SCHOOLS AND TRAINING CENTERS

Belgium

Antwerp Mime Studio

Jan Ruts, Director
Sergeyselsstraat 24 B.2140 Borgerhout, Belgium
+32 (0) 3 /236 37 13
mimestudio@tiscali.be
www.mimestudio.be

Professional day and evening classes on all aspects of mime, including training systems of Decroux, Meyerhold, Grotowski, Stanislavski, Chekhov, Lecoq, Laban, Tanaka, and Butoh dance. Advanced classes in analytic and dynamic movement, psycho technical acting, play and improvisation, training in nonverbal voice work, postmodern dance, acrobatics, and other stage arts.

VZW Agape Dance Movement Therapy
Niek Ghekiere, Director
Oude heirweg 60, 8851 Koolskamp, Belgium
+32 (0) 51 74 80 98
info@agapebelgium.be
www.agapebelgium.be

Classes in Dance Movement Therapy utilizing authentic movement, Chase, LMA, Bartinieff Fundamentals, character analysis, movement and touch, and psychodrama.

Canada

Giuseppe Condello Corporeal Mime
Apt. #20, 130 Macpherson Ave., Toronto, Ontario M5R 1W8, Canada
(416) 720-8048
corporealmime@me.com
www.corporealmime@me.com

Corporeal mime, movement, acting, Hatha Yoga, private teaching and coaching, directing, lecture/demonstrations, performance.

Omnibus
L'Ecole de Mime de Montréal,
1945 Rue Fullum, Montréal, Québec, Canada H2K 3N3
+1 (514) 521-4188
+1 (514) 521-3391 fax
information@mimeomnibus.qc.ca
www.mimeomnibus.qc.ca/ecole.html

Beginning to advanced training in corporeal mime technique and nonverbal dramaturgy. Movement for the actor and stage performer and the relationship of movement to text and other stage elements.

Vancouver Moving Theatre
Producer: Downtown Eastside Heart of the City Festival
Chinatown PO Box 88270,
418 Main Street
Vancouver, BC V6A 4A5
Canada
604-628-5672
vancouvermovingtheatre@shaw.ca
www.vancouvermovingtheatre.com
www.heartofthecityfestival.com

Advising, mentoring, Institutes: providing leadership training in principles and practices that engage with and build community. Workshops: tailored for specific events and in a variety of disciplines.

England

London International School of Performing Arts
The Old Lab, 3 Mills Studios, Three Mill Lane, London E3 3DU, United Kingdom
+44 (0) 20 8215 3390
+44 (0) 20 8215 3392 fax
welcome@lispa.co.uk
www.lispa.co.uk
  The physical and vocal training program includes movement analysis, acrobatics, a physical approach to the dramatic use of time, rhythm and space, and a dynamic study of the human body through plastic representation, painting, sculpting, and writing are offered as an approach to creative expression.

Théâtre de l'Ange Fou & International School of Corporeal Mime
Corinne Soum and Steven Wasson
Belgravia Workshops, Unit 207, 157-163 Marlborough Road, London N19 4NF, UK
(44) 020 7263 9339 tel/fax
infoschool@angefou.co.uk
www.angefou.co.uk
  Professional training in Dramatic Corporeal mime

France

Jorge Gayon, Etudes du Mouvement
5 Impasse des Lilas, 31360 Roquefort sur Garonne, Toulouse, France
+33 5 61 97 34 26
+33 6 32 14 58 23
jorgegayon@mac.com
info@mouvement-matiere.org
www.mouvement-matiere.org
  Master classes in movement for dramatic expression and applied choreology for the actor based on Laban's active movement analysis (LAMA) and Decroux corporeal mime. Classes in French, Spanish, and English.

Ecole Internationale de Théâtre Jacques Lecoq
57 Rue du Faubourg St. Denis, 75010 Paris, France
33 (0) 1 47 70 44 78
33 (0) 1 45 23 40 14 fax
contact@ecole-jacqueslecoq.com
www.ecole-jacqueslecoq.com
  Training in mime, pantomime, *commedia*, clown, buffoon, masks, tragedy, chorus, melodrama, movement in relation to music, movement in relation to writing, and movement in relation to dance. For actors, writers, stage directors, sceneographers, architects, dancers, and educators. Summer workshops.

Ecole Philippe Gaulier
7 Rue de Bouray, 91510 Janville-sur-Juin, France
01 60 82 09 74/08 70 27 84 69
06 76 66 40 12 cell
01 60 82 09 74 fax
philgaulier@aol.com/miyazakio@aol.com
www.ecolephilippegaulier.com
  Clown mime acting classes with master clown/mime Philippe Gaulier to learn to perform in order to better entertain. Classes in French and English.

Hippocampe Mime Corporel
2 Passage de la Fonderie, 75011, Paris, France
33 01 43 38 79 75
Info@hippocampe.asso.fr
www.hippocampe.asso.fr
  Regular corporeal mime classes and periodic corporeal mime workshops with Thomas Leabhart and Luis Torreao.

Pas de Dieux Compagnie
166 bis Rue de la Roquette, 75011, Paris, France
33 1 48 05 22 98
won@pasdedieux.com
www.pasdedieux.com
  Physical theatre training with Leela Alaniz and guest artists Thomas Leabhart, Phillip Zarrilli, and Luis Graells.

Germany

Mime Centrum Berlin
Schönhauser Allee 73 D-10437 Berlin, Germany
+49-30-44 65 18 60/61
+49-30-44 65 18 62 fax
info@mimecentrum.de
www.mimecentrum.de/info_en.htm
  Conducts theatre research and offers space for training, short-term workshops. Provides information on training and international exchange with links to European and world mime centers, movement theatre workshops and theatre research in Argentina, Australia, Belgium, Canada, Denmark, France, Great Britain, India, Italy, Netherlands, New Zealand, Norway, Spain, Sweden, Switzerland, and U.S.A.

Italy

Centro Internazionale di Formazione Ricerca E Creazione Teatrale
International Center for Theatrical Formation, Research, and Creation
Yves Lebreton, Instructor

Via Casciani 3, 50025 Montespertoli, Italy
+39 05 71 6088 91
+39 05 71 60 95 80 fax
teatro@yves-lebreton.com
www.yves-lebreton.com
   Relationship between actor's art and corporeal theatre. Open to actors, dancers and all persons interested in energetic body corporeal mime and body voice training. Instruction in Italian and English.

Netherlands

MAPA: Moving Academy for Performing Arts
Stichting MAPA
Oude Nieuwstraat 13 – I, 1012 TD Amsterdam, The Netherlands
+31 20 427 88 46
+31 6 534 60 268 cell
+31 20 427 44 92 fax
info@mapa.nl
www.mapa.nl
   A postgraduate mobile training program with theatre workshops dedicated to the professionalism of innovative artists.

Poland

The School for Modern Mime
Teatr Na Woli-Warsaw, Poland
The Goldston Mime Foundation
P.O. Box 974-Old Chelsea Stn., New York, NY 10011
917-776-4333
Goldmime@aol.com
www.goldmime.com
   A three-week summer intensive that provides participants with a curriculum that spans the breadth of the modern art of mime.

Spain

Centro Moveo for Training and Creation
Calle Llull 48 Atico 2, 08005, Barcelona, Spain
0034 93 300 25 08
info@moveoteatro for mime training
info@moveoteatro for mime creation
www.moveo.cat
   A performing arts center that trains, creates, and investigates physical theatre and Etienne Decroux corporeal mime. Full-time courses and periodic workshops

RESOURCES FOR OTHER TRAINING CENTERS

For links to worldwide theatre, circus, and dance schools/workshops not specialized in a specific physical theatre style and links to styles of Decroux, Lecoq, Meyerhold, Grotowski, Laban, Butoh, and other physical theatre systems, visit the International Physical Theatre Site or click on http://www.freewebs.com/ physicaltheatre/schoolsandworkshops.htm and click on The Moving Theatre, International Site on Physical Theatre.

For physical theatre companies, centers, and mime teaching resources visit http://artslynx.org/theatre/physical.htm

For information about other national and international movement training centers and workshops, professional and vocational courses, performance degrees, and postgraduate classes, visit *Total Theatre*: www.totaltheatre.org.uk

The *Association of Theatre Movement Educators*: www.atmeweb.org or Atmeweb .org/membership and on membership information page click on members' websites.

Lorin Salm's *World of Mime Theatre, Information and Resources, Schools and Workshops*: www.mime.info

Le Centre National du Mime: www.mime.org

Corporeal Mime in the World: www.mimecorporel.net/festivals/festivals.htm

Physical Theatre, Mime and Pantomime: http://www.artslynx.org/theatre/physical.htm

Also see *From the Greek Mimes to Marcel Marceau and Beyond* by Annette Lust, Lanham MD: Scarecrow Press, 2003, Appendix A, Schools and Centers for Movement Training.

For information about artists and companies creating and teaching movement, dance and mask theatre, puppetry, clowning and beyond in New York, visit: :http://nycphysicaltheatre.com/artistscompanies.aspx

For links to national and international pantomime schools, theatres, and artists visit: www.pantomimes-mimes.com/pantomime-artist.php and click on links.

For information on clown classes, workshops, events, and conventions, face painting, juggling, and magic in the U.S.A., Canada, Europe, and the Asia Pacific region see website: http://clownevents.com/

For a list of international clown circus schools visit www.clownevents.com and click on clown schools at clown events website. Also visit Arts: Performing Arts: Circus: schools and Arts at www.dmoz.org/Arts/Performing_Arts/Circus/ Schools/ and Performing Arts: acrobatics: schools and training institutions at www.google.com/Top/Arts/Performing_Arts/Acrobatics/Schools_and_Training_Institutions.

PUPPETRY RESOURCES

Training in puppetry arts is available in workshops by individual puppeteers and at puppetry festivals in the United States and internationally. For more information contact: The Puppeteers of America www.puppeteersofamerica.com and the Union Internationale de la Marionnette www.unima.org.

University and specialized educational programs emphasizing puppetry arts include:

FRANCE: Institut International de la Marionnette, Charleville-Mézières www.marionnette.com

UK: The Central School of Music and Drama, London www.cssd.ac.uk

U.S.A.: University of Connecticut www.drama.uconn.edu/Puppetry/Puppet_home.htm

For a full list of U.S. and international puppetry programs please refer to: www.unima-usa.org/scholarships/schools.

Puppetry videos and DVD titles may be found in the Appendix F Videography and online video clips of puppet companies are available at www.YouTube.com

Recommended books on puppetry:

Bell, John. *Strings, Hands, Shadows: A Modern Puppet History*. Detroit Institute of Arts, 2000.

Blumenthal, Eileen. *Puppetry: A World History*. Abrams Books, 2005.

Taymor, Julie. *Lion King, The: Pride Rock on Broadway*. Disney Editions, 1998.

Appendix E

Publications, Organizations, Festivals, and Resource Centers

SUPPLEMENTARY BOOK PUBLICATIONS

Babson, Thomas W. *The Actor's Choice: The Transition from Stage to Screen*. Portsmouth, N.H.: Heinemann Drama, 1996.

Casciero, Thomas, ed. "Laban and the World of Theatre," in *The Journal of Laban Movement Studies* (2009). Issue is dedicated to Laban movement studies and their relationship to the discipline of theatre. Articles on research, methods, historical perspective, applications to theatre practices, and the development and execution of pedagogy or training methods.

Eldredge, Sears A. *Mask Improvisation for the Actor Training and Performance: The Compelling Image*. Evanston, Ill.: Northwestern University Press, 1996. History of the mask, neutral and character masks, mask improvisation training and exercises.

Erion, Polly. *Drama in the Classroom*. Fort Bragg, Calif.: Lost Coast, 1997. Simple exercises, theatre games, pantomime, improvisations, and creative activities.

Foreman, Jennifer. *Maskwork*. Portsmouth, N.H.: Heinemann Drama, 1999. Techniques and materials for mask construction, with photos by Richard Penton.

France, Charles Engell, ed. *Baryshnikov at Work: Mikhail Baryshnikov Discusses His Roles*. New York: Knopf, 1976.

Frost, Anthony, and Ralph Yarrow. *Improvisation in Drama*. London: Macmillan, 1990.

Gwinn, Peter, and Charna Halpern. *Group Improvisation: The Manual of Ensemble Improv Games*. Colorado Springs: Meriwether, 2003.

Harer, John B., and Sharon Munden. *The Alexander Technique Resource Book*. Lanham, Md.: Scarecrow, 2009. Reference guide to the basic principles and benefits of the Alexander technique to enhance performance in physical activities.

Hurt, James, ed. *Focus on Film and Theatre*. Englewood Cliffs, N.J.: Prentice-Hall, 1974. Essays by critics, filmmakers, authors, playwrights, and actors on the relationship and differences between film and theatre.

Lane, Richard. *Swashbuckling: A Step-by-Step Guide to the Art of Combat and Theatrical Swordplay*. 2nd ed. New York: Limelight Editions, 2003.

Loui. Annie. *The Physical Actor: Exercises for Action and Awareness*. New York: Routledge, 2009. Exercises to develop the actor's strength and flexibility based on the author's training with Decroux, Carolyn Carlson, and Jerzy Grotowski. Includes the use of contact improvisation in working with texts.

Moffat, Marilyn, ed. *The American Physical Therapy Association Book of Body Maintenance and Repair*. New York: Henry Holt, 1999. Nine common injuries; how to avoid injury; illustrated exercises for strength and flexibility.

Napier, Mick. *Improvise*. Portsmouth, N.H.: Heinemann Drama, 2004. An experienced director/teacher brings out the student's creativity in the art and practice of improvisation.

Olsen, Mark. *The Actor with a Thousand Faces*. New York: Applause, 2000. Group work, the use of masks, and games.

Potter, Nicole, ed. *Movement for Actors*. New York: Allworth, 2002. Essays by renowned movement teachers and directors who reveal a broad range of modern movement techniques, including exercises.

Robinson, Davis Rider. *The Physical Comedy Handbook*. Portsmouth, N.H.: Heinemann Drama, 1999.

Robinson, Lynne, and Helge Fisher. *The Mind Body Workout: Pilates and the Alexander Technique*. London: Pan Books/Macmillan, 1998. Workbook combining the Alexander technique and pilates method.

Suddeth, J. Allen. *Fight Directing for the Theatre*. Portsmouth, N.H.: Heinemann Drama, 1996. Staging and acting fights safely.

Tufnell, Miranda, and Chris Crickmay. *A Widening Field: Journeys in Body and Imagination*. Alton, UK: Dance Books, 2005. A handbook for working in creative arts emphasizing the feeling, moving body as the basis for imaginative activity.

White, Edwin, and Marguerite Battye. *Acting and Stage Movement: A Complete Handbook for Actors and Professionals*. Colorado Springs: Meriwether, 1985. Concise course in all phases of acting and stage movement.

Whitelaw, Ginny. *Body Learning: How the Mind Learns from the Body: A Practical Approach*. New York: Perigee, 1998. How to reduce stress, increase energy, be aware, and focus.

JOURNAL PUBLICATIONS

The following information was current at the time of publication. Permission has been given for providing direct links to the website www.annettelust.com and to e-mail addresses.

ATME Newsletter, a publication of the Association of Theatre Movement Educators. A biannual digital newsletter of member articles, included with ATME membership. It provides information on conferences, workshops, movement training, job opportunities, and an exchange of methods and philosophies through the newsletter and the e-mail interchange of the *Atme_Talk Listserv Forum*, Department of Theatre Arts, 600 Lincoln Ave, Eastern Illinois University, Charleston, IL 61920, www.atmeweb.org. Examples of the newsletters from 2001 to 2009 may be found on http://www.atmeweb.org/resources/newsletters.shtml.

The Journal of Laban Movement Studies, an online journal that publishes scholarly articles, book reviews, and reports of scholarly conferences, archives, and other projects of interest to the field. Articles may present current research, scholarly reviews, or an application to a practice, research, or teaching methodology. Scholarly articles are peer reviewed. Subscription included with Laban/Bartenieff Institute membership. Laban Institute of Movement Studies, 520 Eighth Avenue, Suite 304, New York, NY 10018, Tel: 212-643-8888, fax: 212-643-8388, info@limsonline.org, and www.limsonline.org.

Mime Journal, an annual journal publishing articles on Decroux corporeal mime and mime-related modern movement forms. Editor Thomas Leabhart. Pomona College Theatre and Dance Dept., 300 E. Bonita, Claremont, CA 91711, 909-621-8700, tleabhart@pomona.edu, and http://projects.pomona.edu/mime/.

Mimekrant, a mime journal published in French and Flemish by the Mime Centre of Flanders, Belgium, info@mime.be, and http://www.mime.be.

Movimimo, a mime journal published in Spanish by Victor Hernando of the Centro de Investigaciones del Mimo. Villa Juncal 2426, 1417 Buenos Aires, Argentina, vicsol@hotmail.com.

The Physical Actor, a website publication with a mission to develop dramaturgy of actor-based theatre by connecting scholarship with practice. Originally published as a journal for one year in four volumes, back issues 1–4 are available for $5. Edited by Liz Korabek-Emerson, 900 State St., Portsmouth, NH 03801 603-501-0240. For inquiries, go to www.physicalactor.org.

Telondefondo; Revista de Teoria y Crítica Teatral, a semester publication at Universidad de Buenos Aires containing Theatre Theory and Criticism, book and theatre reviews, essays and interviews. An open-access journal on the internet with abstracts on line in Spanish and English. Faculdad de Fhilosofia y Letras (UBA), 25 de mayo 221(1002), CABA, Argentina. Tel. (+54-11) 4343-5981/1196, editor@telondefondo.org, and www.telondefondo.org.

Total Theatre, a magazine of articles on mime, physical theatre, visual performance, and current world movement theatre. Subscription included with Total Theatre Network membership. The Power Station, Coronet St., London NI 6HD, UK, 44 020 7729 7944, info@totaltheatre.org.uk, and www.totaltheatre.org.uk.

FESTIVALS AND RESOURCE CENTERS

For information about festivals and resource centers visit Lorin Eric Salm's *World of Mime Theatre* website: www.mime.info/ or www.mime.info/calendar.html#festivals.

Le Centre National du Mime: www.mime.org.

Mime Centrum Berlin: www.mimecentrum.de.

Corporeal Mime in the World: www.mime-corporel.net/festivals/festivals.htlm and www.pantomimes-mimes.com/pantomime-festival.html (click on links).

Also see Bari Rolfe, *Mimespeak and Mime Bibliography*, ed. Bari Rolfe and Annette Thornton (Lewiston, N.Y.: Edwin Mellen, 2008), which includes all of the original references plus updates of Bari Rolfe's *Mime Directory/Bibliography*, with titles of mime books, scripts, films, and reference works. See as well Annette Lust, *From the Greek Mimes to Marcel Marceau and Beyond* (Lanham Md.: Scarecrow, 2003).

Appendix F

Selected Videography and DVDs

MIME, MOVEMENT, IMPROVISATION, AND NONVERBAL COMMUNICATION

Many of the titles in this list may be obtained in DVD format, and a number of them may be obtained from Insight Media, 2162 Broadway, New York, NY 10024-0621, 1-800-233-9910 or 212-721-6316, custserv@insight-media.com, www.insight-media.com, and from PBS Home Video, 1-800-645-4727, www.shopPBS.com.

Information on silent such classics as *The Art of Buster Keaton, City Lights, The General, The Gold Rush, Modern Times, Silent Shakespeare, The Cabinet of Dr. Caligari, The Passion of Joan of Arc*, and others, and acclaimed performances on film, including expressive acting movement, such as Laurence Olivier's *King Lear, Hamlet*, and *Henry V*, Orson Welles's *Othello*, Richard Burton's *Hamlet*, among others, may be obtained from Facets: 1-800-331-6197, sales@facets.org, or www.facets.org.

For more information on films and videos on Mime Theatre, visit *The World of Mime Theatre*: www.mime.info/FilmVideo.html.

INSTRUCTIONAL

Acting the Part. Brett Wood describes how to develop both improvised and scripted parts, stressing movement and demonstrating methods used in basic acting skills. 1996. 30 min. DVD.

Acting for the Screen. Explores the differences between stage and screen acting. 1994. 21 min. DVD.

Acting Techniques of Kutiyattam. Eye exercises and facial expressions, gesture, and basic body postures in male and female characters. 1980. 55 min. DVD.

Acting Techniques of the Noh Theater of Japan. Basic postures, gestures, and the symbolism of hand and fan movements in Noh Theatre. 1980. 30 min. DVD.

The Acting Workshop. Jeremiah Comey teaches the essentials of acting from scripted dialogue to improvisation, useful in auditions and performances. 1999. 52 min. VHS.

The Actor's Technique. Presents the Stanislavsky, Suzuki, Laban, and Lee Strasburg acting methods' use of movement. 1994. 31 min. DVD.

Acropolis. Commentary and narration by Peter Brook on Jerzy Grotowski's theatre concepts in his book *Towards a Poor Theatre*. 1968. 60 min. VHS.

Alexander Technique: First Lesson. Jane Kosminsky demonstrates how the Alexander technique helps performers move better. 2000. 74 min. DVD.

Alive and Kicking: The Marriage of Dance and Text: Kenneth King's Writing in Motion. Excerpts from a performance that marked the publication of Kenneth King's *Writing in Motion*. 2005. 34 min. DVD/VHS.

Alive and Kicking: Physical Theater: The Joe Goode Performance Group. Excerpts of interview and performances of Goode's *Wonderboy* and *Maverick Strain* that integrate puppetry, storytelling, dance, text, and song. 2009. 2 DVDs, 45 min. each.

Andrei Serban: Experimental Theater. Excerpts and a workshop of Serban's experimental productions and views on theatre. 1978. 27 min. VHS.

The Art of Mime. Techniques and principles of illusion pantomime, corporeal mime, and mime with masks demonstrated by E. Reid Gilbert and Robin Pyle. 1991. 30 min. Bip and Style Pantomimes by Marcel Marceau. 1975. 4 vols. 30 min. each. VHS.

Aspects of Commedia dell'Arte. Voice and gestures of mask characters of *commedia* demonstrated by world master Giovanni Poli; scenes in Gozzi's *The Green Bird*. 1960. 14 min. DVD.

Aspects of Neo-Classic Theater: Racine's Phèdre. Paul Emile Deiber of the Comédie Française directs French neoclassical theatre scenes. 1972. 13 min. VHS.

Bali: Acting Techniques of Topeng: Masked Theater of Bali. John Emigh introduces the masked theatre of Bali and how masks may be used in interpreting character. 1980. 38:48 min. DVD.

Basic Stage Combat. Fundamentals of stage sword fighting. 2004. 20 min. DVD.

Behind the Mask. History of the mask and construction of papier mâché and leather masks. 1990. 59 min. DVD.

Blocking a Scene: Basic Staging with Actors. How to approach your first directing project. 1990. 90 min. DVD.

Body Language: An International View. Gestures, facial expressions, and body language of different cultures. 1999. 25 min. VHS.

Body Language for Actors: Portraying Different Cultures. How to play characters representing other cultures. 2007. 31 min. DVD.

Body Language: Beyond Words. How gestures and movement mirror inner feelings, send messages. 2008. 25 min. DVD.

Body Language: Introduction to Nonverbal Communication. Demonstration of how movement and gestures communicate feelings. 1993. 30 min. DVD.

Body Language Skills. Patti Colombo demonstrates situational exercises and how to develop characters and attitudes through body movement. 2002. 47 min. DVD.

Bringing Literature to Life. Techniques for introducing English students into dramatic study. 2004. 60 min. DVD.

Peter Brook. Brook discusses his views on cross-cultural performances, improvisation, and working with young actors. 1973. 27 min. VHS.

Peter Brook: The Empty Space. Brook's directing methods and demonstration of exercises. 1975. 60 min. VHS.

Brother Bread, Sister Puppet. Excerpts of Bread and Puppet Theater's street theatre, political satire, stilt walking, papier-mâché puppetry, and masks. 1993. 60 min. DVD.

Bunraku: Masters of Japanese Puppet Theater. The story of Bunraku and ancient tales of Japan through puppeteer Tamao Yoshida and chanter Sumitayu Takemoto. 2001. 52 min. DVD.

Butoh: Body on the Edge of Crisis. Explanation of this Japanese theatre of improvisation. 1990. 89 minutes. DVD.

Butoh: Body Weather Farm. Unpublished photographs and insights into the training practices at the Body Weather Farm, home to Min Tanaka and his company Mai Juku. 2009. DVD-ROM. Also see on YouTube their Dance on Rice Planting.

Characterization. Laban method demonstration hosted by Mariette Rups-Donnelly on the use of movement to create character. 1996. 30 min. DVD.

Chekhov and the Moscow Art Theater. Stanislavsky method demonstrated by Yuri Zavadski directing American actors. 1982. 13 min. VHS.

Ryszard Cieslak: The Body Speaks. Actor Cieslak demonstrates Grotowski's Polish Laboratory body exercises. 1975. 55 min. DVD.

Combat for the Stage. Basics of stage combat, how to use weapons, execute stage falls, and choreograph stage combat. 1988. 96 min. DVD.

Commedia dell'Arte. The theoretical and practical teachings of *commedia* expert Antonio Fava; performance of Pulcinella by Fava and his students. 1997. 53 min. DVD. Also see video clips on YouTube of *Punchinella's War* (Fava and Merve Engin) and *Masks of the Commedia dell'Arte* (*commedia* characters in scenes).

Commedia by Fava: Commedia dell'Arte Step by Step. *Commedia* characters, movement, masks, and scenarios. The value of *commedia* in acting and to create the comedic genre. 2006. 258 min. 2 DVDs.

A Commedia dell'Arte Hamlet. Scenes from Hamlet using *commedia* techniques and pantomime led by Michael Alaimo. 1964. 27 min. DVD.

Commedia dell'Arte: The Story, the Style. The tradition of commedia dell'arte and origins of characters such as Pantalone, Colombina, and Pulcinella. 2007. 75 min. DVD.

Creating Physical Theater: The Body in Performance. Games and techniques that generate physical action, explore the relationship between text and action, and show the influence of Artaud, Stanislavsky, and Brecht on physical theatre. 2006. 120 min. DVD.

Creative Drama and Improvisation. Unleashing the imagination with exercises and improvisations. 1990. 90 min. DVD.

Dance Class for the Actor. Introduction to musical theatre dance such as disco, Broadway-hat, cabaret, showbiz, jazz, Latin, waltz, and modern dance. 2002. 2 vol. VHS. 70 min. each.

Dance for Camera: Anthology One. Dances designed for the camera. 2005. 36 min. DVD.

Dance of the Spirits: Mask Styles and Performance. The masked dances of the Burkina Faso in West Africa. 1988. 30 min. DVD.

Les Deux Voyages de Jacques Lecoq. Lecoq's two-year training program at his International School, and reflections on forty years of movement teaching and research. 2006. 175 min. DVD.

Discovering Your Expressive Body. Exercises on integrating the total body, based on the work of Irmgard Bartenieff. 1981. 60 min. VHS.

Dr. Faustus: An Exploration of Voice, Sound, and Body. Performance of Christopher Marlowe's Dr. Faustus with exercises and ideas for voice, sound, and body work. 2008. 103 min. 2 DVDs.

Drama: Mime. Styles of the great mimes, body movement, facial expressions, creating a mime piece, costume, makeup. 1995. 32 min. DVD.

Drama: Warm-up and Improvisation. Warm-up routines, the value of improvisation, breathing, and relaxation. 1995. 36 min. DVD.

Enfin Voir Etienne Decroux Bouger. Daniel Dobbels, *Le Silence des Mimes Blancs.* Editions La Maison d'à Coté. 2006. DVD. Also see *Enfin Voir Etienne Decroux Bouger* (*Finally See Etienne Decroux Move*) video clip on YouTube.

Expressive Movements with Classical Music. 2005. 55 min. DVD.

The Essence in Theater. Techniques for developing movement for characterization in acting and choreography in dance shown by Jean Sabatine. 1986. 3 vol. 114 min. each. VHS.

Expressive Gestures: Alternatives to Realism. Theatre practitioner Kristza Doczy focuses on imaginative gestures in nonrealistic performance. 2005. 60 min. VHS/DVD.

Face-to-Face: Guide to Performance Makeup. Demonstrates applying stage makeup, creating a character, special effects, and fantasy makeup. 1993. 300 min. VHS/DVD.

The Feldenkrais Method: Basic Lessons in Awareness through Movement. Lessons for all ages and levels on posture, sitting, breathing, and different parts of the body. 1988. 120 min. VHS.

Film Acting. Acting for film and the differences between acting for stage and for screen. 2004. 30 min. DVD.

First Lesson: An Introduction to the Alexander Technique. Jane Kosminsky demonstrates how the Alexander technique helps performers move better. 1999. 74 min. DVD.

Gesture Performance: Dealing with Disability, Working with the Hearing Impaired. Hearing impaired actors at the Moscow Theatre School for the Deaf learning physical expressiveness at rehearsals. 2000. 37 min. DVD.

Uta Hagen's Acting Class. Hagen's approach to acting, in which doing is more important than thinking or feeling. 2001. 2 DVDs, 90 min. each.

How to Write and Produce Your Own High School Musical. 2003. 38 min. DVD/VOD.

Improvisation for the Theatre. Improvisational exercises for beginning to advanced actors. 2003. 33 min. DVD.

An Introduction to Kathakali Dance-Drama. Performance and explanation of the training techniques of South India's dance-drama. 2000. 26 min. VHS.

Isadora Duncan Dance. Technique and performances of eighteen of Duncan's dramatic dances. 1995. 60 min. VHS.

Isadora Duncan: Movement from the Soul. Documentary on the life and choreography of Isadora Duncan. 2006. 59 min. DVD.

Kabuki for Western Actors and Directors. How Western actors and directors can use Kabuki techniques to enhance their performances. 1980. 38 min. VHS/DVD.

Laban for Actors: The Eight Effort Actions. Rudolph Laban's system of analyzing movement to add variety and clarity to the actor's physical training. 1997. 31 min. DVD.

Laban's Legacy. Concepts of Laban and his protégés, who relate Laban's theories to actor training and dance. 2006. 112 min. 4 DVDs.

A Language for Movement. The labanotation of Nijinsky's *Afternoon of a Fawn* in order to recreate his original piece. 1993. 24 min. DVD.

Pierre Lefevre on Acting. The use of neutral and character masks to explore the physical, vocal, and inner life of a character. 1992. 39 min. DVD.

Murray Louis in Concert-Dance Solos. The modern dance career of Murray Louis from 1953 on. 1989. 52 min. VHS.

Makeup for the Theater. Period makeup and creation of characters, old age and fantasy faces, and the creation of hairpieces. 1989. 2 vol. 60 min. each. VHS.

Mask Exploration. Stephanie Campbell demonstrates international mask methods, how to conduct mask workshops and work with character masks. 2008. 60 min. DVD.

Mask Exploration: Mask Making. Basic mask-making skills with paper plates and bags, pie tins, cardboard, balloons, and clay. Historical masks and the use of plaster gauze. 1991. 2 vol. 85 min. DVD.

Maskmaking with Foil. How-to demonstrations and decorating masks with feathers, jewels, and other accessories. Use of masks in different cultures. 1999. 20 min. VHS.

Master Classes in Directing: Joanne Akalaitis. The director of Mabou Mines demonstrates her physical method of approaching a text and the complex physicality in a rehearsal of Jean Genet's *The Screens.* 1991. 40 min. VHS.

Master Classes in the Michael Chekhov Technique. A psycho-physical technique in which movement and gesture are related to the psychology of a character. 2007. 3 videodiscs. 390 min. DVD.

Mastery of Mimodrame. Todd Farley, graduate of Marcel Marceau's International School of Mimodrama, reveals the art of building a character and creating gestures and illusions. For beginners, with useful information for advanced mimes. 2007. 55 min. DVD.

The Method. Introduction to the Stanislavsky and Strasberg acting methods. Relaxation and basic sensory and concentration exercises. 1995. 120 min. DVD.

The Method 2. Stanislavsky's method presented by Lorrie Hull with exercises, improvisation techniques, and memory demonstrations. 2009. 120 min. DVD.

Mime over Matter. Basics of mime with exercises for students, 1988. 101 min. DVD.

Mime Spoken Here: Illusions and Exercises. Climbing, walking in place, stairs, ladder, and other illusion exercises. 1991. 120 min. DVD. See Montanaro YouTube video *How to Mime a Walk.*

Mime Spoken Here: Spontaneity and Invention. Tony Montanaro and twelve mimes, actors, jugglers, and storytellers mime and improvise. 1991. 120 min. DVD.

Mindful Movements. Zen Master Thich Nhat Hanh guides viewers in understanding the links between mind and body. 2007. 38 min. DVD.

Movement. Kirsty Reilly teaches the basics of movement for acting and freeing the body to interpret a part. 1996. 30 min. DVD.

Movement for the Actor. Dawn Mora of Northwestern University demonstrates movement and corresponding emotional states. 1993. 75 min. DVD.

Moving Images: Experiential Learning and the Physical Theater. Refers to Ron East's book on physical theatre and discusses acrobatics, improvisation, and masks. 2000. 35 min. DVD.

A Moving Presence: Ruth Zaporah and Action Theater. Ruth Zaporah's improvisation method and solo performances. 2008. 68 min. DVD.

Mudras: Hand Gestures of Sanskrit Drama. Demonstration of hand gestures coordinated with eye movements. 1980. 38 min. DVD.

Musically Acting: Acting in musical theatre and opera and how this influences an actor. 2004. 30 min. DVD.

Neutral Mask: A Foundation for the Theatrical Experience. Ron East explores the use of the neutral mask as a training device for actors. 2008. 60 min. DVD.

Jay O'Callahan: A Master Class in Storytelling. How both voice and movement make a story work. 1983. 33 min. VHS/DVD.

The Open Theatre: Fable. Demonstration of acting exercises and an excerpt from *Fable.* Andre Gregory shows how he incorporates acrobatics, circus performances, and Grotowski's ideas into training. 1975. 28 min. VHS.

The Open Theatre: Terminal. Acting exercises and excerpt from *Terminal.* 1970. 28 min. DVD.

Performing Shakespeare. Includes physical exercises based on an exploration of words and phrases through the development of a scene from *Hamlet.* 1990. 120 min. DVD.

Period Movement: Early and Late Renaissance. Boston University Judith Chaffee's workshop demonstration of Renaissance movement and dance. 2005. 35 min. DVD.

Period Movement: Restoration. Boston University. Judith Chaffee demonstrates Restoration and Victorian movement, dances, and the use of props. 2005. 35 min. DVD.

Physical Theater. Training drawn from Eastern and Western movement and theatre with Cheryl Heazlewood, who in her Butoh and Beyond Company blends Butoh with Western performance. 1996. 50 min. DVD.

Physical Theater 2: A Workshop in Biomechanics. Biomechanics expert Ralf Rauker shows how to establish bodily equilibrium to reach totality on stage. 2003. 58 min. DVD.

The Physical TV Company. Australia's Physical TV Company, founded in 1997 by Karen Earlman and Richard James Allen, features three pieces for the camera. 2005. 30 min. DVD.

Playing Period. Period movement from medieval to twentieth century. 1995. 30 min. 2 DVDs. 30 min. each.

Poetry Alive. How to stage a poetry performance and bring movement into poetry. 2004. 2 DVDs. 60 min. each.

Puppetry as Creative Drama. Marie Hitchcock shows puppetry techniques, the relationship of creative drama to puppetry, and construction techniques for marionettes and hand puppets. 1984. 46 min. DVD.

Puppets for Theater. Use of life-sized puppets in theatre and creation of animals and characters from *Alice in Wonderland*. 2000. 50 min. DVD.

Puppet Schmuppet. The origin of puppetry and demonstration of finger, hand, marionette, shadow, and ventriloquial puppets. Punch and Judy and puppet performances. 1990. 50 min. DVD.

Puppetry: Worlds of Imagination. Artists in American Puppet Theatre and influence on theatre, opera, music, and dance. 2001. 44 min. DVD.

Bari Rolfe: Movement for Period Plays. Ancient Greece through Victorian/Edwardian; manners, social graces, movement in clothing, basic dance steps. Book and optional videotape shows salutations and basic dance steps. 1985. Book and VHS. Persona Books, Oakland, Calif.

The Silent Message: Nonverbal Communication. Nonverbal communication and how to interpret silent messages. 1994. 30 min. DVD.

Skills for Actors: Circus Skills. Jean-Luc Martin of Cirque du Soleil and juggling champion Mark Nizer teach tumbling, handstands, trapeze walking, and juggling. 2002. 47 min. VHS.

Spirit of Commedia. The Rome Luoghi dell'Arte Company depicts the origin of *commedia*, improvisation, masks, and role in contemporary theatre. 2005. 60 min. DVD.

Stage to Screen. How stage productions are adapted to the screen and how stage and screen acting differ. 2004. 30 min. DVD.

The Story of Mummenschanz. Performances and interviews with company founders Floriana Frassetto and Bernie Schürch. 2007. 3 hrs. DVD/PAL. info@mummenschanz.com.

Super Swordfighting: Beginner. Introduction to the creation of choreographed swordfighting. 2008. 65 min. DVD.

Julie Taymor: Setting a Scene. Taymor's visual and directorial devices, including blocking and gesture. 1992. 30 min. DVD.

Theater Games: Workshopping Body Language in Shakespeare. Participants demonstrate theatre games that bring physical expression to Shakespeare's works. 2005. 92 min. DVD.

Theater and Inspiration. Performances and interviews with mime artist Tony Montanaro, Marcel Marceau, Karen Montanaro, and other mimes, jugglers, and performers. 2006. 56 min. DVD. www.filmsbyhuey.com.

Unarmed Stage Combat. Beginning and advanced theatrical fight sequences. 2006. 149 min. 3 DVDs.

Using Drama in the Literature Class. Improvisation, role-playing, and ways to dramatize literature. 2004. 60 min. DVD.

The Vocabulary of Film and TV. Basic film vocabulary. 2004. 27 min. DVD/VOD.

FICTIONAL

Alegria: Cirque du Soleil. Circus acts of the Cirque du Soleil. 2003. 93 min. DVD.

Alice in Wonderland: A Dance Fantasy. Ballet, mime, acrobatics, and theatre. 1993. 27 min. DVD.

Beckett on Film. Beckett's plays, including *Act without Words I and II.* 2002. 10 hrs. 4 DVDs.

Charley Bowers. Short films of the comic animator and puppeteer of the 1920s–1940s. 2004. 4 and 1/2 hrs. DVD.

Charlie Chaplin Collection, Charlie Chaplin Classics. Vol. 1 *The Kid, Pay Day, The Bank, The Pawn Shop,* and others. 2003. 5 hrs. on 4 videos/DVD. Vol. 2 *City Lights, Monsieur Verdoux, The Circus,* and others. 2004. 23 hrs. on 12 DVDs.

Chaplin Mutual Comedies. Restored Chaplin films, including *The Floorwalker, The Fireman, The Vagabond, The Pawn Shop,* and *The Immigrant.* 2006. 5 hrs. on 2 DVDs.

Children of Paradise. Marcel Carné's classic film depicting pantomime and melodrama in Paris in the 1840s. In French, English subtitles. 1946. 186 min. VHS/DVD.

Chinese Take Away. Anna Yen's stories of mother and grandmother combining storytelling, circus, clowning, and magic. 2003. 67 min. DVD.

City Lights. Silent 1931 classic of Charlie Chaplin as *The Little Tramp* who falls in love with a blind flower girl. 2000. 90 min. DVD.

Classic Television. Groucho Marx, *You Bet Your Life,* performing in the 1950s. 2003. 90 min. DVD.

Jane Comfort. Dance, song, and puppetry in Comfort's theatre/dance piece *Underground River.* 1998. 29 min. DVD.

The Complete Mr. Bean. Rowan Atkinson in fourteen episodes of slapstick comedy. 2003. 5 hrs. DVD.

Deli Commedia. Dancer Merce Cunningham combines commedia dell'arte, dance, and slapstick. 1985. 18 min. DVD.

The General. Silent Civil War comedy with Buster Keaton. 1927. 76 min. VHS/DVD.

Goat Island. A performance art company that combines dance, movement, music, visual images, and text in *From Annenberg* that toured in the UK. 1997. 30 min. DVD.

The Gold Rush. Silent Charlie Chaplin 1925 masterpiece. 82 min. DVD.

The Golden Age of Comedy. Comedy sketches and vaudeville from the 1940s through the 1950s with Bob Hope, Red Skelton, Abbott and Costello, Milton Berle, and other TV favorites. 2005. 6 and 1/4 hrs. on 4 DVDs.

The Green Bird. Performance of Gozzi's play directed by Giovanni Poli with stock *commedia* characters. 1982. 35 min. DVD.

L'Histoire du Soldat. Anna Sokolow's choreography of Stravinsky's 1918 piece that blends music, narration, and dance about a soldier who loses his soul to the devil. 1957. 27 minutes. VHS. 2004. DVD.

Bill Irwin: Regard of Flight. Mime-clown-dancer Bill Irwin satirizes the frustrations of an entertainer in his renowned vaudeville/comedy. 1982. 60 min. VHS. Also see video clips on YouTube of *Regard of Flight, Bill Irwin Clowns Around,* and *The Clown Bagatelles.*

Kurt Jooss. Kurt Jooss's dance drama *The Green Table.* 2000. 59 min. DVD.

Kyogen Classic: Poison Sugar. Stylized mime of *Busu,* a popular Kyogen play performed in Japanese with English subtitles. 1992. 28 min. DVD.

Lady and the Tramp. Disney's children's film about a cocker spaniel that falls for a stray mutt called Tramp. 1999. 76 min. DVD.

Last Dance. A dance-theatre piece by the experimental dance group Pilobolus and author Maurice Sendak inspired by the 1944 children's opera *Brundibar* first performed by the inmates of Terezin. 2006. 60 min. DVD.

The Laurel and Hardy Classic Collection: Spooktacular. Four shorts from Laurel and Hardy's Hal Roach Studio years. 1934. VHS.

The Laurel and Hardy Collection. Stan Laurel, Oliver Hardy, and Virginia Karns. 2003. DVD.

Marx Bros: The Silver Screen Collection. All four Marx brothers perform in their films from 1929 to 1933. 2004. 6 hrs. 45 min. DVD.

Masters of the French Stage: Jean-Louis Barrault and Madeleine Renaud. Performance of Barrault and Renaud of a scene of Moliere's *Misanthrope,* French poetry recitations, and a pantomime with Barrault. 1969. 30 min. DVD.

Meet Marcel Marceau. Marcel Marceau's tributes to Buster Keaton, Harpo Marx, Stan Laurel, and Chaplin along with Marceau's Bip skit. (1965, U.S.A.) 2007. 52 min. DVD.

Modern Molière: Tartuffe. A modern adaptation of Tartuffe set in Los Angeles. 2007. DVD.

Modern Times. Silent Charlie Chaplin comedy in which Chaplin is victim of the industrial boom. 1936. 89 min. DVD.

Molière and the Comédie Française. Comédie style in scenes of Molière's *Tartuffe* and *Le Misanthrope* directed by Jacques Charon. 1986. 17 min. DVD.

Mr. Bean: The Big Box of Beans. Rowan Atkinson in the complete set of Mr. Bean's adventures. 1999. 6 vol. 5 hrs. 54 min. DVD.

Mr. Bean's Holiday. Rowan Atkinson in Mr. Bean's mime/slapstick adventures in southern France. In English and French. 2007. 1 hr. 30 min. DVD.

Mr. Hulot's Holiday. Jacques Tati's mime/slapstick film about the eccentric character's seaside holiday. In French. English subtitles. 1953. 87 min. DVD.

Mummenschanz: The Musicians of Silence. 2001. 54 min. DVD/VHS/PAL. info@mummenschantz.com.

Peter Pan. Disney's 1953 film. 2007. 76 min. DVD.

Pinocchio. Disney's 1940 film of a puppet that comes to life. 2004 DVD. 1999 VHS. 88 min.

Red Skelton: America's Greatest Clown. Ten episodes with Skelton's comic screen characters. 2006. 4 1/2 hrs. 2 vol. DVD/VHS.

Silent Shakespeare. Historic silent early shorts of seven Shakespeare plays such as *Midsummer Night's Dream, Twelfth Night, The Tempest,* and *Richard III* filmed from 1899–1911. 2000. 88 min. DVD.

The Three Stooges 75th Anniversary. Five feature movies, cartoon classics, video clips, and family interviews. 2006. 265 min. DVD.

Three by Martha Graham. Three original dances by Graham. 2005. 87 min. DVD/VHS.

The Unknown Marx Bros. Marx brothers comedy clips. 1993. 126 min. DVD.

Vaudeville Videos. American music hall, circus, and burlesque with clowns, jugglers, comics, dancers, and more. 1980. 2 DVDs. 60 min. each.

Yes, I Am Not Iktomi. Depicts the humor and visual language of Native American storytelling. 1999. 27 min. DVD.

For information on other theatre videos and DVDs and on search engines, visit www2.lib.udel.edu/subj/film/resguide/theatre.htm and click on links.

For a more extensive list of mime, pantomime, acting, *commedia*, silent era comedies, and other movement related videos and films, see Annette Lust's *From the Greek Mimes to Marcel Marceau and Beyond* (2003).

Also see Bari Rolfe's *The International Mimes and Pantomimes Mime Directory* Vol. 2, Bibliography (1978), and *Mimespeak and Mime Bibliography,* edited by Bari Rolfe and Annette Thornton (2008), for titles of books, scripts, films, and reference works on mime.

Visit the website of *The World of Mime Theatre,* www.mime.info/FilmVideo. html, for videos of Marcel Marceau, abstract mime, corporal mime, Yass Hakoshima, and Robert Shields, among other mime artists and companies.

Selected Bibliography

For a more extensive bibliographical list, see Bari Rolfe, *Mimespeak and Mime Bibliography*, ed. Bari Rolfe and Annette Thornton Lewiston (New York: Mellen Press, 2008), which includes all of the original references plus updates of Bari Rolfe's *Mime Directory/Bibliography* (Madison, University of Wisconsin Press, 1978), with titles of books, scripts, films, and reference works on mime; Lorin Eric Salm's World of Mime Theatre website, www.mime .info/; Annette Lust's *From the Greek Mimes to Marcel Marceau and Beyond* (Lanham, Md.: Scarecrow, 2003); and the Association for Theatre Movement Educators website, www .atmeweb.org/ (click on Movement Specialities and Bibliography).

Adix, Vern. *Creative Dramatics: A Workbook of Games, Poems, Improvisation, and Acting Stories.* South Jordan, Utah: Encore Performance, 1986.

Adrian, Barbara. *Actor Training the Laban Way: An Integrated Approach to Voice, Speech, and Movement.* New York: Allworth, 2008. Rudolf Laban's physical and vocal movement theories.

Albee, Edward. *Everything in the Garden.* In *The Actor's Scenebook,* ed. Michael Schulman and Eva Meckler. New York: Bantam, 1984.

Alberts, David. *Talking about Mime: An Illustrated Guide.* Portsmouth, N.H.: Heinemann Drama, 1994. Short history of mime, solo and group exercises, original performance pieces.

———. *The Expressive Body: Physical Characterization for the Actor.* Portsmouth, N.H.: Heinemann Drama, 1997. Movement in creating a character.

Anderson, Sherwood. *The Triumph of the Egg.* In *10 Short Plays,* ed. M. Jerry Weiss. New York: Dell, 1963.

Andrews, Richard, trans. *The Commedia dell'Arte of Flaminio Scala.* Lanham, Md.: Scarecrow, 2009. Translation and analysis of 30 scenarios.

Anouilh, Jean. *Thieves' Carnival: A Play in Four Acts.* New York: Samuel French, 1952.

Appel, Libby. *Mask Characterization: An Acting Process.* Carbondale: Southern Illinois University Press, 1982. Mask exercises for acting, clowning, and other mask work.

Ayckbourn, Alan. *Bedroom Farce.* In *The Actor's Scenebook,* ed. Michael Schulman and Eva Meckler. New York: Bantam, 1984.

Baldwin, James. *Go Tell It on the Mountain.* New York: Dial, 1963. Prose passages that may be dramatized.

Barba, Eugenio. "Words or Presence." *Drama Review* 16, no. 1 (1972): 47–54. Physical training and creativity.

Barba, Eugenio, and Nicola Savarese. *A Dictionary of Theatre Anthropology: The Secret of the Performer*. New York: Routledge, Chapman, 1991. Research at Barba's International School of Theater Anthropology on body techniques, training, dramaturgy, and design with photos and illustrations.

Barlanghy, Istvan. *Mime: Training and Exercises*. Trans. Hugo Kerey, ed. Cyril Beaumont. London: Imperial Society of Teachers of Dancing, 1967; New Rochelle, N.Y.: Sportshelf, 1967. Dance-related mime and character study.

Barrault, Jean-Louis. *Mise-en-Scene et Commentaire sur Phèdre*. Paris: Editions du Seuil, 1946.

——. "Propos sur la pantomime." *Formes et Couleurs* 5 (1947).

——. *The Theatre of Jean-Louis Barrault*. Trans. Joseph Chiari. New York: Hill and Wang, 1961. Translation of Barrault's *Nouvelles Réflexions sur le Théâtre*. Paris: Flammarion, 1959. Reflections on theatre and mime.

Benedetti, Robert. *Action! Acting for Film and Television*. Boston: Allyn and Bacon, 2001.

——. *The Actor at Work*. Boston: Pearson, Allyn and Bacon, 2004. The ninth updated edition of Benedetti's textbook in which the author includes the actor's physical training.

Berry, Marcia. "A Method for Utilizing Beats and Transitions in Whiteface Pantomime." Condensed version of doctoral dissertation presented July 2007 at Regent University, Virginia Beach, Va., and in classes in the Communication Studies Department, Azusa Pacific University.

Bestland, Sandra J. "Margolis: Using the Body as a Dramatic Tool," *Movement Theatre Quarterly* (Fall 1993): 11–12. Margolis training method.

Bieber, Margarete. *The History of the Greek and Roman Theatre*. Princeton, N.J.: Princeton University Press, 1961. History of ancient theatre and mime and pantomime.

Bogard, Travis, ed. *Eugene O'Neill, Complete Plays 1932–1943*. New York: Library of America, 1988.

Bowman, Walter Parker, and Robert Hamilton Ball. *Theatre Language Dictionary*. New York: Theatre Arts Books, 1961. Definitions of mime and pantomime.

Brennan, Richard. *A Practical Introduction: Alexander Technique*. Rockport, Mass.: Element Books, 1997.

Britannica World Language Edition of Funk and Wagnall's Standard Dictionary. 4th and 5th eds. Vol. 1, 2. Chicago: Encyclopaedia Britannica, 1959; New York: Funk and Wagnalls, 1961. Definitions of acting, actor, and theatre.

Broadbent, R. J. *A History of Pantomime*. New York: Citadel, 1965. From ancient Greece to eighteenth-century English pantomime.

Bruford, Rose. *Teaching Mime*. London: Methuen, 1966. Exercises, solo, and mime plays.

Bu, Peter. "Mimes, Clowns, and the Twentieth Century?" *Mime Journal* 1, no. 3 (1983): 9–58. Rebirth and multiple forms of contemporary mime.

Bufano, Remo. *Pinocchio for the Stage*. New York: Knopf, 1929. Pinocchio stories for mimed dramatization.

Callery, Dymphna. *Through the Body: A Practical Guide to Physical Theatre*. New York: Routledge, 2001. Exercises related to the theories and practices of twentieth-century theatre animators and teachers Jacques Copeau, Antonin Artaud, Etienne Decroux, Meyerhold, Jerzy Grotowski, Peter Brook, and Jacques Lecoq.

Carrico, Mara, and the Editors of Yoga Journal. *Yoga Journal's Yoga Basics*. New York: Henry Holt, 1997. Basic yoga postures, breathing, and relaxation.

Carrington, Walter. *The Act of Living: Talks on the Alexander Technique*. San Francisco: Mornum Time, 1999. Twenty-nine talks, from breathing to balancing the head, body pain, and gravity.

———. *Thinking Aloud.* Berkeley, Calif.: North Atlantic Books, 1995. Talks on teaching the fundamentals of the Alexander technique.

Chamberlain, Franc. "Gesturing toward Post-Physical Performance." In *Physical Theatres: A Critical Reader*, ed. John Keefe and Simon Murray. New York: Routledge, 2007.

Champfleury, Gautier, Nodier, et Anonymes. *Pantomimes*, ed. Isabelle Baugé. Paris: Cicéro, 1995. In French. Original nineteenth-century pantomimes performed by Deburau at the Théâtre des Funambules.

Chekhov, Anton. *The Vaudevilles and Other Short Works.* Trans. Carol Rocamora. Lyme, N.H.: Smith and Kraus, 1998. Selected scenes from *The Bear, The Jubilee*, and *The Marriage Proposal* for mime and improvisation.

Chekhov, Michael. *Etre Acteur: Technique du Comédien.* Paris: Pgymalion/Gérard Watelet, 1997. In French. Translated by Elisabeth Janvier and Paul Savatier as *To the Actor: On the Technique of Acting.* New York. A handbook for actors and all stage artists, including a chapter on the psychological gesture.

———. *To the Actor: On the Technique of Acting.* New York: Routledge, 2002. Revised and expanded edition.

Chisman, Isabel, and Gladys Wiles. *Mimes and Miming.* New York: Thomas Nelson, 1951. Mime training and mime plays.

Christoffersen, Erik. *The Actor's Way.* New York: Routledge, 1993. Odin Teatret actors' training techniques and how mental action is related to physical action.

Comey, Jeremiah. *The Art of Film Acting: A Guide for Actors and Directors.* Burlington, Mass.: Focal, 2002.

Conable, Barbara. *How to Learn the Alexander Technique: A Manual for Students.* Portland, Ore.: Andover Road, 1995.

Cooney, Barbara. *The Little Juggler.* New York: Hastings House, 1961. Based on the thirteenth-century legend of the juggler of Notre Dame, a minstrel juggler, tumbler, and dancer who offers his talents to the Virgin Mary and her son.

Courlander, Harold. *Negro Folk Music U.S.A.* New York: Colombia University Press, 1963. Ballads and songs for mimed dramatization.

Craig, Edward Gordon. "At Last a Creator in the Theatre." An Etienne Decorum Album. *Mime Journal* (2001). An appreciation of Etienne Decroux's corporeal mime.

———. *On the Art of the Theatre.* London: Heinemann, 1924.

Critchley, Macdonald. *Silent Language.* London: Butterworth, 1975. Gestures in the theatre, dance, everyday life, and various professions.

Curtis, Paul J. "Exploring Silent Acting." *Dramatics* 44 (May 1973): 22. Author's use of mime in the theatre.

Dalcroze, Emile. *Eurhythmics, Art, and Education.* Trans. Frederick Rothwell. New York: Benjamin Blom, 1972. Rhythmic movement in mime and its relation to the arts and education.

Decroux, Etienne. *Words on Mime.* Trans. Mark Piper. *Mime Journal* (1985). Drama Pub. 1987. Translation of *Paroles sur le Mime* by Decroux, his technique and philosophy of mime and theatre. Origins of mime, comparisons with dance, and its use for actors.

De Marinis, Marco. "The Mask and Corporeal Expression in Twentieth-Century Theatre." *Mime Journal (Incorporated Knowledge)* (1995): 14–37.

Dennis, Anne. *The Articulate Body: The Physical Training of the Actor.* New York: Drama Book, 1995. Actor exercises, technique, and mask work.

Despot, Adriane. "Jean-Gaspard Deburau and the Pantomime at the Théâtre des Funambules." *Educational Theatre Journal* 27, no. 3 (1975): 364–76. In French.

Dobbels, Daniel. *Le Silence des Mimes Blancs.* Editions La Maison d'à Côté, 2006. In French. Story of mime from Debureau to Etienne Decroux. DVD of Etienne Decroux, master of Marcel Marceau, performing and teaching.

Dorcy, Jean. *The Mime*. Trans. R. Speller Jr. and Pierre de Fontnouvelle. New York: Speller, 1961. Essays by Decroux, Barrault, and Marceau.

Duchartre, Pierre-Louis. *The Italian Comedy*. Trans. Randolph T. Weaver. New York: Dover, 1966. Important work on the history of Italian comedy. Illustrations, characters and scenes, and extensive bibliography.

Eldredge, S. A., and H. W. Huston. "Actor Training in the Neutral Mask." *Drama Review* 22, no. 4 (1978): 19–28. The Lecoq use of the neutral mask for actor training.

Enters, Angna. "The Dance and Pantomime: Mimesis and Image." In *The Dance Has Many Faces*, ed. Walter Sorrel. Cleveland: World Publishing, 1951. The fusion of mime and dance.

———. *On Mime*. Middletown, Conn.: Wesleyan University Press, 1965. Enters's views and work in mime.

Faulkner, William. *Sanctuary*. New York: Modern Library, 1931. Prose passages that may be dramatized and mimed.

———. *Requiem for a Nun*. New York: Random House, 1951. Play sequel to *Sanctuary*.

———. *The Marionettes*. Charlottesville: University Press of Virginia, 1977. Faulkner's one-act play.

Feder, Happy Jack. *Mime Time: Forty-five Complete Routines for Everyone*. Colorado Springs: Meriwether, 1992.

Felner, Mira. *Apostles of Silence: The Modern French Mimes*. Cranbury, N.J.: Associated University Presses, 1985. Essays on Copeau, Decroux, Barrault, Marceau, and Lecoq.

Five Comedies of Medieval France. Trans. Oscar Mandel. New York: Dutton, 1971. Includes *The Washtub*, an anonymous French farce.

Fleshman, Bob, ed. *Theatrical Movement: A Bibliographical Anthology*. Metuchen, N.J.: Scarecrow, 1986. Bibliography and essays on movement and performance in Western and other cultures by specialists in theatre, dance, psychology, history, anthropology, and other disciplines.

Fo, Dario. *The Tricks of the Trade*. London: Methuen, 1991. Fo's *commedia* and improvisational theatre.

Fowlie, Wallace. *Pantomime: A Journal of Rehearsals*. Chicago: Henry Regenery, 1951. Mime and pantomime in theatre and dance.

Frakes, Jack. *Acting for Life*. Colorado Springs: Meriwether, 2005. A textbook on acting, including physical, pantomime, and improvisation exercises.

Gelabert, Raoul. "Etienne Decroux Has Much to Teach Us." *Dance Magazine* 33 (September 1959): 66–67. Contribution of mime master Decroux.

Giraudoux, Jean. *Ondine*. Trans. Maurice Valency. In *The Actor's Scenebook*, ed. Michael Schulman and Eva Meckler. New York: Bantam, 1984.

Goby, Emile, ed. *Pantomimes de Gaspard et Charles Deburau*. Paris: E. Dentu, 1889. In French. Original Deburau pantomimes.

Gordon, Mel, ed. *Lazzi: The Comic Routines of the Commedia dell'Arte*. New York: PAJ, 2001. Over 250 *commedia* comic routines.

———. "Lazzi: The Comic Routines of the Commedia Dell'Arte." In *Physical Theatres: A Critical Reader*, ed. John Keefe and Simon Murray. New York: Routledge, 2007. Contains *commedia* lazzi scenes.

Gousseff, James W. *Pantomimes 101*. Woodstock, Ill.: Dramatic, 1974. 101 pantomimes and how to produce a pantomime.

———. *Pantomimes 102*. Woodstock, Ill.: Dramatic, 1981. 102 new pantomimes and how to produce a pantomime.

———. *Street Mime*. Woodstock, Ill.: Dramatic, 1993.

Grantham, Barry. *Playing Commedia*. Portsmouth, N.H.: Heinemann Drama, 2001. A guide to *commedia* techniques.

———. *Commedia Plays: Scenarios, Scripts, Lazzi.* London: Nick Hern, 2007.

Graves, Russel. "The Nature of Mime." *Educational Theatre Journal* 10, no. 2 (1958): 101–4. Mime and speech.

Green, Paul. *Quare Medecine.* In *10 Short Plays*, ed. M. Jerry Weiss. New York: Dell, 1963.

Grotowski, Jerzy. *Towards a Poor Theatre.* New York: Simon and Schuster, 1968. Grotowski's theatre laboratory, voice, and physical exercises.

Hagen, Uta, and Haskel Frankel. *Respect for Acting.* New York: Wiley, 2008. Physical approach to acting.

Hall, Edward T. *The Silent Language.* New York: Doubleday, 1990. Intercultural communication.

Hamblin, Kay. *Mime: A Playbook of Silent Fantasy.* New York: Doubleday, Dolphin, 1978. Introductory mime games and exercises with illustrations.

Hampden, John, ed. *Ballads and Ballad Plays.* New York: Thomas Nelson, 1931.

Harrop, John. *Acting.* New York: Routledge, 1992. Section on the use of improvisation and movement to release creativity and discover meaning.

Harwood, Eliza. *How We Train the Body.* Boston: Walter H. Baker, 1933.

Hawthorne, Nathaniel. *The Scarlet Letter.* New York: Dodd Mead, 1900. Prose passages for mime and dramatization.

Hendricks, Gay. *Conscious Breathing: Breathwork for Health, Stress Release, and Personal Mastery.* New York: Bantam, 1995. The value of conscious breathing, mental and physical healing, beginning and advanced breath lessons.

Hobbs, William. *Fight Direction for Stage and Screen.* Portsmouth, N.H.: Heinemann Educational, 1995. Guidelines for fight scenes on stage and screen and fight notation. Brief history of swords.

Hoyer, Karen. "Mime That Speaks." *Movement Theatre Quarterly* (Fall 1995): 9. The use of movement in speaking theatre in current Chicago productions.

Hunt, Douglas, and Kari Hunt. *Pantomime: The Silent Theatre.* New York: Atheneum, 1964.

Huston, Hollis. *The Actor's Instrument: Body, Theory, Stage.* Ann Arbor: University of Michigan Press, 1993. The actor's use of the body and its relation to the playing space.

Inge, William. *Come Back, Little Sheba.* In *The Actor's Scenebook*, ed. Michael Schulman and Eva Meckler. New York: Bantam, 1984.

Johnstone, Keith. *Impro: Improvisation and the Theatre.* London: Methuen Drama, 1992. Johnstone's invaluable guide to improvisation and mask work.

Jones, Brie. *Improve with Improv.* Odessa, Tex.: Brooklyn, 2002. A guide to improvisation and character development.

Jones, Winifred. *Nine Mime Plays.* London: Methuen, 1940.

Kamin, Dan. *Charlie Chaplin's One-Man Show.* Metuchen, N.J.: Scarecrow, 1984. Reprint, Carbondale: Southern Illinois University Press, 1991. Chaplin's contribution to cinema and his use of mime.

———. *The Comedy of Charlie Chaplin: Artistry in Motion.* Lanham, Md.: Scarecrow, 2009. An in-depth analysis of cinema's greatest mime artist, with a postscript on how Kamin trained Robert Downey Jr. for his Oscar-nominated performance in *Chaplin*.

Kane, Leslie. *The Language of Silence.* Cranbury, N.J.: Associated University Press, 1984. Silence in the theatre of Maeterlinck, Chekhov, Bernard, Beckett, Pinter, and Albee.

Keller, Betty. *Improvisations in Creative Drama: A Program of Workshops and Dramatic Sketches for Students.* Colorado Springs: Meriwether. 1988.

Key, Mary Ritchie. *Non-Verbal Communication: A Research Guide and Bibliography.* Metuchen, N.J.: Scarecrow, 1977. Information and titles on nonverbal communication in life, the arts, animals, etc.

Keysell, Pat. *Mime Themes and Motifs.* Boston: Plays Inc., 1980. Mime study and teaching.

Kipnis, Claude. *The Mime Book*. Odessa, Tex.: Brooklyn, 2002. A functional "how to" book with exercises to develop a mime technique.

Laban, Rudolf. *The Mastery of Movement*. Boston: Plays Inc., 1971. Section on the stage arts developing from mime.

Lawson, Joan. *Mime: The Theory and Practice of Expressive Gesture with a Description of Its Historical Development*. New York: Dance Horizons, 1973. Short history of mime and technique of gestures for dancers and actors, with ballet illustrations.

Leabhart, Thomas, and Franc Chamberlain, eds. *The Decroux Sourcebook*. New York: Routledge, 2008. Key material on Etienne Decroux and corporeal mime.

———. *Etienne Decroux*. New York: Routledge Performance Practitioners, 2007. Overview of Decroux's life and work, analysis of his *Words on Mime*, and corporeal technique exercises.

———, eds. *Mime, Mask, and Marionette*. *Mime Journal* (1978–1980). Articles on mime and mime related subjects.

———. *Modern and Post-Modern Mime*. New York: St. Martin's, 1989. Contributions of Copeau, Decroux, Barrault, Marceau, Lecoq, and late twentieth-century mime artists to modern and postmodern mime.

———, eds. *New Mime in Europe*. *Mime Journal* (1983). Articles by Peter Bu and European mimes, with photos.

———, eds. *New Mime in North America*. *Mime Journal* (1980–1982). Articles and photos on new mime companies in North America.

Leach, MacEdward, ed. *The Ballad Book*. New York: Harper, 1955. Ballads that may be dramatized.

Lecoq, Jacques. *The Moving Body: Teaching Creative Theatre*. In association with Gabriel Carasso and Jean-Claude Lallias. Trans. David Bradby of Lecoq's *Le Corps Poétique* (2000). New York: Routledge, 2002. Lecoq's views on performance, improvisation, masks, movement, and Lecoq exercises.

———. *Theatre of Movement and Gestures*, ed. David Bradby. London: Routledge, 2006. Translation of Lecoq's *Le Théâtre du Geste, Mimes et Acteurs*. Writings by Lecoq and his disciples on Lecoq's vision of acting, mime, and masked performance.

Lessac, Arthur. *Body Wisdom: The Use and Training of the Human Body*. New York: Drama Book Specialists, 1981.

Lifar, Serge. "The Mime and the Dancer." In *Opera Ballet Music-Hall in the World*, vols. 4–44. Paris: International Theatre Institute III, 1953.

Loeschke, Maravene. *All about Mime: Understanding and Performing the Expressive Silence*. Englewood Cliffs, N.J.: Prentice-Hall, 1982. Illustrated introduction to mime, performance techniques, and creating mime.

Lugering, Michael. *The Expressive Actor*. Portsmouth, N.H.: Heinemann, 2007. Body and voice exercises and improvisational studies.

Lust, Annette. "Etienne Decroux: Father of French Mime." *Mime Journal* 1 (1974): 14–25. Contribution of Decroux to modern mime and theatre.

———. "Etienne Decroux and the French School of Mime." *Quarterly Journal of Speech* 57, no. 3 (1971): 291–7. Decroux's contribution to French mime.

———. *From the Greek Mimes to Marcel Marceau and Beyond*. Lanham, Md.: Scarecrow, 2003. A chronicle of the many aspects of mime.

———. "From Pierrot to Bip and Beyond." *Mime Journal* (1980–1982): 9–15. Evolution of nineteenth-century pantomime to twentieth-century mime.

———. "Mime in North America." *Total Theatre* 6 (Spring 1994): 14–15. Twentieth-century mime forms and artists in Canada and the United States.

———. "On the Meaning of Mime and Pantomime." In *Theatrical Movement: A Bibliographical Anthology*, ed. Bob Fleshman. Metuchen, N.J.: Scarecrow, 1986. Meanings of mime and pantomime throughout the centuries.

Marash, Jessie. *Mime in Class and Theatre*. London: Harrop, 1950.

Marceau, Marcel. *L'Histoire de Bip*. Paris: L'Ecole des Loisirs, 1976. In French. The story of Marceau's Bip character.

Martin, Jacqueline. *Voice in Modern Theatre*. New York: Routledge, 1991. The spoken word and the visual and physical elements in twentieth-century directorial vision.

Mawer, Irene. *The Art of Mime*. London: Methuen, 1960. Short history, mime technique, and mime and impromptu scenes.

Mehl, Dieter. *The Elizabethan Dumb Show*. London: Routledge, 1982. The role of pantomime in Elizabethan theatre; description of period dumb shows.

Mic, Constant. *La Commedia dell'Arte*. Paris: La Pléiade, 1927. In French. Important work on the commedia dell'arte.

Mitchell, Theresa. *Movement from Person to Actor to Character*. Lanham, Md.: Scarecrow, 1998. Exercise program to connect person, actor, and character.

Murray, Simon. *Jacques Lecoq*. New York: Routledge Performance Practitioners, 2002. Lecoq's life and teaching methods, with exercises demonstrating his approach.

Murray, Simon, and John Keefe. *Physical Theatres: A Critical Introduction*. New York: Routledge, 2007. An overview of the physical in twentieth-century theatre.

——, eds. *Physical Theatres: A Critical Reader*. New York: Routledge, 2007. Essays that trace the development of physicality in theatre.

Naremore, James. *Acting in the Cinema*. Berkeley: University of California Press, 1990. Study of movie actors, including Chaplin, Marlene Dietrich, James Stewart, Cary Grant, Marlon Brando, and James Cagney, and their use of theatrical to natural acting styles.

Nicoll, Allardyce. *The Development of Theatre*. 5th ed. London: George G. Harrap. 1968. Section on mime.

——. *Masks, Mimes, and Miracles*. New York: Cooper Square, 1963. Critical study of mime from the Greeks and Romans through commedia dell'arte.

——. *The World of Harlequin*. Cambridge: Cambridge University Press, 1987. Critical study of Harlequin and commedia dell'arte.

Noverre, Jean G. *Letters on Dancing and Ballets*. Original treatise published in Lyon, 1760; French edition, 1803. Trans. C. W. Beaumont, 1930. Alton, U.K.: Dance Books, 2004. Use of mime in ballet.

Pardoe, T. Earl. *Pantomimes for Stage and Study*. New York: Appleton, 1931.

Parker, David. *The Collector*. In *The Actor's Scenebook*, ed. Michael Schulman and Eva Meckler. New York: Bantam, 1984.

Perrault, Charles. *Famous Fairy Tales*. New York: Franklin Watts, 1959. Stories adapted by David Stone from the original Perrault versions of *The Sleeping Beauty*, *Cinderella*, *Puss-in-Boots*, and other tales.

Pezin, Patrick. *Etienne Decroux, Mime Corporel-Textes, Etudes et Témoignages*. Saint-Jean de Védas, France: L'Entretemps, 2003. Study of Etienne Decroux's work through an imaginary interview, biography, testimonies by former Decroux students, stage directors, and those who knew him. In French.

Pisk, Litz. *An Actor and His Body*. New York: Theatre Arts, Routledge, 1987.

Pound, Louise, ed. *American Ballads and Songs*. New York: Scribner's, 1972. Popular ballads and songs that may be dramatized and mimed.

Rémy, Tristan. *Clown Scenes*. Trans. Bernard Sahlins. Chicago: Ivan R. Dee, 1997. Classic clown routines for class or performance.

Rice, Elmer. *Three Plays without Words*. New York: Samuel French, 1934.

Ring of Words: An Anthology of Song Texts. Selected and translated by Philip L. Miller. New York: Norton, 1973. Songs for mimed dramatization.

Robinson, Alan Young. "Physicalizing *The Little Prince* by Saint-Exupéry." *Movement Theatre Quarterly* (Summer 1994): 12–13. Interview with stage director A. Lust on the use of movement in an adaptation of the book by Saint Exupéry.

Rolfe, Bari. *Actions Speak Louder than Words: A Workbook for Actors.* Berkeley, Calif.: Persona Books, 1992. Introductory workshop with movement exercises, play scenes, and improvisations.

———. *Behind the Mask.* Oakland, Calif.: Persona Books, 1977. Introduction and exercises to mask work, with photographic illustrations.

———. "Commedia Dell'Arte and Mime." In *Theatrical Movement: A Bibliographical Anthology,* ed. Bob Fleshman. Metuchen, N.J.: Scarecrow, 1986. Essays and bibliography on commedia dell'arte and mime.

———. *Commedia dell'Arte: A Scene Study Book.* San Francisco: Persona Books, 1977. Scenes and *lazzis* for classroom and other purposes.

———. *Farces, Italian Style.* Oakland, Calif.: Persona Books, 1981. Short plays for the classroom and performance.

———. "Mime in America: A Survey." *Mime Journal* 1 (1974): 2–12. History of American mime.

———, ed. *Mime Directory/Bibliography.* Vol. 2. Madison: University of Wisconsin, International Mimes and Pantomimists, 1978. Books, articles, scripts, films, and reference works on mime.

———. *Mimespeak and Mime Bibliography,* ed. Bari Rolfe and Annette Thornton. Lewiston, N.Y.: Mellen, 2008. *Mimespeak* is a collection of Rolfe's essays; *Mime Bibliography* includes all of the original references plus updates of Bari Rolfe's *Mime Directory/Bibliography,* 1978, with titles of books, scripts, films, and reference works on mime.

———. "The Mime of Jacques Lecoq." *Drama Review* 16, no. 1 (1972): 34–38. Lecoq mime training.

———, ed. *Mimes on Miming.* San Francisco: Panjandrum, 1978. Interviews and contributions of famous mimes.

Roose-Evans, James. *Experimental Theatre.* New York: Universe Books, 1973. Dramatic movement in theatre and dance from Stanislavsky to Peter Brooke and Martha Graham to Alwin Nickolais.

Rovine, Harvey. *Silence in Shakespeare.* Ann Arbor, Mich.: UMI Research Press, 1987. How silence contributes to content and characterization in Shakespeare and other playwrights.

Royce, Anya Peterson. *Movement and Meaning: Creativity and Interpretation in Ballet and Mime.* Bloomington: Indiana University Press, 1984. An anthropologist's analysis of the meaning of mime and ballet and the nature of performance.

Rozinsky, Edward. *Essential Stage Movement.* Miami: Physical Theater, 2010. Stage movement for actors based on the Stanislavsky actor training method.

Rudlin, John. *Commedia dell'Arte: An Actor's Handbook.* New York: Routledge, 2000. Origin of *commedia* and a guide to *commedia* techniques.

———. *Jacques Copeau.* Cambridge: Cambridge University Press, 1986. French stage director Copeau's use of *commedia* and masks.

Sabatine, Jean. *Movement Training for the Stage and Screen: The Organic Connection between Mind, Spirit, and Body.* New York: Back Stage Books, Watson-Guptill, 1995. A training program with basic physical exercises and a step-by-step exploration of character study to integrate mind, spirit, and body through movement.

Salerno, Henry F., ed. and trans. *Scenarios of the Commedia dell'Arte*: Flaminio Scala's "Il Teatro delle Favole Rappresentative." New York: New York University Press, 1967.

Sand, Maurice. *The History of the Harlequinade.* 2 vols. Philadelphia: Lippincott, 1915. Reprint of the 1862 original. Reprinted as *The History of Harlequin.* Oxford: Blom, 1958. *Commedia* characters with illustrations.

Saxon, A. H. "The Circus as Theatre: Astley's and Its Actors in the Age of Romanticism." *Educational Theatre Journal* 27, no. 3 (1975): 299–312. Development of theatre elements, with a section on mimetic scenes in the circus.

Schechner, Richard, Mathilde La Bardonnie, Joel Jouanneau, and Georges Banu. "Talking with Peter Brook." *Drama Review* 30, no. 1 (1986): 54–71. Interview with Brook on his collective staging of the *Mahabharata*. Section on the actor's eyes and gestures as more important than scenery.

Schulman, Michael, ed. *Great Scenes and Monologues for Actors*. New York: Avon, 1998. Scenes for mimed dramatization.

Schulman, Michael, and Eva Mekler, eds. *The Actor's Scenebook*. New York: Bantam, 1984. Scenes for mimed dramatization.

Schwartz, I. A. *The Commedia dell'Arte*. New York: Institute of French Studies, 1993. The *commedia* tradition in France.

Séverin. *l'Homme Blanc*. Paris: Plon, 1929.

Sheets-Johnstone, ed. *Giving the Body Its Due*. Albany: State University of New York Press, 1992. Essays by psychologists and therapists on body knowledge and by dancer Sally Ann Ness on the intelligence of the body.

Silva, Mira, and Shyam Mehta. *Yoga: The Iyengar Way*. New York: Knopf, 1997. A manual with 100 yoga postures, breathing, and meditation, including the philosophy and history of yoga.

Simon, Neil. *Barefoot in the Park*. In *The Actor's Scenebook*, ed. Michael Schulman and Eva Meckler. New York: Bantam, 1984.

———. *The Prisoner of Second Avenue*. In *The Actor's Scenebook*, ed. Michael Schulman and Eva Meckler. New York: Bantam, 1984.

Sklar, Deidre. "Etienne Decroux's Promethean Mime." *Drama Review* 29, no. 4 (1985): 64–75. The ritualistic element of Decroux's art.

Souriau, Paul. *The Aesthetics of Movement*, ed. and trans. Manon Souriau. Amherst: University of Massachusetts Press, 1983.

Spolin, Viola. *Improvisation for the Theatre: A Handbook of Teaching and Directing Techniques*. Evanston, Ill.: Northwestern University Press, 1999. New edition with exercises, games, and scenes for adults and children.

Stanislavski, Konstantin. *An Actor's Handbook*, ed. and trans. Elizabeth Reynolds Hapgood. New York: Theatre Arts, 1963. An alphabetically ordered acting handbook.

———. *An Actor Prepares*. Trans. Elizabeth Reynolds Hapgood. New York: Routledge, 1989.

Stolzenberg, Mark. *Be a Mime*. New York: Sterling, 1991. Introduction to mime and makeup, with illustrated exercises and short mime pieces.

Storey, Robert. *Pierrots on the Stage of Desire: Nineteenth-Century French Literary Artists and the Comic Pantomime*. Princeton, N.J.: Princeton University Press, 1985. Pierrot's role in romantic and modern theatre and literature. An extensive list of nineteenth-century pantomime scenarios in Paris libraries.

Sutcliffe, Jenny. *The Complete Book of Relaxation Techniques*. Allentown, Pa.: People's Medical Society, 1991. Over thirty methods of relaxation techniques.

Sutton, Julia, and Rachelle Palnick Tsachor, eds. *Dances for the Sun King: André Lorin's Livre de Contredance*. Annapolis: Colonial Music Institute, 2008. Dance instruction manual and collection of thirteen notated dances from 1685–1687, ordered by and presented to Louis XIV.

Toomey, Susie Kelly. *Mime Ministry*. Colorado Springs: Meriwether, 1986. An introductory handbook in mime training and preparing mime programs for mimes of all ages, with Christian song interpretations, scripture, and message skits.

Turner, Craig. "Contemporary Approaches to Movement Training for Actors in the U.S." In *Theatrical Movement: A Bibliographical Anthology*, ed. Bob Fleshman. Metuchen, N.J.: Scarecrow, 1986. Description and annotated bibliographies of contemporary movement styles.

Udall, Nicholas. *Ralph Roister Doister, a Comedy*. Jointly published with *The Tragedy of Gorboduc* by Thomas Norton and Thomas Sackville. Elibron Classics. Chestnut Hill, Mass.: Adamant Media, 2001.

Viguier, Rachel. *Gestures of Genius: Women, Dance, and the Body*. Stratford, Ontario: Mercury, 1994. Female freedom of expression and mental and emotional liberation through dance and body movement.

Walker, Katherine Sorley. *Eyes on Mime*. New York: John Day, 1969. History and technique of mime in ballet, theatre, and the cinema.

Wangh, Stephen. *An Acrobat of the Heart*. New York: Random House, 2000. A physical approach to acting inspired by the work of Jerzy Grotowski.

Warton, Thomas. *The History of English Poetry*. Vol. 1. New York: Johnson Reprint, 1974. Reprint of the 1824 original, with a section on mimes and minstrels' performances in the Middle Ages.

The Weavers' Songbook, ed. The Weavers. New York: Harper, 1960. Songs with music for piano and guitar that may be dramatized and mimed.

Weep Some More, My Lady. Collected by Sigmund Spaeth. Garden City, N.Y.: Doubleday, Page, 1927. Songs for mimed dramatization.

Weller, Stella. *The Breath Book: 20 Ways to Breathe Away Stress, Anxiety, and Fatigue*. London: Thorsons, 1999. Basic exercises and diagrams.

Wilford, Lee, and Richard Schechner, eds. *The Grotowski Sourcebook*. New York: Routledge, 1997.

Williams, Tennessee. *Vieux Carré*. In *The Actor's Scenebook*, ed. Michael Schulman and Eva Meckler. New York: Bantam, 1984.

Wilsher, Toby. *The Mask Handbook*. New York: Routledge, 2007. A practical guide to origin of the mask, making and using a mask, writing and directing maskwork, exercises.

Wilson, Albert E. *King Panto*. New York: Dutton, 1935. The history of pantomime.

———. *The Story of Pantomime*. London: Home and Van Thal, 1949. Pantomime from the eighteenth to the twentieth centuries.

Wright, Richard. *The Outsider*. New York: Harper, 1933. Prose passages for mimed dramatization.

Yakim, Moni, and Muriel Broadman. *Creating a Character: A Physical Approach to Acting*. New York: Applause Theatre Books, 2000. How the actor can make characters come to life physically.

Zaporah, Ruth. *Action Theater: The Improvisation of Presence*. Berkeley, Calif.: North Atlantic, 1995. A twenty-day program of improvisation exercises, stories, and anecdotes.

Index

About the Author

Annette Lust is the author of *From the Greek Mimes to Marcel Marceau and Beyond*, a definitive work that chronicles the many visages of the art of mime and that received the Choice Outstanding Academic Book 2000 Award and the George Freedly Memorial Award Finalist Place in 2000. Lust is a professor emerita at Dominican University of California in San Rafael, where she has taught courses in mime, theatre production, dramatic literature, and French language and literature. For her teaching and publications on the French School of Mime, she was awarded the French government Palmes Académiques in 1973. In 2004, her biannual Bay Area Fringe of Marin Original One-Act Play and Solo Festival, produced at Dominican University since 1990, received a San Francisco Bay Area Theatre Critics Special Award. Her movement fantasy play *Vinaigrette* and her pantomime *The Robot's Revenge* won first place at the Fringe of Marin Festival in 2008 and 2009, and *The Robot's Revenge* received a San Francisco Bay Area Theatre Critics nomination for best original piece in 2010. She is a member of the San Francisco Bay Area Theatre Critics Circle, awarding local theatre productions and artists, and she writes articles on international theatre festivals and theatre book reviews for the Association of Movement Theatre Educators and other theatre journals.

ABOUT THE MOVEMENT CONSULTANT

Movement consultant **Jo Tomalin** is a professor of theatre arts performance at San Francisco State University, where she teaches acting, movement, and voice in the Theatre Arts Department. In addition to her role as movement consultant, Tomalin assisted in the editing of *Bringing the Body to the Stage and Screen* and the production of the website, and she contributed an essay on puppetry. Originally from England, Tomalin has directed and acted in many productions in the San Francisco Bay Area. She trained in movement and physical acting at the Laban

About the Author

Centre, Goldsmith's College at London University, and at the École Internationale de Théâtre Jacques Lecoq in Paris. In 2006, Tomalin received a doctorate in instructional design for online learning from Capella University in Minnesota.

ABOUT THE EXERCISE ILLUSTRATOR

C. Yeaton received a MFA in theatre arts design from San Francisco State University in 2009.